NAPOLEON AND HIS TIMES

NAPOLEON AND HIS TIMES:
Selected Interpretations

selected and edited by

Frank A. Kafker

James M. Laux

University of Cincinnati

ROBERT E. KRIEGER PUBLISHING COMPANY
MALABAR, FLORIDA
1989

Original Edition **1989**

Printed and Published by
**ROBERT E. KRIEGER PUBLISHING COMPANY, INC.
KRIEGER DRIVE
MALABAR, FLORIDA 32950**

Copyright © **1989**, by Frank A. Kafker and James M. Laux

All rights reserved. No part of this book may be reproduced in any form or by any means, electronic or mechanical, including information storage and retrieval systems without permission in writing from the publisher.
No liability is assumed with respect to the use of the information contained herein.
Printed in the United States of America.

Library of Congress Cataloging-in-Publication Data

Napoleon and his times : selected interpretations / selected and
   edited by Frank A. Kafker, James M. Laux.
     p. 356
   Bibliography: p.
   ISBN 0-89874-935-2 (Paperback)
   ISBN 0-89464-324-X (Cloth)
   1. Napoleon I, Emperor of the French, 1769–1821—Personality.
2. Napoleon I, Emperor of the French, 1769–1821—Influence.
3. France—History—Consulate and Empire, 1799–1815. 4. France—History—Consulate and Empire, 1799–1815—Historiography.
I. Kafker, Frank A., 1931– II. Laux, James Michael, 1927–
DC203.9.N214 **1989**
944.05'092'4—dc 19   88-661
                                                                              CIP

10 9 8 7 6 5 4 3 2

CONTENTS

PREFACE ix

CHRONOLOGY xi

1. NAPOLEON'S CHARACTER 1

   The Roots of Personality
   Harold T. Parker 2

   Napoleon in Action: The Egyptian Campaign
   J. Christopher Herold 22

   Napoleon as Administrator
   Harold T. Parker 37

   A Romantic Tempered by Realpolitik
   Georges Lefebvre 40

2. JUDGING THE COUP D'ETAT AND THE EARLY
   CONSULATE 47

   The Death of Liberty
   Albert Leon Guerard 48

   The Restoration of Order and National Unity
   Albert Vandal 50

   The Voters
   Claude Langlois 57

   A Dictatorship Protecting a New Elite
   Albert Soboul 66

3. THE CONCORDAT 71

   A Compromise for Mutual Advantage
   Jean-Marie Leflon 72

   An Unnecessary Papal Victory
   Alphonse Aulard 86

4. THE RESPONSIBILITY FOR THE WAR OF 1803 91

   The Continental Images of Britain
   Arnold David Harvey 92

Both Sides Responsible
    Georges Lefebvre   104

The British Largely Responsible
    André Fugier   113

5. THE DOMESTIC OPPOSITION   121

A Survey
    Jean Vidalenc   122

An Example: Resistance to Conscription
    Eric A. Arnold, Jr.   139

6. THE COMMON PEOPLE IN FRANCE   149

A Survey of Peasants and City Workers
    Jean Tulard   150

An Example: The Parisian Wage Earner
    Raymonde Monnier   156

7. THE EFFECT OF THE CONTINENTAL BLOCKADE ON BRITAIN   169

A Challenge Easily Overcome
    Eli F. Heckscher   170

A Serious Cause of Social and Economic Dislocation
    François Crouzet   179

8. NATIONALISM AND THE DESTRUCTION OF THE NAPOLEONIC EMPIRE   193

An Introduction
    Robert B. Holtman   195

The Spanish Uprising: A Patriotic Revolt
    Rafael Altamira   200

Mixed Motives for Spain's Revolt
    Robert B. Holtman   208

The German Uprising: Prussia in Arms
    Heinrich von Treitschke   210

Mixed Motives for the German Revolt
    Hajo Holborn   214

An Empire Foiled by Traditionalists
    Owen Connelly   217

CONTENTS vii

9. THE MAIN CAUSES FOR THE DEFEAT IN RUSSIA 229

   Napoleon: The Warrior and His Army
     Gunther E. Rothenberg 230

   A Freezing Winter
     Napoleon 240

   Napoleon's Errors of Judgment
     David G. Chandler 246

10. NAPOLEON AND THE ARTS AND SCIENCES 257

    Medicine
      Dora B. Weiner 258

    Science and the Arts
      Maurice P. Crosland 265

11. NAPOLEON'S LEGACY 271

    A Legend
      Jean Tulard 273

    Institutions
      Jacques Godechot 278

    Napoleon and the Jews
      Abram Leon Sachar 296

    Military Affairs
      Gunther E. Rothenberg 301

    Women and the Family
      Marcel Garaud and Romuald Szramkiewicz 307

    No Turning Point
      Louis Bergeron 317

ANNOTATED BIBLIOGRAPHY 327

ABOUT THE EDITORS 339

MAPS

1. Europe in 1812 xvi
2. Bonaparte in Egypt and Syria 23
3. Spain 1808 201
4. The Russian Campaign 1812 242–243
5. Survival of Aristocratic Landownership in 1803 319
6. Landownership in 1803 by Members of the Pre-Revolutionary Parlements 320

PREFACE

Although the Duke of Wellington defeated Napoleon at Waterloo, he has lost the battle for the attention of the public. People have found Napoleon a more fascinating, complicated, and influential figure. This anthology, we hope, will demonstrate why.

Its main aim is to introduce readers to eleven important historical problems relating to Napoleon. These elucidate his own times and ours, for many of the issues discussed concern perennial subjects in political, military, religious, social, and intellectual history. In some instances, the individual selections within a chapter complement each other; in others they conflict. In any case, we have chosen readings that are long enough to show not only the authors' viewpoints, but also the main arguments and evidence used to support them; and we have not confined ourselves to just two contrasting interpretations when others might be considered equally cogent. We hope that readers will see that some of the explanations and analyses offered here are more convincing than others and that they can arrive at preliminary conclusions on at least some of the historical problems presented. Our introduction to each chapter is intended to suggest guidelines for reading the material, and our extensive bibliography provides recommendations for further investigation.

This anthology does not seek to favor any one view or school of Napoleonic studies; instead we have tried to include selections by historians of different national backgrounds, political persuasions, religious beliefs, and historical methodologies. What we have required is that they present their points of view informatively and clearly. In our search for such selections, we have not limited ourselves to those easily accessible or already in English. Eleven of the selections, for example, are our own translations from the French.

As in our companion volume, *The French Revolution: Conflicting Interpretations*, the spelling, capitalization, and punctuation of the individual authors have been retained. We as editors have supplied titles for each selection. When we have added explanatory material to any selection, such additions have been enclosed in brackets. To distinguish these brackets from the author's brackets in the original text, we have italicized the contents of author's brackets.

We are pleased to acknowledge the help of Professor Kornel Huvos, our friend and colleague at the University of Cincinnati. He has always been willing to share his great learning with us.

F.A.K.
J.M.L.

CHRONOLOGY

1768
May 15   France purchases Corsica from Genoa.

1769
August 15   Napoleon Bonaparte born in Ajaccio, Corsica.

1779   Napoleon goes to France, attends schools at Autun and Brienne.

1784   Napoleon leaves Brienne and enters the Ecole militaire in Paris.

1785   Napoleon's father dies in February; in November he arrives in Valence as second lieutenant in artillery regiment.

1786–1793   Napoleon divides his time between active service in France and long leaves in Corsica.

1789
May 5   Estates General convenes at Versailles.

1792
April 20   France declares war on Austria.
August 10   King Louis XVI overthrown.
September 21   Convention proclaims the French Republic.

1793
June   Napoleon and rest of Bonaparte family flee Corsica for southern France.
September–December   Captain Napoleon Bonaparte commands artillery besieging Toulon and is promoted to brigadier general when siege is successful.

1794
July   Robespierre overthrown and the Terror ends.
August 6–20   Napoleon under arrest as a suspected terrorist.

1795

	Napoleon in Paris.
February 21	Convention separates Church from State.
October 5	Napoleon helps suppress royalist insurrection of Vendémiaire in Paris.
October 26	Napoleon named commander of Army of Interior.

1796

March 2	Napoleon named commander of (French) Army of Italy.
March 9	Napoleon marries Josephine de Beauharnais.
April	Napoleon's first Italian campaign begins.

1797

April 18	Armistice of Leoben concluded with Austria, favorable to the French.
September 4	Directors purge the legislatures of conservatives.
October 17	Treaty of Campo Formio with Austria, favorable to the French.
December 6	Napoleon arrives in Paris as commander of (French) Army of England.

1798

March	Napoleon and Talleyrand persuade Directory to invade Egypt.
July 1	Napoleon's expedition lands at Alexandria.
August 1	British naval victory in Battle of Nile.
July–December	Formation of Second Coalition led by Britain, Russia, and Austria against France.

1799

August 23	Napoleon leaves his army in Egypt and sails for France, landing on October 9.
November 9–10	The coup d'état of Brumaire ends the Directory and makes Napoleon First Consul.
December 25	Constitution of year VIII put into effect and Consulate established.

1800

January 6	Bank of France established.
February 17	Law passed reorganizing national administration.
March 14	Pius VII elected Pope.
June 14	Napoleon wins Battle of Marengo over Austrians.
December 3	Moreau defeats Austrians at Hohenlinden.
December 24	Attempted royalist assassination of Napoleon.

1801

February 9	Treaty of Lunéville with Austria, favorable to the French.
March 23	Alexander I becomes Tsar of Russia.
July 16	Concordat signed with Pope Pius VII.
August 20	French army in Egypt surrenders to British.

1802

March 25	Peace Treaty of Amiens with Britain.
Spring	Chateaubriand publishes *The Genius of Christianity*.
April 26	Amnesty for most émigrés.
May 1	Law passed reorganizing primary and secondary education.
May 19	Creation of Legion of Honor.
August 2	Plebiscite approves Napoleon as Consul for Life.

1803

January 23	Napoleon reorganizes the Institute to weaken his critics there.
April 12	Employee unions and employer associations prohibited; *livret* (passbook) required for many workers, by decree of December 1.
May 3	Louisiana territory sold to United States.
May 18	Hostilities recommence with Britain.
November 30	San Domingo proclaims independence from France.

1804

March 21	Civil Law Code (Napoleonic Code) promulgated.
March 21	Execution of Duke d'Enghien.
May 18	Napoleon proclaimed Emperor of France.
June 25	Execution of royalist conspirator Cadoudal.
December 2	Napoleon's coronation.

1805

May 26	Napoleon crowned King of Italy.
August 9	Formation of Third Coalition: Britain, Russia, Austria.
October 20	French victory at Ulm.
October 21	At Trafalgar, Nelson defeats Franco-Spanish fleet.
December 2	At Austerlitz, Napoleon defeats Austrians and Russians.
December 26	Treaty of Pressburg with Austria, favorable to the French.

1806

January 23	Death of William Pitt.
March–June	Joseph Bonaparte, King of Naples; Louis Bonaparte, King of Holland; Joachim Murat, Grand-Duke of Berg.
July 12	Creation of Confederation of the Rhine.
August 6	Dissolution of Holy Roman Empire.
October 14	French victories over Prussia at Jena and Auerstädt.
November 21	Berlin decree establishes Continental Blockade.

1807

June 14	French defeat Russians at Friedland.
June 25– July 9	Napoleon and Alexander meet at Tilsit.
July 22	Creation of Grand Duchy of Warsaw.
November	French army in Spain and Portugal; Peninsular War begins.

1808

March 17	Napoleon reorganizes public education with decree on the Imperial University.
March 27	After French annex some papal territory, Pope excommunicates Napoleon.
May 2	Spanish uprising in Madrid.
July 7	Joseph Bonaparte, King of Spain.
August 1	Murat, King of Naples.
October	Erfurt conference; Napoleon and Alexander meet; Napoleon has lunch with Goethe.

1809

April 9	Austria goes to war against France.
May 17	French seize rest of Papal States and Rome.
June 11	Pope Pius VII re-excommunicates Napoleon.
July 6	Pope arrested by French forces.
July 6	Napoleon defeats Austrians at Wagram.
December	Napoleon divorces Josephine.

1810

1810–1811	Industrial depression in France.
April 1	Napoleon marries Marie-Louise of Austria.
July 9	Holland annexed to France.
August	Bernadotte becomes ruler of Sweden.
December 13	Annexation of north German region to France.

CHRONOLOGY

1811
1811–1812   Agricultural depression in France.
March 20   Birth of Napoleon's son, King of Rome.
March–May   Luddite riots in England.

1812
June 18   United States declares war on Britain.
June 24   Napoleon invades Russia.
September 14   French army enters Moscow.
October 19   French army begins retreat from Moscow.
October 23   General Malet's abortive coup d'état begins.
November   Continental Blockade ends in failure.
December 5   Napoleon leaves remnant of French army in Russia.
December 19   Napoleon arrives in Paris.

1813
March 27   Prussia begins German war of liberation.
June 21   Wellington defeats Joseph Bonaparte at Vitoria, Spain.
October 8   Wellington enters southern France.
October 16–19 Napoleon defeated at Leipzig.

1814
March 30   Paris surrenders to Allies.
April 6–11   Napoleon abdicates.
May 3   Louis XVIII enters Paris.
May 3   Napoleon arrives on Elba.
November 1   Congress of Vienna opens.

1815
March 1   Napoleon lands in France.
March 20   Napoleon enters Paris.
June 18   Battle of Waterloo.
June 22   Napoleon abdicates a second time.
October 15   Napoleon arrives on Saint Helena.

1821
May 5   Napoleon dies.

1840   Napoleon's remains brought to France and buried in Les Invalides.

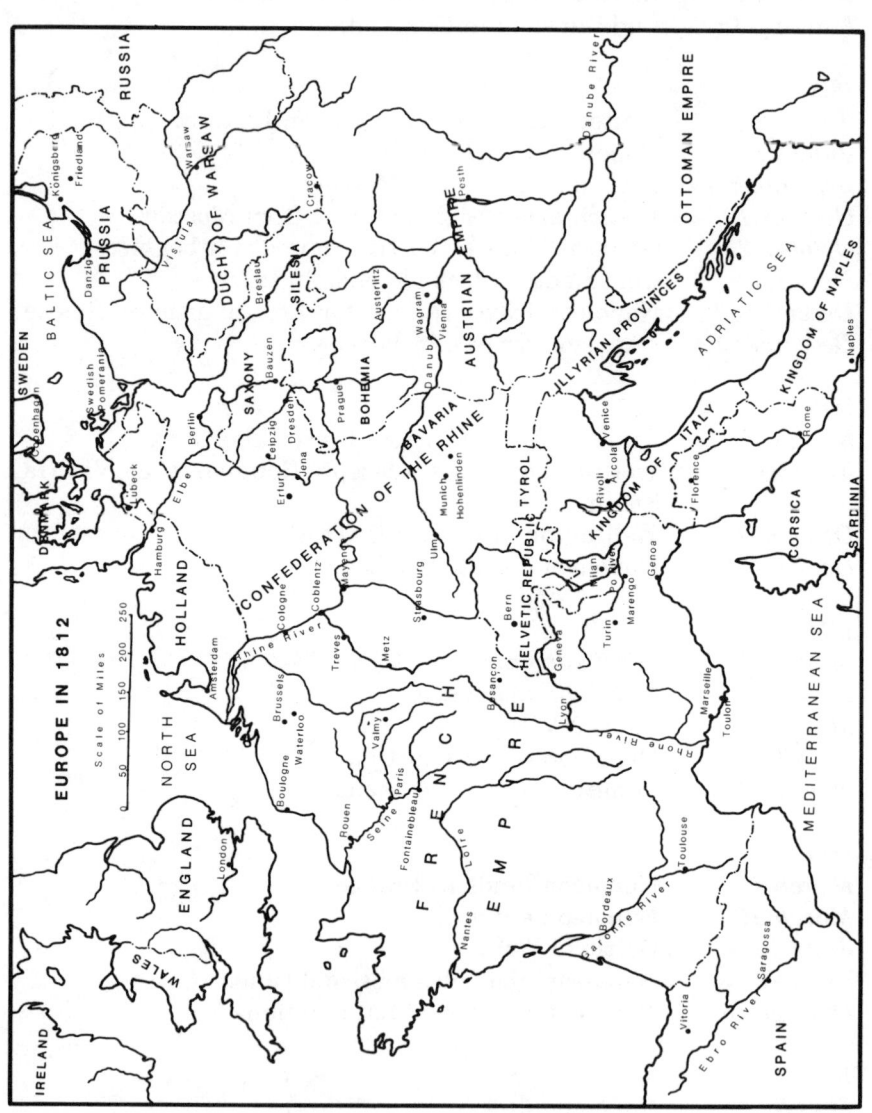

1
NAPOLEON'S CHARACTER

Historians can try to understand a complicated person like Napoleon in many ways. Harold T. Parker studies his family relations, childhood, schooling, early career, and work habits. A rather sympathetic picture emerges. Domineering, manipulative, generally incapable of intimacy, Napoleon was also self-confident, disciplined, persevering, intelligent, imaginative, able to handle stress, and very industrious, a man of great potential. J. Christopher Herold discusses Napoleon as a young general in Egypt. Like Parker, he notices Napoleon's energy and taste for learning, but he sees too a brutal, heartless, blasphemous deceiver, an egocentric with little regard for the lives of others. Georges Lefebvre attempts to capture the permanent traits of Napoleon, those present in maturity as well as youth. He portrays somebody fascinating and extraordinary, a man of action and words, a realist and dreamer, a *philosophe* and romantic, an enlightened despot and a follower of the Revolution, a person combining admirable and despicable qualities.

While studying these selections, the reader ought to keep in mind certain points: good judges of character are observant, well-informed, critical, yet balanced, seeing a person in relation to time and place, and searching for the underlying causes of behavior; less reliable judges of character make hasty critical remarks and vague superficial ones based on biased sources, little evidence, much speculation, and stereotypes.

Harold T. Parker (1907–), a professor's son, received his Ph.D. in history from the University of Chicago and taught at Duke University from 1939 until his retirement in 1977. Among his publications are The Cult of Antiquity and the French Revolutionaries *(1937),* The Bureau of Commerce in 1781 *(1979), and* Three Napoleonic Battles *(rev. ed., 1983). Parker has been especially interested in Napoleon's psychological development and outlook, as the following article indicates.*

THE ROOTS OF PERSONALITY
Harold T. Parker

I do not know much about Napoleon's childhood, but then neither does anyone else. We do know that he was born on August 15, 1769, the second son of Charles and Letizia Bonaparte, in Ajaccio, Corsica. Beyond that the evidence concerning his childhood, the first five years so precious to psychologists, is so slight that much of it can be presented here.

From Harold T. Parker, "The Formation of Napoleon's Personality: An Exploratory Essay," *French Historical Studies* 7 (1971–1972): pp. 6–26. The entire article is reprinted with revisions by the author and with the permission of the author and the editors of *French Historical Studies*.

This article is a revised version of a paper read to the Society for French Historical Studies, March 28, 1969.

There are nearly as many definitions of personality as there are personality theorists. As Joseph Katz observes: "Freud saw personality as consisting of three major systems—id, ego, and superego—that interact to determine behavior. . . . Allport defined personality as 'the dynamic organization within the individual of those psychophysical systems that determine his unique adjustment to the environment.' Bronfenbrenner, integrating various theories of personality, defined it as 'a system of relatively enduring dispositions to experience, discriminate or manipulate, actual or perceived aspects of the individual's environment (including himself).' Common to this sample of definitions is the notion that personality refers [*to quote Nevitt Sanford*] 'not to behavior itself but to dispositions that underlie behavior,' and that 'the dispositions of personality constitute an organized totality, a more or less enduring structure that interacts with the environment.' This idea, that personality refers to an organized, interacting system of underlying dispositions (e.g., goals and ways of realizing them, impulses and means of controlling them, ways of experiencing, thinking, and evaluating)" is adopted as the basis of this essay on the *formation* of Napoleon's personality.

The bulk of the available historical evidence for this enterprise is found in Frédéric Masson and Guido Biagi, *Napoléon inconnu: Papiers inédits (1786–1793)*, (Paris, 1895), which published the papers from the youth and early manhood of Napoleon, and

In 1813 Emperor Napoleon smilingly chided his two-year-old infant son: "Lazy bones, when I was your age, I was already beating up Joseph," Napoleon's elder brother.[1] Later, in 1817, Napoleon at St. Helena confided to his intimates a few childhood memories. He frequently spoke of his mother and said to his physician, Antommarchi, "She was all her life an excellent woman, and as a mother was without equal."[2] On another occasion, observing the "tenacity" of little Bertrand, the son of his aide, he remarked: "I was as stubborn as he at his age; nothing stopped or disconcerted me. I was a quarreller, a fighter; I feared nobody, beating one, scratching another, making myself redoubtable to all. It was my brother Joseph who most often had to suffer. He was slapped, bitten, scolded, and I had already complained against him before he had time to recover himself. But my quickness was of no avail with Mamma Letizia, who soon repressed my bellicose humour. . . . She was both tender and severe; she punished wrongdoing and rewarded good conduct; she recognized impartially our good and bad actions."[3]

In the same year, 1817, Joseph was writing his memoirs at Point Breeze, New Jersey. He recounted that on one occasion when the two boys were at school together at Ajaccio, one-half of the class were made to act the part of the Romans, while the other half were Carthaginians. The master placed Joseph, the elder, with the victorious Romans and Napoleon among the defeated Carthaginians. Napoleon begged Joseph to change places with him, to let him be on the winning side, which Joseph willingly did. But then the little Napoleon was remorseful all the way home that he had been unjust to his brother.[4]

Toward the end of her life, in 1834, Napoleon's mother, at the age of eighty-four, dictated a few reminiscences to her companion, Rose Mellini. She early noted in Napoleon, she said, an "esprit de princi-

---

Arthur Chuquet, *La Jeunesse de Napoléon* (Paris, 1897), which added other information. Although this evidence is insufficient to enable us to describe Napoleon's personality as a totality at any moment of time prior to 1796, when he came under steady public gaze, it is probably sufficient to enable us to notice when the major underlying and enduring dispositions of his adult personality came into existence and under what circumstances. In preparing this essay I am indebted to the counsel and suggestions of Professor Irving Alexander of the Department of Psychology of Duke University and Professors Owen Connelly and Joseph Shulim of the history departments of, respectively, the University of South Carolina and Brooklyn College. They are not responsible, of course, for the use I have made of their suggestions.

[1]Paul Bartel, *La Jeunesse inédite de Napoléon* (Paris, 1954), p. 33.
[2]Norwood Young, *The Growth of Napoleon: A Study in Environment* (London, 1910), p. 77.
[3]*Ibid.*
[4]Joseph Bonaparte, *Mémoires et correspondance politique et militaire du roi Joseph* (Paris, 1855), I, 40–41.

pauté"—a spirit of mastery.⁵ She nursed all her children except the infant Napoleon, who was put out to a wet nurse.⁶

Such family reminiscences of 1813, 1817, and 1834 were in each case set down long after the event, but they were apparently independent and they agree. Together with family records the reminiscences enable us to establish that:

> the infant Napoleon entered the family as the second son and the second child to live, Joseph (b. January 7, 1768) being one and two-thirds years older, the third child, Maria Anna (b. July 14, 1771), being nearly two years younger; five other children followed;⁷

> the parents were young and very much in love; they had been married (June 2, 1764) when Charles (b. March 27, 1746) was eighteen and Letizia (b. August 25, 1750) was not yet fourteen; she was still eighteen when Napoleon was born;⁸

> the father, strong, manly, and handsome, conducted the negotiations with the outside world but within the family the mother was dominant and the father was indulgent and easy-going;⁹

> the mother was a famous beauty ("brown chestnut hair, brown-black eyes, nose straight and rather long, mouth refined and expressive, good teeth, small ears, hands, and feet, a lovely complexion, white, with a delicate peach tint to the cheeks, an expression that was serious and reflective, with a touch of nobility, of refinement, and an aspect of steadfastness of character") and her beauty endured through the years; she took no nonsense from her children and commanded their respect and affection;¹⁰

> the first two children were lost in infancy; Joseph, the third child and the first one to live, was very much wanted, Letizia nursed him, he slept in the parents' room until he was age three and a half when he was put out for Maria Anna; he was a pretty, likeable baby and boy, and the relations between his mother and him were always warm and close;¹¹

> Letizia tried to nurse Napoleon, a small, delicate baby, but the milk failed, and he was suckled by a wet-nurse and slept with her in a back room; the relations between the nurse and Napoleon were always warm and affectionate;

> in his first months Napoleon had a sweet and gentle disposition,¹² but from at least age two he became irritable, self-assertive, quarrelsome, violent, quick in sizing up human situations and in responding, rivalrous, though also affectionate and remorseful.¹³

⁵Bartel, *Jeunesse inédite*, p. 33.
⁶Arthur Chuquet, *La Jeunesse de Napoléon* (Paris, 1897), I, 72.
⁷Young, *Growth of Napoleon*, p. 81.
⁸Chuquet, *Jeunesse de Napoléon*, I, 45, 51.
⁹*Ibid.*, 44–45, 58–59.
¹⁰*Ibid.*, 45–46, 50–51; quotation from Young, *Growth of Napoleon*, p. 45.
¹¹Chuquet, *Jeunesse de Napoléon*, I, 72; Owen Connelly, *The Gentle Bonaparte: A Biography of Joseph, Napoleon's Elder Brother* (New York, 1968), pp. xiii, 5–6.
¹²Bartel, *Jeunesse inédite*, p. 31.
¹³These qualities appear in the stories at the beginning of this article. The coincidence

THE ROOTS OF PERSONALITY

Now, in terms of modern psychology what might the data mean? In general the family was warm and affectionate, and its members were usually supportive of each other. From that support might come self-assurance and even clannish pride. Specifically, it might be speculated that the trusting relationship with the wet nurse gave the infant Napoleon a trust in himself and laid the foundation for a fundamental self-assurance that would sustain him in later events. However, Napoleon's position in the family was challenging. When he emerged from these early relations with the nurse he discovered, so to speak, that he was a member of two triangles (Napoleon, Mother, Joseph; Napoleon, Mother, Charles) in which the adored mother had warm and close relations with Joseph and with Charles of a type from which he was excluded. Simply to secure her attention and win her applause he began to assert himself—to jump up and down, to compete with Joseph, and to play tricks. However, in granting approval she early set standards: you do not win my favorable attention by tricks but by performance and achievement. He was thus bound to his mother not by reciprocal warmth and closeness but by a satisfaction of his own needs for approval. He was also given a slant toward obtaining approval through achievement. And achievement in the early years meant overtaking his brother and being the victor, even though Napoleon might be remorseful at being victorious over Joseph, whom he liked.

Thereafter, the early growth of Napoleon depended on his companionship with Joseph and their interrelations with the mother. Let us consider two brothers, aged five and three, playing together.[14] Five performs a gymnastic feat on the sofa, perhaps in the mother's presence. Three imitates it, with success but with difficulty. Both are in a standard learning situation: the acquired drive for both is desire for mother's approval; the cue for five is the sofa and mother's presence, and his response is to perform the feat; the cue for three is mother's presence and his brother's performance, which he imitates; the reward for both is mother's applause. Both children will learn from a succession of such incidents. However, five with a secure superiority will grow up to be assured, self-satisfied, mild, and, since he is pressed by the younger, perhaps a capable man. Three has had to assert himself, to strain after an uncertain prestige, and to force his abilities by exercise, in order, on occasion, to capture the mother's attention. In any case, as an adult Joseph had the self-confidence of one who had enjoyed an assured position in childhood. He was capable, and he

---

of his weaning with the arrival of the third child, Maria-Anna, whom the mother nursed, may have set Napoleon off.

[14] Young, *Growth of Napoleon*, p. 82.

enjoyed having public approval, but he did not drive for it. Napoleon, of course, was self-assertive and drove to overtake and to overcome.[15]

It might also be speculated that Napoleon's early self-assertiveness grew out of the rivalry of the child with the father for the mother's attention. There may have been indeed an oedipal situation, but there is little evidence to prove it. The importance of the father in the formation of Napoleon's personality may lie elsewhere. Charles Bonaparte was an intriguer and a self-promoter. He supported the Corsican hero, Pasquale Paoli, in the war of Corsican independence against the French. But when the Corsicans lost, he did not follow Paoli into exile in England but joined the winning side. He assiduously cultivated the favor of the French governor, Marbeuf, while seeking to keep on good terms with Marbeuf's enemy, Narbonne. He established his family's claim to nobility for eleven generations, became a deputy of the Corsican nobility in the Corsican States-General, was elected to the Commission of Twelve that acted for the nobility between sessions, and in 1777 was leader and spokesman of a three-man Corsican delegation that waited on the king at Versailles.[16] Through the influence of Marbeuf he was able to secure in 1778 the appointment of Napoleon as royal scholarship pupil in the French preparatory school of Brienne. He inspired each member of the family to have pride in being a Bonaparte, which was another reason for Napoleon's self-assurance, and he set an example of aggressive, persevering, self-serving intrigue in the invidious French and Corsican cultures. By the time Napoleon left Corsica for France as a child of nine he must have been aware of his father's importance in Franco-Corsican relations and of some of the adroit maneuverings by which this position was maintained.

For the child of nine, small and slight for his age, scion of a person of importance in a little world, Brienne was a shock. The French minister of war, Saint-Germain, had decided that 650 young gentlemen, poor but noble, would be educated at the king's expense in twelve *collèges* or preparatory schools. Those who appeared most gifted would then be admitted to the Royal Military School at Paris. The French conquest of Corsica had just been completed in 1769. To conciliate the Corsicans a few scholarships were granted to sons of relatively impecunious Corsican nobles. Napoleon was the first Corsican recipient of one of these scholarships. There was nothing military about the *collège* of Brienne. It was a typical French boarding school,

---

[15] The sense of sibling rivalry with Joseph persisted into maturity. The story is told that Napoleon, emperor and master of Europe, "blackened with rage when his old nurse said Joseph had been a *joli enfant* [nice-looking child] while he had not" (Connelly, *Gentle Bonaparte*, p. xiii).
[16] Chuquet, *Jeunesse de Napoléon*, I, 44–45, 56–59.

taught by a Catholic teaching order, the Minims. There were 110 pupils of whom fifty were royal scholars. Instruction in the ancient classics was stressed. No Greek was taught, but Latin was the chief study, year after year, for six years. The other subjects were French composition, elementary mathematics, German, geography, and history. One of the strictest rules at the "military" schools was that except in rare cases of extreme urgency no boy was ever to leave the school during the six years for which he was entered; he could not go home. In September there was relaxation: only one lesson a day and freedom for long walks, but there were no holidays. Parents at long intervals might be permitted to enter the school to see their boy, but he could not leave it to see them. It was an intense, monastic life.[17]

Napoleon was a *child* of the south: he was transported to a climate that was cold and damp. He spoke Italian: the lessons were conducted in French, which he was just learning. He was a Corsican, a member of a conquered people: he was scorned and derided by his fellow French students. He was by French standards a poor, provincial noble: the sons of French aristocrats snubbed him.[18] His very self-assurance and self-assertiveness may have provoked the older French boys to torment him. More profoundly, he may have been subjected to French ways of managing children that a young Corsican would not immediately understand. In any case, living alone in the midst of the enemies of his country, the conquerors of his nation, he was thrown back upon himself. Resourceful, he developed mechanisms of defense that enabled him psychologically to keep going in a situation of stress and to emerge stronger for the experience. He minimized his contacts with other inmates of this school-prison. He rarely joined their sports; he had only one or two friends, Charles Le Lieur and perhaps Bourrienne [his future private secretary]; over two or three summers he built a garden and arranged the plants, vegetation, and palisades to form a bower of seclusion to which he could retire.[19] He learned to control his rage. As a boy in Ajaccio he had always been flaring into anger and into street fights. At Brienne such angry outbursts would only amuse his tormentors, and though he might still flare out on occasion, he usually kept his temper.[20] He accepted the Corsican identity thrust upon him: yes, I am a Corsican, and I am proud of it; today we are vanquished, but tomorrow we shall be free. Paoli was his hero. "Paoli will return," he cried one day, "and if he cannot break our

---

[17]*Ibid.*, 85–89.
[18]*Ibid.*, 116.
[19]*Ibid.*, 118; Bartel, *Jeunesse inédite*, pp. 81–83, 245, 247, 248, 249, 255; Bourrienne, *Mémoires*, ed. Désiré Lacroix (Paris, n.d.), I, 21.
[20]Bartel, *Jeunesse inédite*, pp. 245, 247; Chuquet, *Jeunesse de Napoléon*, I, 119, 120; Young, *Growth of Napoleon*, pp. 86–87.

chains, I shall go to his aid as soon as I am strong enough and perhaps the two of us together will deliver Corsica from the odious yoke it bears."[21]

He had won his mother's approval through achievement, and now he worked at those subjects which interested him. He was excellent in mathematics, good or very good in history and geography, and deficient in Latin, a subject he refused to study seriously as having no practical value. During play hours he read, borrowing book after book from the school library, chiefly history books, and particularly Plutarch. Work paid off in knowledge and sense of accomplishmnt, in prestige, in tangible reward, and presumably, in reduction of anxiety. He had learned to read (in Italian) at the primary school of Ajaccio, and now at Brienne he became practiced in French and also in mathematics. At successive exhibitions he was quizzed first on arithmetic, then on geometry and algebra, and finally on trigonometry and conic sections. He came to be known as the ablest mathematician of the school and its most indefatigable reader.[22] After five-and-a-half years at Brienne he was one of those selected to advance to the Royal Military School at Paris.[23] He worked, and he also dreamed and planned. He dreamed of the liberation of Corsica and of his heroic rôle in it. In his last year he may have planned a history of Corsica, for he requested his father to send him histories of the island.

Notably, under stress Bonaparte turned neither to religion, which might have afforded consolation and support, nor to sexual pleasure, which might have taken the edge off his hostilities. He received his first communion at Brienne, was confirmed during his year at the Royal Military School, and always dutifully attended daily chapel, but at some point his childhood belief dissolved to be succeeded by a vague, inoperative deism.[24] There were homosexual "nymphs" at Brienne, but he was not attracted.[25] Later, after graduation, when heterosexual opportunities became available, he remained chaste,

---

[21]Chuquet, *Jeunesse de Napoléon,* I, 117; this quotation may seem too pat, but it is confirmed by a caricature of Napoleon, drawn by a fellow cadet at the école militaire in Paris in 1784 or 1785. It represents Napoleon standing, a severe determined look upon his face, with both hands on the top of an upright musket whose butt rests on the ground. A smaller figure, behind him, an old man whose nose nearly reaches his chin, is pulling him back by his wig. Underneath is written: "Bonaparte flies to the aid of Paoli to draw him from the hands of his enemies." (*Ibid.,* 262–63.) See also Bartel, *Jeunesse inédite,* p. 246.

[22]*Ibid.;* Bourienne, *Mémoires,* I, 21; Chuquet, *Jeunesse de Napoléon,* I, 124, 126–30, 141–42.

[23]*Ibid.,* 142–43, 145.

[24]*Ibid.,* 113–14, 204; II, 25–26; Bartel, *Jeunesse inédite,* pp. 259, 263.

[25]*Ibid.,* pp. 79–80; Chuquet, *Jeunesse de Napoléon,* I, 113.

perhaps from memory of the perfect woman, his mother.[26] His personality remained integral, basically self-assured and self-assertive, sturdy and aggressive, but with aggressiveness finding outlets and significance in work and in dreams and plans.

Napoleon left Brienne for the Royal Military College at Paris on October 30, 1784, at the age of fifteen. The patterns of behavior that had been set and hardened under five-and-a-half years of stress at Brienne continued at the Royal Military School. To be sure, his withdrawal from association with Frenchmen moderated. There was a certain camaraderie among the cadets of the school and probably greater acceptance of the Corsican who had established his right to be there. Also, once he had forged a personality that stood up under stress he could be more at ease with himself and, hence, with others. He made friends among the French cadets and had one chum, Alexander des Mazis.[27] However, he still identified with Corsica and dreamed of its heroic liberation by Paoli and himself.[28] He worked, even harder than at Brienne, and was again rewarded in knowledge, prestige, and advancement, thus confirming a habit of industry already formed. He again was known as "one of the ablest mathematicians of the school," and he passed his certifying examination for a commission as second lieutenant in the royal artillery after only a year of study instead of the usual two or three.[29]

He left Paris to join his regiment La Fère at Valence on October 30. One is tempted to say that for the next seven-and-three-quarters years, until June 11, 1793, he led a double life, had a double identity, and wrote two literary styles. One life was that of an officer in the French royal artillery. When not on leave to Corsica, he resided with his regiment at the garrison town of Valence from November 1785 to September 1786; at the artillery school of Auxonne from June 1788 to September 1789 and again from February 12, 1791, to June 14, 1791; then again at Valence from June 16, 1791, to the end of August 1791. He performed his duties punctually, conducted exercises and experiments, wrote analytical, intelligent, and cogent reports, learned the new strategic theories of mobile warfare of Bourcet and Guibert, and received the gratifying praises of the commandant of the artillery school, Baron du Teil, for intelligent work and accomplishment.[30] He continued his companionship with Alexander des Mazis, the chum of the Royal Military College, and he made other friends within the

---

[26]Bartel, *Jeunesse inédite*, p. 261; Henri Bertrand, *Cahiers de Sainte-Hélène: Journal 1818–1819* (Paris, 1959), p. 67.
[27]Bartel, *Jeunesse inédite*, p. 256; Chuquet, *Jeunesse de Napoléon*, I, 232, 260–62.
[28]Bartel, *Jeunesse inédite*, p. 259; Chuquet, *Jeunesse de Napléon*, I, 262.
[29]*Ibid.*, 227, 259, 260.
[30]*Ibid.*, 280–82, 348–55.

regiment and in town. He had come from an affectionate family, and now that he was more at ease he was, in his personal relations with Frenchmen, chatty, amiable, grateful.[31] In off-duty hours he read and read, chiefly history, political science, and Rousseau, taking notes and gaining knowledge.[32]

Yet all the while he was leading another life, having another identity, and writing another literary style, that of an imaginative dreamer and actor for Corsica. After a day of dutifully and punctually obeying orders in the French Royal Army, Bonaparte would retire to his room to write an analytical declamatory essay à la Rousseau, proving that by the social contract the Corsicans could justly shake off the hateful yoke of the Genoese and now that of the French, "Amen."[33] Or, perhaps after chatting amiably one evening with his landlord and landlady, he would retire to compose a declamatory essay on suicide: how can one go on living when one's country is subdued and one is condemned to live among a people whose vain and corrupt manners are so different from one's own![34] A little later, he contrasts the republican love of country with the love of glory to the detriment of the latter, thus rejecting the invidious values of the society in which he moved.[35] At Auxonne, after he had completed his second memoir for Du Teil, he wrote out a gory fantasy of a single Corsican knifing a band of French marauders and consuming their bodies in fire.[36]

Notably, he usually composed these fantasy-essays while on garrison in France. In Corsica he was acting out the fantasy. His first Corsican leave began on September 11, 1786. He had left his Corsican home at the age of nine. He now returned to Ajaccio, a young second lieutenant of seventeen, short, dark, and energetic. He now adored once again his mother, a vital, mature southern beauty and widow at thirty-six. He resumed relations with Joseph, who also had had a French education, at the *collège* of Autun. As the oldest son Joseph was now the head of the family, but Napoleon, with the prestige of a French commission, had drawn even with him. Affectionately they

---

[31]*Ibid.*, 283–89, 340–45; Masson and Biagi, *Napoléon inconnu*, I, 272–80. There are many pleasant tales of the young Bonaparte's residence at Valence and at Auxonne. Here is one. When the regiment was transferred from Valence to Auxonne, his landlord, M. Bou, and his fiftyish daughter, Mlle. Bou, bade him farewell. "We shall never see you again," said M. Bou, "and you will forget us." "You and Mlle. Bou," replied Bonaparte, placing his hand on his heart, "are lodged there, and in that place memories do not change garrison." And he meant it, and he remembered them the rest of his life. (Chuquet, *Jeunesse de Napoléon*, I, 283–84.)

[32]*Ibid.*, 308; II, 1–7, 15–22, 33–34.
[33]Masson and Biagi, *Napoléon inconnu*, I, 141–44.
[34]*Ibid.*, 145–46.
[35]*Ibid.*, 185–92.
[36]*Ibid.*, II, 75–83.

together declaimed the tragedies of Corneille, Racine, and Voltaire. Living in his Corsican dream Bonaparte gathered materials for the history of his native land and began to write it.[37] His second Corsican leave started in September 1789. When he reached home, France was free, but Corsica was still in subjection. He organized a revolutionary club in Ajaccio, persuaded it to draft a petition to the National Assembly, and fomented a riot in the port of Bastia to support the petition. The petition precipitated the decision of the Assembly to accord equality to Corsica, as a French department, and to recall Paoli from exile.[38] Bonaparte was a leader in the action, Paoli was returning, and presumably he would accept Bonaparte as his youthful aide and collaborator.[39] The dream, it seemed, was becoming real.

But the ensuing events did not follow the script. From the first Paoli chose other Corsicans than Bonaparte as his close advisers. Paoli, a perspicacious old man in his sixties, could sense in Bonaparte's love of country the challenge and ambition of a self-assertive love of self, and he was in no mood to share his undoubted moral leadership over the Corsicans with a youngster. Besides, while Paoli and a few Corsican "pures" had spent twenty years of exile in London, the Bonapartes had bowed and scraped to the French and eaten at the conqueror's trough.[40] Bonaparte, to win the old man, defended him in a pamphlet from the calumnies of an enemy; Paoli coolly observed that such calumnies had better be left unanswered.[41] Bonaparte asked Paoli for documents to complete his history; Paoli replied that he was too busy and tired to ransack his archives, and besides, writing history was not for young people.[42] Bonaparte, participating in the island quarrels, imagining all sorts of schemes, using ruse, calumny, and violence in the face-to-face contacts of mobile, unstructured, intense island intrigues, secured his election as lieutenant-colonel of a Corsican battalion of volunteers; Paoli remained indifferent.[43] Meanwhile, Bonaparte kept open the French route, returning to France often enough to keep his commission in force.[44] Meanwhile, too, Frenchmen were becoming acceptable to him as they recovered the vigor of a free people, granted equality to Corsica, and accorded him promotion in the regular army to first lieutenant and then to captain.[45] The war of

[37]Chuquet, *Jeunesse de Napoléon*, I, 293–94; Bartel, *Jeunesse inédite*, p. 261.
[38]Chuquet, *Jeunesse de Napoléon*, II, 79–92.
[39]*Ibid.*, 75.
[40]Masson and Biagi, *Napoléon inconnu*, II, 333–34.
[41]Paoli to Bonaparte, April 2, 1791, *ibid.*, 199.
[42]*Ibid.*
[43]*Jeunesse de Napoléon*, II, 245–59, III, 14; Marcel Mirtil, *Napoléon d'Ajaccio* (Paris, 1947), pp. 111 ff.
[44]Chuquet, *Jeunesse de Napoléon*, II, 260; Masson and Biagi, *Napoléon inconnu*, II, 197.
[45]Chuquet, *Jeunesse de Napoléon*, II, 93, 243, III, 87.

France with other European powers and the emigration of noble officers were opening a route to his ambition for a professional career. Frenchmen were moving into a position once occupied by his mother: a respected but not intimate source of satisfaction of his need for approval and applause. Bonaparte, to be sure, remained loyal to Paoli until April, 1793.[46] When, however, a local Corsican quarrel flared in that month and placed the Bonapartes among the anti-Paolists and when in May the dominantly Paolist Corsican legislative assembly expelled Bonaparte and his family from Corsica and condemned them to Corsican execration, Bonaparte realistically accepted defeat and sought a career in France.[47] After that, with the death of his adolescent dream of fighting for his native land, he could regard most events, people, and institutions impersonally. Freed from the lesser prejudices of factional and national feeling, he could regard ordinary men as figures to be used swiftly and imaginatively for the accomplishment of his ambition.

At first his ambition was for advancement in the army. After performing various military missions in 1793 he distinguished himself by his activity and intelligence at the siege of Toulon and attracted the attention of the deputy Barras. He received the gratifying promotion to general of a brigade and was given command of the artillery of the Army of Italy. But after the overthrow of Robespierre the officers of that army were suspect as Jacobins. Bonaparte was recalled to Paris and ordered to proceed to the Vendée and there take command of an infantry brigade. "Here he would be engaged as an officer in an arm not his own, in a civil war at once desperate and inglorious, against irregular bands of royalist nobles and peasantry. He came to Paris and then boldly refused to go. . . . After a heated argument with the Commissioner of Public Safety he was struck off the army list for refusal to proceed to his post."[48] In the ensuing days of gloom and unemployment in Paris, Bonaparte spent his time paying calls, keeping up his connections, cultivating the society of Barras. Several memoir accounts describe him at this period: the memoirs of the Duchesse d'Abrantès, who was a child of eleven years in 1795 and whose mother the young Bonaparte frequently visited; those of Bourrienne, a former companion of the Brienne days; and those of Thiébault, an army officer who observed him at Paris headquarters. They all describe him as short, dark, energetic, intense, rather poorly dressed, socially awkward, diffident, fundamentally

[46]Jean Defranceschi, "Paoli et les frères Bonaparte," *Problèmes d'histoire de la Corse (de l'Ancien Régime à 1815) (Actes du Colloque d'Ajaccio 29 octobre 1969)* (Paris, 1971), pp. 141–43.
[47]*Ibid.*, p. 144; Chuquet, *Jeunesse de Napoléon*, III, 126–27, 142–43, 153–54.
[48]Herbert Fisher, *Napoleon* (New York, 1913), p. 24.

friendly and good-natured but ambitious to command.[49] In moments of frustration in Corsica he had proposed to enlist in the British service in Bengal.[50] Now, fantasy-like, he thought of visiting Turkey to offer his services to the Grand Seignior, or more practically he planned to go there as chief of the French military mission.[51] The lucky accident of a Paris [right-wing] insurrection and his success [as a republican general] in subduing it on 13th Vendémiaire (1795) rescued him. He was restored to the army, and due largely to the influence of Carnot he was given command of the Army of Italy.

Two days before he left Paris to take command, he married a woman older than himself, a thirty-two-year-old widow named Josephine. Bonaparte may have married his mother. Josephine was a brown-eyed southern charmer and to an infatuated man a fading Josephine at thirty-two may have resembled a vital Letizia at thirty-six. However, Josephine was not Letizia. She had been born in 1764 on the island of Martinique, the daughter of the supervisor of a sugar plantation. She never received much education—"a little feathery instruction at a West Indian convent," and that was all. At the age of fifteen she was brought to France by her aunt, who was the mistress of the Marquis de la Ferté Beauharnais and who married her niece to the Marquis' son, Alexandre, then seventeen. The household was quite irregular—Alexandre had married the niece of his father's mistress, and all four lived in the same residence. Josephine, young, ignorant, and impressionable, began like her aunt to enjoy life and to have friends. A tall, slender girl of considerable sweetness and charm, she was pliable and adopted the immorality of her group, apparently without any shock. As Alexandre grew up he realized the irregularity of his position, denounced Josephine's aunt and then Josephine, and denied the paternity of one of the two children she had. There was a separation but no divorce. During the Revolution first he and then she were arrested and sent to the Carmelite prison. Alexandre was guillotined, but after seven months Josephine was set at liberty. She was now a widow with two children to support. She was generous, and she had a natural and an extravagant taste for clothes; they were her form of self-expression. So, falling in with the current immorality of the

---

[49]Duchesse d'Abrantès, *Mémoires de Madame la Duchesse d'Abrantès, ou souvenirs historiques sur Napoléon, la Révolution, le Directoire, le Consulat, l'Empire, et la Restauration* (Paris, 1831), I, 245–46, 276–85, 316–17; Bourrienne, *Mémoires*, I, 46–51; Baron Thiébault, *Mémoires de général baron Thiébault* (Paris, 1896), I, 532–33. [Napoleon seems to have been five feet six and a half inches tall, about the average height of a Frenchman in 1800. He appeared short in the midst of his Guard, whose considerable height was enhanced by their tall headgear, and in the midst of his generals, who were robust fellows.—Eds.]
[50]Chuquet, *Jeunesse de Napoléon*, III, 26.
[51]Young, *Growth of Napoléon*, p. 344.

new ruling group in France, she became the mistress of General Hoche and then of the deputy Barras. She finally attracted and married Bonaparte, five years her junior.

Bonaparte was infatuated. The honeymoon of two days was just long enough: it left him in transports. From the army he wrote Josephine the most passionate letters. Indeed, his passion for her may have been a factor in the ensuing Italian campaign. His desire to please and impress her may have inspired him to exalted efforts "which the senile generals opposed to him could not by any woman's smiles by galvanized into" emulating.[52] However, Josephine had married him to provide security for her children. She not only did not love Bonaparte, she scarcely even cared for him. Put off by his awkward aggressiveness, she was even a little afraid of him. While he waited feverishly for the mail, as soldiers do, she seldom answered his letters or dropped only a line or two, "cool as friendship," as Bonaparte remarked. She delayed coming to his camp in Italy and, once she arrived, planned on returning. She was having her own pleasant affairs with other men in Paris. Gradually it dawned on the young Bonaparte that he was not receiving the response, the devotion which he desired. Finally, when in Egypt he learned circumstantially from his family of her latest affair, he was bitterly disillusioned. If Josephine was false, who could be true? He continued to live with her, but the old feeling was gone. Instead of a passion she was only a comfortable tranquilizing habit. The intensity of Bonaparte's initial passion, his slowness to recognize Josephine's infidelity, and the bitterness of his disillusionment may indicate an oedipal relation. The failure of his first and only serious venture toward intimacy and sexual union with a woman no doubt accentuated his drive for power and accomplishment.

The new French government, the Directory, had entrusted Bonaparte in the winter of 1796 with the command of one of its main armies, the army that was assembled in the Ligurian Alps for the invasion of Italy. It was no ordinary army that Bonaparte took over. "Its soldiers, its officers, its generals were hardened veterans. They were survivors of a multitude whose ranks had been thinned again and again by fighting, by hardships, by disease," and by desertion.[53] Its divisional generals had been selected by war. The young Bonaparte faced the problem of imposing his personality and will on the generals. The mobile improvisations employed in the face-to-face contacts of Corsican intrigues were inadequate. To solve his problem Bonaparte adopted the rôle of commanding officer and a manner of reserve, brevity, and command.

---

[52]*Ibid.*, p. 350.
[53]Spenser Wilkinson, *The Rise of General Bonaparte* (Oxford, 1930), p. 79.

THE ROOTS OF PERSONALITY

Three incidents reveal his new approach. An old comrade met Bonaparte at Marseilles, as the latter was proceeding to his post. The old friend moved to embrace him, but a glance from Bonaparte checked him. As Bonaparte approached the Army of Italy, its seasoned generals, Masséna, Berthier, and Augereau, "decided they would ignore the young upstart," to them merely a political appointee. "Augereau especially, a large blustering man, said that he would show this 'General Vendémiaire' his proper place. On April 11, near Genoa, the old generals had their first interview with young Bonaparte. The new general kept them waiting. Then he came quietly into the room, in his general's uniform, hat on head. 'He began to speak at once. In a hard voice, in brief, precise, trenchant phrases, he gave his orders, explained what he proposed to do, and with a gesture dismissed his subordinates.' The generals said not a word but saluted and went out. It was not till he was outside that Augereau recovered his voice. With a loud oath, he said to Masséna: 'This little runt of a general frightened me. It is impossible to understand how he made me feel that he was the master from the moment he looked at me.'"[54]

After the army crossed the Alps, a deputation from Milan, headed by the diarist Melzi, waited upon the young general at Lodi on May 11, 1796. Melzi wrote in his journal:

> General Bonaparte entered; upon seeing us, his countenance assumed a willed expression of severity. Here is the dialogue which followed, half in French, half in Italian, between him and me, who had been named the spokesman of the delegation.
>
> Me.—The town of Milan sends us to present you its wishes for peace and friendship. It wishes openly to express to you the admiration which your luminous qualities as well as your zeal for the service of the French army have inspired. The sincerity of its sentiments and of its past conduct, exempt from any kind of wrong toward France, give it hope that you will be the protector of its tranquility, its laws, its property, and its religion.
>
> Bonaparte.—Your powers?
>
> Me.—Here they are.

---

[54]As recounted in Carl Becker, *Modern History* (New York, 1931), p. 261. Another version of the episode has it that Bonaparte entered the room with a portrait of Josephine in his hand. His extreme youth, his low stature, his thin and sallow face, and his eagerness to talk about his bride lowered him in the esteem of the generals. However, assuming a rôle, "a moment afterwards he put on his general's hat, and" wrote Masséna, "he seemed to have grown two feet. He questioned us on the position of our divisions, on the spirit and effective force of each corps, prescribed the course which we were to follow, announced that he would hold an inspection on the morrow, and on the following day attack the enemy." The generals saluted and went out. (Fisher, *Napoleon*, p. 36; Ramsay Phipps, *The Armies of the First French Republic and the Rise of the Marshals of Napoleon I* (London, 1935), IV, 11–12.

Bonaparte (after having fixed his eyes on the paper longer than it was necessary to read it).—I receive with interest the expression of the sentiments of the town of Milan but (and he made his tone dry and severe) I cannot dissimulate my surprise at your arming at my approach.

Me.—Milan has not armed and does not dream of doing so.

Bonaparte.—How's that? Do I not have in hand the edict of the archduke ordering you on his departure to call out the militia?

Me.—The edict to which you make allusion indicates, general, that the only object of the militia is to preserve internal order.[55]

Bonaparte assumed a manner of reserve, brevity, and command to impose on others. The manner was really imposed on him first by the army and then by society, that is, if he was to have his way. French officers and other Frenchmen reared in an authoritarian family and under authoritarian government, would understand and obey only a person who gave orders. Had Bonaparte been reared in contemporary American society, where the father is only a discussion leader and a politician must be one of the boys, he would have assumed another manner to get his way. In any case he assumed this manner to impose on others, and the manner eventually imposed on him. Joseph, his brother, observed that Bonaparte had two characters: a private one, rather sunny, chatty, amiable, friendly, and the artificial one, of authority. That was true. But with the years the public one ceased to be artificial. The manner became the man, the man became the Emperor, and the public character devoured the private one. As political activity more and more filled his life, his political character was exercised more, his amiable one less, until he became the political, calculating man.

Applying the methods of Guibert with amazing resourcefulness, Bonaparte led his army to brilliant victories over the Austrians in the north Italian plain, and eventually he compelled them to sign the peace of Campo Formio (1797). But as he took over the government of the Italian natives, he was ignorant of civil administration, and he knew nothing of Italians. He was entering, like conquerors before and since, a tangle of motives and personal relationships that were largely unknown to him, and some of his early experiences were strange. In the interview at Lodi with the Milanese deputation he tried to tempt them with the offer of liberty, the greatest gift within the power of the great French Republic to bestow. He said, "What do your people desire?" Melzi replied, "Tranquility." Bonaparte: "And nothing else?" Melzi: "And have you sought for anything else in your

[55]Albert Pingaud, *Les Hommes d'état de la République italienne, 1802–1805, notices et documents biographiques* (Paris, 1914), p. 11.

revolution and your victories?"[56] There was no meeting of minds here. Bonaparte indicated that the Milanese might desire the freedom of a democratic republic. The deputation did not appear interested. Four or five days later Bonaparte, now in Milan, asked another municipal delegation what the dispositions of the Milanese were with regard to liberty. He was told that the people had no notion of liberty. Still trying for his own purposes to set these people in motion Bonaparte instigated the overnight formation of a democratic club of obscure Milanese. They in turn organized a "civic festival" with parades celebrating liberty after the French revolutionary manner. The populace at this time regarded their antics with a "tranquil irony." The word "liberty" and a festival which in France had evoked delirious enthusiasm from millions of people, in Italy moved at first very few.[57]

In his quandary the young Bonaparte, brilliant but green, improvised. He talked, watched the faces of these mystifying Italians, and revised his talk. He acted, provoked response, and revised his action. Or he failed to act, was caught, and recovered. He also read Frederick the Great, a practical prince of his own century. Bonaparte gradually elaborated during his two years in Italy strategies for the manipulation of people as individuals, as groups, and en masse from outside and from above and for the purposes of control. Perhaps unification of his Corsican tactics with his new imposing manner fulfilled once again his need for applause.

The Italian experience was crucial in the development of Bonaparte's career and personality. The campaign rendered him famous and popular in France. The smashing victories over superior enemy forces and the booty he and private soldiers sent to France made him the hero of the hour. The campaign also enlarged his ambition. He had gone forth from Paris simply desirous of being a successful general. His successes led him to dream of greater things, of mastering France. He confided to a civil official, Miot: "I should not want to leave the Army of Italy except to play an [*independent*] role in France resembling the one I am playing here, and the time is not yet ripe." After the peace, on the way back to France, he told the same individual that he was no longer capable of obedience. "I have tasted supremacy, and I can no longer renounce it."[58] At the same time the day-to-day manipulation of the Italians had given him strategies for mastery and affirmed in him the habit of manipulating people not intimately as persons but externally as facts or figures for the achievement of his career.

[56]*Ibid.*, p. 13.
[57]*Ibid.*, pp. 17–19.
[58]Count Miot de Melito, *Mémoires de Comte Miot de Melito* (2nd ed.; Paris, 1873), I, 156, 184.

The Italian experience thus completed the formation of the main lines of his personality. Madame de Staël described him as she remembered his appearance upon his return to Paris in December 1797:

> I saw him for the first time, [she later wrote], upon his return to France after the treaty of Campo-Formio. When I was a little recovered from the confusion of admiration, a pronounced sentiment of fear followed. Yet at that Bonaparte had no power; he was even believed to be menaced by the suspicion of the Directory; so that the fear he inspired was caused only by the singular effect of his personality on almost all who approached him. I had seen men very worthy of esteem; I had likewise seen ferocious men. There was nothing in the effect which Bonaparte produced upon me that could recall to me either the one or the other. I perceived rather quickly, in the different occasions I had of meeting him, that his character could not be defined by the words which we commonly use; he was neither good nor violent, neither gentle nor cruel after the manner of individuals of whom we have any knowledge. Such a being, having no fellow, could neither feel nor excite fellow-feeling; he was more or less than a man. . . .
> Far from recovering my confidence by seeing Bonaparte more frequently, I was constantly intimidated by him more and more. I felt that no emotion of the heart could act upon him. He regarded a human being as a fact or a theory, and not as a fellow creature. He did not hate any more than he loved; there was only himself for himself; all other creatures were figures [to be manipulated]. The force of his will consisted in the imperturbable calculation of his egoism; he was an able chess-player for whom the human race was the opposite party. . . . Every time that I heard him speak I was struck by his superiority; yet it had no resemblance to that of men instructed and cultivated by study or society, such as those of whom France and England can furnish examples. But his discourse indicated a tact for circumstance, like the hunter for his prey. . . . He was man who could be natural only in a position of command.[59]

A human personality, it has been said, is a running function in time. One such function started running on August 15, 1769, in Ajaccio, Corsica, and was named Napoleon Bonaparte, an ego seeking satisfaction, a stubborn ego as it turned out. His life in a warm, affectionate family and his relations with his wet nurse gave him a basic self-assurance. From the time he was weaned his development can be explained by either one of two major hypotheses. One hypothesis derives Napoleon's fundamental dispositions from the combination of a basic oedipal drive with partial applause—winning achieve-

---

[59]Madame la Baronne de Staël-Holstein, *Considérations sur les principaux événemens de la Révolution française* (2nd ed.; Paris, 1818), II, 196–98, 210. First two lines of the quotation slightly abridged to fit the context. Madame de Staël-Holstein wrote this passage in 1815, which was published posthumously in 1818, and she may have read into her impressions of 1797 the effect of her later experiences with Napoleon. However, it may be noted that when Napoleon read the passage at Saint-Helena, he remarked on April 8, 1819: "Her portrait of me is true, that is, she saw me like that; that is the impression she received of me [*at that time*]" (Bertrand, *Cahiers de Ste.-Hélène*, p. 328). He did not necessarily accept the estimate, but he recognized that she would think that way in 1797. To me the passage catches the essence of his personality as it had been stabilized by that year.

ments and successes. The theory runs as follows. The child, Napoleon, wishing to dispossess father and possess mother, drove to have her sole attention but never quite obtained it. Yet he received enough applause for his achievements to encourage him to keep on trying. He sought to outbid Joseph, whom mother liked. He may have succeeded momentarily and repeatedly in attracting the mother's approval, but he could never be sure that she did not prefer Joseph. And besides, even if he won over Joseph, there was always father, whom he could not dispossess. The unconscious wish for mother, the disposition to drive for her approval while knowing one can never fully obtain it, and the encouragement of repeated partial successes was displaced on to other objects in later life and came to form a pattern of behavior. Thus, Corsica became mother, Paoli, the father to be dispossessed, but while momentarily Napoleon won Corsican attention, he did not displace Paoli in Corsican affection. Josephine became mother, the other men in her life the father to be replaced, but Napoleon did not make it with Josephine. Or again France became mother, the potential source of applause, but despite Napoleon's astonishing achievements he could never be sure that he had her, and yet his rewards encouraged him to continue. The combination of an unconscious oedipal drive with repeated, partial successes will explain both his never-satisfied, ever-expanding ambition for ever more unattainable goals and his continuing effort. The way the drive was manifested and expressed was affected by the configurations and resources of the culture and the running events of his life, the schooling at Brienne, the acquisition of knowledge of the new strategies at Auxonne, the opportunities opened by the French Revolution, the accident of 13th Vendémiaire, and the experiences of army command and of governing north Italians.

A second hypothesis would recognize, to be sure, the importance of the drives and dispositions of Napoleon's early years, but it would add that Napoleon's personality was not fully formed by age five. Rather, it was formed en route through many years in a continuing psychological-social process which closed out the fulfillment of some potentialities while accentuating the development of others. This theory, like the first, starts with his life in an affectionate family and his relations with the wet nurse, which gave him a basic self-assurance. But, the second theory continues, his early position in the family as an outsider in the relations of the adored mother with Joseph and perhaps with Charles nurtured the desire to secure applause from people with whom he was not intimately connected and through self-assertive achievements. Later events confirmed this central drive while atrophying the more friendly aspects of his character. His very self-assertiveness later put off some of the people he most wished to win—the aristocratic Brienne classmates, Paoli, Josephine. Resourceful, he invented and borrowed from the culture ways to cope with himself and with other members of the human race. He learned to control his rage, to find satisfaction and praise in work accomplishment, to dream, to fantasy, and to plan, to use available theories of mobile warfare and a seasoned army to win military victories, and to contrive strategies for the management of people from above and by appeal, usually, to egoistic motives. Meanwhile, French society in revolution, by opening careers to talent, loosening the bonds of law and tradition, engaging in war and losing its noble army officers, and passing from one political regime to another, was offering opportunities and occasions to the fulfillment of his ambition and enlarging its scope. By 1797 the values he had accepted for his own life and the rôles and strategies he was employing in managing others coincided with his basic self-assured, self-assertive personality and with the salient values of an invidious, competitive French culture.

In this psychological-social process in which Napoleon's personality was formed, one is impressed by the importance of rejection—the relative inattention of the mother, which the infant might interpret as rejection and which provoked self-assertiveness for applause without associated reciprocal warmth and closeness; the harassment of the Brienne classmates, which fixed the patterns of control of rage, work accomplishment, and proneness to dreams, fantasies, and plans; Paoli's antagonism, which killed the adolescent Corsican dream and focused his energy on a career; and Josephine's infidelity, which closed out his one serious attempt to reach trustful sexual intimacy with a woman. Napoleon was badly hurt four times. No wonder, whether "friendly" and "amiable" or reserved, he kept a distance from human beings. One is also impressed by the importance of rewards—in the mutually trustful relationship with the nurse, which gave him a basic assurance; in the praise and recognition accorded his work, at Brienne, the Royal Military School, and the artillery school at Auxonne, which fixed habits of industry; and in the successive army promotions from second lieutenant of the third and lowest degree to commander of the Army of Italy, which confirmed the focus of his energy on a career in a competitive military structure and endorsed his final acceptance of the values of an egoistic culture. A self-assured, self-assertive, outwardly oriented ego seeking satisfaction, continually coming into contact with people, at times rejected and trying something else, at other times rewarded and continuing what was rewarded, finally reached a solution that coincided with both its central drive for approval and society's values.

One is in addition impressed that this is the story of an ego which failed to achieve satisfying intimate human relationships and which learned to cope with and to master other members of the human race instead. One gains the impression that in these years Napoleon was rarely automatically liked (he had to "win" or "charm") and seldom loved. Of himself he later remarked, "I have never loved anyone except Joseph, and him only a little." Failing in intimate relationships, he learned to find satisfaction in work and mastery of other human beings. Since outside of work relationships and the army he never really understood other people, he contrived strategies to manipulate them as figures for the purpose of control.

What was it like to be Napoleon? What were the inner qualities of his psychic life? We shall never really know, but we can guess. To be Napoleon was to be fundamentally deep down self-assured, quick and wary, quick and meditative, quick to perceive aspects of a social situation, quick to imagine a multiplicity of manipulative responses, some realistic, some wild, and yet meditative in selecting responses and planning; to be desirous of approval, first of mother, then of France, and finally of posterity; to enjoy praise, to enjoy having power over human beings, to enjoy dreams and fantasies that through work could be turned into plans, and to enjoy work and accomplishment. The expedition to Egypt, the Napoleonic Code, the Continental System, and the Grand Empire itself were the achievement of a hardworking, contriving dreamer whose patterns of behavior and underlying dispositions had been set before he came to power.

J. Christopher Herold (1919–1964) was born in Czechoslovakia and studied in Geneva before emigrating to the United States in 1939. He also received his bachelor's and master's degrees from Columbia University. While pursuing a career as an editor, first at Columbia University Press and then at Stanford University Press, he wrote many books, including the following on the Napoleonic era: The Mind of Napoleon *(1955),* Mistress to an Age: A Life of Madame de Staël *(1958),* Bonaparte in Egypt *(1962),* The Age of Napoleon *(1963), and* The Battle of Waterloo *(1967). Thanks to Herold's literary skill, his books appeal to the student and general reader as well as to the professional historian.*

NAPOLEON IN ACTION: THE EGYPTIAN CAMPAIGN

J. Christopher Herold

It was Talleyrand, rather than Bonaparte, who persuaded the Directory to adopt the Egyptian scheme. The moment seemed opportune: England had withdrawn her fleet from the Mediteranean in 1796, and the Continent was at peace. (At any rate, France had been able, in the early months of 1798, to overrun with impunity the Swiss Confederation and the Papal States and to transform them into the puppet Helvetic and Roman Republics, without any power coming to the aid of either.) No time was lost. On March 5 [1798] Bonaparte submitted his plan for the conquest of Malta and Egypt to the Directory; on May 19 the expedition began. The main convoy left from Toulon, to be joined by three other convoys, from Genoa, Ajaccio, and Civitavecchia. Together the armada consisted of almost four hundred ships, including thirteen ships of the line, and covered from two to four square miles when on the open sea. Aboard were about 34,000 land troops (for the most part veterans of the Army of Italy), 16,000 sailors and marines, and at least 1,000 civilian personnel, including administrative officials and 167 members of the Scientific and Artistic Commission. Also aboard was a treasury of 4,608,908 francs, which was about enough to meet the army's payroll for four months. (Of this fund, 3,000,000 francs had been confiscated from the treasury of Berne [a canton of the Swiss confederation].) Obviously, the Direc-

---

From J. Christopher Herold, *The Age of Napoleon* (New York: American Heritage Publishing Company, 1963), pp. 67–83. Reprinted by permission of the American Heritage Publishing Company, Inc.

Figure 1 Bonaparte in Egypt and Syria.

tory expected Egypt to pay for the expense of being conquered, just as Italy had.

In sending this armada to Egypt, the Directory was undoubtedly pleased to have found distant employment for a politically ambitious general and his obstreperously Jacobin troops. Bonaparte, on the other hand, saw in the Orient a field of activity worthy of his genius. "Europe is a molehill," his secretary Bourrienne quotes him as saying. ". . . Everything here wears out; my glory is already past. This tiny Europe does not offer enough of it. We must go to the Orient; all great glory has always been acquired there." Did he really think of conquering India as well as Egypt, as Bourrienne asserts? He may well have dreamed of that possibility—but he knew for a certainty that a few victories in Egypt would prove useful to his ambitions after his return to France.

The preparations for the campaign were completed with the utmost haste and secrecy. The fact that a huge fleet was being fitted out at Toulon could not escape the British government; however, the French government, by leaking contradictory information to the press, managed very adroitly to confuse the British. Twelve days after the French fleet had left Toulon, William Pitt, the British prime minister, still believed that its destination was Ireland; many others thought it was England, and an invasion hysteria swept the country. To be on the safe side, the British Admiralty dispatched a squadron to the Mediterranean, with the mission of finding and destroying the French fleet. Its commander was Admiral Sir Horatio Nelson.

Bonaparte's first objective was Malta, held since 1530 by the Knights of St. John of Jerusalem, or Knights Hospitalers, a military and religious order consecrated to the profitable task of raiding Moslem shipping. Its great days were past, and in 1798 only some three hundred knights (most of them French) were left on the island. On June 12, after a day's token fighting, the knights surrendered the island to the French Republic in exchange for lifetime pensions. Bonaparte set up a provisional government, established a garrison, liberated the Turkish and Moorish galley slaves, ransacked the Arsenal, and removed from the Church of St. John about six million francs' worth of treasures. Napoleon having thus dealt with Malta, the armada sailed on June 19 for its next destination, Alexandria.

Two days before Bonaparte's fleet left Malta, Admiral Nelson's fourteen ships of the line anchored in the Bay of Naples. The British minister, Sir William Hamilton, suggested that the French might be off Malta. Nelson set off in hot pursuit, guessing the destination of the French to be Egypt. Sailing at twice the speed of the slow French convoy, he unwittingly passed it at a few miles' distance during the foggy night of June 22–23. From then on, the unsuspecting quarry trailed the impetuous pursuer. On June 29, in the morning, Nelson was off Alexandria and found no sign of the French; he left the same day, in the direction of Crete; the same evening, the French frigate *La Junon*, sent ahead of the main fleet by Bonaparte, anchored off Alexandria and took aboard the French consul. Two days later—July 1—the entire French armada arrived in sight of the city. The people ashore, says an Arabic chronicler, "when they looked at the horizon, could no longer see water but only sky and ships; they were seized by unimaginable terror."

The weather had been fairly rough during most of the six-week crossing. The troops were almost all seasick, squeezed together like cattle, and reduced during the last lap of the journey to eating rotten salt meat and wormy biscuit, and drinking fetid water. Most of them could not swim; none had been trained in landing operations; nobody had thought of equipping them with such elementary necessities as water flasks. Bonaparte, informed by the French consul at Alexandria that Nelson's fleet had just left, ordered an immediate disembarkment, before Nelson had a chance to return, on the treacherous coast west of Alexandria. Sick, starving, exhausted, the troops spent more than twelve hours landing during a stiff gale. Shortly after midnight, without artillery, they began their march on the city. By 11 A.M. they had taken Alexandria. Had they not done so, they would have died of thirst. Two days later, with most of the equipment not yet unloaded, the army began its march to Cairo.

The troops had been told that they would find villages, food, and water; instead, they found only desert, ruined hovels, mirages, sandstorms, and cisterns filled in by the Bedouins. At one well thirty men were trampled to death in a stampede for a few drops of brackish water. Stragglers were mutilated and killed by the ever-present Bedouins. Scores of men lost their wits and shot themselves. In vain did Generals Desaix and Jean Louis Reynier, who commanded the vanguard divisions, plead with Bonaparte for rations, medicine, and draft animals; all he sent them was reams of his proclamation to the Egyptians. The entire army was seized by a sense of despair and abandonment that never quite left it throughout its stay in Egypt.

By July 11 all the French forces save the garrisons left at Alexandria and Rosetta were assembled at El Rahmaniya, on the Nile. The sight of the river drove the men mad with joy. Some stayed in it for hours; some died from a surfeit of water. After two days' rest the army resumed its march to meet the enemy at the village of Shubra Khit.

Who was the enemy? The Mamelukes, the troops had been told, but they hardly knew who the Mamelukes were. The Mamelukes (the word means "bought men" in Arabic) were a warrior caste that had ruled, or rather misruled, Egypt since the middle of the thirteenth century. Originally imported from the Caucasus as young slaves by the Ayubite sultans of Egypt to serve them as soldiers, they soon overthrew the dynasty and set up their own. When the Ottoman sultan Selim I conquered Cairo in 1517, Egypt became nominally a Turkish province governed by a pasha, but the actual government remained in the hands of twenty-four Mameluke beys, or princes, and their *kachefs*, or subgovernors. It was they who held virtually the entire cultivated land in military fee and collected the rent from the fellahin, or peasants. Out of their huge revenues they paid a fraction to the pasha of Cairo, who sent it on to Constantinople as tribute. At times they ceased paying tribute altogether until the sultan sent an army to reason with them.

All in all, there were about ten thousand Mamelukes in Egypt. Although they imported wives, mainly from Georgia and Circassia, and had innumerable concubines of every race and color, they rarely produced offspring and down to the last man practiced homosexuality. To replenish themselves they bought boys nine to ten years old—mostly from Georgia and Armenia, though there was a sprinkling of Russians, Germans, Greeks, and Negroes among them—and brought them up as warriors. Each Mameluke was a mounted one-man arsenal and had at least two servants-at-arms on foot. His usual equipment consisted of a musket, a brace of pistols, several javelins, a scimitar of damascene steel, and an assortment of battle-axes, maces, and daggers. Nothing exceeded his courage except his arrogance, ignorance, cruelty, and greed. For a long time the only enemy the Mamelukes had fought was their Turkish overlords, but they kept themselves in practice by fighting each other, the beys being chronically engaged in a struggle for supreme power. At the time of the French invasion that power was held jointly by Ibrahim Bey, who governed Cairo, and by Murad Bey, who controlled the customs receipts and resided at Giza.

Even before landing, Bonaparte had caused to be printed aboard his flagship *L'Orient* a proclamation to the Egyptian people, in Arabic. The French, he declared in flowery language, came as friends and liberators and as allies of His Majesty the Sultan (may God perpetuate his rule!) to punish the Mameluke tyrants. "Henceforth, with God's help, no Egyptian shall be excluded from high office . . . . Those who are the most intelligent, educated, and virtuous shall govern, and thus the people shall be happy." Religion and property, he promised, would be protected.

Bonaparte's assertion that the French came with the blessings of the sultan was not a deliberate lie. It had been agreed before Bonaparte left Paris that Talleyrand would go in person to Constantinople in order to explain to the Sublime Porte why the French occupation of its richest province should be regarded as a friendly and helpful action. Perhaps Talleyrand could have persuaded the sultan to accept his point of view if he had gone; but he never went, and when another ambassador was appointed in September, Turkey had already declared war on France. These developments Bonaparte could not foresee. At the time he was marching to Cairo, he had no reason to expect that he would have to fight any enemies other than the Mamelukes.

At daybreak of July 13 there burst upon the weary French army simultaneously the sound of the *Marseillaise* and the sight of the Mameluke cavalry—some three or four thousand of them—supported by about ten thousand men on foot. The French drew in their breath with astonishment. General Nicolas Desvernois, who was at that time a mere lieutenant, recalled the moment in his *Memoirs:* "In the background, the desert under the blue sky; before us, the beautiful Arabian horses, richly harnessed, snorting, neighing, prancing gracefully and lightly under their martial riders, who are covered with dazzling arms, inlaid with gold and precious stones. Their costumes are brilliantly colorful; their turbans are surmounted by aigret feathers, and some wear gilded helmets . . . . This spectacle produced a vivid impression on our soldiers by its novelty and richness. From that moment on, their thoughts were set on booty."

With all its dash and glitter, the Mameluke cavalry was devoid of discipline or method; as for the foot soldiers, they could be discounted altogether. The combat at Shubra Khit set the pattern for all future encounters. The French divisions formed in squares several ranks deep and waited for the attack. The Mameluke cavalry charged with incredible speed and fearlessness, trying now this, now that side of the squares, only to be repulsed by a murderous point-blank fire of musketry, grapeshot, and cannon balls, and eventually sped off, leaving the foot soldiers to fend for themselves. Thus, though invariably defeated when they gave battle, they were never caught.

The painful march was resumed immediately. On July 21, at 2 P.M., during the worst heat of the day, the French reached Embaba, on the left bank of the Nile opposite Cairo and ten miles north of the pyramids of Giza, which loomed in the haze. Here Murad Bey's army was awaiting them, supported by some Turkish regulars (mostly Albanians) who had entrenched themselves in a strong position at Embaba. Another army, under Ibrahim Bey, was waiting on the right bank but never had a chance to join in the battle. After only one hour's rest, Bonaparte ordered his divisions to advance, hoping to cut off Murad's retreat. As at Shubra Khit, the Mamelukes charged swiftly and wildly for about one hour, then fled south. Several hundred of them, cut off from the rest, withdrew to the fortified position but were thrown into the Nile, where most of them drowned. The Albanian infantry and artillery was cut down in a frightful carnage. That night Bonaparte slept at Murad Bey's country house in Giza, while his army sorted out the fabulous loot left on the battlefield. Murad retreated south; Ibrahim Bey, taking the Turkish pasha with him, fled with his army toward Syria.

To dramatize the event, Bonaparte chose to call the battle at Embaba the Battle of the Pyramids. According to him, the enemy's strength was seventy-eight thousand men, or three times his; actually, it must have been equal or inferior to the French. Before the battle, he says, he addressed to his troops the famous words, as he pointed to the pyramids, "Soldiers, forty centuries look down upon you." There was no occasion when he could have addressed his entire army, but he may have said something of the sort to some officers standing near him. The victory was not decisive, since the larger part of the enemy forces escaped intact, with their leaders; but the report of it in Europe and America, coupling Bonaparte's name with the magic of the pyramids, produced an impression worth several great victories. Almost overnight in Europe, and ultimately in America, all things Egyptian became the rage and Bonaparte's prestige rose to new heights.

Bonaparte entered Cairo on July 24. One week later, in the early afternoon of August 1, Admiral Nelson and his squadron discovered the French fleet at anchor in Abukir Bay. Despite the late hour, he ordered an immediate attack, thus catching the French commander, Admiral François Brueys, with one-third of his crews on shore. Nevertheless, Brueys' position was very strong—thirteen battleships extending in a mile-long line and presenting more than five hundred guns toward the sea. It would have been stronger still had Brueys anchored his ships closer to shore. Defying the shoals, several of the British ships bearing down on the French managed to turn [go around] the head of the French line and to attack it from the shoreside; others maneuvered into positions between the French ships. Within a couple of hours the ships of the French van and center, with the British guns blazing at them within pistol range, were so many floating shambles, while the rear, under Admiral Pierre Villeneuve, stood by inactive. Brueys was wounded early in the battle but refused to leave the bridge; soon after, a cannon ball carried away his thigh and killed him. About the same time, Nelson received a severe head wound.

The battle reached its climax about ten at night, when Brueys' flagship, the huge *L'Orient*, caught fire and blew up with an explosion that shook the shore within a fifteen-mile radius. For ten minutes the thousand guns of the two belligerents fell silent; then the battle recommenced and did not cease until two o'clock the following afternoon. Eleven French battleships had been captured or destroyed; two others, and two frigates, managed to escape. About seventeen hundred French sailors, including one admiral and three captains, had been killed. What happened in the inferno of the explosion to Captain Louis Casabianca of *L'Orient* and his ten-year-old son—the boy who stood on the burning deck—nobody could tell for sure; not a shred was found of either, and the official reports are no more explicit than Mrs. Hemans' slightly confused poem. But there could be no doubt that the Battle of the Nile—as Nelson chose to call it rather fancifully—had cut off Bonaparte's army from the homeland.

On August 19 Nelson departed from Abukir Bay, leaving behind a small cruising squadron to blockade the Egyptian coast. Bonaparte's first reaction to the disaster was, in essence, to shrug it off and to blame it—quite unfairly—on Brueys. True, the army was now cut off, but it was intact; it would double its efforts and establish itself permanently in Africa and perhaps even in Asia.

To Nelson it seemed that with the destruction of its fleet the position of the French army in Egypt was hopeless in the long run. The larger part of the French army shared this belief, and so, especially, did the highest ranking officer after Bonaparte, General Kléber. In retrospect historians must adopt the same position, but in the circumstances such as he knew them in 1798 Bonaparte had good reasons for refusing to regard himself as doomed. The British blockade was not completely effective. With a little good will the Directory could maintain regular communications with Bonaparte and even send occasional reinforcements and supplies. Another fleet might be fitted out. He still believed that Talleyrand had gone to Constantinople and that Turkey would remain neutral. In fact, anything might happen and change the situation for the better—and at worst his presence in Egypt would have considerable nuisance value when a peace with England was eventually negotiated. All these hopes, though reasonable, turned out to be illusory. With the destruction of its fleet, the French army in Egypt was doomed.

The Battle of the Nile had wide repercussions. In September, yielding to English and Russian pressure, Sultan Selim III declared war on France. Czar Paul of Russia, who had declared war after the French seizure of Malta, now was able to send his Black Sea fleet into the Mediterranean and to seize, after a long naval siege, Corfu and the other French-held Ionian Islands. King Ferdinand of Naples, emboldened by Nelson's victory and encouraged by Nelson personally, attacked the French forces in Italy; it was only a matter of time before Austria joined the new anti-French coalition. In Ireland the uprising of the United Irishmen, inadequately supported by French units, was crushed; this defeat, combined with the loss of its Mediterranean fleet, determined the Directory to abandon the idea of invading the British Isles and to employ the Army of England to fight the Vendéan royalists, who had risen once more. In fact, the entire plan of which the expedition to Egypt was a vital part had gone awry. Bonaparte was not informed of all this until several months later; even then, for some time, he pretended not to know it.

Bonaparte received the news of the destruction of his fleet on August 13, 1798; he left Egypt to return to France one year and one week later. The intervening period, despite all its dramatic happenings and heroic accomplishments, may be characterized as a year of make-believe. He made believe that he controlled Egypt, when in fact he never controlled more than Cairo and a few other key cities. In the rest of the country his troops, unless operating in large numbers, were constantly exposed to ambushes and massacres by Bedouin tribes and by embattled peasants. He made believe that he was in Egypt with the approval of the sultan for three months after the sultan had declared war and vowed his destruction. He set up divans, or local governing councils, in Cairo and in the provincial capitals, but the function of the divans was to serve as buffers between the French administration and the population rather than to govern. He encouraged the sheiks of the Divan of Cairo to believe that he and his army were about to embrace Islam and that his coming had been predicted in the Koran; the sheiks did not believe a word of it, but they dutifully passed on the good word in their proclamations to the populace, which did not believe it either. In October, 1798, when the people of Cairo, led by some fanatics, rose in rebellion, he magnanimously forgave the sheiks of the Divan, who had had no part in the uprising, and at the same time wrote to one of his generals: "Every night we have about thirty heads chopped off, many of them belonging to the ringleaders. This I believe will serve them as a good lesson."

In his financial make-believe General Bonaparte displayed true virtuosity. The treasury was chronically empty, the soldiers were not always paid, but he somehow made do by forced loans, pledging anticipated customs receipts, pawning the revenues of crops not yet sown, farming out tax collection, exacting special contributions from the merchant communities, levying fines, and confiscating property on an infinite variety of pretexts. All the same, when he departed in 1799 he left his successor, Jean Baptiste Kléber, in the red by twelve millions. His army, almost to a man, was seized by an epidemic of homesickness and despair; almost one-third of his forces was afflicted with the Egyptian eye disease; a goodly proportion contracted syphilis and gonorrhea; all were bored and short of wine and liquor; and in December bubonic plague made its appearance. Yet to the Directory he wrote: "We lack nothing here. We are bursting with strength, good health, and high spirits." And when the plague struck in earnest, he made believe that it was just "a fever with buboes" and would go away if manfully ignored. He was cut off, abandoned by his government, losing strength every day, faced with a hostile population, and ringed by enemies. To maintain such fictions in the teeth of such realities borders either on true heroism or on sheer madness.

By January, 1799, Bonaparte could no longer blink the fact that the sultan had declared war, since a Turkish army was preparing to invade Egypt through Syria. He resolved to head off the Turks, conquer Syria—that is, modern Israel, Jordan, Syria, and Lebanon—perhaps even to recruit an army composed of Christian Arabs and Druses and then march on to Constantinople. Later in his life, in his conversations and memoirs, he suggested that he might have marched as far as India and founded an Asiatic empire; it is quite likely that he had such dreams even in 1799, but he must have realized the inadequacy of his means, and his objectives for the time being were probably more limited.

The Syrian expedition was hastily prepared and ill-supplied. At first all went well. Jaffa fell after a brief one-day siege, some two thousand soldiers of the Turkish garrison were put to the sword, and the town was sacked in an orgy of rape and murder. Two or three thousand Turks who held out in the citadel surrendered the next day on the promise that their lives would be spared; in the course of the three days following, they were taken to the beach and shot, bayoneted, or drowned. "Among the victims," says a French eye-witness, "we found many children, who in the act of death had clung to their fathers." The nauseating massacre had been ordered by Bonaparte personally: there was not enough food to feed the prisoners. (It is true that only a few days before the capture of Jaffa, the French had been reduced to eating their horses and camels, and that what food they found they in Syria was just enough for themselves.)

The massacre was still in progress when Bonaparte summoned the pasha of Acre, a ferocious old man who called himself Djezzar ("the Butcher"), to surrender to the French and trust their mercy. "Since God gives me victory," Bonaparte wrote, "I wish to follow his example and be merciful and compassionate, not only toward the people but also toward the rulers." No sooner had this blasphemy been uttered than the plague in the French army struck with redoubled violence.

The fortress of Acre was an indefensible medieval stronghold, held during the Crusades by the Knights Hospitalers after it had been captured from Saladin by Richard Coeur de Lion. There was no reason to expect that it could withstand Bonaparte's army of thirteen thousand. But Djezzar Pasha was as obstinate as he was cruel. Among his garrison there was a contingent of European-trained Turkish gunners; the walls of Acre, however old, were thick; and two other remarkable men helped Djezzar to organize the defense. One was Captain Sir William Sidney Smith of the English navy, a somewhat histrionic firebrand who had crossed Bonaparte's path once before, at Toulon in 1793, when he volunteered to set fire to the ships the Allies had to leave behind in the harbor. He now was accredited to the Porte as an envoy plenipotentiary and was also in command of the squadron cruising off Egypt and Syria. The other man was Colonel Louis de Phélippeaux, a former classmate of Bonaparte's at the Ecole Militaire in Paris, who had emigrated during the French Revolution, helped Sidney Smith to escape from a French prison in 1798, and been commissioned in the British Army. Even before the siege of Acre began, Sidney Smith had intercepted the French siege artillery, which came by sea. The captured siege guns were installed in the fortress and Phélippeaux, an expert artilleryman, took charge of the preparations for the defense. (He exerted himself so unstintingly that he died of exhaustion toward the end of the siege.)

Without waiting for a new shipment of siege guns to arrive, Bonaparte ordered one assault after another, each murderous and futile. The trenches were filling up with rotting corpses, which could not be removed, and each new wave of assailants had to step over their decomposing brothers. Meanwhile the plague continued to rage. On May 20, after a two-month siege, Bonaparte gave it up and began his retreat to Egypt. Of his 13,000 men, at least 2,200 had been killed in action and by the plague, and about 2,300 were ill or crippled. Bonaparte, Kléber once remarked, was the kind of general who needed a monthly income of ten thousand men.

The retreat was a nightmare lit up by flaming fields and villages—for Bonaparte wanted to lay waste the land to slow down the pursuing Turks. In Jaffa he ordered about fifty incurable plague patients to be poisoned, an order only imperfectly carried out if carried out at all. At the same time he saw to it that his return to Egypt should look like a triumph. When they marched through a town, the troops were preceded by their bands playing and by the captured flags waving. Prisoners of war and trophies were sent ahead to Cairo, along with bulletins of victory. All this Bonaparte topped off with his proclamation to his own men: they had accomplished their mission gloriously, he told them; Acre had been razed, except for the citadel, which was not worth taking; now they must return to Egypt to defend it against a possible hostile landing. On June 14 Bonaparte and the more presentable part of his army entered Cairo in triumph, with palm fronds in their hats; at this point, make-believe bordered on the sublime. A civilian member of the expedition, describing its horrors in a letter to his mother, concluded his gruesome report with the words: "The report of the commander in chief, which I enclose, will prove to you how much a man must lie to be in politics."

On July 15 Bonaparte received word from Alexandria that the Turkish army that he had destroyed in his bulletins had just landed at Abukir. He wasted no time; ten days later, with a force of about ten thousand men, he attacked the Turks, who were still entrenched near the beach, and drove the larger part of them into the sea, where they drowned—a sight he described as terrible and beautiful. The Turkish landing, with an inadequate force, was an ill-advised operation, undertaken in all likelihood on the rash promptings of Sidney Smith, whose squadron stood by during the battle. Bonaparte, by doubling the number of the Turks in his report to the Directory, transformed a foregone conclusion into a spectacular victory. A man must indeed lie to be in politics, and Bonaparte's projects at the time were decidedly political.

Shortly after the battle, two French officers had gone aboard Smith's flagship to arrange for an exchange of prisoners. Smith obligingly presented them with a set of European newspapers that brought Napoleon up to date on recent events. Although some of the bad news must have been familiar to him, he affected great surprise and indignation as he read it. Austria had declared war in March. Her armies, under Archduke Charles, were driving the French out of Germany, while the Russians and Austrians under Field Marshal Alexander Suvorov were routing the French in Italy. France herself was in a political and financial crisis. Delightful tidings! The fruit was ripe for the hero to come and pick. Taking only half a dozen men into his confidence, Bonaparte prepared to leave for France. About three in the morning on August 18, 1799, he slipped out of Cairo with a handful of chosen men; on August 23 he sailed from Alexandria with two frigates and a couple of smaller craft, the coast being temporarily clear of English ships. After a stop at Ajaccio—the last time he ever saw his native city—he landed at Fréjus on October 9, preceded by the report of his latest victory.

Bonaparte's administration of Egypt has been much praised by his admirers. The objective mind will find difficulty seeing in it anything but a succession of ineffectual makeshifts, but the overall conception was impressive, and equally impressive was the energy, the quick decisiveness with which Bonaparte addressed himself to every practical problem, be it political, administrative, fiscal, religious, legal, or military. Undoubtedly he was the artist, and his critics mere critics. Many of his projects—dams, an improved and expanded irrigation system, the Suez Canal, the introduction of new crops and industries—were carried out in the following century by Mohammed Ali and his successors. Bonaparte could not realize them, partly because he lacked the time and the means; partly because he never enjoyed the confidence of the uneducated population and of the skeptical, conservative elite; partly because the imperious needs of the day forced him to adopt measures directly contrary to his long-term aims. In two respects, however, he was the originator of very positive achievements: he attached to his expeditionary force a large scientific commission, and he ordered General Desaix to undertake the conquest of Upper Egypt as far south as Aswan.

The inclusion of a scientific commission seems to have been Bonaparte's own idea. The commission—about 170 men strong—consisted for the most part of technical personnel: engineers, mechanics, surveyors, cartographers, interpreters, printers, architects, surgeons, pharmacists. However, there were also a number of physicists, chemists, mathematicians, astronomers, geologists, zoologists, archaeologists, economists, artists, musicians, and poets. Some of them were, or later became, men of the first rank in their field: the mathematicians Monge and Fourier, the chemist Berthollet, the economist Say, the zoologist Geoffroy Saint-Hilaire, the geologist Dolomieu, the physicist Malus, the artist Vivant Denon.

Shortly after capturing Cairo, Bonaparte established, on the model of the French National Institute, the Institute of Egypt, which included the more distinguished members of the Scientific Commission, several generals (among them Bonaparte, elected vice president), and a few civilian administrative officials—all French. Both the Commission and the Institute had their headquarters in a group of fine houses in a garden district at the edge of Cairo. Here were their library (to which the local population was welcome), their laboratories, their workshops, their observatory, their museum, their zoological and botanical collections, their aviary, their agricultural-experiment station, their artists' studios, their printing plant, their living quarters, and their meeting hall. Freed from the social distractions of Paris, the scholars gave themselves over with adventurous zeal to their various pursuits, which ranged from simple practical questions submitted to them by Bonaparte (could the army's baking ovens be improved? could beer be brewed without hops?) to the study of the fish of the Nile, of mummified cats and birds, of desert insects, of Oriental music. Field teams were assigned to such tasks as surveying the Isthmus of Suez, compiling detailed topographical maps of Egypt, and exploring the ruins and antiquities. The result of their labors was a monumental and possibly unique work, the *Description de l'Egypte*, in ten volumes of text and fourteen magnificent volumes of plates, published between 1809 and 1828.

As might be expected, it was in the domain of archaeology that the savants' labors bore the most fruit. Until the arrival of the French in

1798, Egypt was known only through the unreliable accounts of travelers, from Herodotus to Savary. The hieroglyphs were as yet undeciphered. The key to an understanding of ancient Egypt was found in 1799, when a French captain of engineers stumbled on the Rosetta Stone, inscribed with an identical text in Greek and in hieroglyphic and in demotic characters. It was only thirty-two years later that Jean François Champollion fully deciphered the Egyptian text, but the impetus that brought the new science of Egyptology into existence was given by Bonaparte, when he ordered General Desaix to pursue Murad Bey in Upper Egypt and to bring the provinces from Beni Suef to Aswan under French control.

Desaix's campaign is one of the great epics of modern times. For eleven months, with only three thousand infantry, one thousand horse, and a few guns, the thirty-year-old general pursued the elusive Murad and his Mamelukes in a succession of forced marches and countermarches that totaled well over three thousand miles. Desaix never caught Murad, though he defeated him several times and at one point forced him to retreat deep into the Sudan. His division was chronically out of shoes, medicine, and ammunition, and one-third of his men was suffering from purulent ophthalmia. Yet despite their hardships, Desaix's men experienced an exhilarating sense of adventure and discovery. Their marches took them, repeatedly, through the monumental ruins of Dendera, Luxor, Karnak, the Valley of the Kings, Hermonthis, Edfu, and Philae, and they could inscribe their names beside those of Roman legionaires. When, one day at sunrise, they were confronted by the breath-taking sight of Thebes spread out before them, the entire division halted spontaneously to applaud and to present arms, while the bands struck up.

With the vanguard of the division there rode a civilian in his fifties whose chief baggage consisted of a vast portfolio and a supply of pencils. Denon, known until then only as an amiable courtier at the Versailles of Marie Antoinette and as a gifted illustrator and pornographer, was discovering a new world. It is difficult to say which sentiment prevailed in him—enthusiasm over the glories of ancient Egyptian art and architecture or frustration at having to pass by the ruins at the speed of an army in hot pursuit. On his first visit to Thebes he barely had time to make a few sketches; fortunately, he returned several times at greater leisure. Soon his portfolio was bursting with sketches of sights and of details; it was through his eyes, from his drawings, that the world became acquainted with Egyptian art. Later, another expedition of experts was dispatched to Upper Egypt for a systematic exploration of its treasures, whose grandeur has fascinated men's minds ever since. "The true conquests," Bonaparte had written shortly before going to Egypt, "the only ones that leave no regret, are those that have been wrested from ignorance." The sentence might stand as an epitaph for the entire Egyptian campaign.

As for the ephemeral conquest—Egypt—it was retained for two years after Bonaparte's return to France. Kléber, whom he had appointed to be his successor without even consulting him, was anxious to bring the army back to France before disease and more Pyrrhic victories had annihilated it. By the Convention of El Arish reached with the grand vizier and Sir Sidney Smith, he agreed to evacuate Egypt aboard Turkish transports. The Convention, however, was disavowed by the British government, and Kléber, who had already evacuated most of Lower Egypt, was obliged to reconquer it. On June 14, 1800—less than three months after his brilliant victory at Heliopolis—he was assassinated by a Moslem fanatic. His successor, General Menou, a convert to Islam, boasted that he would defend Egypt to the last man. As incompetent and foolish as Kléber had been able and realistic, Menou was obliged to capitulate, on August 30, 1801, to a British expeditionary force of some seventeen thousand men, which had invaded Egypt simultaneously with a large Turkish army under the grand vizier. Under the terms of the capitulation, the British navy repatriated all the French forces in Egypt—about half of their original strength—with all their arms and baggage. On October 1, shortly before their return, a preliminary peace between England and France was signed at London. This anti-climactic conclusion of the Egyptian adventure took place two years after General Bonaparte had seized the power in France. Futile as it was, the campaign had served the general's personal advancement.

For biographical information on Harold T. Parker, see the earlier selection by him in this chapter.

NAPOLEON AS ADMINISTRATOR
Harold T. Parker

Napoleon, like Philip II of Spain, Louis XIV, and Frederick the Great, was a working executive. Like them he arranged his daily round (schedule) for the achievement of maximum administrative effectiveness.

As emperor he lived on the second floor of the palace of the Tuileries in rooms facing the garden that were arranged for work, convenience, and unobtrusive security. Viewed from the garden, the rooms, left to right, were: his *cabinet de toilette* or dressing room; his bedroom (with a staircase to the empress' bedroom below); the map room with large table on which a map could be fully unrolled; his inner office where he worked in seclusion with his private secretary; an outer office where he met with ministers and other officials; and two outer antechambers for the aides-de-camp and pages of the day.

Generally Napoleon rose at 2 A.M. after a first sleep of four to five hours. In a plain dressing gown of dimity in summer and flannel in winter and with a white bandanna around his head, he walked from his bedroom through the map room into his private office. There he worked silently for two or three hours on administrative papers and problems. The Mamluk Roustan slept on a mattress outside the bedroom door, a deputy valet was close by at all times, and one of the two guards of the office's archives kept a vigil over the files in an alcove off the map room. An aide-de-camp was always on guard in the apartment's antechamber. At about 5 A.M. Napoleon went back to bed for a second sleep.

At 7 A.M. the emperor rose again. Constant (Wairy), the first valet de chambre, dressed him in the uniform of a colonel of Guard Cavalry, while he received his master of the wardrobe (M. de Rémusat or after 1811 M. de Turenne d'Aynac), his personal physicians (Jean Corvisart and A. U. Yvan), and often the grand marshal of the palace, G.-C.-Michel Duroc. After a simple breakfast, consumed in ten minutes, he went into his private office. By 8 A.M. he was down to work.

From Harold T. Parker, "Napoleon I, Daily Round," in *Historical Dictionary of Napoleonic France, 1799–1815*, ed. by Owen Connelly (Westport, Connecticut: Greenwood Press, 1985), pp. 357–358. Copyright © 1985 by Owen Connelly. Reprinted by permission of the publisher.

In the center of the office was a large table at which he rarely sat except to sign letters. On the table were booklets of accounts updated each month: reports of the exact state of his army down to the company level, of his navy down to the least warship, of foreign armies, and of the exact state of his finances. There was also a list of the day's prices of wheat in several cities throughout the Empire. At the corner of the fireplace was a settee; touching it was a small table on which were placed that day's incoming letters and reports. In the embrasure of the office's single window sat his private secretary (Méneval or Fain). Napoleon, on the settee, rapidly read through the incoming reports and letters. Those requiring no action he dropped to the floor; those for immediate action he placed in one pile; those needing further thought or research went in another. Returning to the action pile, Napoleon, pacing up and down, dictated replies smoothly and rapidly, leaving to the secretary the problem of keeping up.

Precisely at 9 A.M. Napoleon interrupted the dictation to hold his *lever* [morning audience] in his outer office. He gave audience first to his palace staff, to whom he issued orders, and then to the *grandes entrées* of members of the imperial family, officers of the crown, chief-of-staff Alexandre Berthier, cabinet ministers, senators, deputies, generals, and other high officials who had been invited. Napoleon spoke very briefly to each one, and unless an official had something urgent to present (in which case he was asked to stay over), the emperor was usually back at his dictation and annotation of ministerial reports by 9:30 A.M. By noon he had given his secretary enough letters to write to keep him busy through the rest of the day.

After a luncheon of never more than fifteen minutes with the empress and often an artist or savant, the afternoon was generally devoted to meetings with commissions and committees, the Conseil d'Etat, the Conseil des Ministres, and special councils of administration. These conferences were usually over by 5 P.M. when Napoleon met with his secretary of state, Hugues Maret, his chief of staff for civil administration. A disciplined expediter, Maret guided the traffic of administrative correspondence. At 5 P.M. he brought for Napoleon's signature the letters that had been prepared during the day. Napoleon was then free for a few moments to chat in the empress' quarters with Josephine (or later Marie-Louise) and ladies-in-waiting.

At 6 P.M. there was dinner with the empress (never more than twenty minutes) and a few moments of conversation or perhaps a game of cards. Then Napoleon, more often than not, retired to his private office for further administrative work, retiring about 10 P.M..

Sunday had a more open schedule, with public attendance at Mass, public review of a contingent of the Guard, and a public court dinner with the Bonaparte and Beauharnais relatives. But for six days a week, during the fifteen years from 1799 to 1814, Napoleon worked (while in Paris) fifteen hours a day at his self-assumed task of founding and organizing an empire.[1]

[1] A.-J.-F. Fain, *Mémoires* (Paris, 1908); F. Masson, *Napoléon chez lui: la journée de l'empereur aux Tuileries* (Paris, 1894); C.-F. de Méneval, *Mémoires*, 3 vols. (Paris, 1893–1894), translated as *Memoirs Illustrating the History of Napoleon I from 1802 to 1815* (New York, 1894); Madame de Rémusat, *Mémoires 1802–1808*, 3 vols. (Paris: 1879–80).

Georges Lefebvre (1874–1959) is generally considered one of the most eminent twentieth-century historians of Europe. The child of a clerk, he was born in northern France and attended local public schools and the University of Lille. For twenty-five years he taught at provincial and Parisian secondary schools. At first he did research in medieval history, but after several years he turned to the study of the French Revolution. In 1924, at the age of fifty, he presented his four-volume doctoral thesis on the peasants of the Department of the Nord during the French Revolution. He then taught at various universities, including the University of Paris, where he held the chair of the History of the French Revolution. He published numerous volumes on such topics as the outbreak of the Revolution and the revolutionary mentality, as well as a survey of the Revolution. In addition, he wrote one major work on the Napoleonic epoch, a survey which first appeared in 1935 and went into a fifth edition before he died. Despite Lefebvre's socialist tendencies, he is by no means one-sided in his view of Napoleon.

A ROMANTIC TEMPERED BY REALPOLITIK

Georges Lefebvre

What sort of a man was he [Napoleon]? His personality evolved in so singular a manner that it defies portrayal. He appeared first as a studious officer full of dreams, garrisoned at Valence and Auxonne. As a youthful general, on the eve of the battle of Castiglione, he could still hold a council of war. But in the final years as Emperor, he was stupefied with his own omnipotence and was infatuated with his own omniscience. And yet distinctive traits appear throughout his entire career: power could do no more than accentuate some and attenuate others.

Short-legged and small in stature, muscular, ruddy, and still gaunt at the age of thirty, he was physically hardy and fit. His sensitivity and steadiness were admirable, his reflexes quick as lightning, and his capacity for work unlimited. He could fall asleep at will. But we also find the reverse: cold humid weather brought on oppression,

From Georges Lefebvre, *Napoleon: From 18 Brumaire to Tilsit, 1799–1807*, trans. by Henry F. Stockhold (New York: Columbia University Press, 1969), pp. 63–68. Copyright © 1969 Columbia University Press. Reprinted by permission of Columbia University Press and Routledge & Kegan Paul PLC.

coughing spells, dysuria; when crossed he unleashed frightful outbursts of temper; over-exertion, despite prolonged hot baths, despite extreme sobriety, despite the moderate yet constant use of coffee and tobacco, occasionally produced brief collapses, even tears. His mind was one of the most perfect that has ever been: his unflagging attention tirelessly swept in facts and ideas which his memory registered and classified; his imagination played with them freely, and being in a permanent state of concealed tension, it never wearied of inventing political and strategic motifs which manifested themselves in unexpected flashes of intuition like those experienced by poets and mathematicians. This would happen especially at night during a sudden awakening, and he himself referred to it as "the moral spark" and "the after midnight presence of the spirit." This spiritual fervour shone through his glittering eyes and illuminated the face, still "sulphuric" at his rise, of the "sleek-haired Corsican." This is what made him unsociable, and not, as Hippolyte Taine would have us think, some kind of brutality, the consequence of a slightly tarnished *condottiere* being let loose upon the world in all his savagery. He rendered a fair account of himself when he said, "I consider myself a good man at heart," and indeed he showed generosity, and even kindness to those who were close to him. But between ordinary mortals, who hurried through their tasks in order to abandon themselves to leisure or diversion, and Napoleon Bonaparte, who was the soul of effort and concentration, there could exist no common ground nor true community. Ambition—that irresistible impulse to act and to dominate—sprang from his physical and mental state of being. He knew himself well: "It is said that I am an ambitious man but that is not so; or at least my amibition is so closely bound to my being that they are both one and the same." How very true! Napoleon was more than anything else a temperament.

Ever since his military school days at Brienne, when he was still a poor and taunted foreigner, timid yet bursting with passion, Napoleon drew strength from pride in himself and contempt for others. Destined to become an officer, his instinct to command without having to discuss could not have been better served. Although he might on occasion have sought information or opinion, he alone was master and judge. Bonaparte's natural propensity for dictatorship suited the normal practice of his profession. In Italy and Egypt he introduced dictatorship into the government. In France he wanted to put himself forward as a civilian, but the military stamp was indelibly there. He consulted often, but he could never tolerate free opposition. More precisely, when faced with a group of men accustomed to discussion, he would lose his composure. This explains his intense hatred of the Idéologues [anti-clerical republican intellectuals]. The confused and undisciplined, yet formidable masses inspired in him as much fear as contempt. Regardless of costumes and titles, Bonaparte took power as a general, and as such he exercised it.

Beneath the soldier's uniform, however, there dwelled in him several personalities, and it is this diversity, as much as the variety and brilliance of his gifts, which makes him so fascinating. Wandering about penniless in the midst of the Thermidorian festival, brushing past rich men and beautiful women, the Bonaparte of 1795 burned with the same desires as others. Something of that time never did leave him: a certain pleasure in stepping on those who had once snubbed him; a taste for ostentatious splendour; an over-tender care for his family—the "clan"—which had suffered much the same miseries as himself; and a few memorable remarks of the citizen-turned-gentleman, as on the day of his coronation when he exclaimed, "Joseph, if only father could see us!" But even much earlier there lived in him a nobler trait, a passionate desire to know and understand everything. It served him, no doubt, yet it was a need which he fulfilled for its own sake, without any ulterior motive.

As a young officer he was a tireless reader and compiler. He also wrote, and it is obvious that had he not entered the royal military academy at Brienne, he could have become a man of letters. Having entered into a life of action, he still remained a thinker. This warrior was never happier than in the silence of his own study, surrounded by papers and documents. In time he became more practical, and he would boast that he had repudiated "ideology." Nevertheless, he was still a typical man of the eighteenth century, a rationalist, a philosophe. Far from relying on intuition, he placed his trust in reason, in knowledge, and in methodical effort. "I generally look ahead three or four months in advance to what I must do, and then I count on the worst"; "all work must be done systematically because left to chance, nothing can succeed." He believed that his insights were the natural fruit of his patience. His conception of a unitary state, made of one piece according to a simple and symmetrical plan, was entirely classical. At rare moments his intellectualism revealed itself by his most striking characteristic: the ability to stand off from himself and take a detached look at his own life, and to reflect wistfully on his fate. From Cairo he wrote to Joseph after having learned of Josephine's infidelity, "I need solitude and isolation. I find grandeur tiring, my feelings drained, and glory dull. At twenty-nine I am completely played out." Walking with Girardin at Ermenonville, he would exclaim shortly therafter, "The future will tell if it would not have been better for the sake of world peace had Rousseau and I never been born." When the state councillor Roederer remarked, while visiting the abandoned Tuileries Palace with Napoleon, "General, this is all so sad," Bonaparte, already First Consul for two months, replied, "Yes, and so is grandeur." Thus by a striking turnabout, this firm and severe intellect would give way to the romantic melancholia characteristic of Chateaubriand and de Vigny. But these were never more than flashes, and he would pull himself together at once.

He seemed to be dedicated to a policy of realism in every way, and he was, in fact, a realist in execution down to the slightest detail. During the course of his rise, he made the rounds of human emotions, and well did he learn to play upon them. He knew how to exploit self-interest, vanity, jealousy, even dishonesty. He knew what could be obtained from men by arousing their sense of honour and by inflaming their imagination; nor did he for a moment forget that they could be subdued by terror. He discerned ever so clearly what in the work of the Revolution had captured the heart of the nation and what fitted in with his despotism. To win the French people, he declared himself both a man of peace and a god of war. That is why he must be ranked among the great realists in history.

And yet he was a realist in execution only. There lived in him an alter-ego which contained certain features of the hero. It seems to have been born during his days at the military academy out of a need to dominate a world in which he felt himself despised. Above all he longed to equal the semi-legendary heroes of Plutarch and Corneille. His greatest ambition was glory. "I live only for posterity," he exclaimed, "death is nothing, but to live defeated and without glory is to die every day." His eyes were fixed on the world's great leaders: Alexander, who conquered the East and dreamed of conquering the world; Caesar, Augustus, Charlemagne—the creators and the restorer of the Roman Empire whose very names were synonymous with the idea of a universal civilization. From these he did not deduce a precise formulation to be used as a rule, a measure, or a condition of political conduct. They were for him examples, which stimulated his imagination and lent an unutterable charm to action. He was stirred less by the accomplishments of his heroes than by the consuming spiritual zeal which had engendered their work. He was an artist, a poet of action, for whom France and mankind were but instruments. How well he expressed his sense of grandeur when, in St. Helena, he evoked memories of the victory at Lodi and the awakening in his consciousness of the will to power! "I saw the world flee beneath me, as if I were transported in the air."

That is why it is idle to seek for limits to Napoleon's policy, or for a final goal at which he would have stopped: there simply was none. As for his followers who worried about it, he once remarked, "I always told them that I just didn't know," or again, more significantly, despite the triteness of his expression, "To be in God's place? Ah! I would not want it; that would be a cul-de-sac!" Here, then, we see that dynamic temperament which struck us at first glance in its psychological manifestation. It is the romantic Napoleon, a force seeking to expand and for which the world was no more than an occasion for acting dangerously. But knowing the disposition of one's means alone is not the mark of a realist. On the contrary, the realist also fixes his goal in terms of the possible, and although his imagination and his flair for grandeur push him on, still he knows where to stop.

That a mind so capable of grasping reality in certain respects should escape it in others, as Louis Molé[1] so accurately observed, can only be due to Napoleon's origins as much as to his nature. When he first came to France, he considered himself a foreigner. Until the time when he was expelled from Corsica by his compatriots in 1793, his attitude had been one of hostility to the French people. Assuredly he became sufficiently imbued with their culture and spirit to adopt their nationality; otherwise he could never have become their leader. But he lacked the time to identify himself with the French nation and to adopt its national tradition to the point where he would consider its interests as a limitation upon his own actions. Something of the uprooted person remained in him; something of the *déclassé* as well. He was neither entirely a gentleman nor entirely common. He served both the king and the Revolution without attaching himself to either. This was one of the reasons for his success, since he could so easily place himself above parties and announce himself as the restorer of national unity. Yet neither in the Old Regime nor in the new did he find principles which might have served as a norm or a limit. Unlike Richelieu, he was not restrained by dynastic loyalty, which would have subordinated his will to the interest of his master. Nor was he motivated by civic virtue, which could have made him a servant of the nation.

A successful soldier, a pupil of the philosophes, he detested feudalism, civil inequality, and religious intolerance. Seeing in enlightened despotism a reconciliation of authority with political and social reform, he became its last and most illustrious representative. In this sense he was the man of the Revolution. His frenzied individuality never did accept democracy, however, and he rejected the great hope of the eighteenth century which inspired revolutionary idealism—the hope that someday men would be civilized enough to rule themselves. He did not become cautious through a concern for his personal safety,

[1] Comte Louis Mathieu Molé was prime minister of France from 1836–1839. Under Napoleon I he held various important prefectural and ministerial posts, and he was an *auditeur* in Napoleon's Council of State. TRANSLATOR.

as were other men, because he was indifferent to it. He dreamed only of greatness through heroism and danger.

What about moral limits? In spiritual life he had nothing in common with other men. Even though he knew their passions well and deftly turned them to his own ends, he cared only for those that would reduce men to dependence. He belittled every feeling that elevated men to acts of sacrifice—religious faith, patriotism, love of freedom—because he saw in them obstacles to his own schemes. Not that he was impervious to these sentiments, at least not in his youth, for they readily led to heroic deeds; but fate led him in a different direction and walled him up within himself. In the splendid and terrible isolation of the will to power, measure carries no meaning.

2
JUDGING THE COUP D'ETAT AND THE EARLY CONSULATE

On November 9–10, 1799 (18–19 Brumaire, year VIII), the government of the Directory was overthrown, and Napoleon became First Consul. To some historians, this event represented a disaster for the French people. Albert Leon Guerard, for example, claims that military dictatorship destroyed for decades any budding democracy, regional autonomy, and religious freedom.

Other historians, like Albert Vandal, regard Napoleon's coming to power as most fortunate. Vandal thinks it was the Directory that imposed tyranny on France and that Napoleon quickly attempted to bring order to a chaotic, faction-ridden, and violent country. By his actions, he restored the French people's confidence in the future. Claude Langlois points out that such confidence did not come easily. Langlois shows that the new government tried to make the public believe it was immensely popular, but many citizens did not know what to expect in December 1799–January 1800 and chose to stay on the sidelines.

Albert Soboul rejects any great man or great devil theory of history. He sees the coup d'état as ushering in a government that had to build on the legacy of the Revolution and that favored the property-holders. This new dominant class included members of the aristocracy, bourgeoisie, and peasantry, but not the urban lower classes.

How does one evaluate a new regime that comes to power by a coup d'état? Does one judge it by an absolute standard, and if so, what should this be? Is personal freedom the most important measure or should one consider such others as the achievement of prosperity, equality, representative democracy, stability at home, and victory abroad? Or should one judge a new government by comparing it to the one that came before or the one that came after? If we make such comparisons, then was the early Consulate a more acceptable form of government than either the Directory or the Life Consulate and Empire?

Albert Leon Guerard (1880–1959) was born in Paris and studied in England as well as France. He taught French in a Parisian high school before coming to the United States in his twenties. During most of his academic career, he was a professor of literature at Stanford University. A witty, elegant, and prolific author, he wrote on many aspects of French history and civilization. His books include Reflections on the Napoleonic Legend *(1924) and* Napoleon I *(1956), both critical of Napoleon and his work.*

THE DEATH OF LIBERTY
Albert Leon Guerard

After the [coup d'état of the] 18th of Brumaire Napoleon destroyed, by a stroke of the pen, all possibilities of local autonomy. At the head of each commune was placed a Mayor, at the head of each "arrondissement" a Subprefect, at the head of each department a Prefect, *all appointed by the central power*, and responsible to that power alone. This was not merely a return to the centralizing policy of the Kings: it was infinitely worse. The Intendant of Richelieu was a useful check on the centrifugal tendencies of a province still imperfectly Frenchified, and a watch set upon the Governor, a great lord still imbued with feudal ideas, who might have made himself dangerous. The Napoleonic Prefect had no such peril to guard against: he presided over the artificial, standardized Department created by the Constituent Assembly. So the power of the Intendant was adequate; that of the Prefect was exorbitant.

What France needed, especially after the great upheaval, was a recrudescence of municipal and provincial life, so that the innumerable problems of the new social order might be settled gradually, through many diversified experiments, and so that the vast body of untrained citizens might serve its apprenticeship in local affairs. Napoleon thought otherwise. Once more his conception was that of the soldier: authority, unique, undisputed, descending irresistibly from above. The notion that the prerogatives of the First Consul or Emperor could find their limit in the constitutional rights of a city or of a department would have seemed as absurd to him as a claim to autonomy advanced by a squad or platoon against a colonel. . . .

[We] need hardly ask what he did with Liberty. His apologists are

---

From Albert Leon Guerard, *Reflections on the Napoleonic Legend* (New York: Charles Scribner's Sons, 1924), pp. 62–63, 71–72, 80.

little concerned with that: they claim that the French did not understand liberty, and never missed it. Liberty is so completely the antithesis of the military mind that Napoleon could not be expected to show any great tenderness for it. We all know by what efficient means discordant voices were hushed, in politics, in literature, and in society. France was without a genuine Parliament, without public meetings, without a free Press. Sermons, drawing-room tattle, and private correspondence were under strict censorship. Silence reigned, interrupted only by a well-drilled chorus of praise, until the colossus tottered. Then the Legislative Body recovered the use of its voice, and raised it with a sharpness which, so belated, was another form of cowardice. By 1814 the Napoleonic regime had completely overtaken that of the Louis [XVI] in the way of despotism. "Lettres de Cachet" had their modern equivalents, and for one Bastille that the people had stormed in its wrath, Napoleon restored eight—Saumur, Ham, If, Lanskrow, Pierre-Chatel, Fenestrelle, Campiano, Vincennes. "My father hath chastised you with whips: but I shall chastise you with scorpions. . . ."

What we are claiming is this: France was still in a state of chaos in 1799—a welter of ruined traditions, baffled idealism, lawless appetites. But out of that chaos, weariness and experience were creating order. Napoleon did but accelerate this restoration of normal life. Even under a Barras[1] it would have taken place, and he does not deserve the exclusive credit that he receives for it. But this very acceleration, sensational no doubt, was a curse in disguise. For Napoleon obtained it by a systematic sacrifice of liberty in all fields. The worst tendencies of the Ancient Regime and of the Revolution towards absolutism were renewed and strengthened: France had a military Robespierre on the throne of Louis XIV. The germs of genuine democracy were, on the contrary, stifled. Free government, local autonomy, independent Churches, all disappeared. The progress of material prosperity may have been hastened by a few years; but the soul of France was shackled for a century.

[1][A prominent revolutionary politician known for his scandalous and corrupt behavior.—Eds.]

Count Albert Vandal (1853–1910), whose father directed the French Post Office during the rule of Napoleon III, trained for the law and then entered public service. But the teaching and writing of history attracted his interest more, and he eventually became a professor of law at the Ecole libre des sciences politiques in Paris. This was one of the few institutions of higher education in the Third Republic that flourished under the aegis of neither the State nor the Church. His great book of diplomatic history, Napoléon et Alexandre Ier *(1891–1896), was followed by his* Avènement de Bonaparte *(1902–1907), which extolled the beneficient work of Napoleon as First Consul.*

THE RESTORATION OF ORDER AND NATIONAL UNITY

Albert Vandal

Although the revolutionaries during their last years in power spurned the Jacobin label and had not reopened that famous club, they still remained infected by the Jacobin spirit—the urge to persecute. Liberty existed for the Jacobins alone; they denied it to others, while ordering everyone to worship it on his knees; they had made the word divine but forbade the real thing. This is why the French welcomed Bonaparte as a deliverer and so easily exchanged the oppression of wretched despots for a lofty and impartial tyranny.

Among the accepted legends about 18 Brumaire, none is more erroneous than the supposition that it brought the death of liberty. For a long time it was a historical commonplace to represent Bonaparte in the Council of the Five Hundred at Saint-Cloud[1] destroying a genuine legality with one stroke of his sword and drowning out with his drum rolls the last gasps of French liberty. Such solemn nonsense can no longer be repeated in the face of some clearly recognized and understood facts. Bonaparte can be reproached for not having established liberty; he cannot be accused of having destroyed it, for the excellent reason that on his return from Egypt he did not find it anywhere in France. Bonaparte could not suppress something that did not exist.

From Albert Vandal, *L'Avènement de Bonaparte*, 17th ed., (Paris: Plon-Nourrit, 1912), 1: pp. 26–27, 432–433, 478–482, 484–485. Editors' translation. The author's citations of sources in footnotes have been clarified.

[1][The château near Paris where the last act of the coup d'état took place.—Eds.]

THE RESTORATION OF ORDER

In the early days of the Directory, amid violent reactionary movements, tension had started to relax and a few liberties were recognized. The death of liberty, however, came not on 18 Brumaire but on 18 Fructidor [September 4, 1797], when the revolutionaries ruthlessly seized dictatorial power again to stop a resurgence of royalism. After this coup d'état against the nation [the people], almost all the liberties constitutionally guaranteed to the French were forcibly snatched away or treacherously withdrawn. . . .

In 1789, people experienced a spontaneous anarchy; a decade later, in 1799, there was a spontaneous reaction against the Revolution that threatened to turn into another form of anarchy, a frenzy of reprisals and revenge.

Bonaparte felt the danger at once, for above all he did not want his name to become a synonym for reaction. The plan that he conceived for the future was great and redeeming; it was that of the kings and political leaders who had previously shaped or reshaped France. Freeing himself from parties, leaving on his right and left the intolerant of all varieties, he would go straight to the people, to the masses, to the millions of the French who had needs more than opinions, who simply sought domestic peace, religious peace, and peace abroad; he would win their loyalty by assuring them these benefits; he would provide national satisfaction as the basis of his government and would build on this bedrock. Among the conquered masses who had rallied to him, he would incorporate and blend together the many men who had plunged into civil disorders because of suffering or anger, because of momentary passion rather than conscious principle; thus, he would take from the parties their essence, their real force, and he would have to deal only with isolated agitators or leaders without troops. Turning then against these, he would hit them pitilessly, and hit them again, and reduce to nothing this remnant of the factions. He would order useful men of all parties to forget; decreeing the abolition of the past, he would command the French to pardon each other and to unlearn hatred; as to ten years of crimes and horrors [during the Revolution], of injuries to one another, he would mostly let bygones be bygones; this is what was called, in the mythological language fashionable at that time, "to make France drink the water of Lethe" [water from a river in Hades that, when drunk, produced amnesia]. Calling on the most extreme elements of the political spectrum to join him, he would offer as the rallying point a strong and just government, a government sufficiently open, sufficiently glorious, so that all Frenchmen of good will could come to a reconciliation and find themselves comfortable in the magnificent breadth of the regime.

He wrote to the legislator Beyts, one of his opponents at Saint-Cloud: "No sensible person can think that the peace Europe still yearns for will emerge from the factions and the disorganization these create. All of you ought to join the great mass of the people. The simple title of French citizen is certainly worth more than that of royalist, Clichyen, Jacobin, Feuillant, and those thousand and one denominations that the spirit of faction produces, and which, for the past ten years, have tended to hurl the nation into an abyss from which the time has finally come to rescue it forever. All my efforts will be directed to this goal. Henceforth that alone will gain the esteem of the thoughtful, the respect of the people, and glory. . . ."[2]

Looking now at domestic France and considering the state of the parties, we should note that the provisional Consulate, by the care it took to remain on the left, succeeded in rallying most republicans to it. The wise members of the party and those who had learned their lesson, the republicans who had always been or now once again became men of order, that is, the moderates of the left, had grounds to rejoice. It was in their name and by placing himself within the scope of their interests that Bonaparte had acted. Truly, all the people of this sort, in the provinces as well as in Paris, were not just greedy guardians of their vested interests and property. Among them were disinterested and sincere individuals, hoping to reconcile order with liberty, representative government, and philosophical progress. Disgusted by the Directory and its shameful behavior, these people, while calling for reform, at first were shocked by Napoleon's reformist conduct and found the saber waving too prominent at Saint-Cloud. Nevertheless, the legislators of their party, their natural representatives, had participated in or approved the decisive act; and some of these legislators thought they ought to provide explanations to their constituents. They sent to several departments public letters and manifestoes in which they defended the coup d'état and justified their part in it.

They said that the situation before the coup of 1799 was intolerable; there was no longer either a constitution or liberty; the Republic was dying of gangrene. To participate in the Coup of Brumaire was to take the only alternative that remained to save the Revolution and return it to the right track. As to the final result, one had to hope that the coup would serve to benefit the principles of the Revolution, that the future constitution would provide all the necessary guarantees in this regard, and that the true republic would finally appear.

On the long-range consequences of the coup d'état, the legislators and the men in public life, although willing to accept the judgment of their fellow citizens, still showed themselves to be a little less positive. They affirmed only their good intentions and seemed ready, according to whether the future proved them right or wrong, to boast

[2]Napoleon, *Correspondance*, 32 vols. (Paris, 1858–1869), VI, letter number 4398.

or to beat their breasts. After praising Bonaparte highly and predicting a favorable future, Le Couteulx de Canteleu, President of the Paris Administration, had been the first to say the following in a public address: "Fellow citizens, if events turn against my intentions and efforts, I place in your hands here in advance my indictment and sentence for dishonor and death." Laussat from Basses-Pyrénées, Lapotaire from Morbihan, and Harmand from the Meuse expressed similar reservations, but hastened to dismiss them.[3] No, Bonaparte would not be a tyrant; his past, his untarnished glory, and his excellent entourage offer guarantees; he has freed himself from pseudo-legal forms only in order to create a true, permanent legality to replace the institutions which had been destroying themselves. Also, because the government since Brumaire justified itself by promises and liberal practices, because actually nothing looked less like the clear and brutal triumph of authoritarianism than the period right after the coup d'état, and because, in addition, nobody demanded many guarantees in this time of general exhaustion, it was unnecessary to do more in the provinces to reassure moderate republican opinion and bourgeois rationalism.

It was against the other half of the republican party, against the Jacobins and demagogues, that the seizure of power was carried out; but Bonaparte had declared right after his victory that there were no vanquished, that he did not wish to know of any. To the purged legislators, to the Jacobins who "showed the least sign of repentance,"[4] he very willingly awarded compensations and profitable, if obscure, posts; he let those whom he had thrown out of windows return by this humble back door. This manner of granting them amnesty was enough to soothe the irritation, to dress yesterday's wound; and the sword of Bonaparte assumed a resemblance to the lance of Achilles, which possessed the marvellous power to cure the wounds it inflicted.

The Jacobins understood that their reign as a party was over, but noticing that the Consulate attacked them less as individuals than the Directory had at certain times, they hoped that their tumble at Saint-Cloud would result in each of them landing on his feet. Controlled and treated gently at the same time, seeing themselves facing a man who would deal militarily with any attempt at resistance and yet excluded no one, they bore no grudge against him. To be sure, the dismissed officials, certain provincial political clubs, and the members of the [conspiratorial and communist] Babouvist organizations

---

[3] See their letters quoted by Alphonse Aulard, "Le Lendemain du dix-huit Brumaire," in *Etudes et leçons sur la Révolution française*, 9 vols. (Paris, 1901–1924), II, 239. Compare with *Le Moniteur*, 25 Brumaire [November 16, 1799].

[4] Archives de Chantilly, Report of Condé's agents, November 20, 1799.

howled in secret. Some more prominent democrats, convinced and perspicacious, complained of the fate of the Republic, which had fallen into the hands of an ambitious man, but they grumbled in obscurity and appeared mainly to ignore public affairs and retire to their tents;[5] others limited themselves to expressing doubts and to relying on "that justice which has always struck ambitious people and traitors."[6] The mass of the greedy only asked to rush under the yoke, provided it was not immediately made too obvious and rigid. Thus, the newly formed Consulate benefited from the fact that a kind of coalition of very different republicans accepted the early effects of Bonaparte's *fait accompli*.

The royalists, on the other hand, felt disappointed because they wanted more of a reaction. The harshness, especially the verbal harshness, directed against them, and the care taken by the Consuls to maintain in principle the laws of the Revolution and to declare that this set of laws was untouchable, rid them of any notion that there would be a very marked change; they said sadly: "It is still the republic of the Revolution and not a national republic."[7] Even so, most continued to hope; they thought the new power, born of an anti-Jacobin movement, would end up sooner or later succumbing to the impulses which originated it, and that, despite everything, reaction was on the march. For the moment they remained observers of Bonaparte, that great enigma. What should one think of this extraordinary and hybrid being? A correspondent of [the counterrevolutionary Prince de] Condé analyzed Napoleon in the following manner: "One-third *philosophe*, one-third Jacobin, and one-third aristocrat."[8] He added, "Not a speck of royalism in him"; and yet he thought that Bonaparte's usurpation [in 1799] would prepare the return of the legitimate monarch by giving back to the French the habit of obeying a master. Others imagined that Bonaparte played an underhanded game and was moving toward a restoration of the monarchy by oblique and indirect means. Each wove a fantasy about him. This universal uncertainty about his intentions served his purposes by keeping alive the most contradictory hopes.

Besides the genuine royalists, there were those we would call today [1902] simply conservatives, moderates of the right, bound to the past by their origins and customs without seeking to repudiate the entire work of the Revolution, rather liberal people, not very republican, but

---

[5]See for example Robert Lindet's letter of 3 Nivôse [December 24, 1799] in Amand Montier, *Robert Lindet* (Paris, 1899), p. 383.
[6]See the letter of Guillemardet, a deputy of the Convention and ambassador to Spain, in *La Révolution française*, June 14, 1902.
[7]Archives de Chantilly, Report of Condé's agents, November 20, 1799.
[8]Ibid., November 16, 1799.

THE RESTORATION OF ORDER

disposed nevertheless to accept any government that would set society back on its true foundations. These people, after an initial moment of enthusiasm and relaxation of tension, suspended judgment. Among themselves, they discussed and calculated future chances. For a long time treated [by the revolutionaries] as defeated and suspect, holding themselves remote from public affairs, they had never managed to ignore politics completely and to stop discussing it. Now in provincial surroundings, in the salons of small cities, and on rural estates where these semi-royalists protected their straitened and precarious existence, they talked only of Napoleon; he captured their imagination, but had not yet overcome their convictions.

If the optimists asserted that, thanks to his genius, he possessed the aptitude to remedy everything, others refused to recognize in him the man with the answers. Because very soon after coming to power, he took up the task of rallying republicans and gave a strong left turn to the rudder, was he not going to reconcile himself some day with the full-fledged Jacobins and fall back into the old groove? Besides, did the fact that he was endowed with military genius and the gift of victory really mean he was also a great statesman? Called to straighten out the frightful legacy of the Revolution and settle that immense inheritance, wouldn't Bonaparte succumb to the difficulties of the task? That is what men of intelligence and ability wondered, men who later would enter the Consular government and constitute the best of its substance. . . .

Support for the new regime came especially from below; it came from the underlying strata of the population and went to Bonaparte personally without regard to colleagues and associates. His party, a party being formed, was all of France that was disgusted with politics and desired to have no more to do with it, a France of workers and ordinary folk, the innumerable mass of small property owners, the people from the demi-bourgeoisie, those involved in industry and farming—the real people, who should not be confused with either the Jacobin rabble or the demagogues of the right. The strength of Bonaparte was to represent the opinion of those who previously had none or no longer had one. These working and peaceful people had not yet received any very positive benefits from him. They liked him anyway, because they saw in him the embodiment of their hopes; they were grateful to him for what they expected from him. Although he lacked real means to act, his colossal reputation sustained him and inspired some confidence in his future works.

A fragile confidence still, an anxious confidence, for people had been deceived too often by appearances of salvation not to fear new disappointments! Therefore, this was nothing like the outburst of enthusiasm which followed great achievements, and gone was the ecstasy of hope that had welcomed the beginning of the Revolution and its first marvels. Ordinary people felt, however, that amid universal decomposition, the disarray of ideas, and the overthrowing of theories, it was now possible to begin something concrete and strong again. The thinkers, political leaders, officials, and men of letters willingly imagined that [Bonaparte's associate] Sieyès was the head and mind of the government and that he was going to arrange the future in a wise manner; several local administrations named Sieyès before Bonaparte in their public records.[9] The instinct of the general public was not deceived a bit; it guessed and discerned the real leader, the one who would know how to command. General Lannes wrote to Bonaparte after completing his tour of the southwest and questioning all levels of the population: "Whatever the merit of those who have shared the peril and glory [of overthrowing the Directory], throughout the regions that I have traveled, one shouts neither 'Long live Moreau'! nor 'Long live Sieyès'! but 'Long live Bonaparte'! Those who love you deeply, *men who will idolize you if you should bring peace*, are the peaceable ones, the property owners, the mass of the nation, all victims of political movements stirred up by the ambitious."[10] In the south, east, and north, in the vast countryside always agitated by muffled tremors, in the innumerable cities and towns still badly protected against Jacobin harassment or counterrevolutionary threats, a feeling of reassurance reawakened because a shaft of light shone from the direction of Paris and was visible everywhere. In the night of misfortune in which France was plunged, millions of eyes turned toward the ray of hope which rose from the center.

[9] Léon de Lanzac de Laborie, *La Domination française en Belgique* (Paris, 1895), I, 306.
[10] C.-L.-M. Lannes de Montebello, *Le Maréchal Lannes* (Tours, 1900), p. 37. At the same time, a Parisian newspaper was writing the following: "It is reported that in a small commune of the department of Seine-et-Oise a virtuous old peasant woman had taken her last cent out of her small purse and offered it to her parish priest while imploring him, with tears in her eyes, to be good enough to say a mass for the preservation of Bonaparte's life." *L'Ange Gabriel*, 26 Frimaire [December 17, 1799].

Claude Langlois (1937–   ) teaches at the University of Haute-Normandie and specializes in religious history. He is the co-author of the Histoire des catholiques en France *(1980) and the author of* Le Pouvoir dans l'Eglise: analyse institutionnelle historique et théologique de la pratique contemporaine *(1973),* Christianisme et pouvoirs politiques: de Napoléon à Adenauer *(1974), and other works.*

THE VOTERS
Claude Langlois

It may seem anachronistic and even inappropriate to claim to set forth the beginning of research about the Plebiscite of the year VIII [December 1799][1] by announcing an important falsification that hitherto has been completely ignored. Isn't an interest in the politics of the Consulate contrary to the current trend of historical research? And is it not presumptuous to try to provide proof of a falsification after 170 years during which historians of different ideologies, whether they were close to the event or benefited from the lapse of time necessary to reach sound judgments, have practically ignored the details of this election? Historians have settled for repeating what Lucien Bonaparte, then Minister of the Interior, was willing to announce, despite the fact that they considered the election somewhat suspect. Even though refuted by [the historian Alphonse] Aulard, the insinuations of the "anti-Napoleonic" pamphleteer Charles Comte continued to cast doubt on the reliability of the voting registers. According to Comte's *History of the Paris National Guard* (1827),

From Claude Langlois, "Un Plébiscite de l'an VIII: documents d'une falsification," *Bulletin de la Société d'histoire moderne* 14th series, no. 19 (1971), pp. 9–13. Printed by permission of the author and the editor of the *Bulletin de la Société d'histoire moderne.* Editors' translation.

[1][This Plebiscite, coming after Napoleon's coup d'état, related to the new constitution published in Paris on December 15, 1799. The law on the Plebiscite provided that voting registers be opened in each locality as soon as the text of the constitution arrived and was posted. All adult males could vote by signing a register and indicating there whether they accepted or rejected the constitution. The registers were open for only three days, although some historians have wrongly stated they were open for a month in certain provinces. Most Frenchmen had voted by December 31, and the last registers were closed on January 5, 1800. Claude Langlois's more detailed discussion of this subject is found in his article, "Le Plébiscite de l'an VIII ou le coup d'état du 18 Pluviôse an VIII," *Annales historiques de la Révolution française* 44 (1972), 43–65, 231–246, 390–415.—Eds.]

57

these registers were open to anyone willing to vote, including women, children, and foreigners, or were filled with lists of copied names without any relation to the actual voters.

If the electoral results of 3,011,007 "Yes" and 1,562 "No" votes are still accepted, it is also because these numbers have not been easy to verify in the archives. To be sure, everything that relates to the Plebiscite of the year VIII, as well as those that preceded it during the Revolution or followed it under the Consulate, can be found in the Archives nationales [French National Archives], B II series. Over four hundred bundles of documents record the votes of the French in the year VIII—from one to ten bundles per department. But in this archival series, there is no complete total of the voters showing how the three million votes were compiled. Therefore, we had to look elsewhere in the archives for documents that may have been preserved. Analogous to the practices of later plebiscites in the year X [1802] and the year XII [1804], we expected to examine two types of records which clearly had to be compared with each other. First of all there were the various registers of the votes in the several ministries where the records were centralized: the Ministries of the Interior, Justice, the Navy, and War. The last two were supposed to receive the votes of sailors and soldiers. The Ministry of Justice collected the votes of civilians who had voted at the offices of clerks of courts, justices of the peace, or notaries. Municipalities sent their voting registers directly to the Ministry of the Interior. Each ministry was to count the votes contained in the registers and send these results to the Ministry of the Interior, which was responsible for totaling the vote and publishing the results. Secondly, there were the official documents sent by the Ministry of the Interior to the "authorities," that is, to the Consuls and ultimately to the representative assemblies.

These two sorts of documents exist, not in private archives, but in the Archives nationales, and they are usually where they should be. . . . The records preserved in the files of the Tribunate [a Napoleonic legislative body] tell us how the three million votes were divided and their origin:

> from the Ministry of the Interior
>   2,211,037 "Yes" and 1,457 "No"
> from the Ministry of Justice
>   243,909 "Yes" and 105 "No"
> from the Ministries of War and Navy
>   556,061 "Yes" and 0 "No"

Let us first examine the votes of civilians. The 244,000 votes collected by the Ministry of Justice raise no problems. The official figures recorded for this ministry correspond to the numbers actually compiled in its offices. This is shown in a large folio volume preserved in the Archives nationales, B II 471, where are listed the 12,000 registers received and the counts derived from them.

But what about the 2,200,000 "Yes" votes from the Ministry of the Interior? The totals of the counts carried out in the offices of this ministry and the official returns do not correspond at all or rather they are connected in a way that reveals clear proof of a falsification of the results. To understand how this falsification worked, we must know how the vote counting was done in the Ministry of the Interior. This task fell to its First Division, which was composed of four sections. Each of these sections had to count and register the votes coming from a group of departments. The First Section was responsible for 25 departments from northern France, including Paris and the Belgian departments. The Fourth Section dealt with 24 departments extending from Brittany to Alsace, including Loir-et-Cher and Yonne, a group that we shall call for short *Brittany-Alsace*. The 25 departments of the southwest were handled by the Third Section; and the last 25 departments, from the southeast, including Corsica, went to the Second Section. On 15 Pluviôse [February 4, 1800], Lucien Bonaparte asked all of the sections to stop counting votes and produce a total so that on 18 Pluviôse the final figures could be announced. Each section thereupon calculated the final returns from the 25 departments for which it was responsible. The official lists, which show the votes counted by the Ministry of the Interior, retain the results by regional groupings.

For three of the four sections we have the total votes as determined on 15 Pluviôse. A comparison of these with the official lists is revealing. This is easy to do for the *Brittany-Alsace* group [Fourth Section]. One has only to compare the summary list found in the Archives nationales, B II 471, with the corresponding sheet of the [Ministry of Interior's] official document found in the Archives nationales IV 7 titled "Grand Summary of the Votes to Accept the Constitution of the year VIII." The number of "reject" votes is the same on both lists. On the other hand, the "accept" votes were systematically raised by 8,000 for each department. The vote in the Aube department was changed from 8,694 to 16,694, the Côte d'Or from 11,053 to 19,053, and so on. The same action occurred in 23 of the 24 departments, except for one important difference. The Yonne, the last department in the alphabetical list, was raised by 16,000 votes. It was necessary to spread 200,000 additional "Yes" votes throughout the list; so the last department received the extra 8,000 that were left over. The Fourth Section had counted 304,513 real "Yes" votes by 15 Pluviôse. The falsification added another two-thirds to that total.

The voting returns of the Third Section for the southwestern departments are in the Archives nationales Flc I 54. This working document bears the heading, "Compilation of Votes on the Constitution, 15 Pluviôse, year VIII: 419,129 acceptances and 301 refusals." The corresponding sheet of the official list for the same departments gives the total as 619,129 "Yes" and 301 "No." The falsification is obvious. In point of fact, each department had its results raised by 7,000 votes. Consequently, in the Vendée, where the vote was the lightest, the "Yes" number climbed from 3,550 to 10,550; and in the Haute-Garonne, which reported the heaviest vote, the "Yes" total changed from 34,403 to 41,403. In this way 175,000 "Yes" votes were distributed. An additional 25,000 votes were added to the total of an item called "not designated by department: 7,577 Yes." These were results sent in directly by communes [subdivisions of a department] without indicating the canton [a larger subdivision of a department] or department, and totaled here. The vote manipulator decided to allot the remaining 25,000 extra votes to this item. In this Third Section, therefore, the vote inflation was "only" about 50 percent of the real vote.

In the southeastern section, some variety was used in the falsification process, and also there were some copying errors that are fortunately easy to detect. In its report of 15 Pluviôse, the Second Section declared a total of 247,698 "Yes" and 272 "No" votes for 23 departments. The results for the two Corsican departments had not yet arrived. But the official figures from the Archives nationales, IV 7, show 554,698 "Yes" votes, or 307,000 added votes, that we prefer to divide into 300,000 and 7,000. The simplest way to spread 300,000 votes among 23 departments is to add 13,000 to each and add 14,000 to the last one. This is exactly what was done. If we look only at the top of the list, the Ain changed from 12,029 to 25,129 [sic], the Allier from 8,251 to 21,251, the Basses-Alpes from 7,937 to 20,937, and so on. It is more difficult to understand why the Haute-Loire [the last department on the list] received 7,000 votes in addition to the 13,000 supplementary ones. We assume that once most of the falsifications were made, this final addition was done to bring the total number of "Yes" votes to a little over 3 million, a number that the manipulators seemed to want.

For the northern departments [handled by the First Section], we had a problem because the totals compiled on 15 Pluviôse cannot be found in the archives. But by personally checking some of the results as of 6 Pluviôse and by making a comparison with the other sections, I have no doubt that for this group of returns the same treatment was applied. The total bonus must have been about 200,000 "Yes" votes spread at the rate of 7,000 or 8,000 per department.

In this way, therefore, a total of 900,000 additional "Yes" votes were deliberately added between 15 and 18 Pluviôse by the Ministry of the Interior, whose sections actually counted only 1,300,000 "Yes" votes in the Plebiscite of the year VIII.

However conclusive this demonstration is—at least for Sections Two, Three, and Four—we considered it necessary to substantiate these findings by direct and indirect means: by counting some voting registers and by a closer reading of the contemporary press so as to see what some journalists, still free from control for a little while, might have thought of the extent of voter participation in the election.

Since it was impossible to count all the voting registers, we sampled them. Of the 22 departments considered, we investigated 18 personally; for the other four, we benefited from the work of investigators who had already completed departmental studies. Therefore, we are dealing with a kind of sample of one out of five departments, and we encountered certain difficulties that should be emphasized before we indicate the results obtained. These were difficulties of a specifically material nature: considering that the voting registers lacked uniformity, our totals, as well as those of the sections of the Ministry of the Interior, include a margin of error of 2 to 3 percent, not to mention misplaced registers accidentally transferred from the bundle of one department to that of another. Another difficulty came from the very short time for counting. Some registers arrived at the Ministry of the Interior after [the deadline of] 15 Pluviôse. They turn up in the departmental bundles, but clearly were not included in the counts made by the ministerial sections which stopped tallying after 15 Pluviôse. For these reasons our verifications could not achieve results that exactly match the totals reached in the year VIII, but the importance of our work is to show a consistency in the divergence between the actual votes and the official totals.

Three of the published departmental studies whose authors counted the votes of this plebiscite concern the *Brittany-Alsace* group. Although the differences in the vote totals for the Alsatian departments are not clear, the results for Ille-et-Vilaine (by Benaerts) and Mont-Terrible (by Suratteau) are about 8,000 votes less than the official totals. The difference for the departments that we personally counted, Morbihan (7,300 votes) and Loir-et-Cher (7,900), produced the same results.

It would be tedious to line up and compare all these figures. For the southwestern group, we verified six departments. The spread between our actual count and the official totals averaged 7,400 votes. We selected four southeastern departments for testing. The spread in each case came to an average of about 500 votes more or less than the 13,000 additional votes officially registered for this group.

In the group of northern departments we examined six. Four showed a spread of about 8,000 votes between our actual count and official totals. The spread declined to 6,000 for the Meuse-Inférieure, which may be explained by the delay in sending the registers to Paris. On the other hand, it reached 10,000 for the Seine department. This lengthy task of counting, that we can only briefly indicate here, fully confirms the falsification discovered in comparing the different lists of vote totals by department.

An indirect verification made by examining the reactions of Parisian newspapers does not have the same conclusive value. Nevertheless, the indications that one can discern in the press do provide some revelations that are not less useful. If we set aside the newspapers devoted to the new regime, at least three articles which commented on voter participation clearly suggest that here and there it was light. For Paris, P.-L. Roederer, although he was a Brumairien [an active supporter of Napoleon's accession to power], expressed concern in his *Journal de Paris* about the lack of voters in the capital and sought the reasons for this in "the cold weather, the scant number of days the voting registers were open, laziness, apathy, the habit of everyone expecting other people to perform duties common to all, the assurance that the new regime would win general approval, and the memory of terror associated with the idea of lists and registers."

Two other newspapers, soon to be closed down for their independent views, used similar language. In Brussels, *The Well Informed* noted its doubts and the pressures exerted on government employees to sign the "Yes" register; in Marseille, the reporter for *The Friend of the Laws* mentioned the climate of political violence that reigned in the Midi [southern France] and made a prediction that proved correct: "The favorable votes in this commune will be limited to a very small number."

Actually, the press published little news about the voting in the provinces, nor did it supply many figures during the vote count. The only significant result released before 15 Pluviôse concerned Paris, for the Consuls had decided that Parisian approval would be enough to put the new constitution into effect. On December 29, 1799, *Le Moniteur* published the victory announcement—Paris voted 32,000 "Yes" and only 14 "No": "Never have we seen so much enthusiasm, because never has there been more approval." This comment was to forget very quickly the 40,000 "Yes" votes for the Constitution of the year I [1793] and the 68,266 "Yes" votes for that of the year III [1795]. It is easy to understand why at the announcement of the results, as Charles Comte wrote, "Everyone was amazed at the tremendous popularity of the events of 18 Brumaire."

At the most, then, Bonaparte and the new constitution could boast of the support of 1,550,000 voters. Should we add to these the unanimous approval of 556,000 soldiers and sailors? Of these, 56,996 "Yes" came from sailors: 242 registers preserved in the Archives nationales, B II series, record their votes. In fact, these registers arrived too late to be counted, and the figure given out was for all naval personnel. If one counts the registers, 34,500 sailors voted; and even these votes are very questionable, for almost always on the large vessels only the officers voted, and to their numbers were added the rest of the sailors on each ship. As for the army, there is no proof that the troops took part in the voting except perhaps for the Paris garrison. There are no registers or any correspondence at the Ministry of War about the vote. The officers and rank and file of the army, estimated at 500,000 men, turned up in the nick of time to make the electoral participation reach three million.

So we see that the falsification, both by the manipulation of the vote count of the departments and by the fraudulent addition of the military vote, managed to almost double the true vote. The real result was *1,550,000 "Yes" and several thousand "No"* (for there was an actual undercount of the negative votes, probably inadvertent). On 18 Pluviôse [February 7, 1800], three months to the day after 18 Brumaire, Lucien Bonaparte trumpeted victory and compared the three million "Yes" votes with the smaller total for the earlier plebiscites in 1793 and 1795. In fact, with this Plebiscite, the Constitution of 1799 was approved by 500,000 more "Yes" votes than that of 1795, but by 350,000 fewer "Yes" votes than that of 1793.

Several questions remain after this description of the falsification of the results and our determination of the authentic figures. In restoring the vote to its real size, we have eliminated the erroneous bloc of votes that raised the total to three million and created the deceitful claim of an unprecedented triumph. At first Bonaparte did not really have the support of a public that threw itself into his arms. In conclusion, we only want to suggest in what areas we must begin to revise the historical record and to reread the known events as a consequence of this discovery.

1) *The weakness of the new regime and the organization of the Plebiscite.* If we look closely at the decisions that led to how the election was organized, how it took place, and how the votes were counted, what is most striking is the feverish haste with which Bonaparte involved himself in a general election and the lack of planning to carry it out. Finally—in contrast to what many historians have asserted without any proof—we see the lack of ways to influence public opinion: without a well-organized administration, the public was often no better informed about the new voting procedures than about the stakes of the election and therefore was not urged to vote as

the government wished. Bonaparte had again found himself at an impasse; and perhaps even more than [during the coup d'état] on 19 Brumaire, it was probably his brother Lucien, now Minister of the Interior, who pulled him out of a bad position by faking the results.

2) *The motives of the voters.* To determine the reasons why the French voted for the new constitution would require another investigation. The explanation, "There is Bonaparte," has too often been repeated. It appears that this election was much less a plebiscite than has been said or believed. In point of fact, on the issues of peace at home and on the frontiers, the weak economic situation, or the religious problem, the provisionally appointed consuls made no moves before the election that might have influenced the vote of those who were wavering. They only made some promises. At the end of December 1799, to support the new constitution by one's vote was everywhere just an act of faith in a regime that had changed nothing regarding the difficult circumstances in which the French found themselves. A wait and see attitude remained the most logical response.

3) *The procedures of the election.* Finally, our examination of the specific procedures of the election illuminates factors that discouraged the large turnout the First Consul certainly sought. In the first place, by the year VIII France had gone through a process of depoliticization among voters that had begun in 1793 and had been accelerated by the practices of the Directory: a return to a limited suffrage; almost annual elections; and above all, an easy disregard of election results, especially those of the year V—the coup d'état of Fructidor [September 4, 1797]—but also those of the year VI [May 11, 1798].

In this already unfavorable situation, the new procedures for the election and the timing of it did not facilitate voting by a massive number of citizens despite the indisputable fact (whose effect should not be ignored) that there was a large increase in the number of polling places. The system of signing one's name in a register led some people to abstain because they feared to be placed on new lists of proscription should the political situation be reversed. Also, the illiterate in many places believed they were excluded from voting because they could not sign their names, although they actually could have had someone do it for them. Moreover, the lack of clear information on who was eligible to vote meant that a considerable fraction of citizens who recovered their suffrage rights as a result of the new constitution did not participate, just as they had not participated in earlier elections under the Directory. To complete the discussion on this point, we mention two additional circumstances frequently criticized by those who presided over the voting registers as discouraging a large turnout: (1) opening the voting registers for only three days immediately

THE VOTERS

after the promulgation of the Constitution and the announcement of an election; and, (2) the poor timing—the end of December—when a harsh winter had already struck all of France.

For us, the conclusions are clear. The voter participation was light, if we bear in mind what the First Consul wanted: an enthusiastic approval of the new policy that would break with the earlier regimes and would surely allow public approval to wipe out the illegality of 18 Brumaire. But the legitimacy that the legislative assemblies had refused to grant and that now was given rather reluctantly by the people did not satisfy Bonaparte. He chose to bend the voting to his point of view by a new application of force. He was wrong to do this on two counts. First of all, although it may appear paradoxical considering the difficult situation in which the election of the year VIII occurred, the actual results should be considered favorable to Bonaparte. The French remained hesitant; still, we can affirm that the new regime profited from a favorable predisposition toward it. More important, this falsification of the results became a trap for the regime and for the First Consul. Two years later Bonaparte would be judged in the Plebiscite of the year X, and this time on accomplishments, not promises. At that point he received the approval of over 3,500,000 Frenchmen. This reveals the ground gained since the year VIII. It was the first time in French political life that those voting totaled over half of those eligible. Two unprecedented facts, but they were concealed by the falsification of the year VIII and even a little by the "touch ups" that were made to the vote on the Constitution of the year XII [1804]. Yet, after all, isn't it normal even in politics for morality at times to have the last word?

Albert Soboul (1914–1982) came from a peasant family that had moved from the south of France to Algeria. After his father died in World War I, he was raised first by his mother and then by an aunt, who was the headmistress of a girls' school in southern France. In the 1930s he attended the Parisian Lycée Louis-le-Grand and the University of Paris. He then began an academic career that was interrupted during the Second World War, when he was dismissed from his post for opposing the Vichy government. After the Liberation of France in 1944, he resumed his teaching and writing. A student of Georges Lefebvre, he gained a reputation as the leading Marxist historian of the French Revolution with the publication, in 1958, of Les Sans-culottes parisiens en l'an II *(of which there is an abridged English translation). Among his many other books are* Le Directoire et le Consulat (1795–1804) *(1967),* La Ier République (1792–1804) *(1968),* Le Premier Empire, 1804–1815 *(1973), and* La France napoléonienne (1983), *which is volume three of his* Civilisation et la Révolution française. *From 1967 until his death, he was Professor of the History of the French Revolution at the University of Paris.*

A DICTATORSHIP PROTECTING A NEW ELITE

Albert Soboul

Almost immediately after 18 Brumaire, dictatorship, personified by Bonaparte, emerged in France. It came on the ruins of representative government, which the republican notables had tried to found by the Constitution of the year III [August 22, 1795]. But this dictatorship had to accept the legacy of social changes brought about by ten years of revolution: if Bonaparte governed as the leader, he governed for the profit of the notables. . . .

The Revolution had enthusiastically pursued the ruin of the landed aristocracy and its privileges. Feudal dues and ecclesiastical tithes were abolished without compensation, the property of clergymen and émigrés sold, and the practice of selling government offices ended with reimbursements paid out in depreciated assignats [first bonds and then paper money]. Any future stability presupposed the recogni-

From Albert Soboul, *Le Directoire et la Consulat (1795–1804)* (Paris: Presses Universitaires de France, 1967), pp. 84–89. Printed by permission of the publisher. Editors' translation.

tion of this state of affairs. However, the aristocracy was not irretrievably despoiled. Many nobles lived through the Revolution without being harmed very much and they preserved their property, property now of the bourgeois type, that is, freed from "feudal" restrictions. Some émigrés were able to safeguard their estates or recover them by false divorces or by repurchases using fictitious names. Thus, a portion of the aristocracy managed to survive and, despite the loss of its titles, to conserve some of its traditional prestige.

The bourgeoisie was radically transformed by the Revolution, its internal dynamics modified. Instead of inherited wealth, which traditionally predominated in its ranks, the wealth of *nouveaux riches*, businessmen, and industrial leaders was substituted. The bourgeoisie of the Old Regime, which had been integrated into the old social structure, largely shared the fate of the aristocracy. Those property-owning bourgeois who lived in the style of noblemen on various sources of income derived from land saw their rents and feudal dues vanish while various kinds of debts owed to them had been paid off long ago with depreciated assignats. The bourgeoisie of office holders, like the nobles of the robe, were ruined by the abolition of their ownership of government positions. The upper bourgeoisie of business was hit by the abolition of the system of farming out indirect taxes, the elimination of the joint stock companies, and the closing of the stock exchange, and also by the price fixing and regulation that in the year II [1793–1794] limited profits. Finally, we must also consider the consequences of inflation. In the year III [1794–1795], the collapse of the assignat prompted debtors to free themselves from their debts by paying the principal back in depreciated paper money. The readjustment of perpetual and life debts by Cambon during the Convention and the repudiation of two-thirds of the public debt (the Ramel liquidation) during the Directory resulted in new blows. However, the bourgeoisie of the Old Regime, if it did not emigrate, conserved the essentials of its fortune to the extent that its capital consisted mainly in landed property, wealth in securities then constituting only a small portion of a family's assets. But after ten years of adversities, this bourgeoisie sought tranquility.

A new bourgeoisie appeared that intended to enjoy its freshly acquired wealth. Businessmen found new opportunities to expand their operations by speculating in assignats, foreign exchange rates, nationalized property, military supplies, and the exploitation of foreign conquests. To be sure, capitalist expansion was slow during the revolutionary period, the size of businesses remained small, and commercial capitalism predominated. Some big concerns did, however, stand out, especially in the cotton industry. But speculation [in raw materials] and the supplying of the armies, more than industrial production, seem to be the source of these new and immense fortunes. Many *companies* [groups of military suppliers] took advantage of the government's weakness to plunder the state: the Lanchère company and the Bodin company specialized in food supplies, the Félice company in clothing, and the Monneron company in transport. In this respect, there was no interruption whatsoever: the plunder continued under the Consulate and the Empire. This is how the bourgeoisie rejuvenated itself, by incorporating these "*nouveaux riches*," the financier Ouvrard being the perfect example.

At a lower level on the bourgeois scale, favorable circumstances during the Revolution permitted numerous tradesmen and artisans to expand their operations, increase the size of their enterprises, and emerge from the ranks of the common people into those of the bourgeoisie. From this middle level, the new ruling class soon recruited officials for public administration as well as members of the liberal professions.

The urban lower classes profited little from the Revolution. Despite some increase in wages, their standard of living dropped due to the persistent unemployment, the disorganization of charitable institutions, and their continuing inferiority before the law as sanctioned by property requirements for voting and by the Le Chapelier law of June 14, 1791, which forbade unions and strikes. Wage-earners were delivered without protection to those who controlled the new economic forces.

The peasantry benefited unequally from the agrarian reforms of the Revolution. Only the land-owning peasants profited from the abolition of the tithe and the feudal dues relating to land. Tenant farmers and sharecroppers, the landless peasants, won some advantages solely from the abolition of serfdom and personal obligations to the seigneur. Owing to the rules on the sale of the nationalized properties, the land-owning peasantry was strengthened, the benefits accruing to those who already owned land, that is, the *laboureurs* (the cultivators of big tracts) and the farmers in regions of large-scale operations. The poor peasantry, although unable to become property owners, still kept the essentials of its traditional rights. The revolutionary legislatures did not dare destroy the rural community by abolishing common land and the collective working of land; enclosures were permitted, not imposed; in this sphere, the Revolution achieved only a compromise. Henceforth, however, a powerful minority of land-owning peasants, attached to the new order, joined the bourgeoisie in its conservative stance.

After ten years of upheavals, the different traits of the new society were already clearly outlined. It was not within the power of one man, even if he were a genius, to modify them: the actions of Napoleon as First Consul and Emperor followed the line of the revolutionary heritage. The desire for order by the property-holders, whether they be the old or new rich, furthered the stabilization of the Consulate. Then began the fusion of the diverse elements of the new dominant class: a rejuvenated bourgeoisie and an aristocracy that accepted Napoleon at one with the land-holding peasantry, so that nation and property ownership were considered identical within the framework of political institutions based on property qualifications for voting.

The joining of the aristocracy to the nation of property owners was made easier by the changed attitudes among the émigrés. The aristocrats who had emigrated and the propertied bourgeoisie were coming together after ten years of revolution. Through the mysterious ties of native land with landed property, they now agreed to identify the soil of France with the French homeland. At the same time, the abolition of feudal dues and ecclesiastical tithes, as well as the acquisition of nationalized properties, reinforced the conservative solidarity of the land-owning peasants with the bourgeoisie. The homeland, an abstract notion in 1789, richer in hope than in reality, became for the propertied a concrete reality: title to the land without any restrictions. Patriotism became something tangible in the attachment to landed property. By an entirely different route, by a return to the values of instinct and feeling, the aristocracy that had emigrated now also equated the homeland with the soil, thereby preparing its joining with the property-owning part of the nation.

The work of Bonaparte could, in this sphere as in others, only respond to the aspirations of all the parties involved. Stabilizing society on the fundamental base of the Revolution, he integrated the returned émigrés into a new social hierarchy; and, while reinforcing the principle of authority, he merged these émigrés into a new order which at first had been constructed against them. Opening the frontiers to the émigrés by the *senatus consultum* [the constitutional amendment] of 6 Floréal, year X (April 26, 1802), Bonaparte declared he wanted "to cement peace at home by anything that could bring the French together and provide tranquility within families." Nothing could rally bourgeois and aristocratic France so much as the guaranteeing of property rights.

3
THE CONCORDAT

From the Middle Ages, French history has been marked by quarrels between the State and the Roman Catholic Church. But now and then they reach a reconciliation. One of the most momentous of these was the Concordat, the agreement of 1801 between Napoleon and Pope Pius VII. It healed a split that had developed between Church and State during the early part of the French Revolution, a split that had helped provoke civil war and brought attempts to create non-Catholic religions as alternatives to Catholicism.

Historians differ on whether the Concordat was necessary; whether it came about largely through the efforts of Napoleon or the Pope; and whether it granted greater benefits to the State or Church. The historian and priest Jean-Marie Leflon regards the Concordat as a wise move for both sides: France had been torn by disorder in the Vendée and elsewhere; now the Church regained legal recognition in the mightiest continental power of Europe, one which also controlled Italy. He describes Napoleon as having initiated the negotiations, but Pope Pius VII as more deserving of praise for his diplomatic skill, character, and vision. The freethinking republican Alphonse Aulard, on the other hand, believes that the legal separation of Church and State instituted in 1795 was working satisfactorily and that Napoleon bears the primary responsibility for a reactionary agreement which greatly strengthened the Church in France for at least a century.

In the last quarter of the twentieth century, the relations between Church and State in France have been relatively calm. Is it possible today to examine dispassionately the antecedents and legacy of the Concordat in order to decide whether or not it was a compromise for mutual advantage by two able statesmen? Or will this controversy always be so enmeshed with religious and political values that it is impossible to come to an impartial judgment?

Monsignor Jean-Marie Leflon (1893–1979), a bookseller's son, was born in northern France. He studied at the seminary of Saint-Sulpice, the Institut catholique, and the University of Paris, where he earned a doctorate in history. A priest and a professor, he became a notable historian of Catholicism. Among his many books are studies of two of the principal negotiators of the Concordat, Pope Pius VII and Étienne-Alexandre Bernier.

A COMPROMISE FOR MUTUAL ADVANTAGE

Jean-Marie Leflon

[After the coup d'état] religious questions were not immediately addressed by Bonaparte, although their settlement was an essential precondition for attaining domestic peace. His power was still not well enough established for him to be able, without risk, to confront and smash the opposition of those political circles that remained very anti-clerical. Besides, how was he to reach an agreement with the priests and the faithful, who were resolutely attached to the legitimate bishops [those who had not supported the Revolution] and to the successor of Saint Peter? The bishops, all émigrés, were not likely to accept the necessary compromises. What could one hope from the Sovereign Pontiff, who was to be elected at the Conclave of Venice, convoked under Austrian pressure, or from the cardinals, who were infuriated by the treatment inflicted on the unfortunate Pius VI by the Directory? Most of them had been persecuted [by the French] at the founding of the Roman Republic [1798]. Therefore, because of these difficulties on both the French and Roman Catholic sides, the First Consul had to wait until the situation evolved further before confronting the problem.

FIRST MEASURES OF CONCILIATION

For the time being, Bonaparte limited himself to half measures. A decree of November 29, 1799 exempted from deportation those priests who had taken all the oaths to the government, renounced their clerical office, or married. Concerning three other decrees published on December 28, the last two simply put into effect measures taken by

---

From Jean Leflon, "La Paix religieuse," in *Napoléon et l'Empire*, ed. Jean Mistler, 2 vols. (Paris: Hachette, 1968), I: pp.98–107. The entire article is printed by permission of the publisher. Editors' translation.

the Thermidorians and the Directory in their liberal periods: restoration of the churches "to the citizens who had held possession of them on the first day of the year II [September 22, 1793]," and authorization of the clerics to practice their faith on the condition that they swear loyalty to the Constitution.

The first decree of December 28 annulled the law closing churches every day except the *Décadi* [the tenth, twentieth, and thirtieth day of the month in the calendar of the French Republic]. Given the unpopularity of the *culte Décadaire* [a religion instituted during the French Revolution], the First Consul could afford this apparently bold step without fear.

All these actions favored a relaxation of tension. They promoted the pacification of the Vendée on January 18, 1800 thanks to the mediation of Bernier, the future negotiator of the Concordat; but they remained insufficient. In fact, Bonaparte had committed the same error as all the revolutionary governments by imposing an ambiguous oath on the clergy. If he had simply confined himself to requiring a promise of loyalty to the government, no question of principle would have been raised. Instead, the wording he adopted implied approval of a Constitution that agreed little with Church doctrine in several of its articles. Therefore, Bonaparte only partially achieved religious peace.

Would Bonaparte be more successful in trying to disarm the cardinals' prejudices against him? They were meeting in conclave in Venice. And would he be able to prevent the election of a papal nominee unfavorable to his government?

On December 30, 1799, a decree ordered splendid homages to the remains of Pius VI, who had died while a prisoner of the Directory. Bonaparte hoped to score a great success by a retraction so dazzling and a disavowal so explicit of the regime overthrown on November 9–10, 1799. This explains the spectacular nature of this "delayed-action" funeral ceremony, arranged to the last detail at Valence. This ceremony was also pictured in a large poster that was carefully sent to their Eminences [the cardinals], meeting in seclusion on the Island of Saint-George in Venice. But if we may judge by a letter of [Cardinal] Consalvi, the effect did not correspond at all to what the First Consul anticipated. "You know," the Secretary of the Conclave wrote on January 22, 1800, "that Bonaparte ordered solemn obsequies for the unfortunate Pius VI. We note that Napoleon has lived in Egypt and learned there to act like a crocodile." Much more effective was the intervention of the semi-official representative of the Court of Madrid, Monsignor Despuig, who succeeded in pushing aside Cardinal Mattei, the candidate of Austria, and, according to his own expression, "to bring forward" his own candidate while using all the others for his own purposes. This was the Cardinal Chiaramonti, who was elected on March 14, 1800 and took the name of Pius VII.

During Napoleon's first Italian campaign [1796–1797] the First Consul had grown to appreciate the new Pope [then a bishop], who had been so understanding, courageous, and pastoral in his diocese of Imola. An agreement with him was possible. However, before seeking an understanding with the Holy Father, Napoleon decided to wait until the battle of Marengo made him permanent master of the situation in France, permitting him to apply pressure on Rome by using his troops as a threat. But Bonaparte's plan was already prepared with the advice of Bernier, who had returned to Paris crowned by his success in the Vendée and who was always ready to serve as an intermediary. When the French army that had massed in the Alps [for the invasion of Italy in 1800] started to move, Bonaparte's decision was definitely reached; and Talleyrand ordered Labrador, appointed Ambassador of Spain to the Holy See, to make the first overtures.

The First Consul sought to give more weight to these proposals by also presenting them personally, once he achieved a military victory [at Marengo]. After investigating the matter fully, he chose as his intermediary the venerable Cardinal Martiniana [the Bishop of Vercelli], whom he already knew and judged to be a less forceful person than Consalvi. Bonaparte stopped at Vercelli on June 25, 1800 before returning to Paris. Playing on the Cardinal's surprise, he revealed his intention to settle the ecclesiastical affairs of France. The good Cardinal could not believe his ears. Bonaparte explained the main lines of his plan and made Martiniana his representative for negotiating with the new Pope. According to Bonaparte, the essential conditions of the future Concordat should include the following: the extinction of the schism in France by the resignation of the unwanted bishops [the Constitutional bishops who had sworn loyalty oaths to the Revolution], whom "he [Bonaparte] no longer wished to hear about," as well as the resignation of the bishops of the Old Regime, most of whom had emigrated more for political than religious reasons; the selection of a "virgin" corps of bishops installed by the Pope; a reduction in the number of dioceses; the Church's renunciation of the property expropriated from it; and the regular payment of a salary to the clergy. These were all the conditions that Martiniana, won over, presented as *discretissisme* (very moderate). If, on these fundamental points, an agreement was reached, Bonaparte would use all his power to reestablish the sovereignty of the Holy Father in the Papal States.

Enthusiastic, the Bishop of Vercelli hastened to send Pius VII, by means of his own nephew, an account of this conversation. The Pope, however, was at first unfavorably impressed. We know this from

Monsignor Despuig, who witnessed his first reactions. The Holy Father expressed annoyance that the First Consul held out as a lure the restoration of the Papal States to win concessions from him of a spiritual nature. He opposed the mixing of the spiritual with the temporal. However, he decided to welcome the French government's overtures with the firm resolve to maintain the distinction between the two systems of values.

The Pope's response to the Bishop of Vercelli combined approval and reservations. The Holy Father received the proposals of the Consul "with the greatest hope" and would accept "willingly a treaty which has for its goal an object so in accordance with our ministry and so in agreement with the wishes of our heart."

The Cardinal was to transmit these conditions to Paris and request full particulars. He would be responsible for carrying out the negotiations; but to assist him "on such a delicate matter," he would be joined by a diplomat from Rome, Monsignor Spina. On the restoration of the Papal States, not a word. This was intentional.

The silence maintained on this matter, crucial for the Holy Father, proves that he had clearly seen on what points the fundamental disagreement between Bonaparte and himself would arise. The difficulties appeared great, but an understanding based on the conditions formulated at Vercelli was not impossible, for the Pope's openmindedness made him aware that compromises were necessary. However, although the Pope intended to serve only spiritual interests and was ready to sacrifice those that were temporal, politics alone motivated the French general in his desire to conclude a Concordat with the Holy See. That policy was not only imposed on Bonaparte by the necessity of restoring religious peace in France, but it was also aimed at conciliating Italy, which he planned to reconquer. Indeed, at Milan on June 5, 1800, in his famous speech before the clergy of that city, he revealed his intention to come to an understanding with the Sovereign Pontiff.

The main reasons for this policy arose especially from the internal situation that the new leader of the Republic had to face in France in order to establish his government firmly and rally the Nation around him. Those who had carried him to power in Brumaire [November 1799] no more intended to reverse the anti-clerical policy of the Directory than the Thermidorians, by overthrowing Robespierre [in 1794], had sought to end the battle against the Church. Napoleon would have preferred not to have to rely on the Church, since he condemned religions for fomenting dissension within the state and for interfering in temporal affairs at the expense of civil authorities. Whereas in Italy Catholicism was not seriously affected by the Revolution, Catholicism in France, although seriously influenced by the revolutionary crisis, still remained vigorous; and dechristianization had clearly failed. After Thermidor [July 1794], the common people, especially in the countryside, had demanded their church, church bells, and priests. Government officials who undertook investigations in various military regions, not at all delighted with what they found, concurred in verifying this. A clear-sighted realism required that such a strongly expressed view be satisfied. "My policy," declared Bonaparte to the Council of State on August 16, 1800, "is to govern men as the great number of them desire. This is the way, I believe, the sovereignty of the people should be understood. It is by becoming a Catholic that I won the war in the Vendée, by becoming a Moslem that I came to power in Egypt, and by becoming an ultramontane that I won people's support in Italy. If I governed the Jewish people, I would rebuild Solomon's Temple."

Moreover, in his eyes, religion, despite the drawbacks that he would prevent from happening, provided the state with great advantages by guaranteeing order and property. From this point of view, Catholicism was the most useful religion. It preached obedience to secular government, urged resignation to unavoidable inequities, and supported morality by the promise of rewards and the threat of eternal punishments. In any event, there was no alternative. Napoleon did not have the power to suppress Catholicism or to substitute another creed; since the French people showed themselves faithful to their old religion, it became essential to take the necessary steps. Far from destroying national unity by arousing people's consciences and by opposing the spiritual to the temporal power, the Church, when disciplined and controlled, would serve, according to Fourcroy's remark, as "a powerful lever for directing men."

The usefulness of this lever would be even more appreciated in that it would encourage the quickest possible end to the civil wars raging not only in the Vendée, but in Normandy, central France, and the Bordeaux region. The aristocratic and royalist counterrevolution would no longer be able to exploit, for its own political ends, the anticlericalism of the government.

It was not enough to grant religious freedom however, for two rival [Catholic] cults opposed each other: on the one hand, that which had remained loyal to Rome and, on the other, that which had sworn allegiance to the Revolution. Anxious to attract all Frenchmen no matter what their beliefs and to eliminate any germ of possible discord, the First Consul wanted to settle this problem permanently, a problem created by the worst error of the National Assembly. He distrusted the Constitutional clergy [those who had rallied to the Revolution], for these democrats and especially their leader Grégoire secretly opposed him despite their official statements. But their traditional servility toward established power assured their obedience to his orders. On the other hand, the refractory clergy would only accept orders from the Pope. Hence, it was necessary to turn to him [the Pope] for help, since to maintain an equal balance, the bishops of the Old Regime and the Constitutional bishops would both have to resign in order to create a new corps of bishops. Now, without courting failure and without risking a repetition of the error of 1790 by fomenting a new schism, it was impossible to bypass the authority of the Holy See. Only the Pope could obtain the resignation of the pre-revolutionary bishops, who were regarded by Catholics as the sole legitimate bishops.

Therefore, Christian spirit did not inspire Bonaparte, but a realism as self-interested as it was practical. To rechristianize France, which the Bourbons would try to do later, during the Restoration, certainly did not enter into his plans. His goal was to use what remained of Catholic sentiment to bolster his own power. Under these circumstances, he could not easily get along with a Pope so fundamentally religious as Pius VII. Besides, the Holy Father had no illusions: his reply to Martiniana, whose strong point was not perspicacity, proves this. The expectations of the Supreme Pontiff would be only too often confirmed; the diplomatic discussions, which began on June 25, 1800, would be long and tedious. They would not reach a conclusion until July 15, 1801.

To insist on resolving the basic disagreements stemming from the different premises of the two parties would have been more than enough to make the task of the negotiators very complex. Now, far from simplifying the affair, the diplomatic style adopted by the First Consul when dealing with the Holy See increased the difficulties, for the tactics he adopted too often scorned the accepted practices of diplomatic chancelleries. The Court of Rome had an immediate foretaste of the insults in store for it. Even though Pius VII, only six days after receiving the message of Martiniana, instructed him on July 10 to transmit to Paris an acceptance in principle, two long months passed before the Cardinal received an acknowledgement, which was sent by Talleyrand [the Foreign Minister] on September 4. Now that letter was as pleasing in its preamble as it was disconcerting by the offhandedness with which the Minister mentioned, as a matter of course, the "sending of the required passport so that Monsignor Spina can come to Paris." The Papal Curia had a perfect right to feel offended that Bonaparte, on his own, transferred the center of negotiations to the capital of France without prior notice or agreement with the Holy See. But much more serious than this impolite behavior was the secret purpose that the Curia believed was behind this tactic: indeed Rome guessed that the First Consul and Talleyrand sought to isolate the Pope's representative in order to exercise direct pressure on him and extract unreasonable concessions. Nevertheless, the Holy See acquiesced to letting him depart; but to counteract Napoleon's maneuver, it took the precaution of limiting his powers. Sent to discuss the articles of the Concordat, the Archbishop of Corinth [Spina] was not permitted either to conclude or sign them: the Pope reserved this for himself.

BERNIER NEGOTIATES

Experience justified only too well these prudent restrictions. For two months Rome heard no news from Spina, who had arrived in Paris on November 5, 1800. The first letter that Consalvi [the Papal Secretary of State] received on January 10, 1801 was dated December 20, 1800; and, as it carried the number 10 on it, one can conclude that the nine preceding letters had been seized by the French post office and sent to the *cabinet noir* [the secret French bureau which opened and inspected mail]. The Prelate was forced to resort to the post office because, lacking money, he had at his disposal only one Roman courier, Livio; and he had to be kept in reserve for extremely urgent matters. As to the nine other letters sent from November 12 on, eight reached the Quirinal [a Papal palace] on the following January 17. We can understand the anger of Consalvi, who was also very uneasy about his own dispatches being subject to similar treatment.

Nevertheless, after familiarizing himself with the successive reports of Spina, the Secretary of State [Consalvi] felt reassured. Of course, the unfortunate Archbishop of Corinth [Spina], isolated in Paris, with only one advisor, the upright Caselli, was grappling with formidable competitors, the minister Talleyrand and his representative, the enigmatic and industrious Bernier. The Curia knew Talleyrand only too well. It usually referred to him as "Autun," and one need not say more.[1] As to Bernier, the baffled Spina reserved judgment. "He seems to be a man of good intentions. What kind of person he really is, I do not know," wrote the Prelate, unfavorably impressed by the shifty look and the coarse features of the former Vendean leader, but fascinated by his wonderful intelligence. In fact, Bernier, not overly troubled by scruples, would in his own way render the greatest services to the Holy See. Convinced that Bonaparte surely wanted the Concordat, he did not grow weary of retying threads as soon as they broke.

At first Spina and Bernier believed that they would rapidly reach

[1][Talleyrand had been the Bishop of Autun before he swore allegiance to the Revolution and was excommunicated in 1791. Later he married a divorced Englishwoman.—Eds.]

an agreement; for the first draft, discussed and amended by them together, won the First Consul's approval. But since this draft was judged by Talleyrand as too favorable to the Church, the French Foreign Minister substituted a second that the representative of Pius VII rejected and for good reasons. The negotiation had come to a halt when the attempt on Napoleon's life in the Rue Saint-Nicaise furthered the recovery of lost ground. At first, this odious attack was attributed to the Jacobins, and the First Consul reacted very vigorously against them. Bernier took advantage of this and prepared a third draft favorable to the Holy See. On his initiative, the Catholic clergy at the same time arranged more and more ceremonies of thanksgiving; and Spina addressed his congratulations to Bonaparte, who thanked him "with effusion created by satisfaction." But Fouché [the Minister of Police], whose anti-clericalism was not disarmed, secretly prepared a dramatic action: when he had decisive proof that the plotters of Nivôse [those behind the Saint-Nicaise attack] belonged to the royalist party, he unmasked them suddenly and even implicated Father Clorivière, the uncle of the main plotter. This entrance on the scene of the Minister of Police scuttled the third draft.

Bernier thus resigned himself to its withdrawal, and on January 14, in the name of the First Consul, he proposed another draft to Spina. "This one was for me a bolt from the blue," wrote the Prelate to Consalvi. This fourth text had been conceived in an entirely different spirit from earlier ones: the government demanded that the representative of the Holy See accept it speedily and sign it as the definitive treaty. The Prelate's instructions, however, did not permit him to sign it. Would a rupture therefore take place? To avoid this, Spina and Bernier then proposed to send, by means of the courier Livio, the draft to the Holy Father, who would decide on the concessions he was willing to make. Bonaparte welcomed this suggestion warmly. But in a rush to reach an agreement so as to synchronize the Concordat with Rome and the peace with Vienna, he undertook to settle everything himself. In a military manner, he dictated his own draft, the fifth, which Livio would carry as quickly as possible to Pius VII. Moreover, as "there was not a moment to lose," the First Consul decided to send a representative to the Holy See provided with full powers, who would discuss the agreement with the Pope and Consalvi and then sign it on the spot. With this purpose in mind, his choice, an excellent one, was the citizen Cacault.

Bonaparte's speedy diplomacy collided with the prudent and traditional slowness of Roman diplomacy. Departing from Paris on February 26, the courier Livio brought back the reply only on May 24. On May 12 the French government, impatient, had sent a real ultimatum; the Curia must, without the slightest amendment, accept the fifth draft within five days; should it not, Cacault would leave Rome and be replaced by French troops under Murat's command. At the papal palace, they refused to yield, and everyone expected the worst. Cacault, by a bold initiative, found the way to save the situation: in accordance with the orders he had received, the French plenipotentiary left within the deadline, but in his carriage he took along Consalvi, whom he had persuaded to go to Paris so as to recommence personally all negotiations.

THE CONCORDAT

So began the second act, much shorter than the first, but no less dramatic. The Secretary of State [Consalvi], welcomed warmly by Bonaparte, who was very flattered by his arrival, began by discarding a sixth draft that Bernier had tried to impose on Spina before the Secretary of State's appearance so that the latter would face a *fait accompli*. The curé of Saint-Laud [Bernier] then produced a seventh draft, which the Cardinal [Consalvi] had to decide on within twenty-four hours. As the latter judged this procedure unacceptable, he therefore hastened to formulate a counterproposal and worked on it all night. But Bonaparte rejected this counterproposal and ordered a return to the sixth. There followed a second counterproposal, which suffered the same fate as the first. Finally, after three days of revising and re-revising, the Papal Secretary of State and Bernier reached an accord.

Then they agreed to sign it on July 13, 1801.

Now came a last maneuver, the most improper of them all and which put everything in doubt. Indeed, the document that was presented to the Cardinal totally differed from the text that had been agreed upon. But discreetly forewarned by Bernier, he would not sign under threat and vigorously protested against such an abuse of confidence. Twenty hours of discussion were necessary before the completion of a new draft, the eighth. A wasted effort, for Bonaparte, to whom it was submitted, threw it into the fire and dictated another, the ninth. He demanded that this one be accepted in toto; and, if not, the Papal representatives were to depart for Rome immediately. But Consalvi remained firm, and a new two-hour discussion did not succeed in overcoming his opposition. Bonaparte now recognized that pushing matters to an extreme would lead to an impasse. So he welcomed favorably the opportune mediation of the Ambassador of Austria, Cobenzl, who suggested a compromise solution. At noon the next day, therefore, a most important conference took place. After negotiations lasting twelve hours, at midnight on July 14, everything was finally resolved; and the six plenipotentiaries affixed their signatures on the final text of the French Concordat.

What were the stumbling blocks that beset this long negotiation? Certain points did not create any disputes: new borders for dioceses; the nomination of bishops by the First Consul with their canonical installation by the Pope; a loyalty oath to the government (and not to the Constitution) that was required for bishops and parish priests; the Church's right to receive endowments; and official prayers for the Consuls.

In regard to other articles, the problem lay in finding the formulas that would safeguard certain principles while sacrificing the interests of some specific individuals and some temporal possessions. As to the question of the removal of the bishops in office, two separate issues arose. Concerning the bishops of the Old Regime, the term "deposed" could not be used, for according to the language of Consalvi, "the massacre of a complete episcopate would be historically unprecedented"; the Pope limited himself to requesting the resignation of those who held the office and to authorizing replacements for those who refused to resign; their seats would not, however, be declared vacant by the Pope. As to the Constitutional bishops, likewise dispossessed, Rome arranged to exclude them without putting them on the same footing as the legitimate bishops, which Bonaparte would have desired and Talleyrand even more so. Similar subtle wording was employed concerning Church properties sold as nationalized properties. If Pius VII renounced in fact their restitution to the Church, he did not intend to recognize the legal right of the civil authority to dispose of them. Therefore, he simply pledged not to bother the new owners. The sole difficulty consisted of inserting in the text the qualification "incommutable," which Bonaparte required so as to guarantee more fully the owners or "their beneficiaries of the rights and revenues of their properties." Instead of this adjective, as expressive as it was inelegant, an editorial strategem permitted Consalvi to introduce the term "in consequence," which implied the incommutability of the engagement made by Rome not to disturb the present holders of this property and thus avoided a legal recognition. These issues caused only minor skirmishes.

On the other hand, an all-out diplomatic battle centered on two articles concerning the status of the Catholic religion in France and the freedom of public worship. Two theoretically irreconcilable conceptions clashed: the Roman conception of the rights and independence of the Church versus the Napoleonic conception (inherited from the Gallicanism[2] of the Old Regime and from the ideology of the Revolution) of the supremacy of the civil power over the ecclesiastical combined with the freedom and equality of all faiths.

---

[2][Gallicanism is a body of doctrine which affirmed that the Roman Catholic Church in France should be largely free from Papal direction.—Eds.]

The position of the theologians required that the Catholic religion, the only true one, be recognized as the state religion. Bernier, a competent theologian, had slipped this recognition into the first draft. But in the second draft, Talleyrand, a no less expert theologian, substituted for this legal recognition a simple *de facto* statement, "the religion of the great majority of the French." Spina tried to obtain "the dominant religion," then, lacking success, proposed "the religion of the government," a clause so much more essential, since the First Consul would have the power to nominate bishops. The adroit Bernier found a *combinazione* [compromise]. In the preamble of the Concordat, he introduced the contested expression "the religion of the government" in a modified form, still favorable to the Church. Suppressed in the eighth draft, the clause would be eventually restored.[3] Thus, it is evident that, as a consequence of the vicissitudes of negotiation and successive revisions, the text of the French Concordat was, like all concordats, a compromise.

We do not see today with sufficient clarity what was new in the treaty reached by Pius VII and Bonaparte given the context of their time. First of all, by recognizing the government of the Consulate, the treaty broke the centuries-old alliance between the Church and the legitimate [Bourbon] monarchy. By the plebiscite of the people, Bonaparte inherited the prerogatives and the rights of the monarchy. This papal recognition consecrated the principles of 1789 concerning sovereignty derived from the Nation [the people]. Furthermore, this Concordat was the first liberal Concordat: the Pope acquiesced to the fact that in a France descended from the Revolution, Catholicism was no longer the State religion, an acceptance of the realities of the situation and which did not imply the submission to another principle of 1789, that which proclaimed the equality of different religious cults.

We can judge from this document how necessary it was for Pius VII to be broadminded and audacious to overturn, to this extent, the direction taken by the Holy See since the collapse of the Old Regime. No less essential was the dispassion of this fundamentally religious Pope. He was willing to sacrifice for the general good. This he did by agreeing to the resignation of the bishops [loyal to the Old Regime], men who had not at all acted in an unworthy way. He also accepted the loss of Church property, which was worth much more than the modest salaries only prelates and priests would receive; and he did not demand any subsidies for chapters [administrative staffs], seminaries,

---

[3][The preamble of the Concordat speaks of Catholicism as "the religion of the great majority" of the French people.—Eds.]

and the poor *deservants* [clergy in charge of such places as chapels and small churches].

But, on the other hand, what benefits! Above all, in exchange for recognizing the Consular government, the recognition by the latter of the spiritual authority of the Pope and his right to install and even depose bishops; the reconciliation of revolutionary France with the Church; the restoration of religion in an old Christian land; and increased prestige for the successor of Peter.

At Rome, however, the Curia judged that these advantages did not compensate for the agreed-upon concessions; and the mood there favored the opposition of the *zelanti* [zealots], who invoked principle to denounce the compromises of the Secretary of State [Consalvi] and the weaknesses of the Holy Father, who was dominated by him. Hence Pius VII had to defeat a very powerful opposition in order to gain approval of the settlement by the Congregation for Extraordinary Ecclesiastical Affairs.

"When the cardinals went to the Congregation that had to decide on the ratification of the Concordat, they were sad and dejected, as on the day they went to Saint-Peter's to attend a *Te Deum* ordered by the General Berthier at the founding of the Roman Republic"; so wrote a priest, Cornus, an émigré in Rome, to the Archbishop of Toulouse, Fontanges. The General Congregation on August 10, 1801 split its vote: 14 cardinals favored ratification unconditionally, 12 ratification with conditions, and 2 were against ratification of the most contested articles. Last-minute and rather unexpected support came from [Cardinal] Antonelli, which assured the necessary majority, for this *zelante* tipped the balance with an overwhelming argument: by recognizing the Pope's right to install and depose bishops, the Concordat was the "death sentence of Gallicanism."

Therefore, Pius VII signed the treaty on August 15, and Bonaparte signed on September 8. The exchange of ratifications took place September 10 at Paris.

THE ORGANIC ARTICLES

Nevertheless, the publication of the Concordat in France was delayed until April 18, 1802, for the Constitution required that it be submitted to the legislative houses, both very hostile to the relaxation of religious tension. To overcome their opposition, it was necessary to purge them of opponents, then to wait for an increase in Bonaparte's prestige generated by the Treaty of Amiens [with Britain on March 25, 1802], which permitted the First Consul to force their hand, and finally, to bring to a vote the law of the cults on 18 Germinal, year X

[April 8, 1802] and to promulgate it throughout the Republic the following Easter.

Now, that law not only included the Concordat signed with the Holy See. Under the pretext of elucidating the police regulations mentioned in Article One overseeing the exercise of religion, Bonaparte, on his own authority, incorporated there the *Organic Articles*. These reintroduced the Gallican principles Bonaparte had sacrificed in the text of the Concordat and made the Church of France extremely dependent on the State.

Title I reestablished the right of *placet* [that is, the government's power to prevent the automatic implementation] of all acts, briefs, and bulls of the Holy See and decrees of general Church Councils; it required the government's authorization to hold provincial Church councils and synods and also the government's authorization for "all functions relating to the Gallican Church" that "any individual who identifies himself as a nuncio, legate, vicar, or apostalic commissioner" might exercise; and, finally, it reaffirmed the appeal of abuses [the right of individual clergymen to appeal to the French Council of State in case of alleged abuses by high Church officials and other ecclesiastics].

Title II encroached on ecclesiastical discipline and even on theology: it suppressed exemptions [that is, the freedom of individual clergymen from control by their bishops]; prohibited bishops, without government authorization, from leaving their dioceses or establishing seminaries and chapters; required the First Consul's approval of the seminaries' regulations; required professors in these schools to teach the Four [Gallican] Articles of 1682; and provided for the administration of vacant dioceses by the metropolitan archbishop, not by the *vicaire capitulaire* [a clergyman] elected by the administrative staff of the diocese.

Title III authorized the adoption of a single catechism and a single liturgy everywhere in France; prohibited the establishment of religious holidays on any day except Sunday and prohibited the performing of a religious marriage ceremony before a civil marriage; required government approval for the nomination of parish priests; regulated preaching; determined the amount of salaries granted to clergy; and regulated the religious endowments that were supported by interest earned on government securities.

In a far from honest way, all of this violated not only the letter but also the spirit of the treaty by reinstituting unilaterally measures that the Roman negotiators had formally rejected. The Holy See made the most vigorous protests against the *Organic Articles* and did not stop calling for their abrogation until the 1905 law separated Church from State. But, like Bonaparte, the succeeding governments, including that of the very Christian King after 1814 [Louis XVIII], persisted in maintaining the *Organic Articles*.

Despite everything, Pius VII never altered his opinion of the inestimable benefit of the Concordat, so much so that he excused the Emperor [for interning him later at] Savona and Fontainebleau. Only he, in a moving letter, intervened with the Allies in 1815 "to lessen the punishment of the unfortunate exile who sees himself wasting away on the rock of Saint Helena": admirable evidence of the Pope's goodness and magnanimity.

Alphonse Aulard (1849–1928) was one of the first great professional historians of the French Revolution. The son of a professor who was also a secondary school administrator, he came from the provinces to Paris and attended the prestigious Ecole normale supérieure. He began his teaching in the field of literature, but his writings on the orators of the French Revolution led to his appointment as the first Professor of the History of the French Revolution at the University of Paris, a post he held from 1891 until his retirement in 1922. For more than forty years he wrote and edited books on the religious and political history of France from 1789 to 1815. His three main works on the Napoleonic era are the Histoire politique de la Révolution française *(1st ed., 1901, which covers the Consulate as well as the Revolution),* Paris sous le Consulat *(4 vols.; 1903–1909), and* Paris sous le Premier Empire *(3 vols.; 1912–1923). As the present selection indicates, Aulard was an anti-clerical who advocated the separation of Church and State.*

AN UNNECESSARY PAPAL VICTORY

Alphonse Aulard

Generally speaking, the system of separation [of Church and State since 1795] had produced an extraordinary development of the religious life in France; an unusual variety of religious groups; never had there been so many altars raised in France as on the eve of the Concordat.

As for the relations of the religious groups among themselves, the Catholics continued to give proof of their intolerance. But the shrewd firmness of the Consulate Government did not allow them to attain to the tyrannical predominance to which they aspired, and so to stifle the other forms of worship. They had to confine themselves, in the use of their legal freedom, to attacking the freethinkers rather than the other mystical cults.

"Freethinking" still counted a great number of adepts in cultivated society; it was apparently in the ascendant in the Institute,[1] especially in the class of the moral sciences; but it was no longer the

From Alphonse Aulard, *The French Revolution: A Political History, 1789–1804*, trans. from the 3rd French ed., 1905, by Bernard Miall, 4 vols. (New York: Charles Scribner's Sons, 1910), IV: pp. 202–206, 226, with some changes in translation.

[1][A learned society sponsored by the government and including some of the leading men of letters, scholars, and scientists of the time.—Eds.]

fashion. Militant rationalists, like Fourcroy, were pronouncing their *mea culpa*; and although this particular scientist declared a preference for Protestantism, it was none the less the Catholics who benefited by his defection. In literature, to glorify Catholicism was already a means of arriving at celebrity, as was demonstrated by the example of La Harpe and Fontanes. Chateaubriand, in March, 1801, published his *Atala*, in which, against the background of a romantic adventure, he exalted the Gospels and the Catholic religion: he thus obtained a literary success the like of which had never been known in France since the day of Voltaire. Among the *bourgeoisie* Roman Catholicism gained ground, but not as an intolerant and exclusive religion. Neither Chateaubriand nor his admirers demanded that the altars of other religions should be overturned. It was only to the uncompromising Papist priests that the continuation of the liberal system of separation seemed intolerable.

Although Roman Catholicism was spreading, while the other cults remained as they were, or even declined, there was still a kind of equilibrium between the groups, and the consequent religious competition was carried on to the profit of consciences and of the State. The *independence* of the State increased still further every day, as Roederer [Napoleon's advisor] remarked. It has been argued that the devotion of a portion of the Papist clergy to the cause of Louis XVIII was one of the reasons why Bonaparte decided to put an end to the system of separation. Since the victory of Marengo, however, this devotion was scarcely dangerous, and those priests who were faithful to the King became every day more rare. It would be more correct to say that the uncompromising royalism of a portion of the Papist clergy was useful rather than hurtful to the State, because that very royalism caused a schism in the most powerful of the religious groups, that one whose numerical advantage was most dangerous to the independence of the State.

As a matter of fact the French Revolution had victoriously, but not without trouble, achieved this result: that the most formidable of all the forces of the past against which it had to struggle, namely the Catholic Church, was now split up into three parts; firstly, the ex-Constitutionals; secondly, the reconciled Papists; and thirdly, the royalist Papists, all of whom quarrelled among themselves; while a large rationalistic sect, the Theophilanthropists, gave, by its persistence, an example of the organisation of free thought as a sect; and the Hebrews, and more especially the Protestants, grown more numerous by means of territorial annexations, acted as a counterpoise. Finally, the altar raised to the fatherland, honored on each *Décadi*, still stood in the principal churches. Nowhere did the Catholic religion reign exclusively. Public instruction remained secular. The State was secular. The State was free, and its own master.

Why then did Bonaparte abandon a system so favourable to the State, advantages that his own policy had so ably confirmed, a condition of things so advantageous to France and to himself? Why did he restore the Church to its old preponderant situation?

Was it because there was a movement of public opinion in favour of the Concordat? Quite on the contrary; so unpopular was the Concordat of 1516, indirectly broken by the Constituent Assembly in 1790, that in common prudence and as a matter of policy the convention which was eventually concluded with the Pope was not given the name of Concordat.[2] Had there still been a free press we may be sure that there would have been a revulsion of feeling against the Concordat, we may almost say a unanimous revulsion. Neither among those close to Bonaparte, nor among his adversaries, nor among any party of the clergy, nor even at the Court of Rome (where no one could have imagined that the head of the French State would spontaneously renounce the advantages of separation) was there any demand for a Concordat.

Was it that Bonaparte, by birth a Corsican and a Catholic, was impelled by pious motives to favour the Roman Church? There is no indication that he ever possessed the quality we call faith.[3] Many of his actions testify to his indifference in religious matters. In Egypt he had honoured the Mohammedan religion as though himself a Mohammedan. Married in a civil ceremony, he resigned himself to undergo the religious ceremony of marriage only upon the eve of his coronation, and then only because it was essential to his coronation. If he went to Mass he refused to communicate. Even upon the conclusion of the Concordat he thought a *Te Deum* sufficient. Roederer tells us that it took the combined efforts of Portalis and Cambacérès [two of his advisors] to persuade him to attend a Mass, and that then they could not persuade him to kiss the patena. He did not confess; he did not communicate; not even (it appears) in the article of death; and his will indicates merely that he died in the religion of his birth.

Impenetrable to the religious spirit, incapable even of envisaging religion from the standpoint of the conscience, he said before Pelet (of Lozère):

> As for me, I do not see in religion the mystery of the incarnation, but the mystery of the social order; religion attributes to heaven an idea of equality, so that the rich shall not be massacred by the poor. Religion, again, is a kind of inoculation or vaccine, which, while satisfying our love of the marvellous, safeguards us against charlatans and sorcerers; the priests are more valuable than the Cagliostros, the Kants, and all the dreamers of Germany.

[2][Officially it was called a Convention.—Eds.]
[3][For an interpretation of Napoleon that believes him to be less of a freethinker, see M. Guerrini, *Napoléon devant Dieu* (Paris, 1960).—Eds.]

AN UNNECESSARY PAPAL VICTORY

He said much the same to Roederer:

> Society cannot exist without the inequality of fortunes, and inequality of fortune cannot continue without religion. When one man is dying of hunger by the side of another who is overfed, it is impossible for him to submit to this difference unless there is an authority which says to him: "God wills it thus: there must be rich and poor in the world; but afterwards, and for all eternity, matters will be otherwise arranged."

That Bonaparte, after having presided over the system of separation with an admirable tact and success, came finally to desire, and then to effect, reunion with Rome—in short, to conclude the Concordat—was no proof whatever of his piety; it was all done with a view to swaying the nation's conscience through the Pope, in order to realise, through the Pope, his dreams of empire—of universal empire. He also foresaw the accessory advantage of ridding himself of the former Constitutional Church, which had remained democratic on account of the electoral system which was its foundation, and of depriving Louis XVIII of his last means of influencing France, and of pacifying La Vendée definitely and finally. . . .

After having himself applied the system of separation of Church and State with as much success as ability, he then disorganised that system by means of the Concordat, the organic articles, and a host of other measures; and gradually restored the Catholic and Apostolic Church of Rome to its old situation as State Church; not in name only, but in fact. Depriving the State of its secular character, mixing up Church and State in the manner of the *ancien régime*, restoring Gallicanism to the profit of his policy, his object was certainly not to subject the State to the Church, but to make the Church an instrument of his imperial ambition, and, as I have said, to govern men's consciences through the Pope. This attempt miscarried, in the sense that Napoleon's throne quickly crumbled beneath him. It was the Catholic Church that was finally victorious, for the State ceased for a long time to be secular, and the Church maintained, and still maintains in France [in 1901], nearly all the privileges she had obtained. Even if these privileges had been lost the Church would nevertheless have retained the formidable numerical preponderance which she gained through the suppression of schisms and the abolition of the rationalistic cults, and the state of dependence into which the Jews and Protestants had fallen; and if the system of separation had been re-established there would no longer have been the competition of the other religious bodies by which the secular State had profited from 1795 to 1802; there would have been no serious resistance to the power of the Roman Catholic Church, which to-day is only held in check by means of secular primary education, and the progressive decay of religious feeling among the rural masses of the French population.

Taking the whole work of destruction and reaction which Bonaparte more or less consciously accomplished, it is the Concordat which stands out as the essential counter-revolutionary measure, both in its consequences and the manner of its application.

4
THE RESPONSIBILITY FOR THE WAR OF 1803

In 1802 France was at peace, the first period of peace since 1792. A year later war began again between Britain and France. This war continued until 1814 with other nations joining the fight alongside England. It resulted in the deaths of millions and the downfall of Napoleon.

Who was responsible for the resumption of this very destructive war? Clearly the English cannot be regarded as simply innocent victims: Arnold David Harvey points out that most continental Europeans detested the English for their alleged abridgements of sea trade, their sense of superiority, their mercenary nature, their religious intolerance, and many other reasons; André Fugier demonstrates that the English and French misunderstood one another and that the English press and leading politicians made the situation worse by libeling and provoking Napoleon; and Georges Lefebvre calls attention to British imperialism. But Lefebvre also discusses Napoleon's poorly conceived actions in 1802–1803 which threatened the balance of power and violated the Treaty of Amiens. By this treaty, England had agreed to restore to France and her allies all territory seized since 1793 (except for Trinidad, a former Spanish possession, and Ceylon, a former Dutch possession) and to restore Malta to the Knights of St. John of Jerusalem. In turn, France, who kept all her continental conquests, led the English to believe that she had renounced any design on Egypt and any further territorial claims on the continent.

Of course, judging war guilt is complicated. Do we hold solely responsible the power that was most aggressive and uncompromising? Or do we blame all those who helped increase tension by their insensitivity to others; or those who did not abide by the spirit as well as the letter of the treaty; or those who first broke off diplomatic relations? Moreover, we must place ourselves in the context of the early nineteenth century when many viewed war as an opportunity for national advancement and personal glory, not as an unmitigated disaster.

Arnold David Harvey (1947–) studied at the University of Oxford and then at Cambridge University, where he received his Ph.D. in history. While teaching at various universities in England and Italy, he has published Britain in the Early Nineteenth Century *(1978),* English Poetry in a Changing Society, 1780–1825 *(1980),* English Literature and the Great War with France *(1981), and many historical and literary articles.*

THE CONTINENTAL IMAGES OF BRITAIN

Arnold David Harvey

"The dominant principle of all the political theorists and writers at the present moment is—jealousy of British power." So wrote the German publicist Friedrich Gentz in 1800.[1] Seven years later the former diplomat William Augustus Miles commented on the wave of indignation that swept Europe following the British attack on Copenhagen in September 1807, "Our Court must have been very badly informed of the temper and feelings of the Continent towards us if it has yet to learn that we are everywhere detested."[2] During the years that Napoleon threatened every state in Europe it was not the French but the British who were probably the most hated nation in Europe.

There were few exceptions to this general antipathy. The Norwegians so disliked the Swedes and the Danes that they were fond of singing Rule Britannia and drinking to "The welfare of Great Britain."[3] A Briton visiting Rotterdam under the pretext of being an American (the Batavian Republic being then at war with Britain)

From A. D. Harvey, "European Attitudes to Britain during the French Revolution and Napoleonic Era," *History* 63 (1978): pp. 356–365. The entire article is reprinted by permission of the author and the editor of *History* with corrections of footnote numbering.

[1] *H. M. C. Reports Dropmore Mss* vol. 6, p. 375 *Mémoire* by Gentz. [H. M. C. designates the Historical Manuscripts Commission.—Eds.]
[2] C. P. Miles, ed., *Correspondence of William Augustus Miles on the French Revolution 1789–1817* (2 vols. London, 1890) vol. 2, p. 358 Miles to C. Long 19 November 1807.
[3] E. D. Clarke, *Travels in Various Countries of Europe, Asia and Africa* (6 vols. London, 1810–23) vol. 5, p. 666.

reported, "such is the respect which the Dutch bear towards us, that we soon found the suspicion of our being English rather increased than damped the civilities we experienced."[4] In Hanover—at that time still ruled by the King of Britain—the poet Coleridge was struck by the enthusiasm for things English which he observed during a visit in 1798:

> At the dinner which was given in honor of Nelson's Victory [*at the Battle of the Nile*] 21 guns were fired by order of the Military Governour, and between each Firing the Military Band played an English Tune—I never saw such enthusiasm, or heard such tumultuous shouting, as when the Governour gave as a toast, "The Great Nation"—By this Name they always designate England in opposition to the same title self-assumed by France.[5]

In other parts of Germany however it was noted that, "Among the other topics which assist the sale of political pamphlets and journals in the empire, there is none more universally resorted to than an indiscriminate abuse of the British Government and all its measures."[6] A young nobleman and his tutor visiting the arsenal at Copenhagen discovered that "they were obliged to pass for Frenchmen, in order to avoid the insults of the sailors."[7] Similarly in Sweden another traveller found. "This anti-English feeling was so general... that I was advised to travel as a German through the country, and in fact did so.[8]"

In Spain, even Britain's intervention in 1808 to help expel the French met with little gratitude, and one British officer reported with surprise, "they do not like us in the least, and they tell us very often (to please us) that they had rather see the French than us."[9] When, after four years co-operation with the Spanish armies, Wellington was appointed generalissimo by the Spanish government, Ballesteros, captain-general of Andalucía, revolted and his partisans denounced England as being as great a threat to Spain as France.[10] In the Spanish cortes, despite the bitter rivalries of the various factions, it was observed that "Jealousy of England was however common to all,

---

[4] J. Carr, *A Tour through Holland, along the right and left Banks of the Rhine, to the South of Germany, in the Summer and Autumn of 1806* (London, 1807), p. 28.

[5] E. L. Griggs, ed., *Collected Letters of Samuel Taylor Coleridge* (6 vols. Oxford 1956–71) vol. 1 p. 424–30 Coleridge to wife, 20 October 1798.

[6] *H. M. C. Reports Dropmore Mss* vol. 4, p. 281 H. Elliott to Lord Grenville 15 August 1798.

[7] R. M. Bacon, *A Memoir of the Life of Edward, Third Baron Suffield* (Norwich, printed for private circulation 1838), p. 15–16.

[8] T. Sadler, ed., *Diary, Reminiscences, and Correspondence of Henry Crabb Robinson*, (3 vols. London, 1869) vol. 1 p 259.

[9] *H. M. C. Reports Lonsdale Mss* p. 234 H. C. Lowther to Earl of Lonsdale, 4 December 1808.

[10] C. Oman, *A History of the Peninsular War* (7 vols. Oxford, 1902–30) vol. 6, pp. 61–2.

and 'Inglesimo' was used as a term of contempt."[11] It was even believed that Britain aimed at prolonging the war in Spain in order to terminate Spanish national independence.[12] In Sicily too Britain's intervention to save the island from French invasion was seen as inspired solely by self-interest. The Queen of the Two Sicilies accused the British representative there (to quote his report)

> for 6 years, it had been our settled plan to take the Country. That *spirituel* Fox had said so, Moore who was a Jacobin *enragé* did not deny it—Drummond *qui parloit comme un fou* [who spoke like a crazy man], Stuart and myself were all working to the same end. . . .
>
> I asked Her Majesty if the having refrained for 6 years from having done that which was always easy to Us, was not a proof of the injustice of that accusation— She answered—No—that would have been too like Bonaparte—Your object has been to do this under the cover of Forms, to save your reputation.[13]

Though France was at various times during this period at war with practically every nation of Europe, the French singled out the British for their special animosity. Vilification of Britain became a key element in Napoleon's propaganda[14] and it was during his reign that the catch-phrase "Perfidious Albion" became common usage.[15] In fact most of "the notions which have been propagated and received with so much avidity upon the Continent, of the ambition and intrigues of England,"[16] derived from French manipulation of public opinion.

Early in the French Revolutionary War the French Convention decreed that no quarter should be given to British and Hanoverian troops, and the address proposed by Barrère to accompany this decree began by explaining,

> England is capable of every outrage on humanity, and every crime towards the republic. She attacks the rights of all nations, and threatens to annihilate liberty. How long will you suffer in your frontiers, the slaves of George, the soldiers of the most atrocious of tyrants.[17]

---

[11] W. F. P. Napier, *History of the War in the Peninsula and in the South of France* (6 vols. London, 1828–40) vol. 6, p. 308.

[12] Duke of Wellington, ed. *Supplementary Despatches, Correspondence and Memoranda of Arthur, Duke of Wellington* (15 vols. London, 1852–72) vol. 8 p 184 A. de la Vega to Wellington 28 April 1813.

[13] P.R.O. F.O. 70/44, Lord W. Bentinck to Marquis Wellesley, 26 December 1811. Fox, Moore and Stuart had been successively commanders of the British army in Sicily; Drummond had been the British diplomatic representative at Palermo, 1801–3 and 1806–9. [P.R.O. designates the British Public Record Office (national archives) in London.—Eds.]

[14] R. B. Holtman, *Napoleonic Propaganda*, (Baton Rouge 1950) pp. 3–7.

[15] H. D. Schmidt, "The Idea and Slogan of Perfidious Albion," *Journal of the History of Ideas* XIV (1953) pp. 604–616, espec. pp. 607–613.

[16] *H.M.C. Reports Dropmore Mss* vol. 6 p. 322 Earl of Carysfort to Lord Grenville, 18 September 1800.

[17] J. Philippart, *Memoirs of General Moreau*, (London, 1814) p. 16. n.

In 1797 at the time of the temporary cessation of war with Austria, Napoleon Bonaparte pointed out,

> The Austrians are dull and greedy: no people less intriguing and less dangerous to our interior affairs than the Austrian people. The English, on the contrary, are spirited, intriguing and active. Our government must destroy the English monarchy or must expect to be destroyed by the corruption and intrigues of these active islanders.[18]

When preparing to meet the threat of the Austrian and Russian armies in September 1805 he referred to the Austro-Russian alliance as "this new league which the hatred and gold of England has woven."[19] On the very eve of confronting the Austrian forces, the best that he could do in the way of whipping up the enthusiasm of his own troops was to issue a proclamation to his army saying that if it had not been for the Austrians, "we would today be at London, we would have avenged six centuries of injury and restored the freedom of the seas. But remember tomorrow that you are fighting the ally of England."[20] After the victory at Ulm a further proclamation prepared his troops for the coming campaign against "This Russian army which English gold has transported from the extremities of the universe,"[21] and his proclamation before the Battle of Austerlitz described the Russians as "those hired servants of England, who are animated by so great a hatred of our nation."[22] When Napoleon was Consul, the French government even issued printed placards announcing *Guerre au Gouvernement Anglais* [War on the English Government] for display in every public office in France.[23]

The principal theme of French propaganda was Britain's commercial supremacy and the methods by which it was achieved:

> English vessels cover every sea: she sends soldiers, arms, gold, agents to the four quarters of the world; there is no colony so remote that her distant expeditions do not threaten it; there is no empire, however much a stranger to European intercourse, to which she does not labour to procure access and to secure exclusive establishments there. Countries Europe scarcely knows have received from England names which she regards as marks of ownership: those still unknown await English appellations; and as she extends the realm of nautical geography, she enlarges at the same time that of English maritime domination.[24]

[18]*Correspondance De Napoléon 1er* (32 vols. Paris 1858–70) vol. 3 p. 392 Bonaparte to Talleyrand 18 October 1797 (27 vendémiaire an VI). My translation.
[19]*Ibid.* vol. 11 p. 263, proclamation 30 September 1805 (8 vendémiaire an XIV).
[20]*Ibid.* p. 324, proclamation 13 October 1805 (21 vendémiaire an XIV).
[21]*Ibid.* p. 343, proclamation 21 October 1805 (29 vendémiaire an XIV).
[22]*Ibid.* p. 441, proclamation 1 December 1805 (10 frimaire an XIV).
[23]*H.M.C. Reports Dropmore Mss* vol. 6, p. 289 J. Edwards to Lord Grenville, 12 August 1800.
[24]A. M. Blanc de la Nautte, comte d'Hauterive, *De l'État de la France à la Fin de l'An VIII* (Paris An IX (1800)) p. 117–8. My translation.

In a pioneer analysis of the British empire as a system of economic exploitation, drawn up on behalf of his French hosts, the Irish exile Arthur O'Connor argued,

> Rome has given us an example of the extent to which dominion may be carried by exacting tribute from the nations she has vanquished; but it has been reserved for Great Britain to unite the passion for domination with the insatiable spirit of mercantile exaction.
>
> An island at one extremity of Europe, with a population of scarcely eleven millions, she bestrides the other three quarters of the earth; one foot on the vast continent of America, the other upon the Indies, she consigns Africa to external barbarism and slavery, that the produce of the Antilles may swell the list of her imports; collecting annually in kind, by a mixt system of commerce, exaction, plunder and tribute, to the amount of 17½ millions from the produce of the different nations she had conquered, which she deals out to the nations of Europe at the exorbitant rate of a monopoly price; making those which are territorially free, but maritimely enslaved, feel a part of the injustice she uses to those unfortunate countries over whose liberties she exercises an uncontrouled dominion.[25]

O'Connor argued that the monopoly was imposed by force of arms and that other European countries, by purchasing colonial goods from Britain, "are paying tribute to maintain that navy which shackles their commerce."[26] War was seen as vital to the British as it enabled them to extend their system: the right assumed by Britain of searching neutral shipping in war-time effectively hampered the trade of peaceable rivals, and a state of conflict gave openings for useful alliances. According to another propagandist, Britain's alliances "have as their chief motive the ambition of opening, in all parts of the world, privileged channels for her trade";[27] the alliance with Turkey for example was aimed at securing India and the Levant, and that with Naples was made in the hope of gaining Malta, "and from that important spot, whether considered as a military post or commercial entrepot, command the trade of Sicily, Italy, the Barbary States, Turkey, and enslave the improvident politics of those countries' governments."[28]

According to O'Connor,

> War affords Great Britain so many means of making the other nations of Europe contribute to defray her expences, that nothing but the inordinate expence at which she makes war could prevent her from finding her interest in making it perpetual.[29]

Such views were not confined to theoreticians: even Napoleon claimed that the ultimate British objective was, "the burning of our fleet, the

---

[25] A. O'Connor, *The Present State of Great Britain*, (Paris, 1804) p. 2–3.
[26] *Ibid.*, p. 7.
[27] Hauterive, *De l'État de la France*, p. 138.
[28] *Ibid.* p. 139–40.
[29] O'Connor, *Present State of Great Britain*, p. 82 n.2.

filling up of our ports, and the annihilation of our industry,"[30] and Soult, the French officer commanding in the South of France in 1814, asked in his proclamation to his troops at Toulouse, "Does there exist upon the face of the globe a point known to the English where they have not destroyed by seditions and violence all manufactures which could rival their own?"[31]

In neutral countries there was a ready audience for such propaganda; from Prussia it was reported,

> The towns want maritime trade and manufacturers. The farflung shipping interest especially headed by the minister responsible for such concerns with active members amongst the people of every class has let itself be drawn by the French party into jealousy against the English, and the feeling has spread to the public because of the high price of sugar, coffee and tea. These folk are infatuated with the absurd idea that there would be maritime trade for every nation which had ports, if the French overthrew English power, and Bonaparte penetrated to India.[32]

The pro-British Gentz regretted the

> ridiculous prejudices in economic matters, which cause the public of *all nations without exception* to believe that the strength of one country necessarily means the weakness of others, that what constitutes the wealth of England constitutes the poverty of the rest of Europe, that the preponderance, as just as it is inevitable, which its industry, its character, and the wisdom of its government give to a country is a hateful monopoly by which it oppresses other countries."[33]

Yet in fact there was sufficient truth in these accusations for them to stick.[34]

Resentment of British economic supremacy was strengthened moreover by the right Britain claimed to interfere with the trade of non-belligerent countries in wartime. The searching of neutral merchant ships for contraband was for a time tolerated but on 25 July 1800 there was a serious incident when the Danish frigate *Freya* was fired on by British warships, after having refused to permit the convoy it was escorting to be searched. Shortly afterwards Denmark joined with Sweden and Russia in the League of Armed Neutrality, an alliance to resist British infractions of the freedom of the seas. The

---

[30]*Correspondance De Napoléon 1er* vol. 11 p. 248 Speech to Senate 23 September 1805 (1 vendémiaire an XIV).

[31]Napier, *History of the War in the Peninsula*, vol. 6, p. 588.

[32]H. M. C. *Reports Dropmore Mss* vol. 4 p. 396, A. de Luc to Lord Grenville, 26 November 1798.

[33]H. M. C. *Reports Dropmore Mss* vol. 6, pp. 375–6 *Mémoire* by Gentz.

[34]The effects of British policy on international trade are discussed in my book *Britain in the Early Nineteenth Century* (London, 1978). Of course the British government was not totally single-minded in its pursuit of commercial advantage; the merchant navy captain who assisted the revolt against the Danish viceroyalty in Iceland because Reykjavik had been closed to British trade, was disowned by the cabinet, cf. W. J. Hooker, *Journal of a Tour in Iceland in the Summer of 1809* (Yarmouth 1811) appendices A. & B. and H. P. Briem, *Sjálfstaedi Islands 1809* (Reykjavik 1936).

British government caused even more bitterness seven years later with the promulgation of a total blockade of the ports of France and her allies. The American minister at London described British policy at this time as "that extravagant system of maritime oppression . . . by which Great Britain every day exemplifies in various modes the favourite doctrine of her infatuated advisers that Power and Rightful Dominion are equivalent terms."[35]

Britain's commercial supremacy, and the "injudicious, wanton, and extravagant aggression"[36] with which she interfered with the trade of other nations, were however only the principal, and by no means the only causes of Anglophobia. There was for example, the arrogance of the British:

> It is no wonder considering the dislike and the reserve which the generality of the English manifest to foreigners, both on their own island, and when they are on the continent, that in return, most foreign nations are far from wishing them well, and seem to rejoice at their misfortunes, thinking it will humble their pride, at which they are offended."[37]

The war in fact encouraged an extraordinary chauvinism in the British, which is perhaps best exemplified by the reports of privateering captains on the behaviour of their crews in action: "My officers and men behaved as Englishmen, steady and collected"; "During the action, my officers, and men behaved as becomes Britons on all such like occasions"; "Every praise is due to my officers and men; they behaved like Englishmen to the last moment"; "to do the crew every justice, they fought like Englishmen," and so on.[38] Visitors to Britain soon noticed the national contempt for foreigners.[39] Britons also showed their conviction of their own superiority by their behaviour when abroad. Even British ambassadors showed themselves more adept at representing their countrymen's arrogance than their diplomatic interests. One envoy referred to foreigners clinging to "a sort of shabby hope that their own vices and degeneracy would in the end be redeemed by our virtues, resources, and constancy."[40] William Fred-

---

[35]Henry Wheaton, *Some Account of the Life, Writings, and Speeches of William Pinkney* (New York, 1826), p. 76, Pinkney to President Madison 31 December 1807.

[36]*Ibid.* p. 72 Pinkney to President Madison 7 December 1807.

[37]F. A. Wendeborn, *A View of England towards the Close of the Eighteenth Century* (2 vols. London, 1791) vol. 1, p. 378.

[38]G. Williams, *History of the Liverpool Privateers and Letters of Marque with an Account of the Liverpool Slave Trade* (1897), pp. 363, 365, 408, 419.

[39]A. G. Goede, *The Stranger in England*, (3 vols. London, 1807), vol. 2 p. 88 (First published in Dresden 1804–5 as *England, Wales, Irland und Schottland . . . aus einer Reise in den Jahren 1802–3*).

[40]*H. M. C. Dropmore Mss* vol. 6, p. 463 Lord Minto to Lord Grenville 6 March 1801.

erick Wyndham, while minister at Florence, was so enraged by the way in which the Grand Duke's Chamberlain had been "talking neutral politics," that he waylaid him one day while riding in the Papal Nuncio's carriage, and horsewhipped him.[41] Another career diplomat, Sir Arthur Paget, managed to make himself obnoxious at the courts of Munich, of Naples, and of Vienna, and a plan to send him to Berlin was given up owing to the protests of the Prussian court and the allied ambassadors at Berlin. But perhaps the most undiplomatic diplomat of the day was Sir Gore Ouseley, who was envoy to the Emperor of Persia between 1810 and 1814. When the Emperor remarked inquisitively, "I have heard that your King is a mere cypher, and can do nothing," Ouseley replied crisply, "He was such a cypher as to be able to make and unmake a hundred such kings as you."[42]

Even when British diplomats were relatively well-behaved, their incompetence was such as to render Britain ridiculous when in a weak position, and obnoxious when in a strong. Often this was in accordance with instructions from Whitehall. For example, Viscount Howick, Foreign Secretary early in 1807, thoughtlessly badgered the Russians to negotiate a commercial treaty and to guarantee the security of Hanover at a time when the Russians were desperate for money and for a military diversion to help them face a French invasion then actually in progress. Having refused the Russian demands for aid, Howick blandly instructed the ambassador to St. Petersburg,

> It must necessarily cause considerable disappointment to his Majesty's Government to learn that notwithstanding the readiness shewn upon all occasions to comply with the Desires of Russia, Difficulties should still be raised on the two points of the Commercial Treaty, and the Guaranty of Hanover.[43]

Nearly all Britain's diplomatic overtures of the period were rebuffed, and the various alliances in which Britain joined from 1793 onwards all derived from Austrian or Russian initiatives.

In spite of Britain's professed role as the champion of legitimacy against the French, the government also lost credit by some striking violations of international law, such as the attack on the Spanish treasure frigates before war had been declared on Spain in 1805, and two years later the unprovoked bombardment of Copenhagen which was instanced by Thomas Jefferson, along with the enormities of

---

[41]Lord Holland, *Memoirs of the Whig Party during my Time*, ed. by his son. (2 vols. London, 1852–4) vol. 1 p. 57; and J. Hutton ed. *Selections from the Letters and Correspondence of Sir James Bland Burges, Bart.* (London, 1885) p. 250 Lord St. Helens to Burges 17 June 1799.

[42]K. L. ed., *Extracts from the Diary of Dr. Robert Lee* (printed for private circulation 1897) p. 21–2.

[43]P.R.O. F.O. 181/6 Viscount Howick to Marquis of Douglas 20 February 1807.

Napoleon, as demonstrating that the period was with the Macedonian and Roman imperial era, one of "three epochs in history, signalized by the total extinction of national morality."[44]

Foreigners regarded the British claim to be fighting for freedom and legitimacy as all the more hypocritical in that they believed that, while enforcing a near monopoly in international trade abroad, the British at home existed either in slavery or in a state of licence and corruption. Brougham for example found that the Swedes "laugh at our liberty, which they call gilded slavery."[45] It is true that before 1789 most visitors to Britain had been impressed by the relative independence and equality which they observed, but even before the spread of French Revolutionary doctrines there had begun to be criticism of the British constitution.[46] Rousseau had pointed the way to this revision of attitudes when he had sneered, a generation earlier,

> The people of England regards itself as free; but it is grossly mistaken; it is free only during the election of members of parliament. As soon as they are elected, slavery overtakes it, and it is nothing. The use it makes of the short moments of liberty it enjoys shows indeed that it deserves to lose them.[47]

And later Friedrich Wilhelm Schütz, in his *Briefe über London* [Letters on London] (1792) had cited the petty tyranny of customs officials, the exclusion of Catholics and nonconformists from public office, and the Press Gang, as instances of how limited British liberty really was. Britain's political decadence was seen as deriving from the commercial morality of Britain. "In England one now speaks of nothing but trade," a German visitor reported, "certain other words which were formerly sometimes heard there, are entirely obsolete. I expect that trade will soon be preached from the pulpits there as the sole doctrine of happiness and salvation."[48] The Swedish historian Eric Gustaf Geijer, who actually became an admirer of the British, originally regarded Britain as "a nation whose thirst for gain and a narrow egotism have stifled everything beautiful and noble."[49] From Russia a visiting Cambridge don reported,

---

[44] T. Jefferson, *Memoirs, Correspondence and Private Papers* (4 vols. London, 1829) vol. 1, p. 87.
[45] Brougham, *Life*, vol. 1, p. 174.
[46] W. D. Robson-Scott, *German Travellers in England 1400–1800* (Oxford, 1953) p. 201 foll.
[47] J. J. Rousseau, *Le Contrat Social*, book 3, ch. 15. cf. W. Austin *Letters from London* (Boston, 1804) p. 21 (misprinted p. 20). "You know the English fancy themselves free, once in seven years . . . ."
[48] F. M. Klinger, *Betrachtungen und Gedanken über verschiedene Gegenstände*, 1801–1802, *Sämmtliche Werke* (12 vols. Stuttgart, 1843) vol. 11, pt. 1. p. 39.
[49] E. J. Geijer, *Impressions of England 1809–1810*, ed. A. Blanck, trans. E. Sprigge and C. Napier (London, 1932) p. 245.

> They consider the English as a mercenary nation. . . . One of their princes thought proper to declare in public, at his own table, where we had been invited to dine, and were of course under protection enjoined by the laws of hospitality, that in England there is not an individual, patriot, or placeman, who is not saleable to the highest bidder. He instanced Wilkes, Gibbon, and Burke, with many others; adding, "English slavery is less justifiable than Russian. One is selfishness; the other submission to the laws."[50]

British party politics were understood to consist merely of the rivalry of corrupt factions, and as such commended themselves neither to the advocates of liberty nor to the supporters of royalist legitimacy. Foreign observers had even less faith than their British contemporaries in the stability of British society, "I hear on good authority that the moves in London to reorganize the Order of the Bath are considered as a government trick containing the germs of the decomposition of the constitution and one likely to demoralise the nation," the chief of the political police in Vienna informed the Emperor Franz I in 1815.[51] The British of course sneered at such rumours; Lord Grenville, when Foreign Secretary, on one occasion wrote to his nephew, "I have just heard from Vienna, that while our communications were interrupted by the frost, a revolution took place in England, Parliament was dissolved on the 2nd of March, never to meet again; and the Customhouse was burnt on the 3rd."[52] Yet the fact that such reports were all eventually disproved did not prevent them from adding to the general belief on the Continent in Britain's political malformation.

One of the features of recent British history had been the political upheavals which during the eighteenth century has sent fresh batches of refugees fleeing abroad in nearly every generation. Whereas in the nineteenth century political exiles from all over Europe came to Britain for refuge, in the previous hundred years the movement was mostly the other way. The descendants of the exiles of 1688, 1715 and 1745, though largely assimilated amongst their overseas hosts by 1800, still constituted a reproach to Britain's political system. There were also the Irish Catholics who fled each year from the perennial injustice of the [harsh, discriminatory British] Penal Laws. Once abroad these Irish did not lose sight of their racial identity. At a St. Patrick's Day dinner held at Burgos in 1809, the guests included, as well as exiles implicated in the 1798 rebellion, former officers of the Irish regiments of Bourbon France, officers of Spanish Irish regiments, and a Prussian officer, son of a man born in Austria,

---

[50]Clarke, *Travels in Various Countries*, vol. 1. p. 93.
[51]M. Glover, "When the Congress Wasn't Dancing," *History Today*, February 1978, pp. 88–96; p. 91.
[52]Duke of Buckingham, *Memoirs Of The Court And Cabinets of George III* (4 vols. London 1853–55) vol. 3 p. 53 Lord Grenville to Earl Temple, 8 April 1800.

of Irish family.⁵³ In Spain the "admiration of and attachment to each other" of generals Joaquin Blake and Enrique O'Donnell was noticed by a British naval officer who afterwards elaborated the paradox that,

> the intolerant religious distinctions of the English Government have deprived us of some of the best blood which the United Kingdom produces; whilst, in unison with the very men thus banished from our service, we have been fighting the battles of foreign Roman Catholics⁵⁴

Some of these Irishmen born in exile spoke no English: Blake and Luiz Lacy for example corresponded in French with British officers in Spain, but Pedro Sarsfield, though born in Spain, spoke perfect English with a pure Irish brogue,⁵⁵ and Maurice Lacy, the Russian commander in the Mediterranean, who had left Ireland in infancy, had what was described as "the strongest brogue I ever heard."⁵⁶ Some of these exiles were well-disposed to Britain. Laval, Graf von Nugent, who had been born in Co. Westmeath and had been adopted by uncles in the Austrian service, was sent as a special envoy to London in 1811, and in Spain both Luiz Lacy and his lieutenant Pedro Sarsfield seemed friendly to the British officers with whom they served (though the good feeling was not reciprocated). But generally speaking the Spanish officers of Irish blood cordially hated the British. The Hon. Sir Henry Wellesley wrote to his brother Wellington with regard to Juan O'Donoju's tenure of the Spanish ministries of State, War and Foreign Affairs that, "the principal and indeed the only feature of General O'Donoju's administration was his persecution of you."⁵⁷ It is difficult to resist the suspicion that the quarrel between Wellesley and Juan O'Donoju was partly a quarrel between an Irish Protestant and an Irish Catholic.

There were of course plenty of exiles from France scattered through Europe by the Revolution; equally, there was dislike for French political institutions and fear of French aggression. Yet France was admired as well as feared. "The successes of France always increase the public prejudice in her favour." it was observed in Stockholm.⁵⁸ The future U.S. President John Quincy Adams wrote, "the fame and glory

---

⁵³S. Gwynn, ed., *Memoirs of Miles Byrne* (2 vols. Dublin, 1907) vol. 2 p. 57.

⁵⁴Lady Bourchier, ed., *Memoir of the Life of Admiral Sir Edward Codrington* (2 vols. London, 1873) vol. 1, p. 191 Codrington to wife 21 October 1810, and vol. 1, p. 216, same to same 25 May 1811.

⁵⁵A. Crawford, *Reminiscences of a Naval Officer during the late War* (2 vols. London, 1851) vol. 2, p. 296.

⁵⁶H. Bunbury, *Narratives of some Passages in the Great War with France, From 1799 to 1810* (London, 1854) p. 190.

⁵⁷Wellington, *Supplementary Despatches*, vol. 68., p. 554. H. Wellesley to Wellington 31 January 1814. Note the hispanicization of O'Donoju's name.

⁵⁸Brougham, *Life*, vol. 1, p. 174.

of the Emperor Napoleon, founded on an almost uninterrupted succession of victories for nearly twenty years . . . had become a sort of *religion* in Europe."[59] In Britain, however, foreigners found nothing to admire. The splendid British victories at sea did little to impress nations with no naval traditions, especially as they seemed to rivet more tightly the shackles of the British commercial monopoly. On land Britain made herself contemptible by her policy of bribery and bungling. It was only after the final defeat of Napoleonic France in 1815 that the attitude of most European nations to Britain began to change from resentment and contempt to the interest and esteem which characterized European feelings towards Britain during the remainder of the nineteenth century.

[59]C. F. Adams, ed., *Memoirs of John Quincy Adams* (12 vols. Philadelphia 1874–7) vol. 2, p. 447, 11 February 1813.

For biographical information on Georges Lefebvre, see Chapter 1, "Napoleon's Character."

BOTH SIDES RESPONSIBLE

Georges Lefebvre

Bonaparte was simply not interested in keeping the peace. "A First Consul," he told Thibaudeau, "cannot be likened to these kings-by-the-grace-of-God, who look upon their States as a heritage. . . . His actions must be dramatic, and for this, war is indispensable." He was careful not to speak these thoughts in public, for the nation would have disapproved. "I have too much at stake to let foreigners take the initiative," but, he added, "they will be the first to take up arms." With such an attitude it was natural that he should encourage them. In any event, by assuring an accumulation of coin, the [French] embargo [of British goods] hastened the military build-up to the point where it became a weapon of war—as it had been during the Revolution.

It seemed more than ever before that the economy and financial structure of England, based on borrowing and inflation, were vulnerable. Such sentiments were repeated by Hauterive in Year VIII [1799–1800] the Chevalier de Guer in 1801, Lassalle in 1803, and by the *Moniteur* [the French official newspaper] itself. Although there existed no doubt of the perils menacing France, the mistake of believing that France, unassisted, could bring the English to economic ruin, was again committed. Bonaparte was overready to share this illusion, since he, a soldier and a dictator, held in contempt this oligarchy of merchants who were without an army and without a government. He would have played both Cato and Scipio to England's Carthage. No more was said of a commercial treaty: vessels were seized because they were found carrying articles of British origin. Meanwhile, France's foreign trade rose from 553 million francs in 1799 to 790 million in Year X [1801–1802]. The English capitalists learned that the economic struggle would continue, and they became disgusted with a peace which profited them nothing.

Since colonial goods were essential to her foreign trade, it became incumbent upon France to salvage the Antilles which were still left to

---

From Georges Lefebvre, *Napoleon: From 18 Brumaire to Tilsit, 1799–1807*, trans. by Henry F. Stockhold (New York: Columbia University Press, 1969), pp. 169–179. Copyright © 1969 Columbia University Press. Reprinted by permission of Columbia University Press and Routledge & Kegan Paul PLC.

her. The Peace of Amiens [with Britain, March 25, 1802] had not yet been signed when Bonaparte dispatched an expedition to San Domingo. Toussaint L'Ouverture was by now in control of the entire island, and had, on May 9, 1801, promulgated a constitution granting himself governing powers under the purely nominal authority of France. Although he surrendered in good faith to General Leclerc, who headed the French expedition, he was arrested on June 7, 1802, and deported to France, where he died in the fortress of Joux on April 7, 1803. At the same time, [the French General] Richepanse reoccupied the smaller West Indian islands. If these Antillean conquests were not worth troubling about, the English were nevertheless truly concerned over Bonaparte's Louisiana project: an expedition was being prepared on the coast of the North Sea to send General Victor to the Mississippi. The flotilla was scheduled to depart in March 1803, but it was delayed. In the meantime, Spain closed the Mississippi to American traffic. Since France and Spain were allies, and Holland a French satellite, the Gulf of Mexico appeared to be at Bonaparte's disposal. And, consequently, so did the contraband of the Spanish Indies, where the French were now in a position to extract advantageous concessions. Nevertheless, these prospects vanished without England having to interfere. The United States, which had for some time coveted Spanish Florida, had no wish to see the French established in New Orleans. The newly elected president, Jefferson, with his secretaries Madison and Gallatin, tried to pursue a Republican programme of peace, disarmament, and reduced expenditures. Even though Jefferson was well disposed towards France, and had been pleased with the signing of the Treaty of Mortefontaine,[1] he could not hold back the tide of public opinion. And so he let it be known that if France remained in Louisiana, the United States would join England in the coming war. On April 12, 1803, Jefferson's ambassador, James Monroe, arrived in Paris with a proposal to which Bonaparte had already decided to agree: the purchase of the Louisiana Territory. The ensuing treaty, signed on May 3, brought Bonaparte 80 million francs, of which only 55 million remained after deducting indemnities owed to the United States and the commissions paid to Hope and Baring, the bankers who handled the transfer.

Insurrection, resulting from the re-establishment of slavery, had already become widespread throughout San Domingo. In Bonaparte's immediate circle, where the advocates of the white planters were many (not to mention Josephine herself), the slave system was being upheld as the most expedient way to revive production quickly in the

---

[1][Signed on October 3, 1800, the treaty of Mortefontaine between France and the U.S.A. ended their undeclared naval war in the Caribbean.—Eds.]

colonies. However, it was not imperative that there be slavery, since even in the colonies where the decree of 16 Pluviôse, Year II,[2] had been applied, both the commissioners of the Directory and Toussaint L'Ouverture himself had already instituted forced labour. Bonaparte was at first inclined to keep this system, limiting himself to the retention of slavery in the islands where it already existed—the Mauritius island group where the Convention decree was considered a dead letter, and Martinique which, having been under English occupation, had never received the decree. Finally, Bonaparte gave in. Indeed, the law of May 20, 1802, explicitly stated that slavery would be "maintained" in the colonies, from which one might have deduced that it was not to reappear in places where it had been abolished. But Bonaparte, deciding otherwise, commanded Richepanse to reintroduce slavery in Guadeloupe, thereby provoking a revolt. In San Domingo, Leclerc declared the measure premature. But the blacks could see what was in store for them, and in September, Toussaint's lieutenants, Christophe and Dessalines, had no trouble raising the island in revolt. The French force, decimated by yellow fever, was rapidly exhausted. Leclerc died. His successor, Rochambeau, a supporter of the planters, lost everything by attacking the mulattoes, whom Bonaparte had already alienated by prohibiting them entry to France and marriage with whites. Port-au-Prince fell on November 19, 1803, and a few besieged garrisons managed to drag out a miserable existence until 1811.

If the English were displeased to see France re-establishing her colonial empire, they might nevertheless have delayed going to war to prevent her from doing so. But to threaten English possessions was altogether another matter, and this was precisely what Bonaparte did. A new grand concept prompted him in the direction of the Mediterranean, that is to say, Egypt. The Treaty of Amiens had at last convinced the Turks to make peace with the French (June 26, 1802) and to open the Dardanelles to French trade. A French agent, Ruffin, immediately set about restoring the consulates in the Levant. Also, pacts had been concluded with the Pasha of Tripoli in 1801 and with the Bey of Tunis in 1802. In August 1802 a flotilla compelled the Dey of Algiers to follow suit. Constantinople was already very concerned about French intrigues in the Peloponnesus, in Janina, and among the Serbs, and there were fears of a possible partition. At the end of August, Colonel Sébastiani embarked on a mission of observation to Egypt, by way of Tripoli, and then went on to Syria, seeking everywhere to establish ties with the native chieftains. Cavaignac had been sent to Muscat, and Decaen sailed for India on March 6, 1803, with an

---

[2][This decree of February 4, 1794 had abolished slavery in the French colonies.—Eds.]

important staff capable of forming sepoy regiments. All this led England to conclude that Bonaparte was planning to launch a new attack against Egypt and India, and that prudence demanded that he be stopped from completing his preparations. Under the circumstances, a British surrender of Malta was unthinkable. But that decision was a clear violation of the Treaty of Amiens.

Bonaparte's continental policy gave the English the pretext they needed. Despite [the Dutch leader] Schimmelpenninck's repeated demands, Bonaparte refused to evacuate Holland, alleging that the conditions of the treaty had not been fulfilled. Although he abandoned the Neapolitan ports and the Papal States, he annexed Elba in August 1802, Piedmont in September, and occupied Parma in October, following the death of its duke. In Switzerland, the last of the French troops had no sooner withdrawn when Alois Reding led a rising of the small mountain cantons on the night of August 27, 1802. A rebel diet was gathered at Schwyz. Zurich, Berne, and Fribourg fell under its sway. The legal government, seeking refuge in Lausanne, desperately granted the rebel peasants of Vaud the abolition of feudal dues, and promised to compensate the proprietors out of public lands: but in vain. The government was thus forced to appeal to Bonaparte for help. The First Consul intervened as mediator on September 30, and imposed a general disarmament. [French general] Ney marched into Switzerland, and the diet, obtaining nothing more substantial than fine words from England and Austria, dispersed. Reding was arrested. A consultative assembly was summoned to Paris on December 10, and a commission of ten of its delegates was appointed to discuss Bonaparte's project for a constitution with four French senators. Bonaparte ordered the commission to draft constitutions for the several cantons, and these were then embodied in the final product, the Act of Mediation of February 19, 1803. Each of the nineteen cantons received its own constitution providing for a limited, property-based suffrage in most cases, particularly in the old aristocratic cantons where it ensured that the rule of the pre-revolutionary urban patriciate would continue. The cantons recovered a large measure of autonomy, the freedom to dispose of public lands, and the right to regulate feudal dues and religious affairs. Reaction was thus enabled to triumph nearly everywhere, religious liberty being guaranteed only in the districts where it had previously existed. All that remained of unity was the equal rights of the cantons, which were forbidden to form alliances, the liberty of the Swiss to dwell and own property throughout the confederation, and the abolition of internal tariff barriers. The feeble central government was composed of a diet, where each canton had one or two votes depending on its importance, and a chief magistracy, the office of Landammann, which revolved among the leaders of the six main or "directorial" cantons, viz. Berne, Basle, Lucerne, Zurich, Fribourg, and Solothurn. Bonaparte appointed the first [Swiss] Landammann, Louis d'Affry, a former officer of the French Swiss Guards, who represented Fribourg. On September 27, 1803, the Helvetic Confederation signed a defensive treaty of alliance with France for fifty years and renewed the stipulations for the recruitment of four regiments of 4,000 men each. But the confederation was left without a standing army, and Bonaparte did not even permit the formation of a general staff.

Meanwhile, in Germany, French influence was making giant strides towards a settlement of the indemnities promised by the Treaty of Lunéville [with Austria, February 9, 1801] to the dispossessed princes of the left bank of the Rhine. The Reichstag had refused to let the question be settled by the Holy Roman Emperor, and had empowered a committee to discuss the indemnity with France. In vain did the Austrian Foreign Minister, Cobenzl, attempt to influence France with an offer of an alliance. Bonaparte and Alexander of Russia had already agreed to regulate the affair together. Actually, all the German princes, headed by the King of Prussia, negotiated at Paris and bribed Talleyrand with a combined sum of 10 to 15 million francs in their separate efforts to obtain choice lands. George III himself accepted the Bishopric of Osnabrück. Dalberg, Elector of Mainz, eagerly took part in the sport. Saxony, having no rightful claim, alone hung back. On June 3, 1802, France and Russia invited the Imperial Diet to ratify the plan worked out at Paris. Austria expressed her disapproval and took hold of Passau, which had been destined by the settlement for Bavaria; but she had to pull out in the face of unanimous protests. It was Bonaparte who rescued Austrian prestige in the end by reserving a place for her in the concluding agreement on December 26. On February 25, 1803, the Reichstag ratified the Imperial Recess.

The new imperial constitution abolished the ecclesiastical principalities and reduced the number of free cities from fifty-one to six, thus completing the process of secularization which had taken place in 1555 and 1648. Prussia acquired the Bishoprics of Paderborn, Hildesheim, Erfurt, and a substantial part of Münster; Bavaria received the Bishopric of Freising, and part of Passau; Baden obtained the towns of Mannheim and Heidelberg, and the right-bank territories of the Bishoprics of Speier, Strassburg, and Basle; other states participated in shares proportionate to their size. Austria, which was least favoured of all, ceded the Breisgau and Ortenau to the Duke of Modena, but gained the Bishoprics of Brixen and Trent and part of the Bishopric of Passau; through Austria's influence, the Grand Duke of Tuscany received the archbishoprics of Salzburg and Eichstädt. Austria confiscated the lands and funds of princes dispossessed in her territories.

For the Catholic Church, the Recess was a catastrophe comparable to that of the sixteenth century: the Church lost nearly 2½ million subjects and 21 million florins in annual revenue; eighteen universities and all monasteries were secularized; and of the clerical electors, only Dalberg of Mainz survived the redistribution, his seat having been transferred to Ratisbon. Austria, apart from her loss of prestige, was forced to contemplate the imminent doom of the Holy Roman Empire because the princes of Würtemberg, Baden, and Hesse-Cassel became electors, thus making the Protestant states the new majority in the electoral college as well as in the diet. The *Ritterschaft* [Imperial Knights] and the knightly orders were also destined shortly to disappear despite Austria's attempts to save them. France could only profit from this reshuffling of German territories, since all of the South German states had turned towards her to oppose the Hapsburgs. Prussia gained much but failed to fulfil all of her aspirations, having to turn down Hanover and a proffered French alliance in order to avoid falling out with England. With the advent of peace, Prussia had lost her domination over northern Germany. Frederick William III met the Russian tzar in Memel on June 10, 1802, this marking the beginning of Alexander's amorous friendship with Queen Louise [of Prussia], which bound him ever after to the Hohenzollerns. But the Prussian king sensed that he was the protégé, rather than the ally, of Russia, and so felt slighted.

England was an impotent witness to these upheavals, which, while they did not violate the Treaty of Amiens, were in her eyes clearly contrary to its spirit. Since Russia and Austria were concerned with the fate of Switzerland, and since Austria was disconsolate over the loss of Germany and Italy, the English were comforted and irritated at the same time: as [Prime Minister] Addington had foreseen, England would find allies. Until October 1802, relations with France remained satisfactory. Addington, who had complaints of his own about the *Moniteur*, even took cognizance of Bonaparte's protests [about the English press] and began civil action against the émigré [anti-Napoleonic] journalist Peltier. As late as September 10 instructions received by Whitworth, the English ambassador in Paris, were still wholly peaceful. But the annexation of Italian territory, and above all the intervention in Switzerland (which made quite as much of a stir as it had in 1798) caused an about face. [The British Foreign Secretary] Hawkesbury expressed his "profound regret." "Although we wish for peace . . ., we must depend on the co-operation of the

French government." "England desires for the continent the status-quo as of the time of the Treaty of Amiens, and nothing but that."[3] In his mind, the idea was being formed that every French gain would necessitate a *quid pro quo*.

The best interests of France were, at the very least, to play for time. She had only forty-three ships of the line, and while she planned to build twenty-three more, they would not be ready until 1804. Bonaparte anticipated war in his instructions to [General] Decaen, but not before the fall of 1804. Nevertheless, he impolitically replied that England "should have the Treaty of Amiens, and nothing but the Treaty of Amiens." Talleyrand's threat that "the first cannon shot could suddenly bring into being a Gallic Empire" and persuade Bonaparte to "re-establish the Empire of the West" only added fuel to the fire. Even so, Hawkesbury did not press matters and allowed the French and British ambassadors, Andréossy and Whitworth, to rejoin their posts. This apparent weakness only served to excite the First Consul more. On January 30, 1803, at the very moment that England was completing its evacuation of Egypt, he published in the *Moniteur* a report by General Sébastiani containing the notable remark that "six thousand men would suffice to reconquer Egypt." This kind of provocation is hard to explain. Although he would tell [his brother] Lucien that he was thus counting on goading "John Bull to fight," he was well aware that France was not ready. In October Talleyrand had also stated that if England was leading the world to believe that "the First Consul had refrained from doing any particular thing because he had been prevented, he would do it forthwith." Such statements were as subversive of the national interest as they were irrational.

Actually, Hawkesbury's peaceful posture was purely temporary. "It would be impossible, under present circumstances, even supposing it were wise policy," he wrote to Whitworth on November 25, 1802, "to engage England in a war over one or another of France's recent aggressions. Our policy must seek to use these aggressions to build a defensive system of alliance for the future, together with Russia and Austria."[4] As early as October 27 he had tendered Russia a definite

---

[3] The translator has failed, despite extensive efforts, to locate the source of these quotes, and so has been unable to render them in their original English wording. TRANSLATOR.
[4] See the previous note. The diplomatic correspondence between Hawkesbury and Whitworth can be found in Oscar Browning: *England and Napoleon in 1803. Despatches of Lord Whitworth*, London, 1887. However, this collection neither contains any passages even remotely resembling the above quote, nor is a dispatch by Hawkesbury dated November 25, 1802, to be found anywhere in the book. Hawkesbury wrote to Whitworth on November 14 and on January 14, but these dispatches make no reference to a defensive system of alliance with Russia and Austria. TRANSLATOR.

proposal of alliance for the preservation of the status quo in Europe. Alexander was then preoccupied in arranging German affairs together with France, and so at first turned a deaf ear. But Bonaparte's Eastern policy at last moved him too: as with the earlier French expedition to Egypt in 1798, it brought Russia and England closer together. Alexander reasoned that if he could not have Malta, it would be better for the English to have it than the French. On February 8, 1803, Hawkesbury therefore learned that the tzar wished the evacuation of Malta delayed. The news, coming as it did following the publication of Sébastiani's report in the *Moniteur*, could not have been better timed. On the 9th, Hawkesbury instructed Whitworth that before evacuating Malta England would demand "a satisfactory explanation" of the conduct of the French government.

There ensued a series of stormy interviews between Bonaparte and the British ambassador, and on February 20, in a message delivered to the Legislative Body, Bonaparte denounced the schemes of the war party in London. On March 8, George III replied in a speech from the throne by drawing attention to French armaments; Parliament responded by calling up the militia. For the moment, England was committed to staying in Malta since the conditions stipulated in the Treaty of Amiens had not been fulfilled: Alexander was clouding his guarantee with reservations that presupposed a rewriting of the terms of the treaty, and Prussia followed suit. But Addington, having decided now to keep the island, took this opportunity to give events a sharp turn. On March 15, he demanded occupation of Malta for ten years, as compensation for French territorial gains. Talleyrand replied by offering to negotiate within the framework of the Treaty of Amiens. Meanwhile, Hawkesbury learned on April 14 that Russia, while declining a new alliance, had promised its support if Turkey were attacked, and that Alexander had repeated his advice over Malta. On the 26th, Whitworth presented Bonaparte with an ultimatum.

This sudden resolve on the part of the English upset Bonaparte's entourage. [The Minister of Police] Fouché was to tell him in the Senate, "You, like us, are a product of the Revolution, and war places everything in doubt." In March it was whispered in Whitworth's ear that in consideration for a bribe the First Consul's family could be persuaded to appease Bonaparte, and that Talleyrand would help provided he received his share. Bonaparte too was upset by Russia's fears: on March 11, he wrote the tzar to reassure him and to entreat him to pacify England. He now requested Russian mediation, and proposed to leave Malta in the hands of Great Britain for a year or two, after which time it would be turned over to Russia. Addington replied that this was unacceptable, and Whitworth left Paris on May

12. The British government reserved the option of treating the diplomatic break as a declaration of war, contrary to continental custom. British men-of-war began to capture French commercial vessels at sea without prior warning, an act which was regarded as one of unqualified piracy on the part of "perfidious Albion."

Alexander had in fact accepted the offer of mediation; aside from being flattered, he was well pleased with the prospect of occupying Malta, thus keeping both England and France out of the East. To [the Russian Ambassador Semen] Vorontsov, who demanded explanations, Addington answered that he had not had time to consult the king. This unyielding attitude, so contrary to previous policy, could only be explained by the intervention of the war party, and perhaps Pitt. It did not create a good impression at home, and the Whigs outdid themselves in denouncing it. It took some time for England to become equal to the occasion, but Bonaparte was so dangerous that national unity was welded much more quickly than it had been at the time of the Revolution.

The responsibility for the rupture has been a subject of much passionate argument. If Bonaparte's provocations are undeniable, it is nonetheless a fact that England broke the treaty and took the initiative to wage preventive war from the moment that she could hope for Russia's collaboration. Britain's justification was the preservation of the European balance of power, but this grave concern did not extend to the sea, since in her eyes God had created the oceans for the English. The conflict between Bonaparte and England was in reality a clash between two imperialisms.

André Fugier (1896–1976) was born at Langres in eastern France. He had planned to become a professional soldier, like his father. Badly wounded during the First World War, he trained instead for an academic career. From 1923 to 1932 he taught history in various secondary schools. After completing his doctoral thesis, Napoléon et l'Espagne, 1799–1808 *(1930), he became a professor at the University of Poitiers from 1932 to 1937 and then at the University of Lyon until his retirement many years later. He was a prolific writer, most notably on the diplomatic history of the age of Napoleon.*

THE BRITISH LARGELY RESPONSIBLE

André Fugier

Napoleon and the British leaders were ill suited to understand each other. Their different political principles and domestic policies led to their conflict just as much as their foreign policies. In the eyes of English liberals, and even tories, the First Consul was a dictator controlling a pack of slaves by the whip. The army served as the instrument of this tyranny. Such a *stratocracy* [a government by the military]—a term that appealed to minds brought up on Hellenism, a term they loved to repeat—violently offended a point of view traditionally suspicious of military oppression. The Irish deputy Grattan referred to the revolutionary demi-brigades and the Napoleonic regiments in the House of Commons in May 1815. His vivid words are typical of their time: "Do you wish to confirm this military tyranny in the heart of Europe?—a tyranny founded on the triumph of the army over the principles of civil government. . . . It was not an army, it was a military government in march, like the Roman legions in Rome's worst time, Italica or Rapax, responsible to nothing—nor God, nor man."[1]

To the Anglican Church, completely tory in its higher ranks, Bonaparte was the man who had restored shameful papism to France. To the Methodists, in their pastors' open-air preaching and in the pamphlets of Hannah More, the First Consul symbolized the spirit of

---

From André Fugier, *La Révolution française et l'Empire napoléonien* (Paris: Hachette, 1954), pp. 177–184. Printed by permission of the publisher. This book is volume 4 of the series, *Histoire des relations internationales*, edited by Pierre Renouvin. Editors' translation. The original English quotations have been restored wherever possible.

[1][Thomas C. Hansard, *The Parliamentary Debates* . . . (London, 1804 ff.), XXXI, cols. 429, 422, session of May 25, 1815.—Eds.]

irreligion and license; he spread rebellion by inciting Christians to leave the station in which God had placed them. This latter outlook was not so different from that of the conservative upper classes. It has been claimed that they sought war in order to impose repressive measures on the rabble, measures which reassured them. In fact, the upper classes were frightened by the great number of seditious posters, the persistence of secret societies, and the conspiracy [for Irish independence] hatched by the Irish colonel Despard, who in 1802 recruited three hundred supporters in a single battalion of the Royal Guard. Malmesbury [the former English diplomat] asserted, "It [Jacobinism] is upon us in full force." But the fear that these circles stimulated regarding the Jacobin contamination was not simply temporary. If they detested Napoleon always and everywhere, it was because he was to them the son of the Revolution—even the Revolution itself—"a Jacobin chief who has attained his end, and exercises the unbounded power he has acquired *like a successful Jacobin*." So wrote Malmesbury.[2] In England, just as in the absolute monarchies, Bonaparte was opposed from beginning to end because he was considered the crowned Jacobin, the leader of that doctrine of social revolution which the *Morning Post* in its issue of February 1, 1803 defined as "a violent usurpation of power and property, from the great and rich, by the bloody desperado."

The press, both the newspapers and the magazines, spread these accusations on a grand scale. The press's power increased during the years of peace. In 1802 two magazines were founded that would exert an important political influence: Cobbett's *Weekly Political Register*, intended for the middle classes, and the *Edinburgh Review*, which adopted a whiggish line. In 1803, the use of steam-powered presses would permit larger press runs of such daily newspapers as *The Times*, *Morning Chronicle*, and *Morning Post*. The legal status that custom gave the press was, if not independence, at least some toleration. Its attacks on the First Consul reached a violence comparable to that shown by the most inflammatory French journals during the Revolution. "That half African, half European nondescript, that Mediterranean Mulatto," were lines that the *Morning Post* printed in its issue of February 1, 1803 and they were not the most intemperate of those appearing.

Bonaparte was very sensitive to this kind of behavior and remained so. The English journalists' persistence in tearing him apart was one of the most important causes of the renewal of violent and lengthy hostilities. Whitworth, the British Ambassador to France, despite his

---

[2][Quoted in Harold C. Deutsch, *The Genesis of Napoleonic Imperialism* (Cambridge, Massachusetts, 1938), p. 143.—Eds.]

antagonism to the First Consul, warned the British cabinet that such behavior would lead straight to a rupture. Bonaparte sought to stop this flood of insults. He sent [the French journalist] Fiévée to London on a mission to buy the silence of certain people. The mission failed. The French foreign ministry delivered to [the British Foreign Secretary] Hawkesbury one protest after another. All in vain. The British cabinet invoked freedom of the press. It is quite true that [Prime Minister] Addington did take action against a pamphleteer and toned down somewhat the *True Briton*, the newspaper of his own party, by threatening it with a loss of subsidies. This Bonaparte could understand. Still, the principles of the English political system were foreign to his way of thinking. In all the rather heated discussions in the House of Commons and in all the electoral campaigns, he believed he saw, according to one of his favorite expressions, "England ripped apart by parties." When in the summer of 1802 Addington called for new elections, which resulted in his personal triumph, the *Moniteur* [the French official newspaper] especially emphasized that Middlesex, to the strains of [the French Revolutionary songs] "Ça Ira" and "La Marseillaise," had elected the extremist Francis Burdett and that the "delirious crowds" had acclaimed him even under the windows of the royal palace. The differences in political and social structures, which grew even more pronounced after 1789 and 1793, left each country dangerously incomprehensible to the other.

Events on the continent led to further grievances. It was not lightheartedly that the English at Amiens had signed a peace treaty that ignored the situation of the French vassal states. Cornwallis [the chief British negotiator] could only reply to the Austrian Ambassador, who explained to him the dangers of Jacobin domination of Italy, "I know it very well, but what is there to be done about it? We are totally unable to do anything on the continent."[3] The difficulty was that Bonaparte regarded this muteness as a sign that the London government had implicitly recognized the situation and that, anyway, it was natural and right that the French Republic exercise such an influence on neighbors created and protected by its arms.

Now, however, England spoke out. It even raised its voice very loudly about disturbances in Switzerland in the autumn of 1802 and the threat which was developing there because of repressive French action. With more determination than has been previously thought, Hawkesbury immediately took measures to protect a free people's right of self-determination and at the same time to safeguard a country so well placed, with its contacts in the German world, for

[3][Quoted in Deutsch, p. 80.—Eds.]

quiet financial operations and for discreet diplomatic contacts. But the threat of war only excited Bonaparte. [The British Under-Secretary of State] Moore, sent on mission to Switzerland, arrived too late; Austria, guessing what was coming, refused to commit itself; and the French troops of [General] Ney, entering Switzerland, brutally solved the problem (October 1802).

Addington anticipated the repercussions. At least such behavior provoked in Europe some salutary reactions. In his eyes, the most important were those taken by the Tsar; and Addington was not wrong as to their meaning or effect. Very quickly, this cabinet, accused of being weak and indecisive, returned to the standard English tactic when faced with a power exercising continental hegemony; and very properly it relied on Russia to restore the balance. We shall see why the Tsar responded to these advances and why he distanced himself from that France with whom he had collaborated on Mediterranean questions and had cooperated in the reorganization of Germany. But his passing into the British camp essentially explains British intransigence and consequently the rupture of the Peace of Amiens.

Hawkesbury's first overtures to Russia date from March 30, 1802; vague and premature, they were not taken seriously. In September, Downing Street [the home and office of the British Prime Minister] directed its embassy to guide the Russians toward a rapprochement with London and Vienna. At the beginning of October, news came of an important change in the leadership of Muscovite diplomacy, which had just been confided to Count Alexander Vorontsov. It was known how much the new chancellor distrusted Napoleon and wanted to remove France from the affairs of the East; besides, he was the brother of the Russian Ambassador in London, Semen Vorontsov, an unmistakable Anglophile. Hawkesbury immediately pursued his plans. He took the Tsar into his confidence on the steps in progress to preserve the independence of Switzerland. Then, on October 27, 1802, he had Warren, the British Ambassador at Saint Petersburg, present the Tsar with a definite offer of an alliance: respective territorial guarantees, mutual help against all aggression, and "an agreement on the most effective means of preventing other innovations in the European system."[4]

At first Alexander Vorontsov did not respond, for the reconstruction of Germany, done in common with France, had not yet brought all its benefits. Finally, looking for something better, Hawkesbury guessed what key would turn the lock: a meeting of minds on the East had to be created. On February 1, 1803 he instructed Warren to propose an

---

[4][We have been unable to locate the original English source for this quotation.—Eds.]

alliance again, but limiting it this time to common action for the protection of the Turkish empire. This was a shrewd move or one based on good information, because at that very moment the Tsar was seriously concerned about the plans that Bonaparte had submitted to him for a joint venture to partition Turkey. Since February 8, Hawkesbury had proof that Russian and British interests were now in tandem: the Tsar advised him not to evacuate Malta. On April 14, 1803, the British received a response from the second offer of an alliance; Alexander would act in concert with Great Britain if Turkey were threatened and again he urged Hawkesbury to retain Malta. The Tsar was definitely won over to the English camp. This modification of the balance of power changed everything.

Until the end of 1802, the rhythm of Franco-English negotiations had been rather slow. The two powers exchanged protests concerning problems having to do with the press, trade, and overseas matters; Hawkesbury had delivered (14 November) some rather uncompromising instructions to Whitworth, the newly appointed British Ambassador to Paris; the King's speech before the new Parliament (November 23) had advised vigilance; the debates following it led to some rather aggressive anti-French speeches by Sheridan, Wyndham, and Thomas Grenville. But really the atmosphere was not yet poisoned, and on November 20 Addington made a truly conciliatory gesture: in accordance with the agreements reached, he gave the order to hand over the Cape of Good Hope to Dutch troops.

On January 30, 1803 a bombshell exploded. The *Moniteur* published the report that Colonel Sébastiani had prepared on his return from his diplomatic mission to the East; and in a blustering and insolent tone, this young [French] officer appeared to set down plans for the reconquest of Egypt from the English troops still occupying it. Bonaparte was therefore again dreaming of Cairo and bragging about it! In reality, he had removed more than one fiery part of the report before publishing it. But he could not control the rage aroused in him by an article in *The Times* that took up again and exaggerated the most unpleasant pages of a libel that had recently appeared about the Egyptian expedition. Though perhaps excusable from his point of view, this angry gesture by the First Consul none-the-less produced a disastrous result. "The town [London] is ringing with M. Sébastiani's report on Egypt," noted Lord Minto. Saint-Petersburg was not less agitated, and Constantinople was scandalized: "What! Sébastiani whom we treated so well."[5]

At this moment, Addington began to gather the fruits of his pro-

[5][Quoted in Deutsch, pp. 120–121.—Eds.]

posals to the Tsar. On February 8, 1803, as we have seen, he received news that Alexander wished to see the Red Coats remain at Malta. Thus armed, he shot off on the 9th his reply to the Sébastiani report: England would evacuate Malta only if it were compensated or Europe restored to the conditions in effect when the Peace of Amiens was signed.

Therefore, the rock of the Mediterranean was at the center of the conflict. And yet, London, which now made such strong claims to keep it, had shown only a tepid interest in it at the time the peace treaty had been negotiated. The motive for this sudden change of mind sprang from what had happened in the affairs of Holland and the Cape of Good Hope. When in 1801–1802, England had restored the Cape to the Dutch, it could believe that with peace the Netherlands would escape French influence, the Cape would not become a protectorate of Bonaparte, and the passage to India would remain free. But now the presence of French troops on the territory of the Batavian [Dutch] Republic and the long occupation of its ports proved, on the contrary, that the Dutch would remain vassals of the Tuileries [the palace of Napoleon] and that the Cape would really be almost French. Suddenly the value of Malta as a passage to India was magnified by London. Even before discussions arose (the end of November 1802) about the new French plans for Egypt, the English government was determined not to leave the island of the Knights [Malta] except with the firmest guarantees. Its note of February 9, 1803 had just said what these were.

The situation became much more perilous when the warmongers in England grew stronger. The principal British ambassadors had always been intransigent partisans—Paget at Vienna, Elgin at Constantinople, and especially Whitworth at Paris, who, with his arrogance, his and his wife's worldly disdain, and his biased reports, did much to strain relations. In about November 1802, Pitt definitely joined the war party. His friends kept telling him that he alone was capable of straightening out Britain's affairs, which were being so badly conducted. He let them talk, for in fact he believed the ministry's policies were deplorable; but he decided neither to enter the cabinet nor to oppose openly his friend Addington. The latter did not feel his situation any less precarious, since he was attacked on both flanks at the same time—by the "Old Opposition" of Fox and the *Morning Chronicle* and the "New Opposition" of Grenville and Windham, followers of Pitt. Addington's credit had become so slight domestically that he did not possess enough power to show himself conciliatory in international affairs. The following hypothesis may be proposed: peace would have been less at risk if Pitt himself had been facing Bonaparte rather than an Addington counting and recounting his slender majority in the House of Commons.

The French side appeared moderate. Some were naturally so, like Andréossy [the French Ambassador], who at London tenaciously battled to keep the peace; perhaps others had reasons that could not be revealed so openly: in March 1803 the British cabinet had placed at Whitworth's disposal £100,000 to buy accomplices in the entourage of the First Consul. With the aid of the Swiss adventurer Huber, a contact had been established with Malouet, who as a planter from Santo Domingo desired a relaxation of tension, then Regnault de Saint-Jean-d'Angély, finally Joseph Bonaparte, and of course Talleyrand. It could not be said that they were actually bribed, but all these people secretly talked to Whitworth, searching for the ways and means to keep the peace.

Interpreting English conditions on February 9, 1803, Bonaparte noted a hardening of the other side's attitude, which surely he had not expected would develop so rapidly and which his military position prevented him from countering. On the diplomatic level, although poorly informed by Hédouville, his Ambassador at Saint Petersburg, he now felt that his Russian counterpart was fooling him. Militarily, he was not ready. Having sent his fleet to every ocean, he paid the price of this boldness and was caught in the act of dispersing his forces, which very rarely happened to him. In return for this very perilous strategy, he had not even profited by creating the dreamed of big base in the Caribbean, because the expedition to Santo Domingo, decimated by yellow fever, turned into a disaster. Besides, if assembled, the French naval squadrons would have been inadequate. Even building as rapidly as possible, only 56 ships of the line would be ready in September 1804, a third or a fourth of what the British had available at the signing of the Peace of Amiens. Therefore, it was necessary to gain time. The *Exposé de la situation de la République*, published on February 20, 1803, attempted this: addressing England, there was some bragging, but a wish for peace; regarding the Tsar, the assurance that the First Consul sought only good things for the Sublime Porte [the Ottoman Turkish government]. But Russian distrust did not dissipate so quickly. As to Addington, he quaked with fear that in the House of Commons the members of Parliament would believe him fooled by these delaying tactics. Besides, he felt Russian support behind him, and on April 14, he received complete assurance of this. Therefore, he decided to charge. A period of noisy provocations began, which led very quickly to ultimatums.

As early as the first half of March 1803 retreat was difficult for either side. On the 8th, before Parliament, George III denounced the alleged naval buildup in France and Holland and recommended bringing military forces up to strength. As London could have expected, and perhaps desired, Napoleon responded harshly on the 13th by some fiery words to Whitworth in front of the whole diplomatic corps at the Tuileries. The British began impressing sailors in London, and the French began building landing craft at Dunkirk and Cherbourg. But the First Consul regretted the scene he had made; it did not fit in with his tactics of the moment and, influenced by Joseph and Talleyrand, he appeared disposed to concessions, while Downing Street, on the other hand, only stiffened its stance. On April 3, 1803 the English made their position clear: their own domination of the Mediterranean by their continued presence in Malta and a balance of power on the continent by French renunciation of control in Switzerland and the Netherlands. On the 13th, the English conceded that they would stay in Malta only ten years, time enough to fortify Lampedusa [a small island between Malta and Tunisia], but they never compromised further. On the 23rd they added a sting to this by an ultimatum that Whitworth delivered verbally on the 26th (he refused to write down anything).

The French response contained enough concessions so that the English Ambassador remained in Paris even though the deadline had passed: Bonaparte accepted the English presence on Malta for three or four years. The followers of Pitt paid no attention to this—they wanted either total capitulation or a diplomatic rupture. On May 7 the British cabinet criticized Whitworth for his weakness, demanded ten years on Malta, and rejected the idea of handing the island over to Russia. When the French refused, the Ambassador left Paris on May 12. At the last minute, he received from the French foreign ministry a Russian offer of mediation that had just arrived; but he persisted in seeing there nothing of substance that would allow for new negotiations. After his departure, Talleyrand sent a final proposal to London: England ten years at Malta, but for France the same at Otranto and Taranto [both in the kingdom of Naples]. This was rejected, and the war party took over.

On May 18, 1803, cannon fire was exchanged off the Island of Ushant [near Brittany.]

5
THE DOMESTIC OPPOSITION

How much domestic opposition was there to Napoleon's government? When measured in comparison to the unrest during the French Revolution, it does not appear great. But that is not the only way to study it. Jean Vidalenc surveys all signs of discontent with the regime from republicans, royalists, and those who became disillusioned with Napoleon. He finds the amount of disaffection considerable. Eric A. Arnold, Jr. concentrates on one example—resistance to conscription—and he concludes that draft dodging and military desertion remained a serious problem from at least 1804 to 1815.

Do these authors exaggerate the extent and effectiveness of the opposition to Napoleon? Is the word "opposition" too vague, since it lumps together guerrilla wars, plots, and assassination attempts with strikes by workers and individual acts of nonconformity? Would the picture become clearer if we divided signs of opposition by time periods, by regions, by social classes, or by other categories? Or should we try to determine how many of these acts of opposition merely irritated the regime and how many constituted grave threats to its stability and continuity?

> Jean Vidalenc (1912–1986), the son of teachers, was educated in Morocco, Poitiers, Lyon, and finally Paris, where he studied with the eminent historian Georges Lefebvre. In 1952 he completed his doctoral thesis on the Department of the Eure from 1814 to 1848 and then taught at the Universities of Aix, Caen, and Rouen. His many publications cover a wide variety of subjects in French history since the Revolution.

A SURVEY

Jean Vidalenc

Opposition to the Consulate and the Empire originated because of the way Napoleon's power had been established. 18 Brumaire was really only a coup d'état whose leader managed to arrogate to himself most of the coup's benefits, leaving only a few crumbs to his associates, all the while ready to reject these same associates. The French people let the grenadiers act at Saint-Cloud in the year VIII [November 1799, to overthrow the Directory], as they let the marshals act at Fontainebleau in 1814.[1] The comedy of the plebiscites, with people required to sign their names in public on either a "Yes" or "No" register, demonstrated only the resignation or the prudence of the voters; and there were not very many voters anyway.[2]

There can be no question that the opponents were taken by surprise, often duped, by the ambiguous circumstances of this new coup d'état against a Directory which its own officials did not even consider worth defending. In both the royalist and the Jacobin camps, the opposition was disorganized by the severe blows that the defunct regime had dealt them and by those that the First Consul struck, perhaps even more forcefully. Nevertheless, opposition survived more than the government admitted; the police of Fouché and Savary[3] knew very well that a number of crimes registered by the courts as ordinary criminal offenses were really political in nature, especially many robberies by gangs of draft dodgers or deserters. The actions of

---

From Jean Vidalenc, "L'Opposition sous le Consulat et l'Empire," *Annales historiques de la Révolution française*, no. 194 (October–December 1968): pp. 472–488. The entire article is printed by permission of the editor of the *Annales historiques de la Révolution française*. Editors' translation.

[1] [Napoleon's marshals persuaded him to abdicate in April 1814.—Eds.]
[2] [Concerning the plebiscites, see the article by Claude Langlois on pages 57–65 of this book.—Eds.]
[3] [Savary succeeded Fouché as head of the police in 1810.—Eds.]

the rural police, of departmental companies, of mobile columns, and of special courts created in over thirty departments forced the regime's opponents to be prudent. Still, the opposition's activity never ceased, even at the zenith of Napoleonic power and prestige. Opposition meant different things to Berliners, who admired the Imperial Guard parading into their city, to the people of Le Havre, who could not cross the estuary of the Seine River because British warships controlled these waters, and to those of Ariège department [in the foothills of the Pyrenees], who saw the castle of Foix threatened by guerrillas a year or more after it was fortified. Often confused, sometimes ambiguous, the opposition occasionally formed a coalition one day among those who would be enemies the next; but when all is said and done, the opposition was effective despite its disparate, and especially clandestine, character. To describe it, therefore, one must often be reduced to accumulating details, which is quite a contrast to the huge paintings by Jacques-Louis David that praise the official aspects of the period.

In these cases, as happens under any autocratic regime, the opposition is known less by the accounts or memoirs of its leaders than by those of its adversaries; and documents describing the opposition are therefore slanted by their authors' prejudices. First, we must remember that Bonaparte's views on matters of propaganda and repression strongly affected the behavior and the written reports of his subordinates. The care that he applied to these tasks appears only too well in the construction of the Napoleonic legend, of which he himself was the primary beneficiary and the first architect. In fact, Napoleon as First Consul, even more perhaps than as Emperor, devoted serious efforts to promoting the idea that the whole population supported him. This should have been enough to discourage opposition from people indoctrinated by a very heavily censored press. As general-in-chief of the Army of Italy [in 1796–1797], he had already known how to amplify his smallest successes so as to create popularity. It is not irrelevant to recall that the Emperor, who never thought it beneath him to submit articles for publication in *Le Moniteur* [the official government newspaper], could still order Montesquiou in December 1812 to carry a bulletin to Paris announcing a victory on the banks of the Berezina River [in Russia]. Even though Napoleon had chosen the bishops with care, he had their letters scrutinized with the same concern for detail as were the comments made by regulars in the Paris bars. At the very least, he never stopped trying to spread the idea of widespread rallying to his leadership and he often claimed enthusiastic support. All this was far from the reality that instead tends to favor an impression more of mere indifference or even of resignation. Opinion really shifted only later, after the passage of time and the fall of the Empire;

then people remembered what he said he had done for them and not his demands for money and men. But the records dating from the Empire, inspired by its leader, clearly give a false idea of the opposition that he encountered.

Largely owing to the political shifts of young General Bonaparte, this opposition was rather diverse from the very beginning. [At the time of the Terror] he had played the card of the republican soldier, the friend or at least the protégé of the younger Robespierre [Augustin, brother of Maximilien]; and Napoleon neglected to acknowledge the decisive assistance offered by his fellow Corsican Salicetti. At times, he reminded people how he had been appointed general to command the government troops opposed to the royalists in Paris in the Vendémaire affair [October 1795]. On the other hand, he let it be understood that, when he had refused a command in western France [May 1795], it was to avoid taking part in a civil war; and he forgot to say he would have been there under orders.

Given this background, republicans loyal to the Jacobin tradition and ardent royalists could at first see in Bonaparte a man capable of assuring the victory of their ideas. The same ambiguity, or confusion, was present upon his return from Egypt [1799], when he declared to the President of the Directory, [Gohier], "I did not hesitate to leave my army so as to share your dangers." To which the Director replied, "General, they were serious, but we escaped them in glorious fashion." What more elegant way to say that Bonaparte had arrived after the victories of [the French generals] Masséna at Zurich and Brune at Bergen. But, courteously, the Director did not point out that the only order Bonaparte had received about returning to France had asked the general to come back at the head of his troops, which would certainly have been more useful than his presence there alone. In addition, it will be recalled that Bonaparte had not been the first general approached to carry out the coup d'état contemplated by Sieyès' friends; and [General] Moreau had said to Sieyès when he learned of the landing of the head of the Army of Egypt at Saint-Raphaël, "There's your man; he will carry out your coup d'état much better than I." This comment showed clearly the disdain of the French commanders in chief in decisive military sectors for the former head of the Army of Italy [Napoleon]. In their eyes, none of his successes had had the crucial importance, either strategic or even tactical, of the battles of Valmy, Fleurus, Hohenlinden, or even Quiberon. As they saw it, the Treaty of Campo Formio [1797] with Austria was due more to the threat [to Vienna by Moreau's French army] coming through Bavaria than to the advance of [Napoleon's] army. These other French generals believed Napoleon's army to be on its last legs and Napoleon, as the Austrians recognized, impatient to negotiate with Vienna in order to win the glory of a peace treaty and the opportunity to forward his ambitions in Northern Italy.

At the time of the coup d'état of Brumaire, however, Napoleon's eventual rivals for power—those who let it happen or who allowed the favorable opportunity to pass—did not form a coherent group. Ultimately they would form three main clusters of opposition that would persist and grow for fifteen years. Roughly speaking, one can distinguish three main varieties, each with many shadings: the republicans, either Jacobins or ideologues [intellectuals]; the royalists or *chouans* [guerrilla bands]; and lastly, the most fluid, but in the long run the most effective group, the malcontents, the deceived, the worn out (to use the phrase that Edmond Rostand in his play *The Young Eagle* applied to Marshal Marmont, Duke of Ragusa, the most representative of this group).

The republicans, perhaps the most serious faction of the opposition, received very close attention from the Consular and then the Imperial police. Until 1815 the police reports continuously mention the quiet but persistent activity of the "anarchists," to use the label that became fashionable, a label that made it possible to avoid raising pangs of conscience in those who still believed, even after the coronation, in the slogan inscribed on coins, "République française—Napoléon empereur." A good example of this discreet, but determined, opposition was Lafayette [returned from emigration in March 1800]. He refused to accept membership in the newly created Legion of Honor. Another was the manufacturer Ternaux, who, after voting against the Life Consulate and then against the Empire, joined the Legion of Honor to prevent military officers from monopolizing it.

Some other republicans went further; and the First Consul distrusted them so much that he struck against them for causing an event in which they were absolutely innocent—the attempted assassination [of Napoleon] on the rue Saint-Nicaise prepared by the friends of [the royalist] Cadoudal [December 1800]. They had hidden an "infernal machine"—a time bomb. It went off at the wrong time and caused 22 deaths and 56 injuries, but did not harm the First Consul. Despite all the findings of the police, Bonaparte stuck to his first announcement, attributing the attack to Jacobins; perhaps this was because the police had arrested some of them in the months preceding the affair. In any event, several Jacobins were executed in January 1801, three months after their arrests and three weeks after the attack. Also, such completely arbitrary decisions allowed him to send Jacobins allegedly responsible for the attack to the Seychelles Islands in the Indian Ocean or to Guiana off the coast of South America. This operation at least benefited Napoleon's regime by depriving a strong opposition of some 130 leaders; and when the royalists were found responsible for the affair, the government did not consider releasing the 130. In contrast, the royalists never sustained such a strong blow to their organizations. Half the republican exiles would die overseas, and the silence about their fate surely had a very frightening effect.

Even so, the republican opposition found reinforcement in the growing doubts of some people who had accepted 18 Brumaire and had even accepted the early political rearrangements, but who now found themselves facing a course of events with which they disagreed. This was the case of liberals who had first sat in the Tribunate [one of the houses of the legislature], but whose criticisms the First Consul regarded as intolerable. As soon as he was elected for life, he purged this assembly of one fifth of its members, including Benjamin Constant, Pierre Daunou, and Jean-Baptiste Say; finally, he abolished it several years later, after he had become Emperor. Napoleon harbored a strong grudge against these ideologues, perhaps because he recognized that they easily saw through his game or simply because he had used them in the early days, when he mentioned his membership in the Institute[4] in his proclamations to the Egyptian population [in 1798–1799]. These Egyptians obviously understood nothing in the proclamations anyway, whether the text was printed in French, in modern Greek, or in Arabic, since so many were illiterate. In any case, he was not merely satisfied to ridicule the ideologues whenever possible, but took great care to have any intellectual who expressed criticism carefully watched. Those with considerable notoriety were placed under house arrest by the police or civil authorities. For example, Madame de Staël was lodged for a time [in Châlons] at the residence of the Prefect of the Marne, de Jessaint; the residence was the former mansion of the intendents of Champagne and had become the prefecture. This allowed the prefect to provide her with facilities unavailable in the town's inns and at the same time check on the identity of her visitors. For less important people, like the academician Lalande, it was sufficient to forbid him to publish a new edition of Sylvain Maréchal's *Dictionary of Atheists* in 1805.[5] And a young medical intern at the Saint-Louis hospital, who had shouted "Vive la République," was imprisoned in an insane asylum, where he actually ended up becoming what he had been accused of. It is also very revealing to note the Imperial regime's progressive restrictions on

---

[4][A learned society sponsored by the government and containing some of the leading men of letters, scholars, and scientists of the time.—Eds.]

[5][The story about Lalande is more complicated. After Lalande published a supplement to Sylvain Maréchal's *Dictionary of Atheists* in 1801, Napoleon warned him, in front of his fellow academicians, never again to publish in favor of atheism.—Eds.]

freedom of thought: it forbade teaching atheism as well as joining the "petite église," which grouped the Roman Catholics opposed to the Concordat; and it did not interfere with clerical constraints on free thought. This ultimately worked against Napoleon.

The same concern with defending the political and social structures of the new regime characterized the action directed against workers' organizations and especially against strikes. The steps taken in 1806 against workers in the building trades who went on strike in Paris (30 were arrested in their beds one morning in October); and those steps taken the following year against stone cutters, or in 1808 against carpenters, differed only from those that followed by the numbers arrested or the length of arbitrary confinement.

Of course, similar actions took place in the provinces. A clothing merchant of Verviers [in Belgium] was detained for three months by an administrative order although, or because, the charges against him were so weak that the courts would have hesitated to convict him. We should add that certain measures penalized the militant republicans less than those whose loyalty was not clearly enough demonstrated in the eyes of government officials. This was the case of Michelet, a small scale printer, who lost the contract to print the *Bulletin of the Armies of the Republic*[6] and apparently could not gain the right to publish a newspaper on politics. He ended in financial ruin when some novels he published were destroyed because passages in them displeased the Duke of Richelieu, whom the Emperor regarded highly although the duke had lived in Russia as an émigré for many years.

To be sure, the authorities managed to limit displays of discontent, especially those by "old fashioned republicans," as they were sometimes called near the end of the reign. Still, a week did not pass without police reports noting some incident which more or less resembled the old period of party politics that the First Consul had tried to dissolve into a national unity and that as Emperor he had tried to blend into the docile unanimity of his subjects. The cases mentioned in these reports extend from simple grumbling to conspiracy. The town of Vigan in the Hérault department [actually in the Gard] agreed to proclaim the decree establishing the Empire only after waiting two hours and only on the demand of the sub-prefect. The peasants of Saint-Germain Lembron, in the Puy-de-Dôme, refused to listen to a Te Deum honoring the government and left the church shouting "Down with Bonaparte, we don't want to pay either the tithe or the *cens* [tax]." This occurred in 1805. In the Var department, the

---

[6][This printer was the father of the historian Jules Michelet, and the actual title was the *Courier of the Armies*.—Eds.]

authorities could do nothing more than report the regrouping of all republican malcontents around the former Director Barras, and the police were unable to infiltrate the group despite all their repeated efforts.

The entire Imperial period was punctuated by gestures, sometimes quite spectacular ones. There was the soldier shot at the Boulogne camp for passing out pamphlets urging the assassination of the recently crowned Emperor; notice of this sentence was posted in public places as far away as Paris to warn "malcontents and fanatics." During 1807, in Paris, the authorities arrested and imprisoned a number of former members of a revolutionary law court suspected of meeting anew with other members of similar opinion. However, officials and the police found themselves somewhat trapped in their surveillance of royalists by the euphoric reports they had submitted earlier insisting on the massive and unqualified support of the entire population in their districts. They were torn between the fear of appearing to lack vigilance and of seeming to contradict themselves by revealing that malcontents still existed. So, many ended by reporting nothing or settled for half-measures. For example, the Marseille police commissioner arrested some suspects from 1805 to 1811, but he did not hold these persons long, and they did not fail to maintain ties among themselves, as well as with Barras and with the English fleet.

Perhaps the most serious signs of discontent were some displays of republicanism several years after Napoleon's coronation and extending until the Restoration, displays which demonstrated the persistence during the entire Imperial period of an ideology that Napoleon thought he had seized for his own benefit. Possibly the most vivid case was that of a man condemned to death by a special criminal court in the Aude department who shouted "Long live the Republic" at the moment of his execution. Five years later a conspirator in the Deux-Sèvres repeated this cry in the same circumstances. Most revealing perhaps is a report from de Girardin, Prefect of the Seine-Inférieure department, who pointed out in November 1813 that "former Jacobins speak very quietly, but sing very loudly some songs that suggest they are considering a revival; I have seen children from 12 to 15 dancing to the tune of the 'Carmagnole' [a revolutionary song], and young men sing the 'Marseillaise'." Although these songs had been prohibited for a long time, even before the birth of some of the singers, there must have been a remarkable persistence of oral propaganda, cautious, yet effective and extensive, in order to give rise to such demonstrations. It was surprising that the prefects and the rural police either saw none of this during the long period of Imperial victories or had decided to report nothing. To be sure, discretion was the rule in many situations, as when businessmen in Rouen quickly received the quotations on the

London Stock Exchange or learned of the misadventures of the French army in Russia well ahead of local authorities.

It was certainly not only the left-wing opposition or businessmen who had relations with Great Britain. Royalists were always very active in many respects. There were first of all the irreconcilables, all those who saw Bonaparte as just another republican general before he became a usurper. Probably the most intransigent representative of this point of view was Georges Cadoudal, who wove many plots; but he had many disciples. The government of the Consulate had to use a large army to stamp out the royalist insurgency in western France. One affair involved the government general Hédouville. At the end of a negotiating conference, which he dragged out past the expiration time of the safe-conduct pass for his opposite number, de Frotté (the commander of the Catholic and Royal Army and, like Hédouville, a count of the Old Regime), Hédouville arrested de Frotté. Perhaps this incident reveals less than the First Consul's order to execute immediately the prisoners being escorted from Alençon to Paris. They were shot at Verneuil, about half-way there. This brutality continued in the actions taken to maintain order in the western departments. There was more leniency in imposing only gradually and moderately certain basic obligations of Napoleonic policy, especially the military draft. On the other hand, to watch over these suspect regions, the government stationed a significant number of soldiers as a garrison on the west coast and even in the interior from Poitiers to Pontivy. All along the coast special military units were supposed to stop any hostile landing and any communication with English warships; night fishing was forbidden from boats or the shore; and every night the ropes that allowed one to climb the coastal cliffs of the Caux region [on the Channel, east of Le Havre] were pulled up.

None of this, however, stopped British propaganda from reaching France or royalist agents from entering the country, even by climbing the legendary sea cliff of Biville [in Normandy]. Furthermore, French experts offered their support to the enemy; some 50 pilots from all the coastal regions served on English vessels and permitted them to sail with ease very close to the French shore, on the Channel, in the Bay of Biscay, and in the Mediterranean. It was fruitless for the French authorities to send out false navigation signals or to exile the families of these pilots to inland regions, for example, from Charente-Inférieure to Dordogne. The English squadrons continued to maneuver easily along the coasts and to send landing parties ashore when they wished; English troops were sent to wreck a coastal artillery battery or, more prosaically, to exchange information or to look for vegetables and even livestock among the farmers in the neighborhood.

Operations against the Emperor, often inspired by royalism, occurred not only in the coastal departments from Zéland [in the Netherlands] all the way to the Var [on the Mediterranean coast]; for example, a symptomatic case was that of some 20 Belgian deserters who reached the Maine-et-Loire department [along the lower Loire River] before being detected; this implied networks in the interior of the country just as well organized as those that allowed the movement of priests of the "petite église" in the Paris region. The case of the Belgians took place during the summer of 1809, after four years of the Empire and its victories. Many other police reports point out the persistence of chronic and shadowy *chouannerie* [guerrilla opposition] that the public authorities pretended was pure and simple brigandage. This was hardly likely considering that the men who stopped stagecoaches were satisfied to take money belonging to the government but did not touch the property of travelers. Also, the Duke of Enghien affair caused ticklish problems.[7] In addition to the resignation of [the writer] Chateaubriand [from the diplomatic service], the dismissal of Belloc, Prefect of the Cher department, took place in 1805, because in a letter he had expressed his regrets over "the assassination of the Duke of Enghien."

Nevertheless, the vigilance of the Imperial police remained ineffective in the face of many royalist conspiracies, for these plotters often belonged to the old political elites and found ways to hold clandestine meetings in their drawing rooms or to visit each other on apparent social calls in which they really transmitted political news or watchwords. All the efforts of [Minister of Police] Fouché and his successor Savary were fruitless in the face of the organization known as Chevaliers de la Foi [Knights of the Faith]. Its members knew how to hatch plots as well as to infiltrate effectively governmental bodies, most importantly the Paris National Guard. Heir to the old leagues and to the royalist coalitions of the revolutionary period, the Chevaliers de la Foi established itself, rather boldly, in one of the hospitals the Napoleonic regime employed to intern political suspects who came from good families and who were not considered dangerous enough to be jailed in less comfortable state prisons. The Chevaliers de la Foi combined [in a five-level hierarchy] the "associates of charity" at the lowest level, whose members did nothing more than say prayers and visit prisoners, with (2) the squires, with (3) the knights who were expected to take an oath of loyalty to the king, with (4) the knights hospitaliers, and, at the highest level, with (5) the knights of

[7][The Duke, a Bourbon prince, was kidnapped from Baden, a neutral country, brought to Paris and shot after being summarily convicted on flimsy evidence of participating in a plot to assassinate Napoleon and restore the Bourbon line to the French throne.— Eds.]

the faith, who were pledged to fight for the restoration of the legitimate monarchy.

This organization managed to resist both the probings of the Napoleonic police and those of its liberal opponents in the subsequent Restoration regime. Not until the historical studies by the Abbé Bertier de Sauvigny after the Second World War was the existence of the Chevaliers de la Foi discovered. The main difficulty that it encountered really seems to have arisen from its very power. It was split by personal quarrels, as were the Catholic and Royal armies earlier [1793–1800], and this delayed the start of military actions against Napoleon. But the Chevaliers de la Foi were still capable of creating a fighting organization modeled on the military divisions of the government and of creating a system of couriers designed to avoid inspection of their mail by the official postal system. Its members took special advantage of the obliging attitudes of certain royalists who had pretended to rally to Bonaparte in order to enter government service, carry on a discreet propaganda there, and, at the same time, keep an effective eye on their overly enthusiastic Bonapartist or republican colleagues. De Fontanes, the first grand master of the University of France, did his best to appoint devoted royalists in his administration. It is revealing also to note that the Empire appointed Pierre-Paul Royer-Collard to the professorial chair of the history of philosophy at Paris. To be sure, this man had sat in the Council of Five Hundred under the Directory, but he was also a member of the "Secret Royal Council," which had worked zealously for Louis XVIII during the Consulate.

In addition, the National Guard in Paris and the provinces had many noncommissioned officers from good families, who were more inclined to serve the King than the Emperor. As for the young men whose age led prefects to appoint them to serve in honor guards usually designed to escort Napoleon if he made an appearance, they had grown up in an atmosphere such that those of the 3rd regiment, stationed in Tours, had proposed to kill the Emperor the first time they stood guard near him. The prefects who had to handle this affair, de Barante of the Loire-Inférieure department and de Kergariou of the Indre-et-Loire, managed to delay any decision until after Napoleon's first abdication at Fontainebleau.

Other royalists, like the Baron of La Frégeolière in the Maine department, were pleased to resume command of *chouan* bands early in 1813. At the other end of the kingdom, Fruchart, sometimes called "Louis XVII," operated north of the Somme River [in Picardy]. His close relationship with the two hundred Cossacks led by the Russian colonel Geismar from February 1814 on demonstrates the strength of this internal royalist opposition. We cannot forget the enthusiasm displayed in Bordeaux, well before the Emperor's abdication at Fontainebleau, when the English forces allowed the mayor, who was a member of the Legislative Body, to proclaim openly the return of the Bourbons. From then on, the Bourbons were assured of a greater consideration by the allied powers.

However, it is always difficult to distinguish authentic royalism from parallel tendencies, which appeared not only in Napoleonic France of course, but also beyond the borders of the pre-revolutionary kingdom and especially in the Italian, Dutch, or North German departments. Nationalism, in its classic, that is, romantic form, was able to merge with the very traditional attitudes of feudal loyalty to the Hapsburgs, the Hohenzollerns, or to some Hanoverian, Hessian, or Saxon ruling family. Moreover, we should not equate French republicans with those who in Hamburg, Genoa, or Venice set themselves up as adversaries of the Emperor and King [of Italy] and who called for the return of the old republics. Still, both of these groups supplied considerable help to Napoleon's domestic opposition in the old departments, an opposition that had to take into account the demands of these auxiliaries when it considered its programs for the future. The displays of interest or even of sympathy expressed toward Spanish prisoners of war throughout the Massif Central also demonstrate the prevalence of feelings less charitable to the prisoners than hostile to the Emperor and favorable to the Bourbons. The royalists, moreover, always pretended that they renounced recent French conquests and often even the older ones of the various French governments since 1789. In addition, Napoleon's unification policies, for example the steps he took to make the Tuscan dialect official throughout the Kingdom of Italy, helped give a new structure to these nationalities that were often unconscious and even unorganized before the French occupation.

Finally, we must take into account the role of the Roman Catholic clergy in the character of the partially internationalist royalist opposition in France and the nationalist opposition among the conquered or vassal countries of the Empire. The Concordat did exist, to be sure, but the pretense of a reconciliation between the Church and the French State was hardly sincere, even when a prelate was a relative of the Emperor, such as [Napoleon's uncle] Cardinal Fesch at Lyon. It was not long before papal bulls arrived to lend additional theological arguments to Napoleon's adversaries. At the same time, the lower clergy, even those not involved with the guerrillas in Spain or in the Kingdom of Naples, encouraged the draft dodgers or deserters, to say nothing of the moral support, at the very least, that the clergy gave to the bands of *chouans* in western France.

However, all these forms of opposition had, because of their very nature somehow, perhaps less importance than the opposition that gradually developed within the very ranks of those who had first been Napoleon Bonaparte's strongest supporters—his advisors or those who simply carried out his desires.

The conditions in which the coup d'état of 18 Brumaire unfolded—the surprise, confusion, and even ambiguity in a country at war—had led many Frenchmen to accept the *fait accompli*, especially because for the moment there was no way to express reservations; and this would have been ineffective anyway. Beethoven's gesture of ripping out the dedication of his heroic symphony, because he refused to see it joined to the name of a republican general who had become a politician, is only one example among many others.[8] Later the same composer dedicated a march to General Yorck, the promoter of Prussia's revival in 1813, and the "Victoria" symphony to Wellington.

The circumstances in which the headmaster, professors, and students of the artillery training school at Châlons-sur-Marne voted unanimously for the Life Consulate in order to protect their careers, although individually a majority opposed it, shows that support, even among those having a very high level of education for the time, often had nothing to do with sincere conviction. Many men who had thus been induced to go along with a formality of which they disapproved clearly did not consider themselves bound by it and more or less openly scoffed at the new regime. When the police noticed this behavior, the critics were the target of various measures, ranging from a warning to imprisonment; this only increased the number of the disgruntled. Criticism aimed at the Emperor's policies was added to reservations about him personally, or about the development of his methods of governing, or even about his personal behavior. As for older men, we should also remember the fact that the police-state aspects of the regime added to their normal prudence and fear of competition from younger men anxious to forward their careers. This led older men to keep their opinions to themselves, but the accumulation of disappointments and wounds to their self-esteem could finally lead to the same doubts and to an open opposition as resolute as that due to political differences.

Of course, we should not accept as active opponents all those who, after the fall of the Emperor, claimed to have been so. Many settled for playing a cautious double game, such as the prefect of the Eure department who listed with equal care the number of conscripts sent

---

[8][Beethoven composed his Third Symphony, the Eroica, in 1802–1804 and dedicated it to Napoleon Bonaparte. When news arrived that Napoleon had made himself Emperor, Beethoven reportedly changed the dedication to celebrate only "the memory of a great man."—Eds.]

to the military depots and the number of draft dodgers and deserters: the first list he sent to the Emperor in February 1814; and the second to the King in April of the same year.[9]

In any case, the nature of clandestine activity does not permit us to conclude that the most inconspicuous and earliest defections were always the most effective. As frequently happens in France, this opposition was based on a variety of motives and was just as divided on what it sought. It mostly agreed on only one point: the removal of Napoleon, who was reproached either for seizing power illegally or exercising it poorly.

The earliest doubts probably arose in the army, even though Bonaparte sought to be the representative and symbol of victorious soldiers in the face of inept and corrupt civilians. Such doubts actually existed before 18 Brumaire: Bernadotte, then Minister of War, had wanted to postpone a meeting with him "until Bonaparte has satisfactorily explained the reasons why he abandoned his army [in Egypt]." This attitude was no different from the remarks and behavior of many generals when they became marshals and saw the Emperor abandon his army once again—this time in Russia. Other complaints grow out of the Concordat, which offended the convictions of many republican soldiers. One colonel said openly, "Fine words, the only thing missing is the million men who gave their lives to abolish what you are reviving"; and we may even point out the attitude of those who, in dress uniform, nonchalantly strolled in the Tuileries gardens while the Emperor's coronation was taking place [in Notre Dame] on the Ile de la Cité. The First Consul was well aware of these reservations, and so he took precautions. Avoiding scandals that would have challenged his public role as commander in chief of the army, which was the basis of his authority over civilians, he sent suspect units of the Army of Italy to Portugal and of the Army of the Rhine to San Domingo, where the 82nd regiment of the line was almost completely wiped out. Suspected generals received assignments to distant posts: Richepanse and Decaen to the colonies, Brune to Constantinople, and Lannes to Lisbon. Only Bernadotte, because of his marriage to Bonaparte's former fiancée [Désirée Clary], was treated gently and ordered only to eastern France. However, men of Bernadotte's entourage were sometimes imprisoned, like Donnadieu, who became a fanatical royalist, or were placed in retirement, like Lahorie, or were detached from active service, like Lecourbe, although Napoleon regretted (but only later, on Saint-Helena) not having made better use of Lecourbe's abilities.

Of course, some suspicious officers were more or less fooled by the

---

[9][Napoleon abdicated on April 6, 1814.—Eds.]

evasive answers of General Bonaparte, who needed their services. Perhaps the best example of this was General Oudet. A man who joined the army at age seventeen, he had not hesitated to seek an audience on the eve of the Battle of Marengo [June 1800] and to explain his reasons in these words, "I want to make sure that you are really the same Bonaparte under whose command we conquered Italy [in 1796–1797] and not an imposter using his name in order to crush the Republic and murder liberty." Promoted to the rank of general on the eve of the Battle of Wagram [July 1809], where his regiment would be wiped out because it was in front of the Austrian artillery, he was killed on the following night, possibly by Napoleon's guards. Two of his subordinates killed themselves on his grave. In fact, Oudet was the best known among the leaders of the mysterious Philadelphs, an association that barely hid its hostility to the Emperor. We notice that "chance" placed the military units that included the most members of this group at the head of the French column, the most dangerous position. Of course, it was no longer possible to send the most suspect troops across the Atlantic. Oddly, Oudet was from Franche-Comté, as were those thoroughgoing liberals who established Freemasonry in the Kingdom of Naples with hidden motives unfavorable to [their kings] Joseph Bonaparte and his successor Joachim Murat.

Malet was also from Franche-Comté. He demonstrated an unquestioned attachment to the Republic, although from a noble family of the Old Regime. Malet had welcomed Napoleon as First Consul, but unconditionally opposed the Concordat and then the Empire. [The writer] Charles Nodier, who knew him personally, described him as formed by nature "to keep tyrants from sleeping soundly." Nodier saw in him a very typical example of those men sickened by General Bonaparte's about-faces. As Nodier put it, "Conformity to revolutionary ways gradually faded among those who had supported Napoleon most fervently and was replaced by an unwavering personal hatred, which, despairing of the old cause, joined any cause that promised triumph and vengeance. The first tyrant to come along would have been accepted by the party of the Revolution against the apostate son of the Revolution who had slain his mother." Although we may question whether republican sentiments really died away, there can be no doubt that men such as Malet did not hesitate to come to a reconciliation with the royalists. A former king's musketeer, he had voted against the Life Consulate and against the Empire when he was the commanding officer in the Charente department. Dispatched to Italy, where he was governor of Rome, he had been relieved of his duties for spreading republican propaganda and jailed when the Philadelphs were tried. In prison he conceived the idea, with the help of a royalist clergyman, to concoct a series of false documents announcing the death of the Emperor; for in October 1812 there had been no news from Bonaparte for several weeks.[10] Malet's attempt at a coup d'état allowed him to emerge from prison and to arrest several officials; at the same time, others put themselves at the service of the provisional government that he established. The coup ended with the execution of Malet and fifteen accomplices, including several army officers and others from the Paris National Guard. When the presiding judge asked him to name his accomplices, he replied, "All of France and even you if I had succeeded."

In fact, the most serious aspect of the Malet affair was the disloyalty to the regime shown by its own officials. They found that its risky adventures endangered their vested interests, from which they had expected to profit after all their earlier efforts. Talleyrand's treason, which had caused the Imperial plans to fail at the Erfurt Conference,[11] was only a prelude to the hesitations of some or the plots of others, to say nothing of those who believed themselves poorly rewarded or misunderstood by the Emperor. Although Admiral Villeneuve, the French commander at Trafalgar, died [a suicide] at the right moment in Brittany after his return through a prisoner of war exchange, General Dupont, defeated [by the Spanish] at Bailen, did not appreciate his disgrace any more than did the Minister of Police, Fouché, who had been replaced by Savary. Napoleon said of his model servant Savary, "I like this fellow very much; he would kill his father if I ordered it." Perhaps Bernadotte's attitude was judged severely by the army;[12] but Murat, even though he was the Emperor's brother-in-law, also hoped to save his throne [Naples], which was threatened by Napoleon's foolhardy continuation of a struggle that was unpopular with all ranks. After Napoleon's abdication, Marshal Lefebvre drew a harsh conclusion about the Imperial saga, "That little bugger wouldn't have been happy until he had every last one of us killed."

Such an attitude was not limited to the high dignitaries of the regime. Of course, there was always a crowd to admire the free entertainment provided by a visit of the Emperor or the Empress. But sometimes it was difficult to find local notables to fill the drawing rooms: in 1811 those of Cherbourg and of Caen were cool toward the

---

[10][Napoleon only began his retreat from Moscow on October 19, a few days before Malet's coup d'état broke out.—Eds.]

[11][At Erfurt in 1808 Napoleon requested the Tsar's support in preventing Prussia or Austria from attacking the French while Napoleon was in Spain quelling the insurrection there. Talleyrand secretly advised Alexander to make no such promises.—Eds.]

[12][After becoming the crown prince and ruler of Sweden in 1810, Bernadotte, a former marshal of France, followed a foreign policy that he judged to be in Sweden's best interests. In 1813 Sweden joined the military coalition against France.—Eds.]

Imperial couple; and when Empress Marie-Louise visited Rouen in 1813, most of them went to their country homes. Above all, from the beginning of the regime, many circles were noticeably indifferent to military victories that did not bring durable peace. The Marquise de la Tour du Pin was surprised at the lack of public reaction in Paris at the procession of July 14, 1800, when soldiers paraded who had been brought back from Italy expressly to present the flags captured at Marengo. The letters of the young François Guizot to his mother in Geneva, upon his arrival in Paris just after Austerlitz [December 1805], contain absolutely nothing about the festivities which followed Imperial victories in those days. From the evidence we have, he was affected by neither the military operations nor by the prestige that the Emperor expected from them. General Noguès, a veteran soldier of the Republic, concluded after Waterloo, "Napoleon destroyed victories in the mind of the public"; and as a technical expert, he cast doubt on the military abilities of the Emperor after 1804. The continuing lack of military success, the failures after 1809, and the shift of the master's favors to the men of the Old Regime (whom Napoleon believed had rallied to him, but who were really only trying to advance their careers or even to betray him) only increased disillusionment. We ought not to forget, besides, the lack of conviction of the marshals and many generals when they left for Russia and even more so during the campaigns of 1813 and 1814. The Emperor's abdication at Fontainebleau ultimately came more from pressure exerted by the general staff on the unhappy leader than from the negotiations with the allied coalition. The allied powers simply contented themselves with confirming the contraction of the French frontiers not to those of the period of the Directory, but to a much earlier period [1791]. The clauses in the Constitution of the year III [1795] that punished those who gave up any territory of the Republic had been among the clauses that had disappeared in the Constitution of the year VIII [December 1799].

It took all the blunders of the restored Bourbons in 1814 to push a certain number of disillusioned republicans and liberals back to the Emperor. Once again they had been deceived by the maneuvers of those they had seen as fellow travellers, in the current sense of the phrase [sympathizers], and recognized that they had been merely used [by the royalists] against the usurper. The new [Bourbon] regime's retention or reestablishment of military conscription and excise taxes, although their abolition had been specifically promised, and the excesses of the White [anti-Jacobin] Terror, which included arbitrary massacres, summary executions, and unjustified imprisonments, aroused a new opposition to the government in power.

Later, with the passage of time and the nostalgia for one's youth, the Imperial government, burnished by propaganda coming from Saint Helena, would enjoy a new prestige. But, fundamentally, the Emperor had summed up the opinion of his contemporaries quite well when replying to a courtier who asked him, in the midst of his victories, what would happen at his death: "They will say '*Ouf*!'"

Eric A. Arnold, Jr. (1939–   ) received his Ph.D. from Columbia University and teaches at the University of Denver. He has published Fouché, Napoleon, and the General Police *(1979) and various articles on the history of revolutionary and Napoleonic France.*

AN EXAMPLE: RESISTANCE TO CONSCRIPTION

Eric A. Arnold, Jr.

Most considerations of the reactions of the French people to the military draft of the First Empire generally give the impression that until 1812 there was no significant opposition to the annual military call-up. But, was there indeed no opposition among Frenchmen during the period before 1812? Did the opposition after 1812 come suddenly into being?

Some of the secondary sources in use today are rather confused on this point. For example, F. M. H. Markham in his two works dealing with the period, *Napoleon and the Awakening of Europe* and his more recent *Napoleon*, leaves one with the impression that problems of draft-dodging, to use an Americanism (the French equivalent being *réfractaire*), or military desertion were non-existent before Napoleon's return from Russia and the subsequent German and French campaigns of 1813 and 1814.[1] In contrast, J. M. Thompson in his biography of Napoleon estimates that from 1799 to 1805 there were as many as 250,000 military defaulters (i.e., either draft-dodgers or men who, having been called up, never reported to their mobilization centers). Thompson continues by saying that after 1805 the French conscription system was tightened to the extent that nearly 100 per cent of those drafted reported to their mobilization

From Eric A. Arnold, Jr., "Some Observations on the French Opposition to Napoleonic Conscription, 1804–1806," *French Historical Studies* 4 (1965–1966): pp. 452–462. The entire article is reprinted by permission of the author and the editors of *French Historical Studies*.

[1] F.M.H. Markham, *Napoleon and the Awakening of Europe* (London: English University Press, 1954), p. 141, and *Napoleon* (London: Weidenfeld and Nicholson, 1964), pp. 129–130. See also Marcel Baldet, *La Vie quotidienne dans les armées de Napoléon* (Paris: Librairie Hachette, 1964), pp. 25–32, chapter entitled "*La Conscription*."

centers and were duly inducted into the ranks of the Napoleonic armies.[2]

The great French historian Georges Lefebvre in his monumental work *Napoléon* takes yet a third position, which is between the extremes suggested by Thompson on one hand and Markham on the other. It is Lefebvre's opinion that the number of military defaulters was about 3.5 per cent of the total of approximately 1,300,000 Frenchmen taken into the Napoleonic armies during the period 1799–1812. Lefebvre admits that there were difficulties arising from the conscription system before 1812, among them civil disobedience, draft-dodging, and desertion. But, in concluding his remarks on this matter, he says: "The nation complied . . . to its military obligations, becoming refractory toward the end, when, with the downfall of Napoleon imminent, the *levée en masse* reappeared."[3]

It seems clear from these contradictions that pre-1812 opposition to the French conscription system is a question open to examination. Among the points that should be considered are: Was there any opposition before 1812? If so, where did it occur? How many men did it involve? Did the French government consider it serious? What steps were taken to correct the situation, and were they successful?

The purpose of this article is to attempt to answer these questions by examining recorded cases of opposition occurring during some period before 1812. The particular interval of time that will be studied is the nineteen-month period from December, 1804 to July, 1806. This selection is an arbitrary one, but perhaps this is its best defense, as it can thus hope to be representative of the pre-1812 period. In addition, this particular period may be said to represent the early bloom of the empire when Napoleon's popularity throughout France was high. The period also includes the great French victories of Ulm and Austerlitz.

The following table lists 119 disturbances arising from conscription, showing the departments of France where they occurred. Each of the 119 cases falls within the stated time interval of nineteen months. The ordering of the departments cited in the list is purely coincidental. These disturbances vary from incidents involving one or two people to community wide troubles.[4] The seven southern depart-

---

[2]J. M. Thompson, *Napoleon Bonaparte* (New York: Oxford University Press, 1952), p. 308.

[3]Georges Lefebvre, *Napoléon* (Paris: Presses Universitaires de France, 1965), pp. 200–201.

[4]Much of the information upon which this article is based was found in the daily bulletins, covering the period 1804–1810, from Joseph Fouché, Napoleon's minister of police until 1810, to Napoleon. These documents have been collected from the National Archives in Paris by Ernest d'Hauterive in five volumes, entitled *La Police secrète du Premier Empire* (Paris: Libraire Académique Perrin et Cie, [I] 1908, [II] 1913).

ments, where proportionally the greatest amount of trouble took place, are marked with asterisks.

Meuse-Inférieure	1	Ariège*	16
Creuse	1	Indre-et-Loire	1
Rhône	1	Haute-Saône	1
Haute-Vienne	1	Gers	1
Lot	3	Beauvais	1
Aude*	2	Seine-Maritime	3
Seine-et-Oise	1	Eure	1
Doubs	2	Marne-et-Loire	2
Orne	4	Saône-et-Loire	3
Aveyron	3	Meuse	1
Var	3	Oise	2
Vaucluse	1	Morbihan	1
Calvados	3	Loire	2
Ardèche*	4	Manche	2
Gironde*	1	Bouches-du-Rhône	2
Haute-Loire	3	Finistère	2
Lozère	2	Puy-de-Dôme	2
Haute-Garonne*	8	Somme	1
Nord	1	Loire-Inférieure	1
Landes*	4	Yonne	1
Basses-Pyrénées*	3	Haute-Pyrénées	1
Corrèze	2	Tarn	2
Ourthe	1	Deux-Sèvres	2
Seine-et-Marne	1	Lot-et-Garonne	2
Pas-de-Calais	4	Hérault	1
Gard	1	Hautes-Alpes	2
Haut-Rhin	1		

From the table it can be seen that difficulties arising from the conscription system occurred all over France, though the most serious and extensive incidents were in the southern departments, those which are either on or near the Spanish frontier. This geographical distribution will be considered later in greater detail.

There were various types of problems stemming from conscription, ranging from civil disobedience to draft-dodging and desertion (desertion as defined at the beginning of this article). With respect to civil disobedience, the most common cases involved attempts, often successful, on the part of townspeople to rescue deserters and draft-dodgers from the authorities. For example, a report from the prefect of Doubs dated December 6, 1804, mentions several towns (which are not named) in which the people resisted the efforts of the gendarmes while they were attempting to arrest some deserters.[5] It was not uncommon for this type of popular action to take the form of violent and armed resistance, as in the case (May 29, 1805) of the department of Aude when nine masked men were reported to have ambushed several gendarmes who were escorting a column of deserters.[6] These cases are not isolated examples; many others of a similar nature could be cited in some detail.

Another serious and common form of civil disobedience was giving aid and comfort to known deserters and draft-dodgers. For instance, in June of 1805 a woman in the department of Seine-et-Oise was brought to law for having provided shelter for numerous deserters.[7] She was severely punished by the local authorities for this crime.

What is particularly surprising about these cases of civil disorder is that there were frequent instances when mayors participated in spite of the fact that they were selected by the government for their loyalty to the regime. A report from the department of Haute-Loire dated June 1, 1805, tells of a certain M. de Fontaride, mayor of the town of Saint-Just, who told a squad of gendarmes escorting deserters through Saint-Just that they would do better to direct their activities against brigands, leaving deserters alone. The report states that this remark was made in the presence of a large crowd of townspeople, many of whom were armed. The assembled mob then proceeded to attack the gendarmes, injuring several of them, and to liberate the deserters. In his report, the prefect stated the opinion that the mayor's remarks to the gendarmes provoked the incident. Fouché sent orders that M. de Fontaride immediately be relieved of his position.[8] A similar case, reported to Fouché by the prefect of Ariège, involved the destruction of a town's civil registers by its mayor.[9]

Similarly, there are reports that *curés* took an active part in disorders. When it is remembered that all French churchmen were ordered by the Pope in the Concordat of 1801 to obey the civil government in civil matters, this is no less surprising than the insubordination of the "loyal" mayors. A case in point involves Bernard, a priest in Oise, who was sentenced to a year in prison and was fined 300 francs because he hid several deserters in the sacristy of his church.[10] Another case is that of a *curé* from Ariège who, in a sermon preached during July of 1805, urged his parishoners to resist all attempts made by the gendarmes to arrest deserters. The prefect of Ariège in his report to

[5]*Ibid.*, I, No. 626. Similar cases: *ibid.*, II, Nos. 28, 79, 158 and 212.
[6]*Ibid.*, I, No. 1407. Similar cases: *ibid.*, No. 1106, II, Nos. 665 and 772.
[7]*Ibid.*, No. 1432. Similar cases: *ibid.*, II, Nos. 90, 145, and 310.
[8]*Ibid.*, I, No. 1425. Similar cases: *ibid.*, II, Nos. 197, 290, and 618.
[9]*Ibid.*, II, No. 1025 (April 18, 1806).
[10]*Ibid.*, No. 560 (December 2, 1805).

Fouché was of the opinion that the intemperate remarks made by the *curé* led to a serious disturbance. Both the *curé* and the mayor were dismissed and the *curé* was disciplined by the bishop.[11]

Draft-dodging was a serious problem representing a significant drain of available manpower; every part of France seems to have been affected. A report from Calvados (January 7, 1806) tells of draft-dodgers who "resist" conscription measures. The report concludes with the statement that such resistance was the consequence of the efforts of foreign *agents provocateurs*.[12] In the department of Gers, where draft-dodging was also serious, the prefect reported (February 12, 1806) that the need for farm labor was an important factor contributing to the problem."[13]

Many different tactics were used by young men to avoid being drafted. According to the Loi Jourdan (1798), the law setting forth the method of conscription, it was permissible for a man to buy his way out of the draft by paying an indemnity, and so frequently was this device used that the amount to be paid nearly doubled between 1805 and 1810.[14] But this right of "buying out" of the army was obviously limited to the fairly well-to-do; consequently, conscription fell more heavily on the poorer classes, who were forced to use their wits in order to avoid the draft.

One of the stipulations of the Loi Jourdan was that every man whose number was called had to have a certificate of good health from a doctor of his own choice, and there are many cases on record of doctors who falsely certified that poor health was a bar to military service. Further, doctors not infrequently "mutilated" men so as to render them unfit for military service. Instances of falsification show perjured certificates stating that the bearer has a hernia, while a common example of mutilation involved the removal of the subject's upper front teeth (thus making it difficult for the recruit to tear open the paper cartridges of the day).[15]

Aside from false health certificates, there were other ways of evading the draft. Cases of the falsification of passports and wedding certificates, as well as the alteration or forgery of service records are recorded. There is even a report of a veteran of the Guard Cavalry who sold his discharge papers to a young man who could thereby avoid the call-up of 1806.[16] In large cities such as Le Havre, Brest, or Toulon,

---

[11]*Ibid.*, No. 107.
[12]*Ibid.*, No. 668.
[13]*Ibid.*, No. 572.
[14]Lefebvre, *op. cit.*, p. 200, says that the average indemnity paid in 1805 was about 1,900 francs, and that by 1810, the average had become 3,600 francs.
[15]D'Hauterive, I, No. 1462; also d'Hauterive, II, No. 516.
[16]*Ibid.*, II, No. 1149.

where there was some industry, men bought certificates for about 15 francs apiece stating that their work was of a strategically important nature.[17] There was a good deal of official involvement in the issuance of falsified exemption certificates (cf. note 9). Examples of such official conniving are numerous, with reports, for example, from Lot-et-Garonne, Hautes-Pyrénées, Ariège, and Manche.[18] There is even one report of a mayor removing the birth registers of his commune for the years 1780–1794.[19]

It is quite impossible, in examining the problem of draft-dodging, to estimate the number of men who successfully avoided the draft during the period that we are considering, for documentation is not complete; at best, any figure stated would be a guess. Nonetheless, a study of the available materials does show that it was a widespread problem which, as we shall shortly see, provoked the sternest countermeasures from the government.

The problem of desertion was also serious. Men, once they had been drafted, frequently deserted while on their way to supply and reinforcement depots where they were to be formally inducted into the army and dispatched to their regiments and posts. Several factors influenced the incidence of desertion: peace rumors, military victories, government measures designed to prevent or discourage it, and the attitude of local authorities, to name a few. Here again it is difficult to arrive at an accurate estimate of the total number of deserters.

Of the three basic forms of disobedience to conscription during the First Empire, it is quite probable that desertion was the most serious crime. A report from Saône-et-Loire (dated January 21, 1806) stated that though the quota for the department was filled, the gendarmes were kept constantly busy hunting down deserters and that nearly 200 had been arrested.[20] The prefect of Morbihan, in a report of February, 1806, stated that there had been seventy-one desertions in his department and that the incidence of desertion appeared to have been greater than in previous years.[21] The prefect of Puy-de-Dôme reported to Fouché on August 7, 1805, that desertion was frequent, even when recruits were escorted by gendarmes.[22] The police commissioner of Brest reported on May 5, 1806, that 120 deserters had been arrested but that there were still many deserters at large.[23]

[17]*Ibid.*, No. 933.
[18]*Ibid.*, No. 372, 879, 1109, and 1203.
[19]*Ibid.*, No. 912 (*Ariège, March 4, 1806*).
[20]*Ibid.*, No. 719.
[21]*Ibid.*, No. 795.
[22]*Ibid.*, No. 102.
[23]*Ibid.*, No. 1077.

From Haute-Garonne came a report (March 18, 1806) mentioning the arrest of 212 deserters, with an added note that there were still over 200 at large.[24]

Serious as these instances of large-scale desertion were, they were nothing in comparison with the rate of desertion in the departments on or near the Spanish frontier. In the department of Ariège, for example, in the nineteen-month interval under consideration, there were no less than sixteen conscription cases, many of them involving desertion. The incidence of desertion along the Pyrénées was high because deserters could very easily cross the border from France into Spain. Moreover, until official complaints were registered in Madrid by the French ambassador, French deserters seem to have been welcomed and protected by the Spanish authorities.[25] So serious was this particular problem (involving first deserters from Ariège, then fugitives from Haute-Garonne, Basses-Pyrénées, Haute-Vienne, Ardèche, Gironde, Landes, and Deux-Sèvres) that the French government was forced to bring sufficient pressure to bear upon the Spanish government that the Spanish closed the frontier to all Frenchmen except those who traveled on diplomatic passports.[26] This step was taken in April of 1806.

How many men actually crossed the frontier? The figures given in d'Hauterive vary from an estimate of 5,000 or 6,000 according to the prefect of Haute-Garonne,[27] to 500 or 600, according to the French ambassador in Madrid.[28] A third estimate, Fouché's own, places the figure at about 4,000 men, which figure represented fully one-half of the quota of the departments involved for the year 1806.[29]

In his consideration of the problem of desertion, Lefebvre estimates that 3.5 percent of the total number of men called up deserted and to substantiate this he cites the records of Côte-d'Or (its desertion percentage being 3.5 per cent of 11,000 men) and Côtes-du-Nord (with a desertion percentage of 3.8 of 19,000 men).[30] Côte-d'Or is a department in the interior of France, so that it would have been quite difficult for deserters to remain out of the reach of the authorities—there was simply no place where they could safely flee. Côtes-du-Nord is on the gulf of Saint-Malo, and it is nowhere near a land frontier. Consequently, any would-be deserters would almost have to have had boats, or at least easy access to them. This limitation would have

[24] *Ibid.*, No. 922.
[25] *Ibid.*, No. 589 (dated December 12, 1805).
[26] *Ibid.*, No. 1006.
[27] *Ibid.*, No. 872 (dated March 4, 1806).
[28] *Ibid.*, No. 1006 (dated April 12, 1806).
[29] *Ibid.*, No. 621.
[30] Lefebvre, *loc. cit.*

effectively restricted successful desertions to the fishing population along the coast, men who owned their own boats, or could easily obtain them. This last remark is a surmise as there are at present no figures to support it. On the other hand, Ariège and the seven other departments mentioned as being the center of serious and extensive desertion were near a land frontier, and until April, 1806, the Spanish authorities were known to have welcomed deserters.

In considering the problem of desertion, one thing remains to be done: to attempt a rough estimate of the numbers of men who actually deserted. Let us first assume that the high rate of desertion in the southern departments, most particularly in Ariège, was considerably above the norm, just as the low desertion rate of Côte-d'Or was probably rather below the average. Therefore, a reasonable monthly average would seem to be about 800 from all over France, or about 9,600 men a year, not counting the undetermined number of men who successfully evaded the draft. If draft-dodgers be added to the total, it may be tentatively assumed that the figure would be in excess of 15,000 men a year. It should be noted here that this figure is based on a monthly average and that during certain months the actual totals fell far short of the average. As a result of the great French victories at Ulm (October 20, 1805) and Austerlitz (December 2, 1805) there appears to have been a high point in patriotic, martial fervor which helped to lower the desertion rate for several months.

And yet, the fact that an average of 800 men deserted every month was serious, and in 1805 the French government, through the intermediary of Fouché's police, applied stringent penalities.[31] The most important of these was the quartering of troops in towns where there had been difficulties involving conscription. Generally, the troops were quartered in the homes of the families of deserters. This practice seems to have been initiated by the prefect of Deux-Sèvres who, in a report dated September, 1805, stated that "the presence of a military force would be sufficient to induce the young men to obey."[32] The custom was emulated by most of the other departments. The idea seems to have met with Fouché's favor, though there is no specifically worded circular to the effect that this policy was to be officially implemented. There is, however, a circular dated December 31, 1805, which states that all prefects are to submit monthly reports to Fouché on conscription. In the event of any difficulties, "appropriate measures will be taken."[33] This is the nearest thing to direct approval of

---

[31] Lefebvre, *loc. cit.*, states that such practices as quartering troops did not begin until 1807. Thompson (p. 308) gives 1805 as the beginning of such practices. D'Hauterive bears Thompson out on this point.

[32] D'Hauterive, II, No. 295 (dated September 25, 1805).

[33] *Ibid.*, No. 648.

the practice by Fouché. By the spring of 1806, the practice was in general use throughout France.

Of all of the countermeasures used by the government, the practice of quartering troops on the families of deserters seems to have been the most effective. For example, there is a report from the prefect of Var dated November 20, 1805, which states that, of the 611 men selected for service, 100 deserted en route. Troops were quartered in the homes of their families, with the result that all but ten of the deserters gave themselves up.[34] Similarly, the prefect of Orne reported on February 26, 1806, that "the most efficacious measure of subduing draft-dodgers or deserters is to quarter troops in the homes of their parents. By this means, the return of 58 such defaulters has been brought about."[35] In a report from the prefect of Haute-Garonne of March 26, 1806, we read that "he [*the prefect*] has used with success the measure of quartering troops in homes of defaulters' parents. Two-hundred and sixty-four have presented themselves. . . . They are being sent in detachments to their destinations."[36]

There were other measures taken by the government. Among them were fines and prison sentences, the usual punishment for conscription offenses being one year in prison and a fine of 500 francs.[37]

It is also evident from the documents that the French victories at Ulm and Austerlitz had the effect of reducing, if only for a few months, the incidence of desertion and draft-dodging.[38] In connection with the French victory at Ulm there is an interesting report from the prefect of Haut-Rhin who noted the favorable effects of the victory upon conscription in his department. The report closes with the observation that "the young men are convinced that it is more advantageous to serve their country than the enemy. . . ."[39]

The evidence discussed here shows that desertion was a serious problem for Napoleon before 1812. An indication of its seriousness is seen in the counter-measures utilized by the government. It is quite probable that the practices of quartering troops, levying heavy fines, and imposing prison sentences lowered the monthly desertion rate. But in spite of these attempts to discourage desertion, it persisted. There was fairly constant opposition to conscription in France during the First Empire and virtually nothing that the government did had the desired effect of completely and finally solving difficulties resulting from this opposition. What appears to be most significant is that

[34]*Ibid.*, No. 648.
[35]*Ibid.*, No. 851.
[36]*Ibid.*, No. 950.
[37]*Ibid.*, Nos. 1117, 1174, and 1189.
[38]*Ibid.*, Nos. 444, 445, 447, 432, 427, 472, 473, and 474.
[39]*Ibid.*, No. 490 (dated November 13, 1805).

elements of the public persisted in violating the laws of conscription and, in so doing, tacitly challenging the Napoleonic system, and that Napoleon was able to do very little to solve this problem. In the opinion of this writer, the existence of this constant, irritating opposition is of greater significance than the actual loss of manpower.

6
THE COMMON PEOPLE IN FRANCE

Did the common people in France enthusiastically favor the rule of Napoleon? Jean Tulard and Raymonde Monnier think so, even though they recognize that many peasants and city workers eked out a desperate existence and that Napoleon did not always support their interests. For example, peasants feared conscription and crop requisitions; and city workers, who were legally forbidden to form trade unions or strike, were treated by the government with suspicion. Yet these disadvantages, Tulard and Monnier argue, were far outweighed by the fact that many common people were better off economically and took pride in France's military victories under Napoleon. Also, peasants felt that Napoleon protected gains that they had won during the Revolution; and city workers felt that he shielded them from lesser government officials and from their employers.

Can one be sure, however, that Napoleon was really popular among the masses? As Monnier points out, it is hazardous to gauge public opinion from police reports to higher authorities. They often told their superiors what they wanted to hear. Pronouncements by the government were even more unreliable. They often served as propaganda to bolster the regime and create a Napoleonic cult. Furthermore, Napoleon suppressed dissent mercilessly, and so peasants and city workers could not freely express what was on their minds. But sometimes they showed their dissatisfaction by draft-dodging or striking. Can an argument be made that the common people in France were less ardent supporters of Napoleon than indifferent to him or even perhaps merely resigned to an authoritarian rule?[1]

[1]See evidence to bolster this point of view not only in the selections by Tulard and Monnier but also in those by Langlois in Chapter 2 and by Vidalenc and Arnold in Chapter 5.

Jean Tulard (1933–   ) is an internationally recognized authority on the Napoleonic epoch. A Parisian and the son of civil servants, he studied at the Lycée Louis-le-Grand and the University of Paris. He currently teaches at three schools in France—the University of Paris-Sorbonne, the Ecole pratique des hautes études, and the Institut d'études politiques de Paris. Since 1974 he has been president of the Institut Napoléon. In addition to his scholarly interest in the history of film and the history of Paris, he is a prolific author of books on Napoleon and his times. Tulard's most notable works include the Nouvelle histoire de Paris: le Consulat et l'Empire *(1970)*, Bibliographie critique des mémoires sur le Consulat et l'Empire *(1971)*, Napoléon ou le mythe du sauveur *(2nd ed., 1977; Eng. trans., 1984)*, and Dictionnaire napoléon *(1987)*. Tulard's knowledge of France from 1799 to 1815 ranges from the daily life of the common people to the actions of their political leaders and from Napoleon's impact on his time to the legends about him created after his death.

A SURVEY OF PEASANTS AND CITY WORKERS

Jean Tulard

Although France was growing more middle class [from 1799 to 1815], it remained profoundly rural. In any case the peasant world offered a wide diversity, from the large landowner who speculated over the sale of his produce to the small tenant farmer whose situation was often difficult. The hold of the notables (whether the old nobility or the new landowners) over the countryside was hardly debatable. All the prefects confirmed their influence and the government did not underestimate it.

Two categories profited from the advance of agricultural production and from the circumstances resulting from war. They were the landowner and the day labourer. The large landowner, thanks to his capital and to the productivity of his lands, grew richer in times of famine, particularly in 1801; at other times he benefited from the increase in trade outlets of which Napoleon's conquests assured him. "The victories of our armies, by extending the limits of the Empire,

From Jean Tulard, *Napoleon: The Myth of the Saviour*, trans. by Teresa Waugh (London: George Weidenfeld and Nicolson Ltd., 1984), pp. 186–192. Reprinted with some changes in translation by permission of the publisher.

considerably benefit the sale of our agricultural produce," Caillot wrote in his *Mémoires*, "so immense quantities of grain passed into nations whose poor land could not produce much of these crops." This accurately describes the position in the north and the east, although not the position on the Atlantic coast.

The day labourers, who made up the rural proletariat (about sixty or seventy per cent of country dwellers were day labourers), profited from the shortage of farm hands due to a more and more demanding conscription. The resultant rise in wages between 1798 and 1815 reached nearly twenty per cent. With improved conditions, they could sometimes even buy property—only a small amount, it is true—in the last sales of national property. Fauchet, the Prefect of the Var, indicates several people in his department who acquired, "by dint of economy and deals which did not overburden them" a little field which they cultivated outside their working hours. In the *arrondissement* [district] of Provins, the 6,271 recorded labourers cultivated 34,680 hectares[1] out of a possible 84,000. It is perhaps not so strange as it might appear that day labourers even had servants—a kind of sub-proletariat of cowherds, shepherds and carters. This improvement in their position gave rise to some irritation: "Day labourers," noted the author of the statistics for the [Department of the] Nord, "have shown themselves to be insolent and daring since army conscription has put them in greater demand." In order to avoid excessive rises [in wages], servants and seasonal labourers such as harvesters were forbidden to form unions.

Circumstances were less favourable for the tenant farmer and share-cropper. Whereas the big farmer, like the landowner, profited from the rise in prices and the increase in trade outlets, the small farmer was confronted by serious difficulties. After a moment of euphoria the rise in the price of grain was barely eighteen per cent between 1809 and 1812, whilst the rise in farm rent for the same period reached thirty-seven per cent. Let us take the case, described by the Prefect of the Meurthe, of a farmer from the *arrondissement* of Lunéville who cultivated a property of twelve hectares. His rent was 1,200 francs; he had to pay a ploughboy and a herdsman, both of whom were employed throughout the year; he had also to be sure of the services of casual labourers in certain seasons. To all this was added maintenance of farm implements, food, and clothing. The farmer's entire expenditure exceeded 3,488 francs whereas his income reached 3,646 francs. Profits came from the sale of grain either in the market or to itinerant merchants who came to fetch it from the farms. The length of leases—from three to nine years—was far too limited and

[1][One hectare equals 2.47 acres.—Eds.]

represented a serious handicap. The situation of the share-cropper or tenant farmer who paid part of his crop in rent was even worse. According to Sismondi, nine-tenths of those who managed their farms were share-croppers. They worked land which was not highly productive and their marketable surplus was not enough to enable them to benefit from the advantages made available by the new state of affairs. Nevertheless their condition was considerably improved: their share was no longer subjected to tithes and was often exempt from tax. In his *Mémoires sur le Métayage*, Gasparin notes that share-croppers were the class in France least burdened with taxes.

Wine growers, usually smallholders, were, however, a particular case. According to sub-prefects' reports, a moderate year producing good-quality wine was preferable to a year of great abundance by reason of the decrease in costs and the increase, on the other hand, of the price per hectolitre.[2] Costs were in fact greater—manure, vine-props, cultivation, casks. Even for the Bordelais [inhabitants of Bordeaux], confronted with the problem of exports to England, the income was low.

Nevertheless, as late as 1809, rural areas remained favorable to the imperial regime which guaranteed a return to security due to the decrease in brigandage, a fairer distribution of taxation, and the maintenance of revolutionary gains (the abolition of feudal rights, and to a certain extent the sale of national property). Unquestionably living conditions in the countryside improved. As early as 1805, Peuchet remarked in his *Statistiques élémentaires de la France*:

> More bread and more meat are eaten in France today than formerly. The country-dweller who knew nothing better than rough food and unhealthy drink, today eats meat and bread and drinks good cider and beer. Colonial commodities (like sugar and coffee) have also spread around the countryside with the increased wealth of cultivators.

And [the prominent Napoleonic official] Chaptal himself recognized:

> The ruinous system for the countryside combined with requisitions and conscription should have made the Emperor odious to the peasants, but that is not the case. They were among his warmest partisans, because he reassured them against the return of tithes, feudal rights, the restitution of property to émigrés, and the oppression of the lords.

The Emperor found this popularity equally among the ranks of the urban proletariat. These town dwellers, artisans, craftsmen, low-paid workers who had been in the forefront during the great revolutionary days of Paris, and who at Lyons had supplied the greater part of the

---

[2][One hectolitre equals 100 litres.—Eds.]

[Jacobin] Chalier's strength, and at Marseilles that of the terrorists, had without much difficulty, rallied to the Empire. The ideals of the sans-culottes were no more than a memory at which only a few police veterans would still tremble. How can such an infatuation for Napoleon—the word is not too strong—be explained?

The legal position of the worker in fact grew worse under the Empire. The law of 22 Germinal Year XI [April 12, 1803] instituted the *livret*, a document which he was obliged to hand to his employer when he was hired and which was returned to him on leaving. This document made the worker dependent on his master and made it possible for the police to supervise migrations of workers. But it is sometimes forgotten that the Minister of the Interior used the scarcity of labor to justify the introduction of the *livret* which was no more than a return to a practice of the Ancien Régime. Firms attempted to entice workers away from other employers; the workers therefore, with no regard for previous agreements, tended to profit from the advantages which this overbidding brought them. The aim of the *livret* was to provide for manufacturers a more or less stable workforce. But the employers, especially in the building trade, were subject to no sanctions and themselves encouraged workers to get around the law by engaging them without the *livret*. Furthermore, attempts made by the police to control the movement of workers through employment bureaux ended in failure.

Any coalition [working men's organization] or union was forbidden by articles 414, 415 and 416 of the penal code. All the same, there were a large number of strikes, especially in Paris. No doubt they were limited to one site or at least to a few elements of one trade, and they lasted no longer than a week. They never took on a political character. They were caused, above all, by the introduction of machinery (at Lille in 1805, at Sedan in 1803) or by the length of the working day. In 1801 the workmen employed to erect scaffolding for the fête of 14 July in Paris demanded a ten per cent increase; the ring-leaders, among them a wine merchant, were arrested by the police; in August 1802 construction was interrupted on the Pont d'Austerlitz. The approach of the coronation provided a pretext for the workmen employed at Notre-Dame cathedral in 1804. The following year the men working in the Louvre refused to have their working day lengthened. The strike of 1805 was more serious and was extended to a large number of public works. There was another strike in August 1807 when the stone-cutters working at the Louvre came out. A very serious incident occurred on the site of the Arc de Triomphe at the Etoile in March 1810 as the result of an accident, which necessitated the intervention of the armed forces. There, it was a matter of spectacular demonstrations—a number of disputes which ended in a compromise.

In October 1806, a police regulation determined a new timetable for public works in Paris: only one hour's break was laid down, between ten and eleven o'clock. Workers refused to return to these old rules; they demanded a snack break for what they called their "meal on stone" in the afternoon. A significant detail: "They claimed that if the Emperor had been in Paris, His Majesty would not have allowed the passing of the regulation." The movement began on 6 October and only ended on the 13th with the agreement that the workers would lunch between ten and eleven o'clock and would have a snack on site between half past two and three o'clock. It was an exceptional case. Repression was often severe, with imprisonment or the sending of ringleaders to the provinces. But the bosses were not spared. When they combined to lower wages, the police immediately obstructed their plans, no doubt more for reasons of law and order than because of any concern for fairness. But such an attitude impressed the workers in the capital favourably and explains the popularity of the Emperor in the worker's districts. So the Parisian paper-manufacturers, to put a stop to the claims of their workers, requested a fixed maximum salary and were shown the door by Dubois, the Prefect of Police. In 1801 and 1810 the rates laid down by the hatters' employers were also nullified.

The conciliation boards, instituted by a law of 18 March 1806 for the purpose of arbitration between employers and workers, were far from being as fair as Napoleon had foreseen. But the worker had sufficient means at his disposal. *Compagnonnages*—workers' associations—although illegal, reappeared. Should they be forbidden? Réal, one of the chiefs of police, recommended tolerance: "*Compagnonnage*, which is a kind of Freemasonry, exists since time immemorial. I despair of fruitfully attacking its essence and limit myself to the prevention of its excesses in so far as that depends on me." Could he have done otherwise? Particularly as the various *compagnonnages* wasted their time in brawls among themselves and took no political action. Hence a certain accommodating attitude on the part of the Imperial Police in the provinces, if not in Paris.

The drain caused by the Napoleonic wars emptied the towns, as well as the countryside, of younger men and caused a grave crisis of manpower. No doubt the proportion was low in comparison to the population which was of a working age, but the most active element and those most in demand were removed. Seasonal immigration, which consisted of some forty thousand workers who came to the capital in search of work in the summer months, began to decline around 1812. On visiting some work sites in Paris in December 1813, Napoleon was surprised to see only old men. "You can find as many old men as you need," replied the contractor, "but they have neither the spirit nor the strength for the work. As for the young, you don't see them any more. Conscription has swept them away." There was no certainty of relief because of the length of the wars.

The worker did not complain so long as he avoided military service. Such a shortage naturally pushed wages up. The rise varied according to the occupation: it was particularly marked in the building trade but much less so in the textile trade. The rise was greater in Paris than in the provinces, which was the cause of so great a seasonal emigration to the capital. The rise was irregular and was interrupted by the crisis of 1810. It can be estimated at more than twenty-five per cent since 1789 (but the cost of living had risen equally, except for the price of bread which, at Napoleon's will, had remained in Paris at less than 18 *sous* [a little less than a franc] for four pounds). A worker in the capital earned between 3 and 4 francs a day, that is to say, taking Sundays and holidays into account, less than 900 francs a year which was not very much in comparison to a councillor of state's 25,000 francs. In the provinces, the average wage of a labourer was 1 franc-20 in 1801; a more specialized worker would earn between 1 franc-60 and 2 francs. But the cost of living was lower than in the capital except for bread.

However, the disappearance of unemployment and a relative rise in wages brought about an improvement in material conditions. Undoubtedly there were many accidents at work and sickness took its toll. In the discouraging report established by the Prefecture of Police in 1807, it is to be seen that life expectancy rarely exceeded fifty in certain occupations (shoemakers, bakers, carders), and suicides occurred frequently. Alexis de Ferriéré remarks in Year IX [1800–1801]: "The workman has marginally improved his diet; he eats meat more often and drinks fermented liquor, his clothes are cleaner and of better quality." Other sources confirm this. The Englishman, Birkbeck, remarked in 1814 that the working class in France was much higher up the social ladder than in England. Besides, Napoleon favoured the establishment of societies for mutual help—for example, the society for the miners of Liège which was decreed on 26 May 1813. The society was financed by a two-per-cent deduction from wages and participation of the employer based on one-half of one per cent of these wages. The experiment heralded the present-day social security system in France.

This comparative well-being and the absence of class consciousness (with the exception of arms manufacturers there were very few large enterprises, the national average being around four men to a workshop) explain, as much as any niggling police supervision, the calm of the worker's districts. A calm which was to last until 1830.

Raymonde Monnier (1932–), the daughter of tradespeople, has a doctorate in history from the University of Paris. Inspired by the work of the noted Marxist historian Albert Soboul, she has written Le Faubourg Saint-Antoine (1789–1815) *(1981), a microscopic study of a Parisian worker's district during the revolutionary and Napoleonic eras. She and Soboul co-authored a* Répertoire du personnel sectionnaire parisien en l'an II *(1985). On the staff of the Institute of the History of the French Revolution at the University of Paris-Sorbonne, she also serves on the editorial board of the* Annales historiques de la Révolution française, *a leading journal on the Napoleonic period as well as the Revolution.*

AN EXAMPLE: THE PARISIAN WAGE EARNER

Raymonde Monnier

It is not an easy matter to sketch the picture of the society that emerged from the Revolution in a Parisian district inhabited by common people, such as the faubourg Saint-Antoine. After a brief appearance in the foreground of the political scene at the beginning of the Revolution, the masses were again cast into the shadows. The people of the poorer districts no longer hold the attention of observers nowadays except for certain picturesque traits. Research devoted to the society of the Napoleonic Empire deals primarily with the middle class and the nobility, the group known as the new notables.[1] The only study of the common people is that by A. Chabert on the fluctuations of incomes from 1798 to 1820.[2] B. Gille has completed a general essay on the common people in the collective work entitled *Napoléon et l'Empire*.[3]

From Raymonde Monnier, *Le Faubourg Saint-Antoine (1789–1815)*, (Paris: Société des études robespierrists, 1981), pp. 245–252, 287–289. Printed by permission of the publisher. Editors' translation.

[1] J. Tulard, "Problèmes sociaux de la France impériale, *Revue d'histoire moderne et contemporaine* 17 (1970). None of the papers presented at the colloquium held at the Sorbonne in 1969 on the occasion of the 200th anniversary of Napoleon's birth concerned the social history of the lower classes.

[2] *Essai sur les mouvements des revenus et de l'activité économique en France de 1798 à 1820* (Paris, 1949).

[3] "Le Monde ouvrier" in Jean Mistler, ed., *Napoléon et l'Empire*, 2 vols. (Paris, 1969), I, 218–227.

A study of the social structures of the lower classes confronts the problem of a lack of sources. The archives of notaries do not include information about manual workers. We have based our research on the archives of the justices of the peace, which contain an inventory or a written summary description of a person's premises after death or bankruptcy. These allow us to estimate the standard of living of different groups of workers.[4] Our research focuses on the period from 1810 to 1814, the last years of the Empire.[5] For this period of five years, we have discovered 242 inventories or descriptions concerning people living in the faubourg Saint-Antoine, including 36 about premises sealed after a bankruptcy and 132 about premises sealed after a death. In 59 cases, the justice of the peace provided only a simple description of the premises; the low worth of the contents did not justify sealing the premises in order to make an inventory. We also have eight descriptions of dwellings after the tenants disappeared, five inventories following requests for divorce, and two inventories after criminal sentencing.[6]

Because of the relatively important number of premises sealed after a death, almost a third of the 242 inventories or descriptions concern widows, people living on their investments, former shopkeepers, or former artisans (78, including 34 of former artisans or former small shopkeepers). Of the 242 inventories or descriptions, about two-thirds or 164 relate to people of the faubourg Saint-Antoine who were still working at the time of their death. A fourth of these were shopkeepers. The largest group is that of artisans, who number 55, representing a third of those who were still working. 59.1 per cent of the inventories or descriptions concern artisans or small shopkeepers. People in business and manufacturing are represented by 13 inventories or descriptions, gardening and farming by ten.

[4]The inventories of premises sealed after a death do not permit a monetary estimate of their values, but they do allow us, by means of the accounts of the premises, furniture, and belongings, to ascertain the tenants' way of life. This can be done as much by the number and uses of the rooms of the apartment as by the presence or absence of debts or, on the contrary, by the presence of food or merchandise, tools, and valuable or everyday objects. The inventories after a bankruptcy are more precise than those after a death and comprise a more or less complete evaluation of assets and liabilities. Under the Empire, the inventories of premises sealed after a death were often necessary, because many young men were in the army and thus absent at the death of a close relative.

[5]Archives départementales de la Seine, D^8U^1, cartons 34 to 42. Carton 66 contains the registers of the lists from 1810 to 1823. The inventories or descriptions are missing for the months of March to May 1810 and for those from July 1812 to March 1813, that is, for a total of 11 months.

[6]Sixty inventories or descriptions were drawn up in 1810, 66 in 1811, 26 in 1812, 35 in 1813, and 63 in 1814, for a total of 250; eight have been discarded because they concern people not from the faubourg Saint-Antoine.

The poorest classes, that is, wage earners employed by industry or trades and wage earners dependent on service to others, are very insufficiently represented: only 25 inventories or descriptions concern them, which is a small number for a numerically important group. These lower strata of the population are difficult to study except en masse: for example, by means of statistics about the indigent or workers in general. Therefore, these few cases are valuable only as examples, but we can provide some nuances to the picture of the life of wage earners during the Empire by relying on other data.

THE WAGE EARNERS

The main tendencies of Imperial policy concerning workers are well known. Legislation reinforced the control of master guildsmen and businessmen over their workers.[7] However, in certain better organized trades, the workers could make the most of their demands, for labor shortages provided favorable conditions for wage earners. A. Chabert concludes that real income from wages rose 25 per cent from 1798–1802 to 1817–1820, with the highest level of wages probably in 1810.[8] This is a general tendency that was not true of all organized trades. Specific indexes for individual occupations clearly indicate a definite pay increase in the building trades (a 21.9 per cent increase in wages); in textiles, on the other hand, the drop in wages during the same period came to more than 40 per cent. In addition, the lack of sources has forced A. Chabert to include in his general index only male wage earners. Given the importance of female and child labor during the Empire, especially in textiles, we question whether we can conclude that there was a general rise in the standard of living of wage earners.

Although surely improving, the material life of workers still remained very precarious, since the economic crisis at the end of the Empire caused an increase in poverty. Finally, even in a period of favorable conditions, the picture must be shaded; for the rise in wages certainly did not affect all organized trades. To understand the disparities better, it is advisable to differentiate among workers in large-scale industry, those who worked on raw materials supplied by others, and journeymen of the crafts.

If one accepts the report of Prefect of Police Dubois about Parisian

---

[7]Compare Chabert, p. 155, and Gille, I, 218ff.

[8]Chabert, pp. 173–264. According to [the French Minister of the Treasury] Mollien, wages remained high in the cities in 1811. (Archives nationales, AFiv 1089 A, letter of October 29, 1811). He claimed that the workers of the cities, never before having "been so well paid," could afford the high price of bread.

workers in 1807,[9] it seems that in traditional trades such as building, which were better organized, the journeyman had the greatest opportunity to earn a decent salary provided he was a good worker. Some workers earned two and even three times more than others; if an ordinary ditchdigger earned only very little—1.5 to 2.5 francs a day, a stonecutter or an ironworker might make three to seven francs a day; and the pay of a marblecutter might reach 12 francs a day.[10] Moreover, we must take into account the seasonal nature of the building trades. For the masons who remained year-round in Paris, "winter is . . . a dead season, because they are unemployed."[11] Among these workers traditions remained strong: their journeymen's association [*compagnonnage*] and their meeting at the work site made them more conscious of their solidarity and common interests. During the Empire, there were many examples of unions in the building trades.

This was not true for journeymen in the luxury trades, for example in furniture or metal working. Furnituremakers, Dubois says in 1807, "do not form unions."[12] The journeyman, often living with his master and working alongside him, came under his sway. As regards the mentality of leatherworkers, the Prefect of Police says, "They are differentiated on the basis of the attitude or example of the master guildsmen who employ them."[13] The wages of these workers in 1807 were not so high as workers in the building trades. The best paid did not earn more than six francs a day (carriagemakers, harnessmakers, and gold- and silversmiths). The wages of a journeyman were about three to four francs: in 1807 that was what carpenter-cabinetmakers, watchmakers, cutlers, and machinists earned. The lowest paid were certain workers in metal trades—nailsmiths, pinmakers, and braziers. In these trades, the artisan was often dependent on the merchant-manufacturer. A turner [lathe worker] earned only two francs a day.

Wage differentials were especially wide in work concerning precious metals. This occupation had a subtle hierarchy among journeymen of various trades who despised each other: "The chiseler who works in metals and the gold- and silversmith who works in the round disdain the worker who inserts precious stones or pearls into objects. He in turn pays their contempt back with interest. Both consider the person who makes or sells jewelry far beneath them. The latter

---

[9]G. Vauthier, "Les Ouvriers de Paris sous l'Empire," *Revue des études napoléoniennes* 2 (1913), 426–451.

[10][One franc per day was about the minimum amount an adult needed for survival.—Eds.]

[11]Vauthier, p. 432.

[12]Ibid., p. 436.

[13]Ibid., p. 442.

would be ashamed to fraternize with the gold- and silversmith" etc.[14] That was why workers' unions, adds Dubois, were "almost impossible."[15]

Then there was the army of those who worked at home in the textile industry, in the garment trade, and in sewing, industries often dominated by merchant-manufacturers. Many of these people were indigent during the Empire. In fact, they earned a wage that was nearly always inadequate. The least poor among them were perhaps the hosiers and weavers: ribbonmakers, workers in gauze, and blanketmakers who engaged in piecework could earn 2.5 to five francs a day. In the last years of the Empire, these wages fell because of the general economic crisis. Shoemakers were the poorest: "A typical shoemaker is paid 25 sous [a little more than a franc] for a pair of shoes. The most any person could produce in a day is one and a half pairs, which would earn about 36 sous." The material condition of master shoemakers, who were themselves dependent upon the merchant-manufacturers, was not much better. "One noticed that many of them bought one candle to provide two workers with light for a whole day."[16] Woman's work was exploited in an even more cruel manner. A seamstress or linendraper earned only ten to twenty-four francs a month in 1807.

The life of workers in the textile factories was no more enviable: the spinners earned only 1.5 or two francs a day. The exploitation of women and children spinners was more oppressive than of those in sewing. In other manufacturing establishments, wages were a little higher; they did not go below two francs a day except for the making of glass: two francs for tobacco; two to three francs for wallpaper (but children only earned a few sous). In the manufacture of faience [a type of pottery], a good worker could earn twice that amount.[17]

Although wages rose a little until 1810, the fate of a large portion of the Parisian workers remained precarious during the Empire. By means of the inventories or descriptions after a death, we see that the standard of living of wage earners in the faubourg Saint-Antoine seems very low. In 17 actions by the justice of the peace concerning the lodging of workers or journeymen, only for six of them was it necessary to seal the premises in order to inventory their contents, that is, only a little more than a third of the number. In the other cases, a simple description sufficed, given the extremely meager furnishings and the slight importance of the documents found there.

[14]Ibid., pp. 440–441.
[15]Ibid.
[16]Archives nationales, F^{12} 502.
[17]Worker agitation in factories does not prove a class consciousness regarding working conditions, but rather points to old forms bound to the traditions of journeymen associations and to the defense of old customs. See for example the disturbances which broke out in 1807 in the Lefevre et Caron factory. Archives nationales, F^7 3126.

The sample includes three workers in factories or in big workshops who appear to have had a decent standard of living: a turner working for Richard-Lenoir [who operated a cotton-spinning factory], a tinworker in a glass and mirror factory, and an apprentice brewer.[18] All three were lodged by their employers in the factory or workshop: the brewer shared a room with another worker; the tinworker had his own room at the factory; and the turner and his wife occupied two rooms at the former convent of Notre-Dame-de-Bon-Secours. In these three cases, the presence of valuable documents or objects required the sealing of the premises. All of them had saved some money, the brewer only about four hundred francs, but the two other workers each had some five thousand francs in gold and silver pieces. All three owned a gold or silver watch. They were the only wage earners who owned objects of some value.

Let us look at the Swiss-born Joseph Hueber. He had moved to Paris in 1769. A tinworker in a glass and mirror factory, he died in 1811 at age 68. He had been ill for some time and was cared for at the factory: his room was very simply furnished, but the furnishings belonged to him. He had nearly five thousand francs in savings, which he had hidden in various places in his room.[19] The number of cases is too small to permit broad generalizations, but these three examples suggest that workers in factories enjoyed some advantages and were not the poorest workers.[20]

On the other hand, the living conditions of the other workers seem worse. The sample covers many different types, including eight journeymen,[21] a worker in gauze, a coachman, and three women living alone (a spinner, a linenworker, and a chairpolisher). For these thirteen cases, only four required the sealing of their premises. For example, concerning the three female workers, a mere description of the premises was sufficient, the furnishings being very meager. Only one of the carpenters was lodged in the home of his female employer; the very sparse furnishings in his room belonged to her. Except for two workers, the lodgings of all the others consisted of one room for

[18]Archives départementales de la Seine, D^8U^1 36, no. 1013; D^8U^1 37, no. 1076; D^8U^1 41, no. 3189.
[19]Archives départmentales de la Seine, D^8U^1 37, no. 1076, July 5, 1811; and Archives nationales, F^7 4804, no. 644.
[20]In glass and mirror factories, the wages of workers were exempt from direct taxes. Provident societies were formed in certain factories. The workers in the wallpaper factory of Réveillon had created a relief fund in November 1789; it counted 104 members in the year XII [1803–1804]. For an initial payment of six livres and twelve sous plus a weekly assessment of two sous, the members received help in case of illness or disability. See the rules of this society in the Archives nationales, F^{15} 3963. An association of the same type existed in the Richard-Lenoir factory.
[21]Two carpenters, an ironworker, a gold- and silversmith, a maker of spurs, a foundryman, a turner of faience, and a marblepolisher.

both cooking and sleeping. The furnishings were always meager, including only the essentials: a stove, a bed, a table, and some straw-bottomed chairs, a buffet for pots and pans, napkins, knives, a wardrobe for clothing, a small chest of drawers containing kitchen utensils, some shabby clothes, and linen, often threadbare. Here for example is the description of the dwelling of Pierre-Louis Melon, a journeyman gold- and silversmith: "Two straw-bottomed chairs in bad condition, a small table made from fir or pine wood, a stove made of faience used for heating, a sandstone water jug in its wicker cover, a wooden bench in poor condition, and a small oak server with four doors. . . ."[22]

The worker lived from day to day; he had no supplies, no valuable objects, and, most of the time, no ready cash. Only four of them had savings, from five hundred to eleven hundred francs. For one of the carpenters, there is a mention of a small gold necklace. The inventories do not mention any debts; it is true that people lent money only to the rich. Pierre Baju, a journeyman ironworker from Limoges, came to the faubourg Saint-Antoine in 1765 at the age of 21. He did not make his fortune there. At the end of his life, he lived in a poorly furnished third-floor room on a courtyard off the Rue de Lappe. Some kitchen utensils, some iron worker's tools, a basket of old scrap iron, and some shabby clothes: these were all his worldly possessions. A widower for two months, he died at the Saint-Antoine hospital on February 19, 1812.[23]

Descriptions drawn up of some of the workers' rooms in the small craft shops on the street are even briefer: a small piece of furniture made of white wood or boxes containing some shabby clothes and coarse linens; and an old cot or a folding bed.[24] The most precious objects that they possessed were the tools of their trade: for the porter, a small hand cart and a pair of hooks; and for the water-carrier, a small horse cart equipped with a large cask.[25] The widow Montié kept in her room all her business goods—two hundred small Maroilles cheeses. Each of the three people had a little ready cash: 13 francs in coins for the cheese merchant; 70 to 80 francs each for the two others.

Domestic servants were in a somewhat different situation. Five

[22]Archives départementales de la Seine, D^8U^1 34, no. 60, February 5, 1810.
[23]Archives départementales de la Seine, D^8U^1 38, no. 1505, March 5, 1812; and Archives nationales, F^7 4804, no. 5138. Among these workers, there is no mention of religious objects. Only two workers possessed devotional books.
[24]Archives deépartementales de la Seine, D^8U^1 34, no. 306; D^8U^1 35, no. 622; D^8U^1 40, no. 2754.
[25]According to the Prefect of Police, 633 carts owned by water carriers moved about Paris daily during the Empire—41 per cent pushed by hand, the others by horses. During the winter, unemployed workers sold hand-carried water. There were two thousand of them. Archives nationales, F^{20} 134, report by Dubois, August 20, 1807.

inventories made after a death concern housemaids, all unmarried. From the provinces, they served the family of their employers for a long time; one of them had worked fifty-six years for the same family. In nearly every case, the presence of documents required the sealing of their premises. Lodged in small rooms in the residences of their employers, they had few personal items. Two had government bonds given to them by their employers; two had a little money. But the other was owed about 1,350 francs in wages.

Therefore, most of these wage earners were very poor. Still they did possess some personal belongings, modest as they were; they had the use of a room. Others were even worse off. Many of the wage earners lived in furnished rooms shared with others. During the Revolution, there were 137 rooming houses in the faubourg Saint-Antoine, almost all in the Montreuil and Quinze-Vingts sections.[26] The inventories made after a death describe these furnished rooms. For example, in the establishment of the widow Bernardin on the Rue de Charonne, a worker could for 4.5 francs a month sleep in one of the nine beds in a large room. The old cots were provided with a straw sack of grey cloth, a mattress, an unbleached linen blanket, and a bedsheet of coarse canvas. The shabby clothes of the tenants were contained in an old commode, a bottom part of a buffet in poor condition, and a white wooden chest.[27] At the establishment of Jean-Baptiste Belhague, innkeeper-landlord on the Rue du Faubourg, a large room on the second floor was furnished with seven old beds provided with bedding of very poor quality; another room on the ground floor in the back of the shop was furnished with three old beds, two folding beds, and a bed of rabbit fur. A room facing the street served as the shop.[28]

Many of the wage earners ate out, since according to a statement drawn up in Pluviôse, year III [January–February 1795], more than half of the faubourg Saint-Antoine's population were fed by caterers.[29] By caterers we really mean wine merchants, tavern-keepers, and owners of hash houses, where workers came "to satisfy their hunger at reasonable prices," those whom Mercier calls the "cheapjack restaurateurs."[30] During the Revolution, the faubourg contained about one hundred cafés or shops run by wine merchants; eighty were located in the Quinze-Vingts section. Their number increased greatly during the Empire: in 1807 the faubourg had more than two hundred

---

[26] Archives nationales, F^7 3688^4, document entitled "The Condition of the Population," 3 Pluviôse, year III [January 22, 1795].
[27] Archives départmentales de la Seine, D^{8}U^1 36, no. 754, January 26, 1811.
[28] Archives départementales de la Seine, D^{8}U^1 40, no. 2506, July 3, 1813.
[29] Archives nationales, F^7 3688^4 4. Sixty-one per cent of the 23,639 people in the faubourg who ate at caterers lived in the Quinze-Vingts section.
[30] L.-S. Mercier, *Le Nouveau Paris*, 6 vols. (Paris, 1798), II, 219.

drinking establishments, cabarets, or hash houses; 45 per cent were in the Quinze-Vingts. It is there that common laborers came to drink and eat their meals. Jouy described these workers at table: "At first I entered the wine merchant's shop, where I found several errand boys and some masons seated around a table lunching heartily on a piece of home-made bread, some cheese, some colored hard-boiled eggs, and a few liters of a local light-red wine."[31]

The condition of workers varied widely during the Empire. It is difficult to conclude that there was a general improvement. If the journeymen in the best-organized artisan trades were able, thanks to favorable circumstances and the shortage of labor, to obtain raises in pay and to experience better material conditions, many others remained very poor and without much hope of social advancement. As an artisan, a capable journeyman could hope one day to set up his own business; in such trades as metal work for example, the original investment was not large. But what hope could a worker entertain who was not self-employed or was a wage earner in a textile factory? His wages, always inadequate, kept him in poverty; and an economic crisis reduced him to despair. Regarding these people, material and moral conditions did not improve during the Empire. This can be verified by consulting the welfare rolls. Also, the situation of unskilled workers was always precarious. . . .

POPULAR OPINION

There can be no doubt that the laboring classes of the faubourg Saint-Antoine were ardently Bonapartist. How can we explain this attachment to the Emperor on the part of the masses and lower middle-class workers who had constituted the bulk of the activists during the Revolutionary days?[32]

From the beginning of the Consulate, Bonaparte benefited from the confidence of the lower classes, who were exhausted by the battles of the Revolution and profoundly disappointed by the republican government. Bonaparte profited from the unpopularity and disrepute of the Directory. At the time of the signing of the Peace of Amiens [with Britain, March 25, 1802], joy was widespread: "It is especially among the people and the working class that the impression is the sharpest and deepest; they speak only of the happiness they owe to the First Consul. . . ."[33] The workers "talk of the First Consul with veneration

---

[31] V.-J. de Jouy, *L'Hermite de la Chaussée d'Antin*, 5 vols. (Paris, 1813–1814), II, 279.
[32] On the opinions of the urban lower classes, compare Gille, I, 218; and J. Tulard, *Nouvelle histoire de Paris: le Consulat et l'Empire, 1800–1815* (Paris, 1970), p. 296.
[33] A. Aulard, *Paris sous le Consulat*, 4 vols. (Paris, 1903–1909), II, 798, police report of 6 Germinal, year X [March 27, 1802].

only; remarks against the government made in front of them would receive a very hostile reception."[34]

Later, the glitter of victories reinforced the popularity of Napoleon, who worked diligently by skillful propaganda to maintain the illusion with the public that he enjoyed broad support and total loyalty. Concerning the working class, the Emperor strove to appear as the redresser of wrongs so that any measure unfavorable to workers was interpreted as having been taken without his knowledge. For example, in September–October 1806, when a strike broke out by workers in the public-works sector as a protest against the police ordinance of September 26 regulating the hours of work, they claimed that "if the Emperor were in Paris, His Majesty would certainly not have allowed the ordinance to pass. . . ."[35]

However, are police reports accurate reflections of public opinion? Official propaganda encouraged popular support and joyous demonstrations in workers' districts. As to official reports of festivals and public attitudes, we must take into account conformity or toadyism. Perhaps these reports conceal the masses' profound indifference to political issues. "The multitude has work and is comfortable. It is content: it loves the Emperor."[36] The absence of disturbances among the common people is explained primarily by Bonaparte's firm and able policies concerning the Parisian masses, whom he distrusted.[37] The police were vigilant, preventing any subversive movement. Attentive to the needs of the laboring classes, the Emperor was careful to assure them food and work during an economic crisis. Favorable circumstances and relative well-being compensated for the aspects of Imperial legislation disadvantageous to workers. As to the lower middle-class artisans, Napoleon showed himself mindful of the interests of small-scale production; he stimulated the luxury trade by official orders, orders which were made, like those in 1811 for cabinetwork, directly to artisan workshops, bypassing the merchant or business middlemen of Paris.

During the Empire, everything combined among the people to create a cult of the Emperor. The Empire meant military victories, Austerlitz, Wagram, and the *Bulletins* of the *Grande Armée*. Until

---

[34]Ibid., II, 806, police report of 10 Germinal, year X [March 31, 1802].
[35]Compare A. Aulard, ed., *Paris sous le Premier Empire*, 3 vols. (Paris, 1912–1923), II, 720, police report of October 3, 1806; and P. Brousse and H. Turot, *Le Consulat et l'Empire*, Vol. VI of *Histoire socialiste (1789–1900)*, ed. Jean Jaurès, 13 vols. (Paris, 1901–1908), 236.
[36]E. d'Hauterive, ed., *La Police secrète du Premier Empire: bulletins quotidiens adressés par Fouché à l'Empereur*, 4 vols. (1908–1963), IV, 340, police report of August 26, 1808.
[37]J. Tulard, "Du Paris impérial au Paris de 1830 d'après les bulletins de police," *Revue de l'histoire de Paris et de l'Ile de France*, 1969, pp. 157–175.

1814, the young men of the lower classes responded enthusiastically to the draft.[38] The young artisans, the apprentices and journeymen of the faubourg Saint-Antoine who had enlisted for patriotic reasons or with the hope of social advancement, and those others who had been drafted, united to maintain, after their return to civilian life, an attachment to the person of the Emperor. Military glory made the lower classes forget the harsh realities of daily existence.

There were however some instances of ill temper as, for example, the noisy reunions of the Conquerors of the Bastille in the year XII [1803–1804].[39] Unhappy about not being admitted into the Legion of Honor, they tried unsuccessfully to gain support for their cause among the people of the faubourg Saint-Antoine, saying "that they would know how to take revenge and to make clear that they alone had made the Revolution and that they remained forever patriots."[40] These demonstrations were infrequent. The lower classes remained devoted to the Emperor.

The popularity of Napoleon is revealed even better at the time he fell from power and also in the Hundred Days. During the first Restoration [1814–1815], the workers' districts showed their hostility to the Bourbons. Prefect of Police Pasquier kept watch especially over the faubourg Saint-Antoine, "where one finds the most hotheads and where there still ferment some remains of the old leaven of the Revolution."[41] On his return from Elba, Napoleon was enthusiastically welcomed by the Parisian common people and lower middle class.[42] Later, the workers expressed repeatedly their patriotism, their devotion to the Emperor, and their desire to defend Paris against the Allies; this was especially true during the great demonstrations of the national guard of the districts on May 14 [1815].[43] For the people living in the workers' districts, Napoleon came to be seen again as the defender of the Revolution against aristocratic Europe.

After 1815, the legend continued to grow. The glorious memories of the Empire built on those of the Revolution. From the taking of the Bastille to the great victories of the Consulate and the Empire and to

---

[38]L. Bergeron, "Recrutements et engagements volontaires à Paris . . . ," in *Contributions à l'histoire démographique de la Révolution française*, 3rd series (Paris, 1970), p. 243.

[39]Aulard, *Paris sous le Premier Empire*, I, 116, 125, 133, 160, 234, 244, police reports of 30 Messidor, 4, 7, 17 Thermidor, and 17, 22 Fructidor, year XII [July 19, 23, 26, August 5, and September 4, 9, 1804].

[40]Ibid., I, 257, police report of 28 Fructidor, year XII [September 15, 1804].

[41]E. Pasquier, *Histoire de mon temps: mémoires du chancelier Pasquier*, 6 vols. (Paris, 1893–1895), II, 337. See also Archives nationales F⁷ 3836, police reports of July 5, 20, 1814.

[42]E. Le Gallo, *Le Cent Jours* (Paris, 1923), pp. 109ff.

[43]Ibid., pp. 303ff.

Napoleon's farewells at Fontainebleau, the popular legend retraced the national epic. The sons of the sans-culottes of 1793 had served in the ranks of the *Grande Armée*. The new generation, nourished on the stories of glory, looked with nostalgia on a recent past that the grayness of the Bourbon Restoration made appear as a kind of golden age.

7
THE EFFECT OF THE CONTINENTAL BLOCKADE ON BRITAIN

By November 1806, the Fourth Coalition against Napoleon was crumbling. The French had defeated Austria, Prussia, and Russia in battle. But Napoleon's armies could not invade Great Britain, as it controlled the seas; therefore Napoleon embarked on a plan (known to historians as the Continental Blockade or Continental System) to triumph over her by economic warfare—by preventing British goods and ships from entering the continent. He believed this would disrupt her economy, cause her political and social instability, and force her to stop fighting. Within a year, most of the continental states had accepted his policy in varying degrees and they continued to do so until the *Grande Armée* was annihilated in the last months of 1812 in Russia.

Eli F. Heckscher regards the Continental Blockade as doomed to failure: British goods could find alternative markets; the Blockade did not aim to choke off the goods Britain needed for home consumption; her credit system was too strong to be seriously disrupted; and the Britain people showed little inclination to revolution. In fact, he thinks the British economy continued to expand from 1806 to 1812. This does not surprise him, because he considers economic blockades ineffectual restraints on the natural course of the economy.

François Crouzet views the Continental Blockade in a different light. He argues that even though British capitalism was resourceful and the country never close to revolution, the Blockade caused very serious economic and social dislocations at times. Moreover, Crouzet holds that had Napoleon not lost in Russia, France could have maintained such intense pressure on Britain that she would have had to leave the war.

How can we explain this difference of interpretation? Does nationalistic pride stand in the way of analysis? Or is one historian better informed than the other? Or do they disagree about the ability of governments to control economic activity?

*Eli F. Heckscher (1879–1952) was one of Sweden's most distinguished historians. After studying economics and history at the University of Uppsala, he taught at the University of Stockholm, the Stockholm Business School, and the Stockholm Institute of Economic History. A prolific writer on public affairs as well as on scholarly matters, he became a strong defender of laissez-faire economics. Thanks to translations of three of his books—*The Continental System: An Economic Interpretation *(1922),* Mercantilism *(rev. ed., 1955), and* An Economic History of Sweden *(1954), much of his research and findings in economic history are well-known to the English-speaking world.*

A CHALLENGE EASILY OVERCOME

Eli F. Heckscher

There remains the question of the effects of the Continental System on the United Kingdom. . . .

LIMITATIONS OF OBSTACLES TO EXPORTS

In order to be able to judge this matter aright, we must realize clearly the serious weakness that existed in Napoleon's position from the standpoint of the Continental System, a weakness that lay in the fact that the very most that he could be expected to attain by his own resources was the closing of the mainland of Europe. The importance of this for his object of smothering the exports of Great Britain probably appears with sufficient exactitude if we reduce the value figures corresponding to her exports to percentages and then divide them into three groups according to countries of destination. The position is then revealed as follows:[1]

From Eli F. Heckscher, *The Continental System: An Economic Interpretation*, ed. by Harald Westergaard (Oxford: Clarenton Press for the Carnegie Endowment, 1922), pp. 324–332, 363–365. Reprinted by permission of Oxford University Press.

[1] . . . The trade with Ireland . . . has not here been taken into account.

A. Domestic Goods[2]

Year	Europe	United States	Rest of world
1805	37.8 per cent	30.5 per cent	31.7 per cent
1806	30.9 per cent	31.3 per cent	37.8 per cent
1807	25.5 per cent	33.4 per cent	41.1 per cent
1808	25.7 per cent	15.0 per cent	59.3 per cent
1809	35.4 per cent	16.2 per cent	48.4 per cent
1810	34.1 per cent	23.9 per cent	42.0 per cent
1811	42.9 per cent	6.2 per cent	50.9 per cent

B. Foreign and Colonial Goods[3]

Year	Europe	United States	Rest of World
1805	78.7 per cent	5.1 per cent	16.2 per cent
1806	72.9 per cent	5.7 per cent	21.4 per cent
1807	80.0 per cent	3.1 per cent	16.9 per cent
1808	71.1 per cent	0.9 per cent	28.0 per cent
1809	83.1 per cent	1.4 per cent	15.5 per cent
1810	76.9 per cent	2.7 per cent	20.4 per cent
1811	83.6 per cent	0.4 per cent	16.0 per cent

This summary shows, to judge by the position immediately before the organization of the Continental System, that at the very highest about one-third of the exports of domestic goods could be affected by the self-blockade of the Continent, although, it is true, there must be added to this three-fourths of the re-exports. It was, therefore, a factor of fundamental importance for Napoleon's success that the United States should also be driven to the establishment of a self-blockade, inasmuch as that would put an end to another third of the exports of British goods. It is impossible to deny that in this matter he received excellent help from the British government itself, when it allowed things to come to an almost unbroken series of conflicts with America, mainly because of the Orders in Council,[4] which as a matter of fact were never more than quite a secondary weapon in the great struggle. This meant that, strictly speaking, everything had been done which was really possible in the direction of preventing British exports; and so far Napoleon had achieved even more than he could have achieved with the resources of his own empire alone.

[2][Exports of goods produced in Great Britain.—Eds.]
[3][Re-exports (British exports of goods previously imported from foreign and colonial lands).—Eds.]
[4][The Orders in Council mentioned here were measures to control maritime trade taken by the British cabinet to counteract Napoleon's Continental Blockade.—Eds.]

But precisely the development thereby created, as it is illustrated in the above figures, shows a limitation in the range even in a course of action which was so surprisingly successful, namely, that it always left trade with the rest of the world undisturbed. We see from the third column of the table how the share of this department of exports with regard to British goods increases in relative importance under the Continental System in comparison with the preceding years; and this tendency will be clear whether the situation is regarded from an English or from a continental point of view. British industry would seek transmarine markets [overseas markets other than Europe] as substitutes for lost European ones; and it would likewise find them, as the increased self-sufficiency of the European Continent would make the rest of the world more dependent upon British supply than before. Of interest in this connexion is the fact that the Continental System gave the impulse for British transmarine exports of calicoes and prints, which had been unheard of before.[5] And in this respect Napoleon was almost hopelessly impotent, for it must have been inconceivable to prevent for any long time the power that commanded all the seas of the world from exporting goods to other continents. Even if the self-blockade of the Continent of Europe had been complete, which was, of course, far from the case, the immediate effect would probably have been to hasten the economic orientation of Great Britain both from Europe and also, to a large extent, from the United States, to the rest of the world; and this orientation, as a matter of fact, has taken place gradually during the last hundred years and has formed one of the most significant changes in the position of Great Britain in the economy of the world. In one of his famous and most overweening utterances (1826), Canning justified British co-operation in the liberation of the South American colonies on the ground that "he called the New World into existence to redress the balance of the Old." In the sphere of economics this British tendency already had century-old roots, and indeed it was precisely what was attempted under the Continental System by the speculative exports [that is, goods for which no orders have been received] to Brazil. When one follows the later development of transmarine exports, one scarcely doubts that this speculative touch would soon have vanished if the blockade of the Continent had become permanently effective. How important the change has been since the time immediately before the

---

[5]A. Jenny-Trümpy, *Handel und Industrie des Kantons Glarus, und in Parallele dazu: Skizze der allgemeinen Geschichte der Textilindustrien mit besonderer Berücksichtigung der schweizerischen Zeugdruckerei* (Glarus, 1899–1902), Vol. II, pp. 370–71, quoted in T. Geering, "Die Entwicklung des Zeugdrucks im Abendland seit dem XVII Jahrhundert," in *Vierteljahrschrift für Social-und Wirtschaftsgeschichte* (1903), 422.

Continental System is shown by the following comparison with the situation immediately before the outbreak of World War I.[6]

A. Domestic Goods

Year	Europe	United States	Rest of world
1805	37.8 per cent	30.5 per cent	31.7 per cent
1913	35.6 per cent	5.6 per cent	58.8 per cent

B. Foreign and Colonial Goods

Year	Europe	United States	Rest of world
1805	78.7 per cent	5.1 per cent	16.2 per cent
1913	56.1 per cent	27.5 per cent	16.4 per cent

The same thing can also be illustrated by the quantity figures, namely, the tons actually shipped to the same groups of countries; but in this case we can deal only with the first half of the nineteenth century, because statistics are no longer compiled in this way.

[C. Per Cent of the Total Weight of Goods Exported from Britain]

Year	Europe	United States	Rest of world
1802	66.97 per cent	7.53 per cent	25.50 per cent
1849	56.00 per cent	16.90 per cent	27.10 per cent

More or less parenthetically it should be observed that at the present time [1922] Great Britain, as a consequence of this, would be considerably less susceptible to being barred from exports to Europe than she was a hundred years ago.

The limitation of Napoleon's possibilities of affecting British exports was thus obvious even during the comparatively few years that his continental empire lasted; and, as far as one can judge, it would have become still more so, in ever-increasing degree, if the Continent of Europe had passed through a long period of insolation. We must now try to form a notion of British economic life under the pressure of the blockade as far as it actually became a reality.

Unfortunately it must be regarded as impossible, in the main, to separate these effects in any kind of inductive way from the general tangle of economic development. Not even in the special category of war measures does the Continental System stand in isolation; that is to say, the effects of the war and the effects of the Continental System do not coincide. Here the self-blockade of the Continent has by its side the Orders in Council and the many other subjects of dispute with the

[6]The figures for 1913 are calculated on the basis of the *Statistical Abstract for the United Kingdom.*

United States, which brought about the closing of that great market to British exports; and they were accompanied also by the burdens peculiar to the war itself, which could not possibly have been without importance even if there had been a complete lack of measures and countermeasures in the sphere of commercial policy. But in addition to all this there was the circumstance that not even this complex of factors could take effect as a whole in anything which could be called, even approximately, a community in a state of economic equilibrium. On the contrary, the economic life of Great Britain would have been in a state of violent transformation quite irrespective of the Napoleonic wars, owing to all the different movements included in the industrial revolution, the effects of which were made still worse by a poor law system which was entirely devoid of guiding principles and was therefore extremely pauperizing. Finally, moreover, the confusion of the British currency caused dislocations which must be referred to yet a third cause, which was in the main independent of the others. It is manifestly impossible, under such circumstances, to arrive at more than rather general conclusions as to the effect of the Continental System on the economic life of Great Britain as a whole.

RATE OF INDUSTRIAL DEVELOPMENT

The main thing is to determine to what extent the industry of the country was hit in the way that Napoleon intended. We ask ourselves, therefore, whether the six years during which the Continental System may be regarded as having been in force (1807–12) exhibited any stagnation or decline with respect to the preceding and succeeding development; if there was, we may possibly see in this an effect of this special cause.

The question is not easy to answer, as the period was so short and so full of ups and downs. But one starting-point might possibly be obtained in the figures for the supply of coal, if such were available; for during the age of coal, coal has usually formed the best common standard of industrial development. As it is, however, we have no figures for the total amount of coal produced, but only for the quantities of coal shipped from Newcastle and Sunderland[7]; while probably the greater part, and the part that underwent the greatest increase, was consumed within the huge cotton, wool, and iron areas that lay on or behind the coal-fields. But in any case the figures (yearly averages) are of interest.[8]

---

[7][Two cities on the northeastern coast of England which shipped coal by sea to markets elsewhere in England or overseas.—Eds.]

[8]The figures have been collected on the basis of the table in G. R. Porter, *The Progress of the Nation* (new ed., London, 1851), pp. 275–6. The other statistical data in this section have been taken, where nothing to the contrary is stated, from the same work.

A CHALLENGE EASILY OVERCOME

Period	Tons	Per cent increase over preceding period
First quinquennial period of the century (1801–5)	2,137,209	—
Period of the Continental System (1807–12)	2,463,890	15.29
First quinquennial period after the peace (1816–20)	2,812,851	14.83

These figures do not in the least degree indicate that the rate of industrial development was retarded under the Continental System, but, on the contrary, they show that the growth was not greater even during the first years of peace; and the figures for the particular years give the same impression. For the cotton industry by itself we have no figures to go by save those referring to the imports of raw cotton; the fluctuations here were very great from year to year. But a summary of the figures for net imports gives the following result:

Year	Pounds	Percent increase over preceding period
1801–5	56,662,421	—
1807–12	79,744,529	40.73
1816–20	130,328,347	89.27

Here, too, therefore, we are confronted with an increase which is even several times greater than in the former case, although it falls far short of the increase during the following peace period, which, of course, is only natural.

Nor does the rest of the somewhat scattered material that is available show any visible signs that the uniquely rapid industrial development which is characteristic of this period was retarded by the Continental System. The population of Great Britain and Ireland increased 13 per cent. between the years 1801 and 1811, as compared with 15¼ per cent. during the following decade; and naturally it was considerably greater for the industrial districts. Calico-printing works quadrupled their production between 1800–14, and the exports of iron increased. Nor did the years of the Continental System form an exception to the general transition to new technical methods which constituted the *primus motor* of the industrial revolution. Thus Cort's son stated in a petition to the House of Commons in 1812 that even at that date 250,000 tons of malleable iron were annually produced by puddling and that Cort's processes had obtained practically general acceptance.[9] The power-loom likewise made progress, though at a considerably slower pace. A great new revolution took place in calico-printing with the year 1808, in that the pattern was transferred to the cylinders from a little steel cylinder instead of being engraved direct; and the lace machine came into existence in 1809, etc.

There was certainly no pause in the industrial revolution, nor any tendency to a backward development of the industrial life of Great Britain toward increased self-sufficiency, such as, in accordance with our previous findings, would have been the consequence of complete success for the Continental System. But, of course, it was not in that way that Napoleon himself thought of this matter; his hopes were limited to dislocations in the system.

EFFECTS OF DISLOCATION OF EXPORTS

It appears that these hopes were not frustrated, but, on the contrary, were very nearly fulfilled through the British crisis of 1810–11. Also it appears equally clear that this crisis cannot be regarded wholly, or even mainly (though certainly in part), as a fruit of the blows of the Continental System against Great Britain; nor was the extent of its effects at all what Napoleon had imagined.

On the whole, we have no reason to regard the economic effect of purely dislocation phenomena as particularly important. It is possible in this connexion that we are too much impressed by the unique experiences of the recent war in this direction; but even if we think of crises occurring during otherwise normal times—even crises of such an incalculable character as the cotton famine in England during the American Civil War—it is striking how soon their traces are swept away by subsequent development. The whole of Napoleon's plan on this point, made out at short sight as it was, cannot be regarded as having had any great prospect of attaining its object, that is, the crippling of Great Britain's military power by undermining the foundations of her economic life.

This, then, holds good of the purely economic effects of the dislocation; with regard to its social and political effects the matter assumes quite a different aspect. Here the political economist can really neither contest nor confirm the process of thought, for the result depends almost exclusively on the character of the people in question. An impulsive race, which has also become accustomed to receiving help from the state in all things great and small, may be led by a mere trifle to overthrow a government, a constitution, perhaps a whole order of society, while another people, which is more phlegmatic and less trained to rely on the state, may leave the conduct of the state entirely

[9]Thomas C. Hansard, *The Parliamentary Debates* (London, 1804 ff), XXI, p. 330.

undisturbed even in times of serious distress and great difficulties. It is quite obvious that Englishmen, especially during the time of the Napoleonic wars, belonged to the latter category; and as Miss Cunningham has justly observed, the rage of the unemployed was directed in the "Luddite riots" against the new machinery (framebreaking), but not really against the government.[10] One can easily imagine that Napoleon, with his experience of the continual *coups d'état* during the French Revolution, could not see this; but this makes no difference with respect to the fact that he made a thorough miscalculation.

But to all this must be added the fact—and this is a very important fact—that the particular kind of dislocation in Great Britain due to the Continental System which was most favourable to Napoleon, was necessarily of a comparatively superficial nature, just because it was a dislocation caused by obstacles in the way of exports and not of obstacles in the way of imports. A failure of exports can always be alleviated by production with a view to accumulating stocks [building up inventories]—supported, if necessary, by public funds; but that is not the case with the failure of imports, for if irreplaceable commodities are irretrievably left outside no measures can be of any avail. . . .[11]

BRITISH CREDIT SYSTEM

. . . It is a quite different and far more searching question, to what extent the British credit system could have been thrown into disorder by the general difficulties and dislocations caused to British economic life by the Continental System in combination with a number of other factors. As regards the credit of the state, nothing of the kind occurred. The system of the national debt was so firmly founded that it resisted the strain without difficulty, though the cost of the revolutionary and Napoleonic wars certainly appears, for various reasons, to have been much greater than would have been the case if the borrowing had been effected in some other way. The private credit system, on the other hand, had not yet attained the same vital position in the economic life of the country as it has now. The new large-scale industry was to a predominant extent based on its own capital, and was mainly extended with the help of its own profits—a fact which is seldom properly emphasized. Consequently, the harm that could be involved by a dislocation of credit can probably be measured by the results of the crisis of 1810–11—that is to say, bankruptcies by

---

[10]Miss A. Cunningham, *British Credit in the Last Napoleonic War* (Cambridge, 1910), pp. 17–18, 27 *et seq.*

[11]It may be allowable to point out how well this result, which was reached early in 1918, is in accordance with later German developments.

the merchants with reaction on the manufacturers from whom they bought their goods. Besides, it is an open question whether the credit system of a country can be regarded as being so delicate as it has long been the fashion to make out. The experience of the recent war has largely suggested that our credit organization has a much more robust physique than anyone had previously suspected.

CONCLUSION

The Continental System had little success in its mission of destroying the economic organization of Great Britain, and most of the things it created on the Continent lasted a very short time. The visible traces that it left in the economic history of the past century are neither many nor strong. Indeed, it is difficult to find any more obvious and lasting effect than that of prolonging the existence of the prohibitive system in France far beyond what was the case, not only in Great Britain, but also in Prussia. Thus there are good grounds for doubting that the material development of our civilization would have been essentially different if this gigantic endeavour to upset the economic system of Europe had never been made. In general, it is true that what sets its mark on the course of economic development—largely in contrast with what is political in the narrower sense—is that which can be used as a foundation for further building, where cause can be laid to cause. Isolated efforts to destroy the texture of economic society, even if they are made with a giant's strength, can generally do little more than retard the process of development, and gradually they disappear under the influence of what may be called in the fine— perhaps too fine—phrase, "the self-healing power of nature" (*vis medicatrix naturae*).

However, the Continental System mainly had immediate ends in view. It was in the first place a link in a life-and-death struggle, where, as is always the case under such circumstances, the thought of the future had to be relegated to the background. The fact that the future effects were small, therefore, is a thing which, strictly speaking, touches the heart of the Continental System no more than it touches the heart of other trade wars. It is true that in all such struggles people count on the most far-reaching and profound effects in the future from the victory that they wish to win to-day; but the only thing that they understand clearly is their desire to win the victory. First and foremost, therefore, the question is, to what degree the Continental System served this its immediate aim.

So far as the answer to this question lies in the sphere of economics, the answer has already been given in the preceding pages, and is mainly in the negative.

François Crouzet (1922–), the son of a history professor who was also a school administrator, studied at the University of Paris, the Ecole normale supérieure, and the London School of Economics and Political Science. Since 1964 he has been Professor of History at the University of Paris, first at the Nanterre branch and now at the Sorbonne. His main field of research is the economic and social history of Britain and France. Combining painstaking research with deft Anglo-French comparisons, he has written extensively on the British economy since 1700. Among his publications are Capital Formation in the Industrial Revolution *(1972),* The Victorian Economy *(1982), and* The First Industrialists: The Problem of Origins *(1985). He is best known for his impressive doctoral thesis,* L'Economie britannique et le blocus continental (1806–1813) *(1st ed., 1958; 2nd ed., 1987), from which the following selection is drawn.*

A SERIOUS CAUSE OF SOCIAL AND ECONOMIC DISLOCATION

François Crouzet

In a very sensible discussion, [Frank O.] Darvall has demonstrated that if a revolutionary movement had arisen in Great Britain in 1812, it would have had a good chance of success, or at least a better chance than at any other moment in recent English history. Actually many circumstances favorable to a revolution came together in the spring of 1812: a very severe economic depression, which had gone on—and without hope of improvement—for eighteen months; a sharp increase in the price of foodstuffs; intense suffering among the laboring population; widespread discontent; a weak, discredited, and unpopular cabinet, yet hostile to any reform and failing to provide the dissatisfied with any reasons to believe that their demands might gain legal approval; an archaic and ineffective system of local administration and police; and finally, the essential factor for a political revolution— a social structure heading toward upheaval due to the effects of an industrial and agricultural revolution, a social structure that had lost its traditional foundations without having found a new equilibrium.

From François Crouzet, *L'Economie britannique et le blocus continental (1806–1813)*, 2 vols (Paris: Presses universitaires de France, 1958), II: pp. 804–808, 853–860, 868–872. Printed by permission of the author and publisher. Some of the footnotes have been omitted or shortened. Editors' translation.

And Darvall does not hesitate to criticize Napoleon's failure to exploit this exceptional situation. He should have come to the aid of the Luddites.[1]

A "revolutionary situation" existed then, but there were no revolutionaries to exploit it. The workers were discontented, even angry and exasperated; and the attitude of the working people in the affected regions supplies plenty of proof of this. The workers applauded the actions of the Luddites, or in any case did nothing to oppose them. But the workers lacked leaders, an organization, and a program. The clandestine trade union associations had no political aims; and the secret "revolutionary" committees were insignificant and inefficient, flooded with police spies. The Luddite gangs of the Midlands and Yorkshire—which had some organization and knew what they wanted—had aims that were strictly job-oriented, limited, and local. These Luddites did not wish to overthrow the government. Their activities were directed neither against the state nor even against the local authorities. They only sought to exert pressure on their employers by menacing them, to spread anxiety and terror so as to gain immediate economic concessions. By no means did the Luddites seek to start a revolution.

In addition, the first condition for a revolution would have been the alliance of the middle class and the proletariat. To be sure, a large part of the British middle class, especially among the industrialists and merchants, held radical and reformist views. During 1812 these middle class reformers participated in vigorous campaigns against the government's policies. But such radical leaders as Whitbread, Burdett, and even Cobbett opposed the use of violence. Moreover, radical businessmen could only regard the Luddite activities with suspicion, if not worse; and these activities even threatened to push them toward the political right. The middle class actually played no role whatsoever in the violent disturbances of 1812. Consequently, Luddism was destined to be simply a desperate revolt of the wretched, not a revolutionary movement. This was so because, in general, despite suffering and discontent, there was no protest based on principle and no revolt against the established order. The discontented, whether bourgeois or workers, and even the Luddites, had only specific and limited complaints, such as those against the Orders in

[1] Frank O. Darvall, *Popular Disturbances and Public Order in Regency England* (London, 1934), pp. 306–312. [The Luddites were organized bands of English rioters who operated in 1811–1812 in the Midlands, Yorkshire, and Lancashire. They often destroyed textile machinery that they blamed for causing low wages and unemployment.—Eds.]

Council or the use of shearing frames.[2] No revolutionary myth intoxicated large segments of the population.

On the other hand, the entire establishment (with some exceptions, notably Lord Byron) united firmly to condemn the Luddite disturbances and to seek their suppression. Despite the caution or ineptness of some local government officials, those favoring the established order demonstrated their resolve to defend themselves in every way; and the army and police were completely loyal.

Consequently, examination of the Luddite movement and the other disturbances of 1812 leads one "to say with some degree of assurance that there was at that time no real danger of a general collapse of order or of a violent overturn of government or society."[3] Great Britain, during this last year of the Continental System, had not yet arrived at the edge of the revolutionary abyss, and an investigation of the disturbances proves only the stability and solidity of the British political and social edifice.

The disturbances of 1812 were, nevertheless, the most extensive, longest, and most serious that England had experienced since the seventeenth century. The authorities were sometimes overwhelmed, and for several weeks certain districts were virtually in the hands of rebels who caused considerable damage, terrorized the inhabitants of these regions, and temporarily managed to force their will on their employers. In the spring of 1812 the suppression of these disturbances required the use of a real army amounting to twelve thousand regular soldiers. This was a larger force by far than any of those employed earlier in similar circumstances. These events also showed very clearly the faults, if not the evils, of the economic and social organization of Great Britain as well as the inadequacy of her archaic system of local government and police. Finally, by the anxieties that these disturbances aroused in the ruling circles, we judge that they exerted some effect on the British government's policy. On this point we depart from the views of Darvall who concluded that neither public opinion, nor Parliament, nor the cabinet were seriously worried by these events and that they took only slight interest in them.[4] To us

---

[2][The Orders in Council were regulations decreed by the British cabinet and having the force of law. Here the reference is to those Orders aiming to control maritime trade in response to the Napoleonic Continental Blockade. They had the effect of so antagonizing the United States that this country prohibited the import of British (and French) goods. Shearing frames were machines used to finish woolen cloth. Workers feared that they would lose their jobs because of these machines.—Eds.]
[3]Darvall, p. 8
[4]Ibid., pp. 319–327.

this judgment does not seem fully justified. It is certainly true that Luddism neither aroused a general panic nor a fear of an imminent revolution. On the local level, however, it is indisputable that at certain times the propertied classes and the local authorities in the areas of disturbances succumbed to panic and believed the most outlandish rumors about the Luddites' revolutionary schemes and their organization. Another symptom is that, from the time of the first disturbances, coined money—not just silver, but copper also—disappeared. In addition, although the press in London and the provinces devoted little space to the disturbances, in several instances it did spread alarming rumors.

As for Parliament, it showed only a belated and limited interest in this problem and engaged only in some short discussions of it. Still, it easily passed five bills that the government proposed, and in June 1812 the two Houses appointed "secret committees" to study the matter. These bodies presented their reports early in July. The documents are interesting for their pessimism and alarmism; prepared at the point when the disturbances were almost over, they stated nevertheless that the difficulties were increasing. They also insisted that the Luddites had a powerful secret organization whose members were bound together by oaths, that they engaged in actual military training, and that they were drafting vast revolutionary programs.[5] On the other hand, the members of the Opposition—although condemning the Luddites in general terms and approving their suppression—did not take the most extravagant rumors seriously and perceived events on a more realistic basis. They understood that the Luddite movement was not at all revolutionary and was of limited extent.[6] Finally the cabinet does not seem to have believed the problem to be important and did not devote much time to it. At the end of January 1812, it discussed the Luddites formally for the first time. Although [Prime Minister Spencer] Percival did, on occasion, consider the problem, full responsibility for the maintenance of order fell to the Home Secretaries, [Richard] Ryder and then [in June 1812 Henry Addington] Lord Sidmouth; and neither of them seems to have exaggerated the seriousness of the disturbances.

---

[5]See ibid., pp. 219–224; Great Britain, Parliament, House of Commons, "Report of the Committee of Secrecy on Papers relating to Certain Violent Proceedings in Several Counties of England," Session of 1812, *Parliamentary Papers*, II, no. 335, pp. 307–314; Great Britain, Parliament, *House of Lords Sessional Papers*, 1812 LIII (no. 158), 8–11.
[6]See Darvall, pp. 221, 339–340; Great Britain, Historical Manuscripts Commission, *Report on the Manuscripts of J. B. Fortescue, Esq., Preserved at Dropmore* [Grenville Correspondence], ed. W. Fitzpatrick and F. Bickley (London, 1927), X, 233, 240–241, 251; *Cobbett's Parliamentary Debates*, (London, 1812), XXI, cols. 602–603, 813–819, 848, 850, 859–864, 972–978, 1084–1086; XXIII, cols. 999–1002, 1016.

Despite this, it cannot be denied that the ruling circles were worried by this proleterian movement, whose secret nature made it especially frightening, . . .[7]

The first question we must consider concerns the effectiveness of the Continental Blockade. To what degree did it have an unfavorable effect on the British economy? To what degree did Napoleon reach the objective that he hoped to achieve by issuing the Berlin decree [November 1806]: "To vanquish the sea by the power of the land," that is, to force England to surrender by closing European markets to it? We must stress immediately that most writers who have approached this problem have maintained that the Blockade never put Britain in very serious danger. Heckscher even insisted that the "dislocations" suffered by the British economy were minimal, if not imperceptible.[8] This attitude, however, can be explained largely by the national prejudices of those who hold it, by their systematic hostility to Napoleon, or by their attachment to certain principles of free enterprise economics. It seems to us that it cannot be sustained by an impartial analysis of the evidence and a dispassionate consideration of the facts.

It is certainly true that during a considerable part of the period of the Continental Blockade [November 1806–November 1812], it was not applied seriously and effectively. This was the situation from November 1806 to June 1807—when economic activity in England was almost normal. This happened again during the second half of 1808 and especially during 1809; so England experienced a phase of recovery beginning in July 1808, then a phase of prosperity, and even a boom that lasted until July 1810. Finally, after the disaster in Russia [October–December 1812], the Blockade broke down and a new phase of recovery got underway in England in November–December 1812. To sum up, for the six years that the Blockade lasted, it was ineffective for a little more than two and one-half years; during this time British goods managed to find their way into Europe in large amounts, and Napoleon's policy did not have a negative effect on the British economy. But this was not the case for the rest of the period, some three and one-half years. . . . From July 1807 to July 1808, that is, from Tilsit to the Spanish insurrection, and then from spring 1810 to the Russian debacle, the Continental Blockade was seriously enforced. Of course, it never was absolutely hermetic (which would have been impossible); but during these two periods British exports to

---

[7]See, for example, *The Letters of King George IV, 1812–1830*, ed. A. Aspinall, 3 vols. (Cambridge, England, 1938), I, 76–77.

[8][See the selection from Eli Heckscher, *The Continental System*, in this book.—Eds.]

France and to its satellites and allies fell to a very low level (especially for manufactured articles); and we can say without exaggeration that Napoleonic Europe was closed to English trade. This closing of Europe had very serious consequences for British economic activity and was made even worse because in 1808 and in 1811–1812, it was accompanied by the closing of the United States market. Exports and industrial production suffered very significant reductions, business failures multiplied, unemployment spread, and social disturbances broke out. We also believe that the Continental Blockade was the source of the recession of 1810, that veritable hurricane that shook the whole British economy, as well as the source of the monetary difficulties England experienced from 1808 until the end of the wars of the Empire [1815] that seriously hindered her war effort.

To put it simply, throughout the years when the Continental Blockade was rigorously applied, Great Britain suffered very unfavorable economic conditions marked by real "dislocations" of economic relationships, by an acute trade and financial crisis in 1810, and by a prolonged and serious depression in 1811 and 1812. To maintain, therefore, that the Blockade was ineffective is a serious error.

It is not less true that, despite this *technical* success, the Blockade ended in failure, even a double failure, both from the *political* and *economic* points of view. First of all, the difficulties that British commerce and industry suffered never led the government to consider capitulation. No, these difficulties did not lead to a defeatist and pacifist movement capable of either dominating the cabinet and the Parliament or overthrowing them. England had her defeatists, to be sure; they turned up among the aristocracy as well as among the common people, but their influence remained limited. On the other hand, the "patriotism" of the establishment and of the majority of the bourgeoisie was never seriously weakened; and in the working class itself agitation "for peace" only temporarily prevailed. To this political and psychological defeat of the Blockade (and which partly explained this defeat) can be added an economic defeat: under the pressure of the Continental Blockade, England experienced serious economic and social difficulties, but her economic and social structure withstood them; there were dislocations and tensions, but no collapse. In short, to reverse the famous epigram, the economic situation of Great Britain was sometimes grave, but never desperate. Neither at the beginning of 1808, nor during the crisis of 1810, nor even in the spring of 1812 (when domestic tensions reached their height) was England driven to capitulation or to revolution; nor, we feel sure, was she at any moment close to being pushed into such a position.

This conclusion brings us to investigate another problem that we have posed: the reasons for the final failure of the Continental Blockade. . . . They may be divided into two groups: exterior causes (from the British point of view, our central concern), that is, the weaknesses of the Continental Blockade itself; and internal causes, that is, the English capacity for resistance. Taking the first aspect, the essential fact is that the Continental Blockade never was applied for a long enough period; this mistake was due primarily to Napoleon himself. . . . The Blockade had a chance to succeed if the closure of Europe (and the United States) to English trade had been maintained for several years. But the Blockade was seriously enforced only during two periods [July 1807–July 1808; spring 1810–last months of 1812]. The first lasted a little less than one year and the second almost two and one-half years. This second period was more effective than the first, but still too short. In both cases the chances for the Blockade to succeed were destroyed by military events—the war in Spain and the Russian disaster—both due to Napoleon's errors. Our study can only confirm the conclusion that earlier historians reached long ago: the unfortunate and even catastrophic effect on the Grand Empire of both Napoleon's intervention in Spanish affairs to dethrone the Bourbons and his attack on Russia.

In fact, the uprising in Spain, unleashed by the coup of Bayonne [May 1808], had enormous economic consequences. It reopened the markets of the Iberian peninsula to English trade (which in some years would absorb very large amounts of English goods); it opened the markets of Spanish America; and it opened the door (by drawing into Spain a large part of the French army and so helping to start the war of 1809 with Austria) to the huge expansion of smuggling in 1809 and early in 1810 on the coasts of the North Sea and the Baltic. In short, it unleashed the British economic recovery that, after the serious depression early in the war, marked the second half of 1808. It also played an essential part in the development of the boom of 1809.

As for the consequences of the attack on Russia and the destruction of the *Grande Armée*, they are too obvious to require detailed discussion. By throwing Russia and Sweden into the arms of England and by provoking the German uprising, these events reopened most of northern Europe to English trade and brought about the sharp economic recovery that began in Great Britain at the end of 1812 and the prosperity that she enjoyed in 1813.

It cannot be denied that these two major errors by Napoleon were the principal causes for the failure of the Continental Blockade and for the ruin of his entire system.[9] We can also mention another error

---

[9]It could be argued, of course, that it was precisely to apply the Blockade more stringently that Napoleon intervened in Spain and attacked Russia and that the "internal logic" of the system required these decisions. But it should be recalled that,

by Napoleon. This can be seen in his policy toward the United States. The closing of Europe to English trade would have been disastrous for England only if it were accompanied by the closing of the immense American market. But Napoleon did not understand the necessity of obtaining the cooperation of the United States. Although this country competed with England (especially for the trade in colonial goods), he saw the American ships as agents smuggling English goods and took unjust and very harsh measures against them, such as the decrees of Bayonne and Rambouillet.[10] These blunders had unfortunate effects on American public opinion and consequently on the policy of the United States. There can be no doubt that they helped reduce the outrage felt by American opinion against Great Britain and that they favored the pro-English party. As a result, they delayed the United States decision to fight against England. When that war finally arrived, it came too late. The Russian campaign had just begun.

But there also were other "external" causes that worked to delay the application of the measures ordered by the Emperor, to reduce their effectiveness, and sometimes even to negate them completely. First of all, there was the corruption of the customs officials, diplomatic consuls, government officials, and soldiers of all ranks who were supposed to enforce the Blockade. It is undeniable that a large number, if not a majority, of the Emperor's agents showed themselves to be corrupt and tolerated or favored more or less openly the growth of smuggling, particularly in Holland and Germany. Because of the corruption of the French authorities, the Berlin decree remained a dead letter until Tilsit [July 1807] and English merchandise flooded into Europe in 1809 while Napoleon was preoccupied with the war against Austria. The baseness, one might even say the treason, of [such high Napoleonic officials as] a Brune, a Bernadotte, a Bourrienne, a Clérambault, and a throng of more obscure people, are perfectly clear; and the consequences were serious.

Less shocking (except when it was the case of members of the Emperor's family—a Louis of Holland or a Murat), but also very important as an explanation of certain weaknesses of the Blockade,

---

before the uprising in Spain, the Blockade was more or less enforced there and trade with England was small. The situation was similar in 1811 and early 1812. Although Alexander of Russia and Bernadotte of Sweden had abandoned the Blockade, their countries did not offer very large markets for English goods. Napoleon's errors of judgment cannot be denied.

[10][The Bayonne decree of April 17, 1808 declared that any vessels claiming United States registry would be considered sailing under false auspices and could be taken as lawful prizes. The Rambouillet decree of March 23, 1810 ordered any U.S. vessels that had been seized to be sold along with their cargoes.—Eds.]

was the attitude of vassal or allied governments. Our study has only confirmed the well-known fact that none of them (except Denmark) applied the Blockade willingly and that only Napoleon's threats forced them not to trade with England; but such threats never stopped them from maintaining a relaxed attitude toward smuggling and of tolerating it, or even secretly favoring it. Often this position simply reflected popular opinion, for public hostility to the Continental Blockade was an important reason for its failure. This is too well known to discuss in detail. We shall mention only that most businessmen on the Continent refused to abide by regulations that might ruin them by completely stopping their normal business relationships. On the other hand, violating the regulations would bring huge profits. The continental bourgeoisie as a whole remained attached to the more advanced capitalism of England. The masses, hurt by distress and unemployment, deprived of wares to which they were accustomed, took a big part in smuggling or at least profited from aiding and abetting it.

It would be only a slight exaggeration to see the Continental Blockade as the battle of one man or almost one (for there were still some faithful subordinates such as Collin de Sussy and Davout) against not only England but against a huge coalition of the greedy and treasonous plus their accomplices. Thus, one is surprised less by its ultimate failure than the successes that it won, especially because it involved a very strong cross-channel opponent.

Indeed, Napoleon's errors and the weaknesses of his system were not the only causes of the Blockade's failure. Much of the credit must go to Great Britain's ability to resist and particularly to the strength of her economic system. Here the key probably was the flexibility, adaptability, and entrepreneurial spirit of businessmen. [There were] many outstanding examples of these qualities that allowed Great Britain's foreign trade to adapt quickly to constantly changing political and military circumstances, . . . to reduce the effects of a closure of a traditional market by quickly profiting from possibilities that the opening of a new one might provide. In a frequently quoted letter, Napoleon complained that in 1809 French exporters had not known how to profit from his march on Vienna by flooding Austria with duty-free French goods.[11] Clearly, the British government never had to make such reproaches to its merchants; and in several cases (the taking of Buenos Aires in 1806, the opening of Brazil in 1808, or the shipping of goods to the Baltic region in 1810), it would have been well advised to urge more prudence and less speculation by them. Yet the

---

[11]Napoleon, *Correspondance*, 32 vols. (Paris, 1858–1869), XIX, 529, letter number 15874.

losses that the British businessmen's adventurous spirit caused them to suffer many times should not hide the essential fact: this attitude, that of a highly dynamic and self-confident capitalism, was one of the principal reasons for the Blockade's failure. To try to ruin the exports of a country whose businessmen and industrialists were motivated by this spirit reminds us too much of the myth of Sisyphus.

But many other factors also contributed to reinforce British resistance. First of all, she controlled the seas, which allowed exporters to take advantage of the slightest breach in the wall of prohibitions that surrounded the continent and to exploit distant markets with ease. Furthermore, the development of credit, a powerful branch of warfare, [must be] emphasized. Finally, the English economic system's productivity, greater than that of its adversary, allowed Great Britain to support without faltering the crushing financial burdens that she maintained until the end of the war.

These were, in our opinion, the principal reasons for the failure of the Continental Blockade. However, we should not consider it inevitable and that the outcome was determined in advance. If Napoleon had returned from Moscow as the victor, Great Britain would have faced a continent united and closed to her goods; at war with the United States, having as markets only her colonial empire, South America, and a part of southern Europe, her industrial production would have dropped to a quite insufficient pace; depression and unemployment would have reached alarming proportions. Who can insist that in these conditions her resistance would have been able to continue very long? Georges Lefebvre put it well: the Russian winter saved her. . . .[12]

The conclusions that emerge from this short analysis are perfectly clear: during the period of the Continental Blockade (and also during the years that immediately preceded it, more precisely, from 1803 on), the investments made in Great Britain went primarily into agriculture, transportation, maritime ports, and construction—not including the building program undertaken by the government for military purposes. Investment in industry, on the other hand, was relatively small, and it does not appear that industrial capacity increased sig-

---

[12]Georges Lefebvre, *Napoléon*, (4th ed.; Paris, 1953), 375–376. We cannot do better than to quote Lefebvre's language: "If he [Napoleon] had come back victorious from Russia, he surely would have applied his decrees with new vigor and new effectiveness, because his power would have been even more far-reaching than earlier. For his enemy [Great Britain], circumstances would not have been favorable. . . . The enterprise [Continental Blockade] had not been foolish, although in the last analysis its success depended on the *Grande Armée*, whose ruin in so brief a time no one could have predicted. It was not the "natural laws" of an unregulated economy that saved England; it was the Russian winter."

nificantly between 1803 and the end of the Napoleonic Wars. Confirming this impression are the production indexes of the major industries. We can state that only in the cotton industry and in metal refining was the level in the period around 1802 significantly exceeded during the 1809–1810 boom. On the other hand, in the other textile industries—especially wool and linen—and in hardware we find that production remained flat over the decade 1803–1813.[13]

In this situation, it is impossible not to conclude that the period of the Continental Blockade was characterized by a clear slackening of British economic expansion, especially by a reduction in industrial equipment. This conclusion completely agrees with the findings of Gayer, Rostow, and Schwartz for the entire period of the wars of the Revolution and the Empire. In fact, these authors estimate that the expansion, the "rate of growth" of the British economy, was much less rapid between 1793 and 1815 than for the period before the wars with France, especially when compared with the years after 1815 (which is the period showing the strongest growth of industrial capacity). Because of the huge loans issued by the state, which diverted capital from productive investment, as well as the "forced" export of capital caused by military expenditures abroad, domestic productive investment was relatively less important than before 1793 and after 1815. Moreover, these investments, influenced by the special wartime conditions, were diverted into certain channels. The conclusions of the Gayer team on the matter of this shift of investments are fully in accord with our own.[14] Except for the period 1798–1803, they estimate that investment in industry was of relatively minor importance. Because of the high prices grain brought throughout the wartime years, there was, on the contrary, a tremendous increase in agricultural investment to improve the output per acre and to expand cultivated land. Similarly, the rise in foreign trade resulted in very large sums invested in merchant shipbuilding and especially in port facilities.

The Gayer team admits, to be sure, that the quantity of investment was considerable in spite of these shifts, but insists that "on balance, the Napoleonic Wars turned investment away from the channels that would have been taken in a period of peace, and were, in fact, followed after 1815."[15] These authors judge that, if the wars had not occurred,

---

[13]Neither the exports of these industries, nor their indexes of output show any significant increase from 1802 to 1812. We point out again that the growth of British exports in this period can be explained largely by the export of cotton goods.

[14]Arthur D. Gayer, W. W. Rostow, and Anna Jacobson Schwartz, *The Growth and Fluctuation of the British Economy, 1790–1850*, 2 vols. (Oxford, 1953), II, 535, 623–624, 646–649.

[15]Ibid., II, 648.

the economic expansion would have been more rapid (and oriented differently) and technical progress would have speeded up. Therefore, they reject the traditional view that from 1793 to 1815 the war and the inflation that accompanied it accelerated the British economy's growth. On the contrary, it is clear to them that these factors slowed down, held back, and distorted the economy. We agree completely with this conclusion, which is especially accurate for the period of the Continental Blockade. The effect of the Blockade on economic expansion was therefore of the same nature as that of the war for the entire period from 1793 to 1815. In addition, because the dislocations and tensions brought by the war to the British economy were raised to their highest pitch during the Blockade, for it represented the paroxysm of the entire period of the French Wars, the Blockade tended to accentuate and worsen the effects of the war. Consequently, the years from 1806 to 1812 were those where the slowdown of the economic expansion was most noticeable.

The social effects of the Blockade were similar to those of the wartime period generally. Just as the working class for the most part bore the cost of the wars against France, so also, thanks to its labor, suffering, and distress, the victory over the Continental Blockade was achieved. But the human cost was very high, not only in the short term, but also for the succeeding generation. The burden of the enormous public debt incurred during the war weighed for a long time on the shoulders of the workers and consumers. The whole country had been mortgaged for the benefit of the new class of government bond holders, the fundholders, in whose favor an immense transfer of national income was arranged. Therefore, the wars and the Blockade seriously aggravated the social problems raised by the Industrial Revolution.

These observations should not lead us to forget that during the entire period of the war, and even during the Blockade, the British economy continued to advance, modernize, and develop. This was a remarkable phenomenon considering the difficult tests, tensions, and dislocations that this economy endured and was indisputable proof of its strength and flexibility. Therefore, it comes as no surprise that contemporaries were misled and that the economic advance of Great Britain in the midst of a desperate war against a powerful and implacable enemy filled them with pride and confidence.

In addition, there can be no doubt that in 1815 England's economic advance over her continental rivals, especially France, was much greater than in 1793. If the war and the Continental Blockade had slowed down England's development, their effects on the economies of the other European countries had been much worse.[16] Such was the paradoxical result of the economic war the Convention had begun against England in 1793, which Napoleon had relentlessly continued for seven years, and which led him to make so many fatal decisions. British capitalism emerged from the test badly bruised, but fundamentally sound and more dynamic than ever. For the next century it would dominate the world.

[16]This hypothesis may be challenged. We are not trying to deny that the economy of the continent made significant progress from 1800 to 1810. But in the French case we judge that this progress worked only to catch up from the consequences of the economic collapse suffered during the revolutionary period. In addition, the crisis of 1810–1811, continued by the depression of 1812–1813, was a major step backward for the entire economy of the continent. We think the wars and the Blockade as a whole did not accelerate England's economic growth, as has often been claimed, but slowed down that of the countries of the continent more than her own.

8
NATIONALISM AND THE DESTRUCTION OF THE NAPOLEONIC EMPIRE

Did nationalism cause the collapse of Napoleon's vast Empire from 1808 to 1813 and did Europe benefit from that collapse? Introductory remarks by Robert B. Holtman help explain the meaning and history of modern nationalism. He thinks that, except perhaps for Great Britain, nationalistic sentiment appeared largely after 1789, when people began to feel more solidarity because of their common language, customs, and values than because of a common religion and social group. The French people led the way, but others—often in reaction to Napoleonic imperialism—developed their own spirit of nationalism.

We shall concentrate on the rise and effects of nationalism during the brief years of the Napoleonic Empire. Rafael Altamira and Heinrich von Treitschke present nationalism as the main cause for the anti-Napoleonic uprisings in Spain in 1808 and Prussia in 1813 that helped topple the Empire. Sympathetic to these uprisings, they stress that people from all walks of life courageously united to defeat the hated foreigners. Robert B. Holtman and Hajo Holborn, on the other hand, consider that nationalistic enthusiasm only partly explains these uprisings and that the Spanish and Prussians had other motives as well. Some felt loyal to a dynastic house and to a common religion, others to provincial leaders among the clergy and aristocrats. Also, regular Spanish and Prussian army troops followed their commanders' orders.

When studying the destruction of the Empire as a whole, Owen Connelly agrees with Holtman and Holborn that one should not ignore that the masses often supported the anti-Napoleonic uprisings in order to maintain their traditional attachment to Crown and Church. But whereas Holtman and Holborn limit themselves to this area of disagreement with nationalistic historians, Connelly goes further. He puts forward a defense of the French Empire, explaining that many of those fighting Napoleon did not follow their rational interests and that the Empire brought invaluable benefits which were later ignored by partisans of a Europe of nation-states. Connelly denies that Napoleon exploited the economies of his satellite kingdoms; instead, Connelly sees Napoleon as a liberal benefactor, encouraging more efficient administration and establishing constitutions, modernized law codes, and religious toleration.

Can these disagreements among historians be resolved? When discussing the motivations of the rebels, should we accept what the people themselves say caused them to revolt? Should we search for unexpressed or subconscious motivations? Ought we to stress social, economic, political, or religious explanations? Furthermore, what standards should be used to judge the Napoleonic Empire: the values of the old order, those of the French Revolution, or those of the nationalistic nineteenth century? Is it better to be governed by a ruler of the same religion as the population and by a dynasty which has been in control for generations? Or by someone who promotes order, reform, equality, and liberty even if that person is a foreigner? Or is it more important that the ruler share the people's language and customs?

Robert B. Holtman (1914–) received his Ph.D. from the University of Wisconsin and taught at Louisiana State University for most of his academic career until his retirement. He is the author of Napoleonic Propaganda *(1950) and* The Napoleonic Revolution *(1967), works that present a balanced judgment of Napoleon's achievements and limitations.*

AN INTRODUCTION
Robert B. Holtman

The dominant political force of the 19th and 20th centuries has unquestionably been nationalism. It has led to a desire for national states by people within heterogeneous empires, by nationalities divided into numerous small states, and by subject colonial peoples. To a large extent the nationalism which has been so important for the last century and a half is an outgrowth of the Napoleonic period.

Nationalism had been mentioned as far back as the end of the Middle Ages. Prior to the French Revolution, however, the term was applied to what we today think of as patriotism, for then, with the possible exception of Great Britain, there were states rather than nations. This patriotism was in general linked with loyalty to the monarch, and it admitted no religious differences. The idea of nationalism seemed to be connected with popular sovereignty and civil equality; the rulers and aristocrats in power during the *ancien régime* in any country therefore naturally opposed it. One student of nationalism says it is inconceivable without preceding ideas of popular sovereignty, and without a revision of classes and castes. Only after subjects became citizens, as in the French Revolution, could modern nationalism arise.

Several characteristics differentiated the new nationalism from the older patriotism. The most important were a feeling of mutual relationship between the government and the governed, and a feeling of community among the governed themselves. This feeling meant a desire to have a sovereign state which would include all like-minded people. (Emphasis should be placed upon the "all"; earlier nationalism or patriotism influenced only the few.) The nation needed features such as language and institutions distinguishing it from other similar groups. The strongest single tie of nationalism was language, with

---

From Robert B. Holtman, *The Napoleonic Revolution* (Baton Rouge: Louisiana State University Press, 1981), pp. 179–185. Reprinted by permission of the publisher. Copyright © 1967.

all its cultural derivatives, such as literature. But other factors might also enter the picture: historical tradition, geographical contiguity, political entity, religion. The new nationalism also differed from the old in that it might embrace people of more than one religion. A common sense of right and wrong was likewise important.

Nationalism is not a natural phenomenon but a cultivated sentiment which is the product of historical factors. The nation or nationality comes first, then the theory. Nationalism also demands that loyalty to the nation must take precedence over any other loyalty— that is why it can accept people of varying religious beliefs. Members of the same nation are, in common with their fellows, ready to make sacrifices, and are more willing to co-operate with one another than with other people. At the same time, of course, there is distrust of the foreigner. In Germany the poet and patriotic pamphleteer Ernst Moritz Arndt demanded the growth of a "general love among Germans" and "hatred against the crafty foreigners."

The wars of the French Revolution and Napoleon were responsible for gradually substituting nationalism for both the cosmopolitanism of the intellectuals of the Enlightenment and the parochialism of the unlettered. The threat of military invasion usually promotes social solidarity. The French, both because they were the revolutionaries and because they were the object of attack by other countries, were the first to develop a feeling of nationalism. Even before he came to power, and very effectively after his accession, Bonaparte favored this evolution. He bolstered French nationalism by centralization of activities, military service, wars—and by victories in those wars.

In his propaganda Napoleon constantly referred to France as the "great nation," rather than as the "great country." Yet he was not a nationalist for the sake of nationalism; he looked on this new force primarily as something that would foster his own cause, first by overcoming factionalism within France. In order for France to remain great, it would, of course, need a united front of its rulers and ruled; thus the role of nationalism became entwined with that of the dynasty itself. Early in the Consulate he wrote,

> I want you all to rally round the mass of the people. The simple title of French citizen is worth far more than that of *royaliste, clichien, jacobin, feuillant*, or any of those thousand and one denominations which have sprung, during the past ten years, from the spirit of faction, and which are hurling the nation into an abyss from which the time has at last come to rescue it, once and for all. This is the aim of all my efforts.

Napoleon further wanted to build up the French nation so as to use it to extend his own control, aided by the beneficent influence of Revolutionary ideas. The Frenchman would of course share Napoleon's glory for the revolutionary transformation of Europe, a transformation involving such reforms as freeing peasants, establishing equality before the law, providing freedom of conscience and a uniform code, unifying the domestic market, and abolishing feudal and provincial autonomies and privileges.

On St. Helena Napoleon said, "There are in Europe more than 30 million French, 15 million Spanish, 15 million Italians, and 30 million Germans. I would have wished to make each of these peoples a single united body." This wish was pure fiction—or legend. In actuality, Napoleon did not recognize non-French nationalism or intend it to be on a par with that of France. In this realm, as in so many others, he was the classicist, the believer in one universal standard. Since France was his base, the standard would be French interests and French nationalism.

> I should like a person of French extraction, even though of the tenth generation, still to find himself a Frenchman. . . . I want to raise the glory of the French name so high that it becomes the envy of all nations. I should like to see the day when, with the help of divine guidance, a Frenchman travelling throughout Europe could always find himself at home.[1]

Thus for France the national ideal was not to be contained within its borders.

Napoleon's attitude toward non-French nationalism resulted in part from his misunderstanding and underestimating it. To him the spirit of nationalism, when it occurred abroad, seemed far less strong, and therefore less dangerous, than religious or political feelings and beliefs. Napoleon thought that people could be won away from national allegiance and united in a great international state.[2] It therefore did not greatly matter to him that nationalism was incompatible with the imperialism he was advocating, and the universal empire of which he dreamed. Especially after 1810 the Napoleonic empire was the negation of nationality outside France. It was in that year that he wrote Eugene:

> My principle is *France first*. . . . It would be short-sighted not to recognize that Italy owes her independence to France—that it was won by French blood and French victories, that it must not be misused. . . . Make your motto too—*France first*.

That later generations of Frenchmen, who claimed Napoleon was merely defending their natural frontiers, should have considered him

---

[1]Quoted in Bernard Schwartz (ed.), *The Code Napoleon and the Common Law World.* New York: New York University Press, 1956, p. 107.
[2]But this international state by conquest would differ greatly from the cosmopolitanism of the Enlightenment, for France would hold first rank.

a nationalist is not surprising. What is surprising is that for half a century or more after his fall liberals in Italy, Poland, Belgium, and even in western and southern Germany and in Spain, tended to forget his desire for domination and empire and to look on him as the defender of nationalities against reactionary kings.

And he did bring to life or resurrect German, Italian, Polish, Southern Slav, and Spanish nationalism. Of these, only two proved to be advantageous to him.

The first was Italian nationalism, to which Napoleon made concessions. He wanted it to be at the *juste milieu*, sufficiently strong to serve as a support against the *ancien régime* rulers, but not powerful enough to threaten his own plans. In addition to the reforms he usually introduced in subject areas, he gave the Italians a flag and an army. Army officers returned from the wars nationalistic minded. The mere fact that he reduced the number of states on the peninsula to three, including the part incorporated into France,[3] tended to induce nationalistic feelings and pride on the part of the Italians. This was more particularly true because one of those parts was titled the Italian Republic from 1802 to 1805 and the Kingdom of Italy thereafter. Napoleon encouraged the exclusive use of the Tuscan dialect, the literary language of Italy. But his image as a promoter of Italian nationalism was dimmed by other actions, such as awarding Italian principalities to his marshals and other high French officials or making such annexations to France as that of Parma in 1806, Tuscany in 1808, and the Papal States in 1809. Much of the later Italian national sentiment was a reaction against rather than a continuation of the Napoleonic regime.

The other people whose nationalistic impulses served Napoleon was the Poles, who had been divided before and during the French Revolution among their neighbors, Russia, Prussia, and Austria. Napoleon's actions led the Poles to hope, and Tsar Alexander of Russia to fear, that he was going to establish a Kingdom of Poland. . . . The Poles remained loyal followers of Napoleon to the end of his reign. Yet at the same time that he led the Poles to believe their support of him would be rewarded at some unspecified future date, Napoleon was very careful never to promise them a kingdom.

In a third area, the engendered nationalism proved to be neither beneficial nor detrimental to Napoleon. This was the case in the Illyrian provinces, which were formed from the Dalmatian holdings taken away from Austria after the campaigns of 1805 and 1809. For the first time since the 14th century various Southern Slav peoples were grouped together. Croatian and Slovenian received the status of

---

[3][The other two were the Kingdom of Italy and the Kingdom of Naples.—Eds.]

official languages. From such facts as these sprang the Southern Slav nationalist movement of the 19th and 20th centuries that brought about the formation of Yugoslavia following World War I and Titoism after World War II.

Nationalism that arose elsewhere, though springing partly from the history of the areas and partly from imitation of France, came mainly as a reaction to Napoleon's domination. As Gneisenau, later the famous reformer of the Prussian army, stated after the crushing defeat of Jena:

> The Revolution has set in action the national energy of the entire French people . . . thereby abolishing the former relationship of the states to one another and the balance of power. If the other states wish to re-establish this balance, they must open and use these resources. They must take over the results of the Revolution and so gain the double advantage of being able to place their entire national energies in opposition to the enemy.[4]

Even though it opposed him, and its development surprised him, Napoleon must be given credit—or blame—for the arousing of national consciousness in such places as Germany and Spain. In the words of Ernest Lavisse, "It is the Revolution he serves, in spite of himself and against himself, when, oppressing Europe because such is his pleasure, he awakens the soul of the Spanish and German peoples." His invasion of Russia undoubtedly increased national solidarity there also.

[4]Quoted in Boyd Shafer, *Nationalism: Myth and Reality*. New York: Harcourt, Brace, 1955, p. 138.

Rafael Altamira (1866–1951) was born in Alicante, Spain, and studied at the universities of Valencia and Madrid. Trained as a lawyer, he held various posts during a long lifetime. These included serving as an editor of a Republican newspaper, secretary of Spain's National Pedagogic Museum, Director-General of Spanish elementary education, a senator in the Spanish legislature, a judge in the Permanent Court of International Justice at The Hague, and a professor of history at Oviedo and Madrid. He has written novels, literary criticism, journalism, and works on teaching, but he is best known as a historian of Spain and Latin America. Reacting against his country's defeat by the United States in 1898, he attempted to restore Spanish pride in their civilization and colonial past with a series of informative works based on considerable research.

THE SPANISH UPRISING: A PATRIOTIC REVOLT

Rafael Altamira

At the Spanish Court in the year 1801 the animosity between Manuel Godoy and the Crown Prince Ferdinand, Charles IV's eldest son, was an open secret. It was rooted in mutual distrust and ambition for power and for influence with the Throne. (Ferdinand was the son of King Charles IV and Queen María Luisa; Godoy was the King's favorite and the Queen's lover.) Rivalry between Crown Prince and Minister was intensified by Ferdinand's marriage to María Antonia, Princess of Naples, an alliance which Godoy had opposed. After her marriage, the new Crown Princess, whose influence over her husband was always great, was the center of the political opposition to Godoy, which was composed of the latter's critics and his personal enemies. This group was the origin of the Fernandista party—the party of Ferdinand—which from the first had the support of Napoleon who not only held Godoy in contempt but was apprehensive about his influence over the King and Queen.

In 1805, the moral effect of [the British victory at] Trafalgar was to arouse the spirit of Spain and cause Godoy to change his policy; that is, to oppose Napoleon, who in 1804 had proclaimed himself Emperor

From Raphael Altamira, *A History of Spain: From the Beginnings to the Present Day*, trans. by Muna Lee (New York: D. Van Nostrand Co., 1949), pp. 524–527, 529, 531–534. Reprinted by permission of Wadsworth, Inc. This translation is from the *Manual de historia de España* (2nd ed.; Buenos Aires: Editorial sudamericana, 1946).

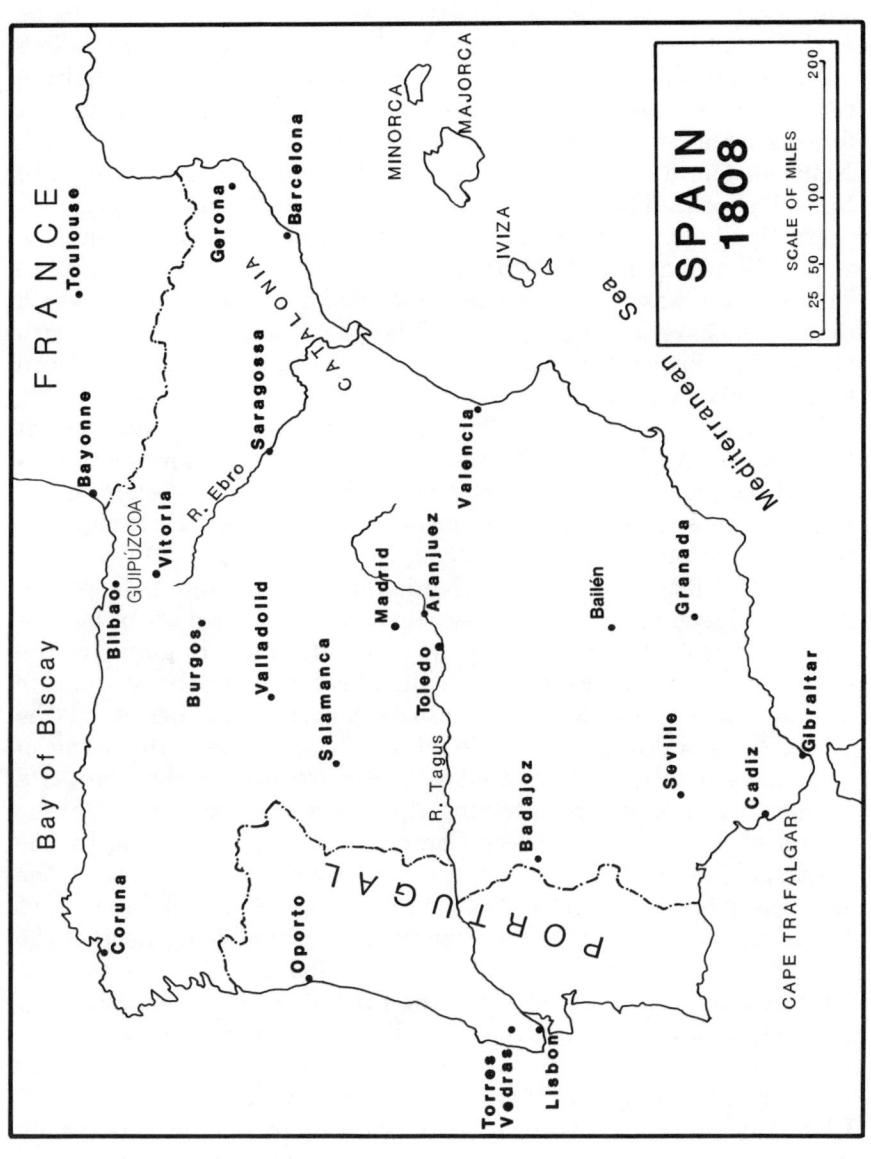

of France. Though Godoy started secret negotiations with the English Government (October, 1806), the highly important Napoleonic victory at Jena (October 14, 1806) caused him once again to become subservient to Napoleon. The latter, without permitting it to be evident that he was aware of the political instability of Charles IV's favorite, had already decided upon Charles' overthrow, and with him, that of the Bourbon monarchy of Spain. The natural point of support for such a plan, if it were to succeed, was the Fernandista party, which Napoleon found very receptive. In July 1807, in fact, Prince Ferdinand himself appeared before the Emperor to request the latter's "paternal protection" and permission to marry a princess of the Bonaparte family. (Ferdinand's wife María Antonia had died the previous year.) This request was formalized in a letter of October 11, 1807, which made transparent allusion to the Queen's adulterous relations with Godoy. The Prince thus sacrificed to rancor and ambition the good name of his own mother.

Not suspecting this accord between Napoleon and his enemies at home, Godoy made every effort to curry favor with the former. Consequently, he agreed to send 1500 Spanish soldiers to the aid of the French troops in Germany; and he persuaded Charles IV to sign two new conventions (at Fontainebleau, November 27, 1806) which involved the fate of the Spanish monarchy even more deeply in Napoleonic schemes. One of these conventions decided upon the conquest of Portugal (which was always inclined to favor England) by the combined armies of France and Spain. Portuguese territory after the conquest was to be carved into three parts, from which would be formed a new kingdom for Charles IV's son-in-law, the King of Etruria; a principality for Godoy; and a territory to be held as a bargaining reserve and exchanged, if possible, for Gibraltar, the Island of Trinidad, and other Spanish territories captured by the English. The preparations for military cooperation began with the entry into Spain of a strong French army under General Junot, days before the signing of the conventions at Fontainebleau. Each of the two rival parties at the Spanish Court (Godoy's followers and the Fernandistas) saw in those incoming French troops an effective ally against the other. Neither Godoy nor Ferdinand, nor the henchmen of either, had the slightest inkling of the truth: that Napoleon's forces would be utilized not only against Portugal but also against Spain. Blissfully unaware, both parties continued to pin their hopes on Napoleon and to confide their plans to him, while they kept up the bitter struggle with each other. One of its episodes in 1807 was Ferdinand's conspiracy against Godoy ("the plot of the Escorial") and, apparently, against Charles IV himself; which proved to be the first step along the path that led to the Crown Prince's speedy imprisonment and trial. The intervention of Napoleon, and possibly that of the Queen, caused the affair to end in a verdict of Not Guilty (January 1808). While this was going on, one French army after another continued to pour into Spain. The allied Franco-Spanish forces, commanded by Junot, invaded Portugal, capturing Lisbon on November 30, 1808. Meanwhile the Portuguese royal family and many nobles and persons of importance embarked on English ships for Brazil.

MARCH 19 AND ITS RESULTS

Finally, the Spanish public began to worry about the movements of the French troops who under one pretext or another were seizing the fortified towns of northern Spain from Guipúzcoa to Catalonia. Godoy himself, at last coming to see Napoleon's intrigues for what they were, proposed to the Royal Council that it demand the withdrawal of French military forces and declare war on France. But the Council and the King, always timorous when it was a question of opposing Napoleon, rejected Godoy's suggestion. The latter thereupon asked to be relieved of his post as Minister, but this request also was denied.

Disillusionment speedily became general when the Spanish Ambassador at Paris informed Madrid of a new demand by Napoleon. The Emperor was now asking that he be ceded certain Spanish provinces in north Spain down to the Ebro, or that his title to the whole of Portugal be recognized, together with concession of a military road across Spain from Irún to that country. The only way out of the difficulty which occurred to Charles IV (it was advised by Godoy and the Ambassador) was to set out for the south of Spain with the intention of following the example of the Portuguese royal family and embarking for America. With that purpose in view, the King and Queen hastened to Aranjuez, as the first stage of their journey; but they got no further. On the night of March 17, 1808 an insurrection broke out there, organized and led by the Fernandista party. The consequences were the downfall, imprisonment, and forced retirement of Godoy on March 18, and abdication of the throne by Charles IV on March 19. Rejoicing became general throughout Spain as the news spread. This was partly because of relief that the extremely unpopular Godoy was now out of the picture, and partly because of a confident expectation that the new broom of King Ferdinand would sweep clean. But public opinion on this point failed to take into account Napoleon's determination, although, as we have said, many Spaniards were increasingly suspicious of the intentions of the French troops.

It would have simplified matters for Napoleon if the royal family had carried out their project of sailing for America. When that plan fell through, Napoleon, while ordering French forces under General Murat to occupy Madrid, instructed them to maintain a prudent reserve with regard to recognizing the new King. Charles IV himself played into Napoleon's hands by entering upon negotiations with Murat, withdrawing his abdication of March 19, and humbly seeking Napoleon's support. The latter, by threats and by deceptions, succeeded in getting the new King Ferdinand VII to leave Madrid. The pretext was that Ferdinand was to meet the Emperor, who sent word that he greatly desired to confer with Ferdinand and was on his way to Spain for that purpose. That this was untrue became clear as soon as Ferdinand and his entourage arrived at Vitoria, the appointed meeting place, only to be informed that Napoleon was not there but awaited them at Bayonne, on French territory. Although the citizens of Vitoria clamored against Ferdinand's leaving Spain for any such purpose, and even cut the traces of the horses drawing the royal coach, the advice of the Ministerial favorite, the canon Escóiquiz, as well as his own trusting nature, impelled Ferdinand to continue the journey. On April 20 he reached Bayonne, and ten days later his royal parents arrived there also. There Napoleon obtained Ferdinand's abdication of the Crown in favor of Charles IV; and immediately thereafter, Charles IV's abdication in favor of Napoleon was obtained also (the Treaty of May 5) on two conditions: first, that the integrity and independence of the Kingdom of Spain should be maintained, with whatever Prince Napoleon should decide to name as its ruler (in his own mind he had already fixed on his brother Joseph Bonaparte, then King of Naples); and second, that the Catholic religion should be respected as the only religion in Spain. By a further treaty (May 10) Ferdinand, in exchange for preservation of his rank as Prince dignitary of the French Empire and an annual income of one million francs in addition to some territorial possessions, agreed to the cession of the Crown made by his father to Napoleon.

MAY 2 AND THE WAR OF INDEPENDENCE

While these humiliating scenes were taking place at Bayonne, there was a reaction in Spain upon which Napoleon had not counted. Popular opinion, supported by the ardent patriotism of some officers of the Spanish army, not so blind to the facts as the courtiers were, viewed with alarm increasing momentarily the successive departure from Madrid of the members of the royal family. They witnessed at the same time the conduct of French military leaders who were conducting themselves in the Spanish capital as though they were in a vanquished country. The growing resentment against all this was augmented by sight of the passiveness with which Spanish officials permitted Napoleon's intentions to be carried out. Tension increased at Madrid and at Toledo when news arrived of Charles IV's protest against the abdication forced upon him at Aranjuez and of Napoleon's refusal to recognize Ferdinand as King of Spain. Several riots and insurrections at Toledo, Burgos, and other cities soon showed that public indignation was running high. The decisive outbreak occurred at Madrid on May 2, 1808, with departure of the little Prince Francisco de Paula (aged thirteen) from the Palace to journey to Bayonne in company of Prince Don Antonio, chairman of the Junta of Government appointed by Ferdinand on leaving Madrid. The crowd that had gathered in the Plaza de Oriente to see this last member of the royal family take leave waited with growing excitement. This increased when word came that at the last moment the young Prince, bursting into tears, had refused to depart from the Palace and Madrid. The smouldering wrath of the people needed only this to touch off the flame. The crowd set upon one of Murat's aides and cut the leather thongs of the coaches. Such was the seemingly slight circumstance that sparked the beginning of the uprising of the Spanish people against Napoleon.

During that same day, May 2, a heroic struggle was staged in Madrid by the populace, who had few weapons, no organization, and only the aid of some artillery and infantry soldiers and officers (Captains Velarde and Daoiz, Lieutenant Ruiz, and others) against the numerous and well-equipped forces of the French garrison. News of this uprising and of the executions that followed (immortalized in Goya's art) caused the revolution of the whole of Spain and initiated the War of Independence: the first instance of a nation's daring to do such a thing as oppose Napoleon's power and prestige though it had no king and no officials of government and no army, since Spanish armed forces were for the time being immobilized by order of the Junta representing Ferdinand VII.

Therewith began a new era in the history of Spain. That war was also one of the first manifestations in Europe of the political movement of nationalities which was to characterize the nineteenth century. The extraordinary vigor and scope of Spanish nationalism, and the unique example that it afforded, in the political life of the period, of a collective determination pursuing its own course, with neither monarch nor political leader to inspire and direct it, claimed the immediate attention of the world. A German patriot, the philospher Fichte, who was at the time, by his *Addresses to the German Nation* instilling into the youth of his country a patriotic sentiment of rebellion against Napoleon's imperialism, pointed out as an example for them to follow the impassioned resistance of Spain to the impositions of a war-lord. . . .

THE WAR OF INDEPENDENCE

The Spanish War of Independence lasted six years, from 1808 to 1814, and in itself was a great surprise to Napoleon. Like the rest of Europe, he had believed that the only opposition to him in Spain would come from the courtiers and the army. Through his own dealings with Godoy and Ferdinand VII, he had learned to despise the former. With regard to the army, he knew his ground and felt no anxiety. But to his astonishment, he found himself confronted by a nation in arms. Nothing in his experience had taught him how to measure such a force as that. Nor did he realize that this uprising of the Spanish people expressed not merely the idealistic but the practical determination of a country that would not tolerate having an alien power decide its fate, but was resolved to settle its own destiny. Rejection of the patrimonial monarchy stirred underneath that determination, although many Spaniards were not yet thinking about this consequence implicit in their act of rebellion against Napoleon and against the abdications at Bayonne. On the contrary, adherence to the patrimonial theory was what caused some army officers who were loyal to the principle of traditional monarchy to join the group of King Joseph Bonaparte's adherents; but the mass of the Spanish people would have no part in such hidebound royalism. And so the people on their own initiative fought the French armies, with no king nor any other national leader to be their guide and example; but fired by those two mighty determinants in mass psychology: love of freedom and love of country. These two sentiments were translated at the moment into hatred for Napoleon the Emperor who had deceived them and disposed of the Crown of Spain arbitrarily without regard for the opinion of the country, and into love and hope for Ferdinand VII their King whom they longed and expected to see restored to his throne. It was this devotion, very general among Spaniards at that time, that caused the people to call Ferdinand "*el Deseado,*" the Desired. And while the people of Spain poured out their blood to maintain the independence of Spanish earth and the Spanish throne, Ferdinand himself was adulating Napoleon and congratulating him on his victories in Spain.

Ignorant of that fact, the Spanish nation with intrepid confidence, defying Napoleon's power and military genius, kept on fighting; at first, alone and unaided; later (1809) with the assistance of English troops that came to join forces on the Peninsula against the Emperor. All Spaniards—merchants, laborers, artisans, students, physicians, lawyers, some members of the nobility, priests, some of the parish clergy, and many women—snatched up what arms they could lay hand on, and began fighting; some in ranks of the regular army, which also rose in rebellion, and others in independent or guerrilla groups, and also in beleaguered cities, as happened during the sieges of Saragossa and Gerona. A moving example of patriotism was the impassioned violence with which the Spanish troops that had been sent to Germany years before, now confined under very strict French vigilance on the islands of Langeland and Fionia and on the peninsula of Jutland, broke through the blockade hemming them in and made their way back to Spain to join the fighting forces. Led by the Marquis of Romana, 9,000 men managed to sail to Sweden and thence to Spain, where they arrived October 9, 1808. The only exceptions to this wellnigh universal patriotism of the Spanish people were the group of Spanish radicals (called the *afrancesados*, or "Frenchified Spaniards") . . . and the Catalán aristocrats, clergy, and bourgeoisie, who in the number of some 40,000 emigrated to Mallorca [Majorca], thereby moving out of range of the sacrifices that the war entailed.

With that improvised fighting force—and before any help came from England—the Spaniards inflicted on Napoleon's troops their two first defeats: the battle of Bailén, July 19, 1808, and the battle of Bruch in Catalonia in the same year. The French Emperor had to come to Spain in person to direct the fighting and repair the disaster. During the six years of warfare, the Spaniards continued to show great endurance and high courage. The two sieges of Saragossa (1808 and 1809) and the siege of Gerona (1809), exemplifying the heroism of a whole people, amazed and confounded the French themselves, just as the siege of Numantia had astonished the Romans. In other countries dominated by Napoleon where also the spirit of independence was stirring, the valiant action of the Spaniards was esteemed at its just value as the dynamic example of a people who fought to establish the right of nations to rule themselves.

For biographical information on Robert B. Holtman, see the earlier selection by him in this chapter.

MIXED MOTIVES FOR SPAIN'S REVOLT

Robert B. Holtman

There is no questioning the national motivation in the Spaniards' fight against Napoleon, but one must be careful not to exaggerate it. The tendency to do so frequently stems directly or indirectly from Madame de Staël, who wrote that in Spain Napoleon "was faced with national resistance, the only kind he could not deal with by diplomacy or bribes. . . . He never understood that a war might be a crusade. . . . He never reckoned with the one power that no arms could overcome—the enthusiasm of a whole people."

Some facts do back up this interpretation. Madrid revolted against the French on May 2, 1808. Although Murat quickly and severely suppressed the uprising, May 2 still remains a Spanish national holiday. Guerrilla resistance increased steadily. Though there were in Spain no theoretical nationalist writings, there was an actual nationalist rebellion, or war for independence, against Bonapartist control. Here for the first time Napoleon seemed to be fighting a people rather than rulers.

This traditional interpretation of the Spanish fighting, though accurate to a point, overlooks several important factors. Dynastic loyalty in Spain was far stronger than in France. The religious element also played a large role, for the peasants were greatly influenced by their parish priests, and it must be remembered that Napoleon at the time was having difficulty with the Pope. The guerrillas were at least as imbued with local patriotism for their province or locality as they were with a feeling of being Spanish.

The uprising was a good deal less spontaneous than Madame de Staël would make it appear. The revolt against Napoleon did not start immediately, and it began in those provinces of Spain which the French did not invade. The nobility and clergy in these areas explained to the masses why they had to be called to arms because of what was taking place elsewhere. These dominant classes unquestionably turned patriotic feeling to their own special interests; the

---

From Robert B. Holtman, *The Napoleonic Revolution* (Baton Rouge: Louisiana State University Press, 1981), pp. 185–186. Reprinted by permission of the publisher. Copyright © 1967.

people were far from unanimous in their answer to their call. The role of the regular army was considerable. The defeat of General Pierre Dupont at Bailén, which caused a sensation throughout Europe because it showed the French were not invincible, was the work of Spanish regulars, not of a popular uprising. If it had not been for Wellington's forces, the Spanish guerrilla resistance would in all probability eventually have collapsed.

Still another feature was the fact that the peasants were fighting for their own food, for the French were in the habit of living off the countryside, requisitioning or seizing supplies from the peasants. This aspect of the fighting naturally grew more important as the campaign became more drawn out.

Heinrich von Treitschke (1834–1896) was born in Dresden, the son of a Saxon military official. He became a professor and writer on history and politics. A fiery nationalist, he initially favored a united Germany under a parliamentary government; but when that choice proved unrealistic, he enthusiastically supported an authoritarian Germany led by the Hohenzollern ruling family of Prussia. His almost total deafness prevented him from being an effective politician for this cause, but he spread the message in his lectures and in his major work, Deutsche Geschichte im 19. Jahrhundert *(5 vols.; 1879–1889), translated as* Treitschke's History of Germany in the Nineteenth Century.

THE GERMAN UPRISING: PRUSSIA IN ARMS

Heinrich von Treitschke

War was declared [between Prussia and France on March 16, 1813]. On the following day Frederick William III signed the Landwehr Law and the *Appeal to my People*. This was the return to truth and to open dealing, as Schleiermacher joyfully declared in a sermon. The people breathed once more, since now all doubt was over and the undue trial of their patience and their obedience was at an end. Never before had an absolute monarch spoken thus to his people. A breath of freedom, such as that which of old had animated the Æschylean warsongs of the Hellenes, breathes through the straightforward and impressive words which the talented [Prussian official] Hippel had written in a good hour. With cordial confidence the king appealed to his Brandenburgers, Prussians, Silesians, Pomeranians, and Lithuanians, speaking to each separately by their ancient tribal name and summoning them to the holy war: "There is no other way, and we must either secure an honourable peace or go down gloriously to destruction. This latter even you will go confidently to meet, for the Prussians and the Germans cannot live without honour!" Now did the people arise, the Prussians great in arms, the people of the fights with the Slavs, of the battles with the Swedes, the fighters of the Seven Years' War, and there happened what had happened in the case of that hero of the Teutonic saga whose wrath flamed up so highly at the sight of

From Heinrich von Treitschke, *Treitschke's History of Germany in the Nineteenth Century*, trans. by Eden and Cedar Paul, 7 vols. (New York: McBride, Nast & Co., 1915–1919), II: pp. 505–508, 511.

his fetters that the chains were molten. There was no doubt or hesitation, no deliberation concerning the overpowering strength of the enemy. All thought like [the German philosopher] Fichte: "It is not for us to conquer or to die, but simply to conquer!" [The Prussian general] Scharnhorst wrote: "However often Napoleon may win battles, the whole situation of the war is such that in this campaign we cannot fail to conquer." The appeal of February 3rd [by Frederick William] had already produced results which no one except Scharnhorst had regarded as possible. It was the proudest moment of his life when in Breslau he led the king to the window and showed him the rejoicing crowds of volunteers, how in picturesque medley, on foot, on horseback, in carriages, an endless train, they pressed onwards towards the ancient gabled houses of the Ring. Tears stood in the king's eyes. Faithfully and conscientiously had he discharged his difficult duty in this long time of trouble, and often had his judgment been a sounder one than that of the war party; what he had lacked was a belief in the sacrificing powers of his Prussians, but this he was now to recover.

Since May 17th the general masses of the population had also been entering the army. The competitive zeal of the various estates rendered possible the greatest yield of soldiers ever known in the history of civilised nations. The impoverished little country increased the 46,000 men of the old army of the line by 95,000 recruits, furnishing in addition more than 10,000 voluntary yagers [also spelled Jägers] and 120,000 men of the Landwehr [national guard], comprising 271,000 men in all. This was one soldier for every seventeen inhabitants, incomparably more than France had formerly produced under the pressure of the Reign of Terror. All was done in a single summer, to say nothing of the strong reinforcements which were subsequently sent to the army. It need hardly be said that the retired officers at once pressed forward in order to restore the honour of the old flag. As soon as General Oppen, at his home in the Mark, heard of the approach of the army of the fatherland, he took down his old sabre from the wall and, like a knight of the old days of the Wendish wars, rode in hot haste with a single squire to join Bülow, his ancient companion-in-arms. Bülow smilingly presented to his officers the Herculean man with the flashing eyes, saying, "This is one who understands how to cut the enemy down," and gave him command of the cavalry. Oppen, once he was at work again, remained happily engaged, never wearying of war, until the entry into Paris. Next to the old soldiers, it was the educated youth who grasped most vividly the seriousness of the time. There glowed in them an enthusiastic yearning for the free and only German fatherland. Not a single student who could wield a weapon remained at home. Professor Steffens left his professorial chair, after an enthusiastic recommendation to his audience to present themselves on the recruiting ground of the yager volunteers. The king also summoned the lost provinces to the colours, saying, "You are no longer bound by an enforced oath from the day when I summon my loyal people to take up arms." Although a mass uprising was as yet out of the question in those unhappy territories, the East Frisians and the Markers at the University of Göttingen hastened to the Prussian regiments; so also did all the students from loyal Halle, which had not forgotten under Westphalian rule its memories of the Old Dessauer and of the good Prussian days. The same spirit animated the schools. From the gymnasia of Berlin alone 370 lads went to the war. Many a young fellow who was physically a weakling, wandered sadly from one regiment to another, rejected again and again, and happy was he who at length secured acceptance from an indulgent commander. The officials reported themselves for military service in such numbers that the king ultimately found it necessary to issue a proclamation to the provincial governments to insure the retention of enough men to carry on the work. In Pomerania, during the summer, the royal authorities had almost completely disappeared, and every circle and every village ruled itself, for good or for evil.

The common people, too, had, amid need and suffering, rediscovered their love for the fatherland. Their souls were stirred by the great passions of public life, stormily moved as never before since the days of the wars of religion. The peasant left his farm, the manual worker left his workshop, making up their minds in a moment as if it were a matter of course; the time had come, and what must be, must be. The king, too, with all the princes, had gone into camp. In a thousand moving traits the loyalty of the common people was displayed. Poor miners in Silesia worked for weeks without receiving pay, in order that their wages might equip a few comrades for the army. A Pomeranian shepherd sold his little flock, his only possession, and then went, well-armed, to join his regiment. It was with admiration that the older generation contemplated all such manifestations to which the universal liability to military service has long accustomed us of a later day. Hundreds of betrothed couples went before the altar to unite their lives a moment before the young husband passed away to battle and death. It was only the Poles in West Prussia and Upper Silesia who did not share the devotion of the Germans; and in a few towns which had hitherto been free from liability to military service the new laws encountered resistance. The German and Lithuanian country people of the old provinces on the other hand, had been accustomed to military service since the strict days of Frederick William I. At the same time, public collections were held everywhere, such as had hitherto been customary only for benevolent ends: this poor quarter of the German nation offered, together with the flower of its young men, also the last poor remnants of its property, for the re-establishment of the fatherland. Of actual cash there was very little available, but what still remained of old ornaments and plate was freely given. In many regions of the old provinces it was regarded as a disgrace, after the war, if any household still possessed silver plate. The common people brought their wedding rings to the mint, receiving iron rings in exchange, with the inscription: "Gold gave I for iron"; many a poor girl sold her hair in order to get money for the war. . . .

But the masses of the people outside Prussia had little sense of the heroic fury of this war. [The German statesman] Stein's hopes for a unanimous uprising of the whole nation were disappointed. It was only in those provinces which had already belonged to Prussia, and in a few regions of the north-west which had been directly under the rule of the Napoleonides [members of Napoleon's family], that the people voluntarily rose in arms as soon as the victorious columns of the liberators drew near. Everywhere else the people quietly awaited the commands of their territorial sovereigns and the logic of completed facts. The dukes of Mecklenburg and Anhalt joined their Prussian neighbours, with whom they were on old terms of friendship. A battalion from Weimar allowed itself to be taken prisoner by the Prussians immediately after the outbreak of the war, in order subsequently, like the valiant hussars of Strelitz, to join [the Prussian General] Yorck's corps. The other members of the Confederation of the Rhine followed the orders of Napoleon, most of them still animated by the ardent zeal of the Napoleonic army. In its first and more difficult half, the German War of Liberation was a war of Prussia against the three-fourths of the German nation that were ruled by France.

Just as had formerly happened in the beginning of the modern German state-building, so now did the re-establishment of the national independence proceed from the north alone. The new political and moral ideals of the awakened youth bore the stamp of North German culture. The old German God, to whom they prayed, was the God of the Protestants; all their activities and all their thoughts were based, consciously or unconsciously, upon the moral ground of the strict Kantian doctrine of duty. It was of momentous importance for many decades of German history that it was only the North German stocks that played any serious part in the finest happenings of this new Germany, whereas it was not until two generations later [1870–1871] that the south had the happiness of taking part in the struggles and the victories of the great fatherland.

Hajo Holborn (1902–1969), born and educated in Berlin, taught history and international relations in Germany before he fled the Nazis in 1934. After settling in the United States, he joined the Yale University faculty as a professor of history, a post he held until his death. One of his generation's foremost historians of modern Europe and especially Germany, he wrote Ulrich von Hutten and the German Reformation *(1937)*, The Political Collapse of Europe *(1951)*, A History of Modern Germany *(3 vols., 1959–1969)*, and other works.

MIXED MOTIVES FOR THE GERMAN REVOLT

Hajo Holborn

On February 3 [1813], Frederick William III had agreed to the formation of ranger (*Jäger*) detachments through the call-up of volunteers from among the propertied class. A week later all exemptions from military service were invalidated. But even though he was arming, the king had not made up his mind whether to fight. When he moved from Berlin to Breslau, the attitude of the people showed him that he had practically no choice. He signed the Russian alliance, and on March 15 Alexander I entered Breslau. Two days later the creation of a national guard (*Landwehr*) comprising all men from the age of seventeen to forty who were not in the regular army or the ranger corps was announced. Universal service through conscription, except for the rangers, was achieved as Scharnhorst and the military reformers had wished. In 1813, Prussia managed to mobilize 280,000 men or 6 per cent of her population. Thanks to the new military organization, and through this impressive striking force, she enhanced her influence among the powers far beyond her slender size. In the spring of 1813, however, the Prussian army was hardly a good army. The national guard was untrained and arms were scarce. But morale was high and the local self-government, entrusted with organizing and equipping the national guard units, proved the value of popular institutions. Yet if the war, after an initial phase, had not been followed by an armistice during the summer, the shortcomings of the army might have proved very serious. It became particularly

---

From Hajo Holborn, *A History of Modern Germany, 1648–1840* (New York: Alfred A. Knopf, 1967), pp. 424–426. Copyright © 1964 by Hajo Holborn. Reprinted by permission by Alfred A. Knopf, Inc.

important that the ranger detachments produced good officers for the national guard. This was one reason why [General, then Minister of War] Boyen could stave off attempts to use the national guard as a mere reservoir for the replenishment of the regular army. He wanted to keep it as a distinct citizens' army. And in battle the national guard regiments fought side by side with those of the regular army.

The general patriotism shown by the Prussian population [in 1813] was in stark contrast to the apathy of 1806, and there can be no question that the reformers had worked hard to bring about this change. They had rightly judged that great moral forces were slumbering in the people which could be activated for the state. Whether they had diagnosed the nature of these forces quite correctly can be doubted. Their own philosophy of life was too idealistic and individualistic, their nationalism too lofty and moralistic to serve as the belief of the masses. Even their political action had looked too far ahead to be immediately cherished by the people. Apart from the reactionary opposition of certain *Junker* circles, the townspeople disliked freedom of trade and had little appreciation of self-government. By 1815, the agrarian reform had hardly gone beyond promises. Though the reformers had a following among the officer corps and upper bureaucracy as well as among the educated groups, they did not dominate these groups completely. . . . Wilhelm von Humboldt, as chief of education in the years 1809–10, had aimed at making the humanism of Weimar the foundation of Prussia's educational system. Great as the results of Humboldt's reforms finally proved to be, they had not as yet produced a general effect, nor had the active interest of the Prussian government in the modern German culture moved the intellectual leaders to support the Prussian reformers' national policies. Goethe, Hegel, and Schelling remained aloof from all efforts of national liberation.

The patriotism of 1813 rested on more elementary forces than the lofty ideas of Stein and Scharnhorst. The reformers recognized this and on their part attempted to arouse popular passions to the full. In April, 1813, Scharnhorst created provincial militias (*Landsturm*) consisting of all men not in the army or national guard. Their function was to act as home defense by all means of popular resistance, for which the Spanish War served as the model. Yet in Prussia the call-up and the arming of the common men met with strong criticism. This appeal to sansculottism [lower-class radicalism] aroused fears among the nobility and bourgeoisie, and care was taken to keep the mobilization of a *Landsturm* on a small scale and control it by placing it under the police authorities. Everywhere the established state authorities directed the popular movement. As a matter of fact, where such agencies did not give the signal and take charge, people failed to act.

It was one of the reformers' bitter disappointments that no uprisings occurred in the states of the Rhenish Confederation and that only the people of "Old Prussia," that is, of the four eastern provinces which formed Prussia between 1807 and 1815, made far more than ordinary sacrifices. Among the Prussian reforms the greater equality among the classes and the improved conditions of army life were most generally important for engendering the common spirit shown by the Prussian people during the war. Hatred of the foreign oppressor and desire for the restoration of normal economic life were the predominant motives of the popular war spirit. Although the hope for further liberalization of the Prussian government and the national liberation of Germany may have played a role in the thinking of a good many educated people, the patriotism of the masses, most of them peasants, did not need these special incentives. They were animated by Prussian loyalties. The dynasty was still considered the supreme authority ordained by God, and it was not modern philosophy but the old religious teachings which served as the justification of political beliefs and actions. The war revealed in general that the traditional forms of religion were much more alive among the people than the literature of the age would indicate. The motto "With God for King and Fatherland" expressed rather well the prevailing sentiment of these years. Monarchism, antiforeign feeling, and a vague nationalism, partly Prussian, partly German, were fused into a quasi-religious obligation.

Owen Connelly (1924–   ) has gained a well-deserved reputation as an authority on Napoleon and his times. After serving in the United States Army and Air Force from 1943 to 1946 and 1950 to 1956, respectively, he earned his Ph.D. from the University of North Carolina in 1960. Since then he has taught at the University of South Carolina for most of his career. A prolific writer, he is the author of Napoleon's Satellite Kingdoms *(1965),* The Gentle Bonaparte: A Biography of Joseph, Napoleon's Elder Brother *(1968),* The Epoch of Napoleon *(1972),* French Revolution/Napoleonic Era *(1979),* Historical Dictionary of Napoleonic France, 1799–1815 *(1985), and* Blundering to Glory: Napoleon's Military Campaigns *(1987).*

AN EMPIRE FOILED BY TRADITIONALISTS

Owen Connelly

After many decades of controversy, scholars seem agreed that Napoleon had no fixed, unchanging, master plan for Europe. Georges Lefebvre saw him as a "man of the eighteenth century" possessed with a passion for rational organization and efficiency, who tightened and extended his control continually until his commitments exceeded his power.[1] André Fugier sees him as a creature of expedients (. . . *il garda l'esprit dégagé* . . .) whose design was a product of accumulating day-to-day decisions.[2] The history of the satellite kingdoms confirms that Napoleon progressively centralized control of his empire until he seemed bent on founding a European government in which national states had no part.

As First Consul Napoleon more than achieved the goals of the defunct Directory—a France of "natural frontiers" (the Rhine, the Jura, the Alps, and the Pyrenees) flanked by "sister republics."[3] His

---

From Owen Connelly, *Napoleon's Satellite Kingdoms* (New York: The Free Press, 1965), pp. 333–345. Reprinted with permission of The Free Press, a Division of Macmillan, Inc. Copyright © 1965 by The Free Press.

[1] Georges Lefebvre, *Napoleon* (4th ed., Paris: 1954), p. 66 and *passim.*
[2] André Fugier, *Napoléon et l'Italie* (Paris: 1947), p. 332. Excellent summaries of the older theses on the Grand Design may be found in Pieter Geyl, *Napoleon, For and Against* (paperback ed.; New Haven: 1963).
[3] He did not restore the short-lived Roman and Parthenopean (Neapolitan) Republics, but with the annexation of Piedmont (1802), France extended beyond the Alps.

system might die with him, however, and the republics were too independent for his taste—even Italy, where he was president. To insure the perpetuation of his government, he made himself hereditary emperor, with the right to adopt heirs. He tightened his system by annexing the Ligurian Republic (Genoa) to France and converting the Italian and Batavian (Dutch) Republics into kingdoms, then expanded it to include Naples, Westphalia, and Spain.

His royal relatives were expected to provide adoptive heirs of suitable rank and serve as obedient viceroys and faithful allies. By 1810, however, Napoleon was convinced that he could father his own heir,[4] and had found a new bride. Moreover, clan loyalty and self-interest had not, as expected, kept the satellite rulers properly submissive. Murat [King of Naples] and Louis [King of Holland] had become nationalists; Jérôme [King of Westphalia], though guardedly, pled for his people; Joseph [King of Spain] ignored the war that sapped the empire's strength to play the king and involve himself prematurely in progressive endeavors. Further, the national spirit developing in Italy and Westphalia, recovering in Naples and Holland, and evident in Spain among *afrancesados* [pro-French Spaniards] as well as rebels, portended ill for the future. It seemed desirable to check its growth by fragmenting the kingdoms into French departments and/or military governments, as the situation dictated, centering all control in Paris and teaching the people loyalty to the empire.

During 1810 Holland was annexed to France, as was a fifth of Westphalia (most of Hanover and part of her original territories). Marshal Davout flaunted Jérôme's authority in what remained of his kingdom. The French garrison in Naples was strengthened, and Murat was systematically humiliated. Three-quarters of Spain was removed from Joseph's control and placed under French military governors, and the annexation of northern Spain was threatened. Napoleon seemed bent on forcing all three remaining kings to abdicate or on removing them.[5] As for Italy, Eugène's viceroyalty was ordered terminated twenty years after the anticipated birth of Napoleon's son. Already designated the "king of Rome," he would inherit

---

[4]He had sired three illegitimate children. The last, born in 1809 to the Countess Walewska, he could be certain was his—and it was a boy.

[5]As we know, "disciplinary" pressure on Jérôme continued into 1811, and on Murat until 1812. Joseph's authority was not restored until March 1812. Meanwhile in January 1812, the valley of the Aran, in northern Catalonia, was added to the French department of Haute Garonne and the rest of Catalonia divided into four departments for administration by French "intendants." La Forest was told to explain to Joseph that Catalonia was *not* annexed to France, however. See the *Correspondance du comte de la Forest*, 7 v. Edited by Geoffroy de Grandmaison. (Paris: 1905–1913), VI, 80 and footnote.

the crowns of both the empire and Italy.[6] France meanwhile had been extended onto the Italian peninsula to include Rome (the "second city" of the empire), and into the Balkans (the Illyrian Provinces), and had absorbed the Hanse cities on the North Sea and western Baltic.[7] The empire seemed destined to become a highly centralized European state, a new "Roman Empire," governed from Paris, and ceremonially, Rome.[8]

NAPOLEON AND THE RULERS

To Napoleon, doing one's duty to France and to a subject state were the same thing. No empire; no kingdoms. At base, the states existed (and had been granted their constitutions) by right of conquest. Naturally the emperor responded with fury when his policies were questioned. Eugène, and to slightly lesser degree, Jérôme, understood his attitude. Louis, Joseph, and Murat accepted his basic proposition intellectually, as they told the emperor *ad nauseam* in their correspondence, but not emotionally. When it came down to cases, they resisted (as best they could) sacrificing national interests for the sake of the empire.

Arguments as to whether Napoleon or his rulers were "right" seem fruitless. The answer depends on one's viewpoint. If one accepts that the perpetuation of the empire was necessary and good, and that the emperor, even if not always right, had to be obeyed to maintain the discipline necessary for survival, then all Napoleon did was justified. If one takes a national viewpoint, then one can sympathize with Louis's view of the Continental System, Murat's outrage at having his invasion of Sicily sabotaged [Napoleon refused to support Murat's attempt to invade Sicily in 1810], or Joseph's complaint that the Spanish would never trust him if he were forced to violate his constitution.

To say that a ruler was more liberal or humane than Napoleon raises questions: Were imperial or national goals more worthy? Did the ends (in either case) justify the means? Would the emperor's

---

[6] Unless a second son were born, in which case he would assume the Italian crown, probably in title only. Eugène was compensated with the Grand Duchy of Frankfurt, and promised a principality in France. See the *Correspondance de Napoléon Ier*, 32 v. (Paris: 1858–1870), XX, pp. 84–85, 249–250.

[7] Imperial fiefs dotted the states beyond, e.g., Berg, Frankfurt, and Erfurt in Germany, Neuchâtel in Switzerland, Ponte Corvo and Benevento in Naples, and Albufera in Spain. Elisa Bonaparte and her husband Prince Bacciocchi governed Piombino and Lucca (outside France) and Tuscany (part of France). The Grand Duchy of Warsaw, governed by the king of Saxony, remained at Napoleon's disposal.

[8] *See* J.-Edouard Driault, *Napoléon en Italie* (Paris: 1906), pp. 676–677. He seems overenthusiastic over the "Roman" aspect of the empire, however.

(hopefully) short-term cruelties have brought Europe greater benefits than the rulers' more humane efforts? Was there any difference between Napoleon's liberalism and that of the rulers, or is it only that the latter disagreed as to implementation? Overall, would Europeans generally have had more liberty, equality, and prosperity (not to speak of unity and power) if they had sacrificed temporarily to allow Napoleon to achieve his vaunted "general peace?" Was the preservation of European national states and the production of new ones in the nineteenth century (which the success of Napoleon might have prevented) "good" or "bad"?

Napoleon, after all, wanted the Spanish rebellion ruthlessly crushed so that Spain, under an efficient, progressive government, could better serve both her people and the empire. ". . . I seized by the hair the chance fortune gave me to regenerate Spain . . ."[9] he said, and doubtless meant it. The Dutch sustained heavy casualties in an economic war, which, if won, would have netted them great benefits. (We shall not attempt to judge whether it *could* have been won.) Who was more humane? Napoleon, or Joseph and Louis?

The emperor granted (even helped to write) constitutions which called for representative bodies, then discouraged their use for fear of weakening the kingdoms and the empire. In installing the *Code Napoléon*, however, Joseph, Louis, and Murat all proved less zealous than the emperor. In Spain it was applied only in the military governments;[10] in Holland only after annexation to France; in Naples never, in its true spirit (though nominally in force after January 1, 1809). Though Napoleon tailored his policies to local conditions,[11] he was generally more forceful about promoting social revolution than his rulers, surrounded as they were by members of the old ruling classes. And as Franklin Ford noted in discussing the period: "The most important change of all occurred in the social structure, and equally important, in the way men conceived the social structure."[12] Who was more liberal—Napoleon or the rulers?

Why discuss the relative merits of Napoleon and his rulers, one might ask. Were not all their governments "illegal"? But where does legality begin? Unhappily history answers: "Usually in force; popular consent comes afterward, often long afterward." Setting aside the

---

[9]Emmanuel de Las Cases, *Mémorial de Sainte-Hélène*, 8 v. (Paris: 1823–1824), IV, 287.

[10]And that part of Catalonia attached to the French department of Haute Garonne in 1812. See footnote 5.

[11]In Germany, for example, he catered to the nobles, since they still had the loyalty of most of the peasants. In return for stomaching the abolition of feudalism they got priority for civil and military posts.

[12]Franklin L. Ford, "The Revolutionary-Napoleonic Era: How Much of a Watershed?" *American Historical Review*, LXIX, No. 1 (October 1963), 24.

AN EMPIRE FOILED BY TRADITIONALISTS

question, the basic issues between Napoleon and his rulers are ageless. How much force is justified to make men "free"? Who is to decide whether they are free? At what governmental level are decisions to be made? If the people are to consent, how? What is the unit of popular consent? Where does enlightened authority end and tyranny begin? The answers depend on one's political faith.

Liberals in the satellites answered the questions we have posed differently. Liberal nationalists were divided for or against Bonapartist rulers, most clearly in Spain, where they had to choose sides in the war, elsewhere less openly. At one extreme old Jacobins opposed any monarchy, at the other, wishful thinkers hoped to liberalize legitimate rulers when they returned. As time passed pan-Germanism and pan-Italianism caught the emotions of increasing numbers. Others were alienated by the suppression of representative bodies and the tightening of censorship. Finally, in the last years, when the rulers had to concentrate almost solely on raising troops and money, the defection of idealists accelerated. Napoleon, who had begun as a Jacobin, seemed to have moved through phases as "enlightened dictator" and "enlightened monarch" to tyrant. The defectors ignored, however, that the liberal schoolmaster of Europe was compelled to abandon teaching to restore order in his class. Enraged by the rejection of his "enlightenment," he was more determined than ever to apply Rousseau's dictum to force men "to be free"—in all of Europe. Napoleon wore the imperial purple, but he no more "betrayed the Revolution" than did Robespierre. Those who allege he did judge by the history of France, not Europe.[13] Ultimately the emperor had not enough force to "free" Europe, and its nations, including France, were cast back into the maw of the Old Regime.

EUROPE

For a time, however, there had been a Europe and Europeans. "Men of practical bent and modern outlook," says R. R. Palmer, "freed from both popular demands and old-noble pretensions . . . protected by armed force, until 1813 . . . worked together at the liquidation of the Old Regime."[14] Among them were men who suppressed their sense of nationality to labor for the empire—for Europe. Reinhard, born a German, trained in the French bureaucracy, served Napoleon in Switzerland, Moldavia, and elsewhere, but also, without losing pride in his origins, maintained a purely imperial outlook as French am-

[13]Jacques Godechot, for all the depth of his erudition, feels that France was not a center of "revolutionary impulsion" from 1797 until 1830. (*La Grande Nation*, 2 v. [Paris: 1956], II, 696.)

[14]R. R. Palmer, *The Age of Democratic Revolution*, 2 v. (Princeton: 1959–1964), II, 571.

bassador to Westphalia. The Piedmontese Prina managed the finances of Italy. The Corsican-French Ferri-Pisani worked in Naples and later Spain. Pierre-Louis Roederer, the model of Frenchman turned imperial civil servant, reformed the finances of Naples and administered the Grand Duchy of Berg. All saw themselves as functionaries of a European government, at home anywhere in Europe. They were Europeans the like of whom would not be seen for a century. Between their time and the 1920's nationalism drowned others of their ilk, and until after World War II muffled the voices of most who saw Europe whole.

"Men of practical bent . . ." says Professor Palmer. True. The intellectuals mostly lost faith in Napoleon. In the earlier stages of his career reformers and literary lights of all nationalities had seen him both as tamer and protector of the Revolution—Goethe and Müller, Bilderdijk, Monti and Cuoco, Llorente and Jovellanos—but sooner or later they were disillusioned. In the last days a few suddenly saw that their choice lay between Napoleon and the return of the Old Regime, and made a gesture. The aging Ugo Foscolo, for example, insisted upon joining Eugène's army. Generally, though, the intelligentsia had defected to the schools which would stir the mentality of the nineteenth century—liberal nationalism or pan-nationalism, romanticism, and conservatism, and for a few leftist Jacobins, socialism. Napoleon had driven them away, but he had not intended to.

The emperor's vision was larger. He planned an empire of departments directed from Paris, but as the number of non-French departments increased, a multinational, multilingual European state would have surely emerged. What began as a French empire would have become Europe, integrated in every respect. There were tariff barriers between France and the kingdoms, for example, but there would have been none, ultimately, between France and her new departments. A "common market"? Why not? The empire, in time, would have been no more French than the Grande Armée of 1812, which, as we know, was two-thirds "foreign." In 1812 Napoleon saw himself fleetingly as leading Europe's legions against those of the Orient.[15] Romantic and farfetched? His defeat destroyed all semblance of European unity and left a power balance which Russia (or the Soviet Union) has played to her advantage ever since. At Saint Helena Napoleon predicted that Russia and the United States would become great powers.[16] He said nothing regarding a unification of

[15]On Napoleon's fixation for the East, see Émile Bourgeois, *Manuel historique de politique étrangère*, 4 v. (Paris: 1893–1926), and F. Prat, *Napoleone e l'oriente* (Milan: 1945).
[16]André Fugier, *La Révolution française et l'empire napoléonien*; vol. IV of *Histoire des relations internationales*. Ed. by Pierre Renouvin. (Paris: 1954), p. 404.

Germany and little about Italian national possibilities—perhaps because he still saw Europe whole.

THE LEGACY OF THE KINGDOMS

In 1814 Ferdinand VII of Spain returned to resume his traditional powers, reject the Constitution of 1812, and viciously smash the Cádiz leaders who had written it—all with the backing of the peasant masses. Westphalians, though remarkably quiet during the last days of the kingdom, cheered the return of their legitimate princes. The Dutch welcomed back the scion of the House of Orange. Italy stood by Eugène until Napoleon fell, but thereafter the Old Regime was restored with minimal difficulty. Neapolitans, listlessly supporting Murat, proved unequal to his "Crusade of 1815," and afterward bent their backs again to the Bourbons.

In the stillness that followed Napoleon's disappearance, the masses of Europe manifested little interest in anything but repose and the reconstruction of their private lives. But the peoples were not unlike graduates who say they "learned nothing in college," but whose every utterance reflects attitudes and ideas acquired there. They had been deeply affected by the years of the empire, and not least the peoples of the satellite kingdoms. It is not remarkable, for example, that the cycle of nineteenth-century Italian revolutions began in Naples in 1820, or that in 1830 the first German rulers to be overthrown (if temporarily) were those of Brunswick and Hesse-Cassel (formerly part of Westphalia) and Saxony (long under close imperial supervision).

"The peoples of Germany, those of France, of Italy, of Spain, want equality and value liberal ideas," wrote Napoleon to Jérôme.[17] What he meant was that they *would* want enlightenment once they tasted its benefits. Unhappily the bulk of the people, who everywhere were peasants, either refused to sample the proffered advantages (as in Spain) or saw immediate benefits outweighed by new burdens of taxation and conscription. In all the kingdoms, nevertheless, feudalism was abolished (technically even in Spain), and serfdom wherever it existed, and, except in Spain, the peasants knew enough to challenge any tampering with these basic reforms.

In all the kingdoms constitutions had been granted, if not strictly applied; Westphalians remembered that even peasants had sat in the *Ständeversammlung* [parliament]; legislative power over taxation had been practiced (Holland, Westphalia, Italy) or promised (Spain and Naples). The *Code Napoléon* had either been applied or held up as

[17]*Correspondance de Napoléon Ier*, 32 v. (Paris: 1858–1870), XV, 166 (November 15, 1807).

a model; equality before the law had become an established principle; jury trial had been introduced; civil and religious liberty had been guaranteed, and minority groups elevated to full, active citizenship (notably the Jews of Holland and Germany). Guilds and other economically privileged groups had been suppressed, and internal tariffs condemned if not abolished. The political and economic power of the churches had been reduced, and the confiscated properties of nobles and churches pledged (if not always devoted) to public welfare and education.

Most important, perhaps, the kingdoms left behind a coterie of trained personnel—bureaucrats, judges, magistrates, soldiers—who were familiar with the most efficient systems extant for the administration of government, finances, the law, and armies. Not until the return of the restored rulers (absent five to eighteen years) did these men fully realize how much their attitudes had changed, and how truly careers had been "open to talent." They, together with liberals and intellectuals, both former enemies and former friends of Napoleonic government, constituted the core leadership of revolutionary movements of the early nineteenth century.

The idea persists that the satellite kingdoms were "robbed" for the benefit of France. One envisions wagons rolling toward Paris with coin for the imperial treasury and revered works of art for the Louvre. To dismiss the latter quickly, many of the paintings and objects were legitimately purchased, and still belong to the French government.[18] As to treasure wagons, many rolled from France into Spain; few indeed came from the kingdoms to France. The states contributed largely by supporting French troops within their borders; much of the money they supplied was spent locally, either by army buyers or the troops themselves, to the benefit of native merchants and producers. Because of the cost of the Spanish War, the French taxpayer's burden was *increased* by the holding of the satellite kingdoms. Moreover, the tax rate in France was always higher than in the kingdoms, which added to the general fear of annexation. Trade agreements favored France, and the Continental System caused distress, but native merchants managed to make immense profits anyway, especially in Italy and Naples. Further, despite economic dislocations, there were some

[18] Admittedly, so do many "stolen" works, however. Louis XVIII did not want to offend the French public by returning them all, and the allies were sympathetic. The conquerors, moreover, could not agree on which works had been "legally" seized. The czar set a precedent by ignoring the whole problem and buying hundreds of confiscated paintings and objects, most of which are now in the Hermitage, at Leningrad. See Dorothy Mackay Quynn, "The Art Confiscations of the Napoleonic Wars," *American Historical Review*, L, No. 1 (April 1945), 437–460. See also Cecil Gould, *Trophy of Conquest* (London: 1965); and Ferdinand Boyer, "Les responsabilités de Napoléon dans le transfert à Paris des oeuvres d'art de l'étranger," *Revue d'Histoire Moderne et Contemporaine*, XI (Octobre–Décembre 1964), 241–262.

permanent gains—new industry, new crops, and much technological improvement.[19] Everywhere, the value of broad tariff-free trading areas was demonstrated, positively on a small scale (Italy, Westphalia, Naples), and negatively on a larger one.

The kingdoms (and the empire generally) also set precedents in problem-solving by legislation (decreed or voted), by which the governments asserted the right, in principle, to rearrange any and all areas of national life. In the long run this legacy, valued property of all contemporary governments, whatever their political systems, would overshadow all others. Napoleon did not originate the process, nor was it a French innovation, though Louis XIV and the Committee of Public Safety had used it most masterfully, and the latter immensely widened its scope. Napoleon and his rulers, however, demonstrated it more fully in more areas than had anyone else before. Aside from constitutions and mandatory administrative, legal, and judicial reform programs, there were laws requiring smallpox inoculation and land redistribution, ordering the establishment of public schools and new industries, granting specific guarantees to minorities, and a hundred other things. Not all were implemented, but success was sufficient to orient progressives toward reform from seats-of-power. Napoleon's answer to all ills—legislate, administer, enforce—has been echoed ever more widely and loudly by every generation since his time.

THE KINGDOMS AND THE FALL OF NAPOLEON

Explanations for Napoleon's fall are legion, and few are without some validity. Most emphasize some factor such as the impact of the Continental System on Russia, Austria's periodic diplomatic humiliations, or the exclusion of Prussia from Germany, which drove her into Austria's arms, all with the sustained opposition of Great Britain in the background. Some prefer to believe that Napoleon, driven by an insatiable will-to-power, ultimately provoked overwhelming opposition—from legitimate rulers, the Church (both as religious force and power structure) and Christians generally, from liberals and conservatives, from nationalities, and the uniformly oppressed peoples of Europe.[20] Whatever the attitudes of rulers, diplomats, churchmen, and leaders of all political factions, however, peasant masses formed

---

[19]To cite one of the newer books, see Rudolph Strauss, *Die Lage und die Bewegung der Chemnitzer Arbeiter in der ersten Hälfte des 19. Jahrhunderts* (Berlin: 1960), p. 8 and passim.

[20]If one ignores or discounts Napoleon's worthy objectives, he fits beautifully into Canetti's picture of the ruler as "survivor," i.e., one whose sense of power requires that not only his enemies but his supporters die, in the last extremity *all* of them. *See* Elias Canetti, *Crowds and Power*. Tr. by Carol Stewart (New York: 1962), pp. 231–234.)

the armies which defeated the emperor of the French. Why did they fight? Whether their authors choose to recognize it or not, the evidence supporting all theses reveals that the peoples were nonrationally, or emotionally, motivated. They fought primarily neither because of the disadvantages of French government, nor to alleviate their suffering, nor for concrete advantages expected from national independence and/or unification. They fought for their ancient states or nations, hereditary rulers, and established churches. They responded to the call of tradition and conscience, or acted out of habit. (Whether this was good or bad, right or wrong is not in question here.)[21] During the "War of Liberation" in Germany, the illusion of a vast popular uprising against the French was given by the progressive defection of the princes (followed by their dutiful subjects) to the allies. Pan-German and liberal propaganda surely contributed to the pervading spirit, but it incited to action only the intellectuals and a few leaders (like Vom Stein's group), who generally favored restoring the major princes, reforming their governments, and linking them in loose confederation. In Westphalia there was little movement until the old princes returned to point the way. In Spain, the rebels, under noble and clerical leadership, had fought desperately for Crown and Church, ignoring the aspirations of the Cádiz liberals. East of the Niemen, the masses had risen to defend "Mother Russia" and the monarchy. The nationalism of the peasants of Austria and Prussia was almost as anachronistic. None could have produced arguments for sustaining or restoring the Old Regime. They did what they *felt* was "right." In Italy and Naples, despite widespread enthusiasm among native leaders for liberalism and pan-Italianism, the common man, reverting to traditional attitudes still common among Italians,[22] displayed a practiced indifference which allowed the restoration of the Old Regime.

One cannot view Murat's defection as an important factor in wrecking the empire; Italy and Westphalia both sacrificed heavily to sustain it. Only in Spain did developments contribute markedly to Napoleon's downfall. "C'est ce qui m'a perdu ["That's what ruined

---

[21] I acknowledge my debt, which is obvious, to the scholarly anti-intellectuals, of whom Professor Crane Brinton of Harvard is the chief exponent among historians. *See* his *Ideas and Men* (Englewood Cliffs, N.J.: 1950), pp. 503–526, and the interpretive sections of *The Jacobins* (New York: 1930) and *A Decade of Revolution* (New York: 1934).

[22] Says Luigi Barzini, Jr.: "The tenacity and eagerness with which the individual pursues his private interests and defends himself against society, his mistrust of noble ideals and motives, the splendid show, the all-pervading indulgence for man's foibles make Italian life pleasant and bearable in spite of poverty, tyranny, and injustice. They also waste the efforts and the sacrifices of the best Italians and make poverty, tyranny, and injustice very difficult to defeat." (*The Italians* [New York: 1964], p. 376.)

me"]," he said at Saint Helena.[23] Clearly the immense cost of the Spanish venture in lives, money, and matériel had greatly weakened the empire before the Russian campaign began. If nothing else, as we know, 300,000 French troops were engaged in the peninsula in 1812, over 200,000 in 1813. One might argue that, considering Russian strategy, they would not have helped Napoleon in 1812, but later, surely, their presence in Germany could have been decisive.

In Spain, moreover, we have the prime example of a people moved by anachronistic nationalism. Unless one wishes to defend an Old Regime of the most medieval character extant (à la Henry Adams), or argue that Spanish self-determination on any terms was better than what Napoleon offered, then they were acting against their own interests. Nevertheless in five years of war (with British aid) they took 300,000 French casualties, cost France a billion francs in specie and probably an additional three billion otherwise, damaged the prestige of French arms and the morale of French soldiery, and inspired other Europeans to resist.

The Spanish war debilitated the empire as did nothing else, and Joseph, in command of French forces at critical times, bears heavy responsibility for its continuance and the eventual loss of Spain. Napoleon's success in 1808–1809 seems to show that Spain could have been conquered if the French armies had been properly directed. Joseph's good intentions, liberalism, personal magnetism, and—yes—goodness are not in question. He loved his people, forgave their rebellion, betrayals, and insults, wept for them, and labored for their welfare. But he lost the war. He was not of the stuff of warrior-kings; he was not a Napoleon. Can we blame him for that? No. We do not. We simply say he lost Spain.

Moreover, Napoleon, ultimately, must be held accountable for the disaster. Aware of Joseph's military incapacity, surely after 1809, he would neither give anyone else overall command in Spain, or come there again himself. Instead he tried to direct the war from Paris, and matters went badly (though largely because the marshals would not cooperate in his absence). In 1810 or 1811 his presence might have spelled victory in Spain. But in 1810 he was busy reorganizing the empire for the benefit of his anticipated son, and so happy with his new bride that he could not bear to leave her. (Genius can ill afford happiness.) In 1811 he was preparing for war on Russia, which, tragically, he considered more important than completing the conquest of the peninsula. In 1812, fearing to trust anyone else, he again gave Joseph the army of Spain. The results were catastrophic, and probably could have been otherwise if Joseph had simply obeyed Napoleon's orders. In the final analysis, however, Napoleon was responsible.

[23]Las Cases, *Mémorial*, IV, 285.

9
THE MAIN CAUSES FOR THE DEFEAT IN RUSSIA

Napoleon's defeat in Russia was one of the most important, if not the most important, reason for his fall from power. Never again did his army attain comparable quality, having lost more than 500,000 soldiers and 200,000 trained horses; and his enemies in Russia, Great Britain, Prussia, Austria, and Spain gained the courage to fight on to victory.

How did this military catastrophe come about? Gunther E. Rothenberg sets the stage. We learn of the strengths and weaknesses of the *Grande Armée* and of Napoleon as its commander in chief. Then Napoleon and David G. Chandler each discuss the campaign. As one might expect, Napoleon blames a circumstance that nobody could control—the harsh winter—and ignores his personal responsibility. On the other hand, Chandler stresses the rashness of the whole enterprise, the inadequate preparations before the campaign even began, the faults in Napoleon's strategy and tactics, and the summer heat as well as the winter cold. In addition, Chandler concentrates more on Napoleon's misjudgments than on the diplomatic and military skillfulness of Tsar Alexander I, the Russian generals, and their troops.

The reader should decide whether the defeat in Russia is one of those complicated events that have multiple causes or whether a few crucial factors led to the debacle.

Gunther E. Rothenberg (1923–) has combined military and academic training to fashion a distinguished career as a military historian. Born in Berlin, he served in the British Army from 1941 to 1946 and the United States Air Force from 1949 to 1955. After receiving his Ph.D. from the University of Illinois in 1958, he taught at various American universities. He is currently Professor of History at Purdue University. His books in military history include two on the Napoleonic era: The Art of Warfare in the Age of Napoleon *(1978 and 1980) and* Napoleon's Great Adversaries: The Archduke Charles and the Austrian Army *(1979).*

NAPOLEON: THE WARRIOR AND HIS ARMY

Gunther E. Rothenberg

From the Revolution, Napoleon inherited huge conscript armies, led by young and ambitious commanders, accustomed to a mobile, offensive, and ruthless way of war. As First Consul and later Emperor, Napoleon imposed his own genius and personality on these armies. He inspired Frenchmen and foreigners alike with fierce loyalty and devotion. As a soldier he stood among the great captains, and under his leadership his armies swept aside all opposition. He won unsurpassed victories and his campaigns, strategy, and style of command are to this day studied by soldiers everywhere. In the end, of course, both his overweening ambitions and his overcentralization, coupled with a neglect of logistics and supply, proved his undoing and he was defeated by attrition and greater numbers.

THE GRANDE ARMÉE

Napoleon's main military instrument was the *Grande Armée*, the Grand Army, designating from 1805 on the principal body of French and allied forces operating under his personal command. Concentrating the bulk of his strength to deliver the decisive stroke at the crucial point, its tremendous offensive impact gave Napoleon a considerable advantage over his enemies. At the same time, the formation of the Grand Army manifested in the military sphere the goal that Napo-

---

From Gunther E. Rothenberg, *The Art of Warfare in the Age of Napoleon* (Bloomington: Indiana University Press, 1978), pp. 126–130, 146–148, 162–163. Reprinted by permission of Indiana University Press and Batsford Limited.

leon already had attained in the political sphere—the concentration of all power in his hand. But it also imposed an important handicap. As an absolute autocrat, Napoleon could not brook any competing authority. Therefore there could be only one main army, and when this was engaged in one theatre of operations, makeshift command arrangements would have to do elsewhere. And in Spain, where except for a brief appearance in the winter of 1808–9, Napoleon did not exercise direct command, the consequences would be costly.

The development of the Grand Army took several years. When Napoleon returned from Egypt and established the Consulate, he carefully observed the Republican injunction against the head of state commanding the field army and this was the major reason for designating the army of Marengo as the "Army of the Reserve." Marengo, and Moreau's victory at Hohenlinden, brought peace and allowed Napoleon to begin restructuring the military forces.

The victories had come just in time. By 1799 the French armies had deteriorated, numbers were down to about 230,000, desertion was rampant, and morale was low. The general inspection held in August 1801 revealed additional shortcomings. "The officers," the report noted, "are apathetic. They know their trade fairly well, but they are sullen and without spirit. And the non-commissioned officers are even worse. The majority is ignorant, pretentious, and slack. These men between 25 and 35 act as if they were 80."[1] A major cause of the low morale was the intense rivalry between the various French armies. Under the Republic and the Directory "each of these armies acquired a history, style, prejudices, and reputation of its own."[2] Especially dangerous was the ill-feeling between Moreau's old Army of the Rhine and the troops who had served with Napoleon in Italy and Egypt. Bad blood, in fact, survived for many years. As late as 1811, Napoleon observed that Marmont would make an excellent replacement for Ney who had clashed with Masséna in Spain, because "both are from the same family; they are of the Army of Italy, while Ney is from a foreign [*i.e. the Army of the Rhine*] army."[3]

Moreau, the victor of Hohenlinden, was Napoleon's most bitter rival and his troops sullen. Soon after the Treaty of Amiens, Napoleon despatched a considerable portion of these units to reconquer San Domingo. A short time later, he discovered Moreau's involvement, together with some other generals, in a plot implicating royalist elements. There followed executions and prison sentences; Moreau

---

[1] J. Morvan, *Le Soldat Impérial*, Plon, Paris, 1904, Vol I, 281–2.
[2] R. W. Phipps, *The Armies of the First French Republic*, 5 vols., Oxford University Press, 1926–39, Vol. I, 4; Vol. IV, 145.
[3] J. J. Pelet, *The French Campaign in Portugal 1810–1811*, ed. D. D. Horward, University of Minnesota Press, Minneapolis, 1973, 504.

was sent into exile. These events paved the way for Napoleon to assume supreme power. In May 1804, France received a new constitution with Napoleon as hereditary emperor.

Since March 1803, Napoleon had been concentrating large forces, designated as the Army of England, in camps and cantonments along the Channel and the North Sea. For the first and only time, troops received intensive training, practised new tactics, and received new equipment. Incompetents were weeded out, deserving officers promoted, and higher formations organized; shortages, however, persisted. There was inadequate transport and too little artillery. Even so, when it went to war in 1805, the Grand Army, as it was now styled, was a finely honed weapon and Napoleon could properly boast that "surely there is no finer army in Europe than mine today."[4] The army of 1805 was the first Grand Army and fought at Ulm, Austerlitz, Jena, and Friedland. In 1808 it shifted a considerable part of its forces to Spain, but was hastily reconstituted in early 1809 to battle at Aspern and Wagram. In 1812 it assembled its greatest strength for the invasion of Russia. After its destruction there, a new Grand Army arose in 1813–14. When Napoleon conducted his last campaign in 1815, he no longer used the title Grand Army; instead his forces were known as the Army of the North.

ORGANIZATION OF THE GRAND ARMY

At the end of 1804, according to a semi-official source, the French military establishment numbered a total of 610,976 officers and men, 472 battalions, 320 squadrons, 8 regiments of foot and 6 of horse artillery, as well as staff, engineer, and supply elements. A modern writer, however, gives a lower estimate. "Including garrison and second-line troops," Chandler states, *"La Grande Armée* probably comprised some 350,000 men by 1805."[5] The lower figure seems closer to the mark.

For strategic and grand tactical purposes, Napoleon institutionalized the corps organization, used experimentally by Moreau. The corps became the smallest force of all arms. Primarily an infantry organization, each corps combined two to four infantry divisions, a brigade or division of light cavalry, several artillery batteries, and a small number of engineer and support troops. The exact number of divisions and guns allocated to each corps varied purposely, both to

---

[4]S. J. Watson, *By Command of the Emperor: A Life of Marshal Berthier*, The Bodley Head, 1957, 9.

[5]S. F. Gay de Vernon, *Science of War and Fortification*, trs. J. M. O'Connor, J. Seymour, New York, 1817, Vol. I, 56; D. Chandler, *The Campaigns of Napoleon*, Macmillan, New York, 1966, 333.

confuse enemy intelligence and to reflect its assignment and the talents of its commander. In 1805, for example, it ranged from Soult's IV Corps with 41,000 to Augereau's VII corps with 14,000 men. Ney's VI Corps, 24,000 strong, three infantry divisions and one of cavalry, supported by 36 guns, was about average. Each corps was to be capable of defeating approximately equal numbers and able to hold against superior forces until reinforced. The system was adopted by Napoleon's allies and imitated by almost all of his opponents.

In 1805 the Grand Army's order of battle comprised seven corps, with one additional allied corps formation. In addition, there were three major formations which Napoleon kept under his own control. There was the Army Cavalry Reserve, six heavy mounted divisions; the Army Artillery Reserve, concentrating almost a quarter of all available guns, and finally the Imperial Guard, the *corps d'élite* of Napoleon's forces, numbering over 7,000 men. For the 1812 campaign, Napoleon modified the army organization, introducing the army group. On that occasion, operating with over 400,000 men exclusive of support formations, the Grand Army moved in three army groups. The central, led by the Emperor, consisted of three mixed corps, two cavalry corps, the Imperial Guard, 47,000 strong with 112 guns, as well as allied contingents. This central group was flanked by two other army groups, the Army of Italy under Eugene and the Second Support Army commanded by Jerome. One Prussian and one Austrian auxiliary corps operated on the extreme northern and southern flanks, while additional corps were in reserve and along the line of communications.

Command and control of the Grand Army was exercized by Napoleon who practised a personal, highly centralized style of command. Imperial Headquarters was constituted of three major divisions. By far the most important was Napoleon's separate personal staff, the *Maison*, performing political as well as military functions. The General Staff of the Grand Army proper, presided over by the efficient Berthier, formed the second major division. The third division, and never able to function as smoothly as the others, was the staff of the Commissary General. Altogether with its subsidiary staffs, bureaus, escorts, and attached personnel, Imperial Headquarters became extremely large, looking, when drawn up for review in 1812, "like a small army."[6] In the field, Napoleon repeatedly tried to reduce the size of Imperial Headquarters and in battle he usually surrounded himself with only a few trusted subordinates and a small escort.

---

[6] M. de Fezensac, *The Russian Campaign of 1812*, trs. L. Kennett, University of Georgia Press, Athens, 1970, 10–11.

For all practical purposes Napoleon was his own operations officer and he made all decisions. Berthier did not participate in the planning. In 1806, Napoleon instructed him to "adhere strictly to my commands. I alone know what I have to do," and Berthier, in turn, told Ney in 1807 that "the Emperor needs neither advice nor plans of campaign. No one knows his thoughts and our duty is to obey." Although Berthier was extremely efficient in his executive functions, this did not shield him from occasional outbursts. "Not only are you no good," his master stormed at him in 1812, "but you are in the way."[7] Berthier's passive role was further underscored by Napoleon's use of a pool of trusted officers attached to his personal staff to serve as observers and to carry out special missions. Staffs also existed at corps and division level, where on occasion, as in the case of Ney and Jomini, an effective partnership developed between a commander and his chief of staff.

Napoleon, as chief of state and at the same time supreme commander, had distinct advantages in maintaining control of planning and operations. At the same time, however, the system had severe limitations. The forces under his command grew from less than 50,000 to over 400,000 men, but he never changed his command system. His system did not produce capable leaders on the highest level, though at the intermediate level he always had a hard core of excellent divisional and brigade commanders. Napoleon was almost unbeatable as long as he could exert direct control over his armies, but he refused until 1813 to nominate a supreme commander in Spain, although very large forces were fighting there. In 1813 and again in 1815 his command control failed, and despite his subsequent complaints about slow or faulty execution of his orders, Napoleon's refusal to train his subordinates to act independently was largely responsible. "Wherever Napoleon was," Fuller commented on the 1813 campaign, "success was assured; wherever he was not, it was disaster."[8]

There was one more crucial shortcoming in Napoleon's system of war—his improvised and ramshackle logistics. Although he did not entirely rely on "living off the land," and frequently, such as in 1800, 1807, and again in 1812, laid down great magazines for the supply of the army, and also made considerable efforts to provide his troops with bread and hardtack, the problem of bringing these supplies forward remained. Napoleonic strategy was based on rapid movement forcing the enemy into a decisive battle. Large wagon trains, even if they had existed, could not have kept pace. The army that marched to the Danube in 1805 carried with it but eight days' rations, bread or

[7] Watson, *op cit.*, 193.
[8] J. F. C. Fuller, *Decisive Battles*, Charles Scribner's Sons, New York, 1940, 642.

hardtack to be used only when the enemy was close and forces had to remain concentrated. During the approach march the various corps, spread over a wide frontage and each allocated a specific sector for foraging, were able to subsist on the country, but in the restricted area around Ulm this method did not work well. And in poor countries—Poland, Spain, or Russia—such arrangements could produce calamities.

Foraging and requisitioning, moreover, aroused local resentments and had adverse effects on discipline. In October 1805, Davout demanded authority to shoot all marauders, and on 14 May 1809, Napoleon decreed that "all stragglers who under the pretext of fatigue have left their units to maraud, shall be rounded up, tried by summary provost courts, and executed within the hour."[9] Even so, march discipline remained poor. Before Wagram, in rich wine country, the French, according to Captain Blaze, broke into the cellars and a considerable part of the army was drunk during the battle. And in Spain, the French alienated the population by their indiscriminate looting. As early as 1807, when Spain was officially an ally, Junot's corps, admittedly mainly recruits, lost all cohesion and looked, so Marbot tells, "more like an evacuated hospital than an army coming to conquer a kingdom."

Napoleon made some efforts to improve his supply arrangements. During the operations of 1806–7 the inadequate system of field transportation provided by civilian contractors broke down completely. In 1807 the French militarized transport and formed nine transport battalions. In addition, Napoleon introduced a network of military staging areas, the *étapes*. However, he always maintained that the security of the rear areas depended upon success at the front and so he did not allocate the *étapes* much manpower. In 1808, for example, there were some 200 such posts between the Rhine and the Vistula, manned by some 75 commissaries, 90 officers, and about 1,000 gendarmes.

Having suffered from short supplies in Poland, Napoleon made his most extensive preparations for the invasion of Russia. Huge amounts of provisions were accumulated in Prussia, but once again it proved impossible to bring these forward to the fighting troops. Moreover, neither Napoleon nor most of his subordinates, except for Davout, took care to preserve supplies. Already on the march to Moscow, provisions ran short and men weakened by hunger and fatigue became an easy prey to disease, losing one-quarter of their combat effectives before ever coming into contact with the enemy.

---

[9]E. Picard ed., *Préceptes et jugements de Napoléon*, Berger-Levrault, Paris-Nancy, 1913, 92.

And when he left Moscow, Napoleon allowed his army to depart with over 40,000 vehicles, most of them carrying loot instead of supplies.[10] In fact, it was this tail impeding the French, which allowed the slowly moving Russians to close. And finally, the total breakdown of discipline in the rear areas, especially at Smolensk and at Vilna, where the advance elements of the retreating troops wasted or destroyed the accumulated supplies, completed the destruction of the Grand Army.

Despite his often quoted pronouncement that "an army marches on its stomach," Napoleon remained essentially an improviser. He could never free himself from the experience of his first Italian campaign when a small, highly motivated army, moving rapidly in a rich countryside had sustained itself from local resources and captured supplies. Failing to acquire a substantial logistical capability, his strategy remained geared to the quick knock-out blow, dictated, at least in part, by the problem of how to keep huge forces in the field without an adequate supply organization. . . .

NAPOLEONIC STRATEGY

Napoleon frequently paid respect to the great captains of the past, to Alexander, Hannibal, Caesar, Gustavus Adolphus, Eugene, and above all, Frederick the Great. He also studied the writings of recent military theorists, Bourcet, Du Teil, and Guibert, and acknowledged his debt to these men. But in his strategy he was basically a pragmatist. Although he often wrote and talked about the so-called principles of war, he never enumerated them. In fact, he once confessed that in war there were "no precise or definite rules." Fundamentally, he told Gourgaud, the whole art of war was "just like all beautiful things, simple; the simplest manoeuvres are the best."[11] Despite his denial of any system, later strategic analysts have tried to deduce meaningful patterns from Napoleon's generalship. Yorck von Wartenburg declared that the operations before Marengo illustrated Napoleon's major strategic principles. They were the use of one major line of advance, careful attention to security in order to screen his intentions from the enemy, the selection of the enemy's main body as his objective, manoeuvre against the flank or rear of the enemy's communications, while safeguarding his own. And Fuller summed it up more succinctly. He reduced the elements characteristic of Napoleon's

[10]*Memoirs of Baron Lejeune*, trans. and ed., A. Bell, 2 vols. Longmans, Green & Co., 1897, Vol. II, 201–2.

[11]E. Picard ed., *Précepts et jugements de Napoléon*, Berger-Levrault, Paris-Nancy, 1913, 23.

strategy to three: unity of command, generalship and soldiership, and planning.[12]

The destruction of the enemy's main field force, rather than the mere occupation of territory or the capture of the enemy's capital was Napoleon's main objective. "There are in Europe," he once observed, "many good generals, but they see too many things at once. I see only one thing, namely the enemy's main body. I try to crush it."[13] Carefully planning a short campaign of annihilation, and able to direct both the strategic and political aspects of the war personally, he made use of the corps system and the well-developed road network of central Europe to force his opponents into one decisive confrontation, *"une grande bataille . . . une affaire décisive et brilliante,"* to be followed by vigorous pursuit which completely shattered the opponents capacity and will to resist while raising the morale of his own troops. This approach, of course, could exact heavy casualties, but Napoleon could draw on the almost unlimited replacement pool provided by conscription while for some years his opponents found such losses unacceptable. The potential of this strategy was most brilliantly demonstrated in the Ulm-Austerlitz and Jena-Auerstädt campaigns. However, if the enemy eluded destruction and if he was able to fall back on strategic depth and reserves, then Napoleon faced severe problems.

Napoleon's strategic deployments were carefully planned to set the stage for the great and decisive battle. Even before hostilities had begun, the Emperor's intentions were carefully shrouded from the enemy. Newspapers were censored, borders closed, travellers detained. Then, when the Grand Army moved, its advance was preceded by swarms of light cavalry, screening its line of advance, protecting its communications, and gathering intelligence about the location of the enemy. The self-contained corps would march along separate routes, deployed to encompass the entire area of operations. At the outset this strategic net would be quite large, about 170 miles wide in 1805–6, and over 300 miles wide in 1812. Then, when the main body of the enemy was located, Napoleon pulled his corps closer together, adopting a loosely quadrilateral formation known as the *bataillon carré*. Frontage was reduced to about one day's march between the corps, until finally the corps' first contact with the enemy engaged him at once and pinned him, while the other corps would hurry to its support. Final concentration was achieved either before or during the

---

[12]Yorck V. Wartenburg, *Napoleon as a General*, Kegan Paul, 1902, Vol. I, 168; J. F. C. Fuller, *The Conduct of War 1789–1961*, Minerva Press, New York, 1961, 44–7.
[13]Chandler, *op. cit.*, 141.

climactic battle. When concentration had been achieved, Napoleon's forces often outnumbered those of his adversaries. He could fight and win when the odds were against him, at Austerlitz, the Beresina, and Dresden for example, but he always attempted to gain local superiority, achieved by exact calculations of time, distance, and the mobility of his forces. . . .

NAPOLEON'S ARMIES: A SUMMING UP

Napoleon's system of warfare was based on theories developed during the *ancien régime* and put, at least partially, into practice during the Revolution. He also profited by the advances in manufacturing, population, and road building. As Liddell Hart stated, eighteenth-century commanders, Marlborough, Frederick, and Saxe, "understood like Napoleon, that rapidity of movement, security of movement, ease of manoeuvre, and efficient supply are the primary conditions for victory."[14] They lacked, however, the physical means to translate their theories into practice.

Napoleon, absolute head of state and commander in chief, was able to achieve the realization of these theories and his short and relentless campaigns restored decisiveness to land warfare. His corps organization was adopted throughout Europe and his strategy became a model for future generations of planners. Both the central position and the manoeuvre on the rear, the indirect approach as Liddell Hart called it, were the basic models for many successful modern operations.

Yet, there were substantial weaknesses in Napoleon's approach and in his armies. Combining all aspects of government and war in one hand led to overcentralization and neglect of detail. When Napoleon failed or when he was absent, difficulties arose that could not be compensated. He had little interest in technology and considering the scope and duration of his wars, there was remarkable little technological change. Communication on the battlefield and in the period of concentration remained haphazard; several of his victories were won only by the fortuitous arrival of detached forces—Marengo, Eylau and Friedland were examples. The chronic indiscipline and the neglect of proper administration could well have been overcome. Davout's corps, with its efficient administration and attention to detail, suggests how the entire army might have been run.

Like all other military institutions, Napoleon's army was to a large degree the product of its historical experience, transformed and made more powerful by the charismatic genius of its leader. It served him

[14]Chandler, *op. cit.*, 141.

well, sometimes better than he deserved, and even in extreme adversity, the hard core of the army remained loyal to him. His memory lived on, and his legend grew, and there were thousands upon thousands of veterans whose greatest experience had been to have served the Emperor.

Napoleon (1769–1821) dated this army bulletin "Molodechno, December 3"; actually he dictated it on the night of December 5, before reaching Vilna, after he had left the remnants of his army. It appeared in the official French newspaper, Le Moniteur universel, *on December 17, the day before he arrived back in Paris. According to his aide, General Armand de Caulaincourt, Napoleon remarked about this report, "I shall tell everything. It is better that these particulars should be known through me than through private letters. Full details now will mitigate the effects of the disaster which have to be announced later to the nation." The reader may decide how forthcoming Napoleon really was.*

A FREEZING WINTER

Napoleon

29TH *BULLETIN* OF THE *GRANDE ARMÉE*

Molodechno, December 3, 1812

The weather was perfect until November 6, and troop movements were executed very easily. Cold weather began on the 7th; every night after that we lost several hundred horses, which died while we camped overnight. By the time we reached Smolensk, we already had lost many cavalry and artillery horses. . . .

The cold, which arrived on the 7th, worsened suddenly; and on the nights of the 14th and 15th, the temperature was 16 and 18 degrees below freezing Réaumur [minus 4 and minus 8.5 degrees Fahrenheit]. The roads were icy. Horses of the cavalry, artillery, and baggage train died every night, not only by the hundreds, but by the thousands, especially horses from France and Germany. Within a few days, more than thirty thousand horses had died; our entire cavalry was now on foot, and our artillery and transport wagons had lost their teams of horses. We had to abandon and destroy a good part of our artillery as well as our munitions and food supplies.

That army, so magnificent on the 6th, was very different by the 14th, for by then it had almost no cavalry, artillery, or transport. Without cavalry, we could not reconnoiter beyond a quarter of a league; at the same time, without artillery, we could not stand firm and risk a battle. We had to march on so as not to be forced into a battle that our lack of ammunition made undesirable; we had to occupy a

---

From [Napoleon], "29e Bulletin de la Grande-Armée," *Le Moniteur universel,* 17 December 1812. Editors' translation.

certain amount of space to avoid being outflanked; and we had to do all this without cavalry for scouting and for keeping the columns linked together. This difficulty, combined with the sudden extreme cold, made our situation most unfortunate. Men whom nature had not hardened enough to withstand all the accidents of fate and fortune appeared shaken, lost their cheerfulness and good humor, and imagined only misfortunes and catastrophes; those whom nature had created superior to everything retained their good cheer and their normal composure and saw a new way of winning glory by surmounting various difficulties.

The enemy, who observed on the roads the traces of this frightful calamity that had struck the French army, sought to take advantage of the situation. He had Cossacks surround all our columns, and like the Arabs of the desert, they carried off the baggage trains and carriages that strayed. That contemptible cavalry, which only blusters and is unable to break through a company of light infantrymen, became redoubtable by force of circumstance. However, the enemy had reason to regret all the serious attempts that he wished to undertake; he was tripped up by the Viceroy [Eugène de Beauharnais], in front of whom he had taken a position, and he lost many men.

The Duke of Elchingen [Marshal Ney], who with three thousand soldiers made up the rear guard, had blown up Smolensk's ramparts. He was surrounded and in a critical position; he broke free with his typical boldness. After keeping the enemy at a distance during the daylight hours of the 18th, while constantly driving him back, Ney moved on the right flank during the night, passed the Dnieper River, and upset all of the enemy's calculations. On the nineteenth, the army passed the Dnieper to Orsha, where the exhausted Russian army, having lost many men, stopped its efforts. . . .

Meanwhile, the enemy occupied all the crossing points of the Berezina; that river is some 250 feet wide; it was carrying a fairly large amount of floating ice; and along its shores was marshland for another 2,000 feet. All this makes it a difficult obstacle to cross.

The enemy general [P. V. Chichagov] had placed his divisions at different passages where he assumed that the French army would want to cross.

After deceiving the enemy by various troop movements on the 25th, the EMPEROR at dawn on the 26th, proceeded to the village of Studenka [about eight miles upriver from Borisov] and immediately had put up in his presence two bridges over the river in the teeth of an enemy division. The Duke of Reggio [Marshal Oudinot] crossed, attacked the enemy, and kept it on the run for two hours; the enemy retreated [southward] to the bridgehead at Borisov. General Legrand, an officer of the highest merit, was severely, but not mortally,

FLOW MAP OF SUCCESSIVE LOSSES OF THE FRENCH ARMY IN THE RUSSIAN CAMPAIGN, 1812
(after C. J. Minard, 1861)

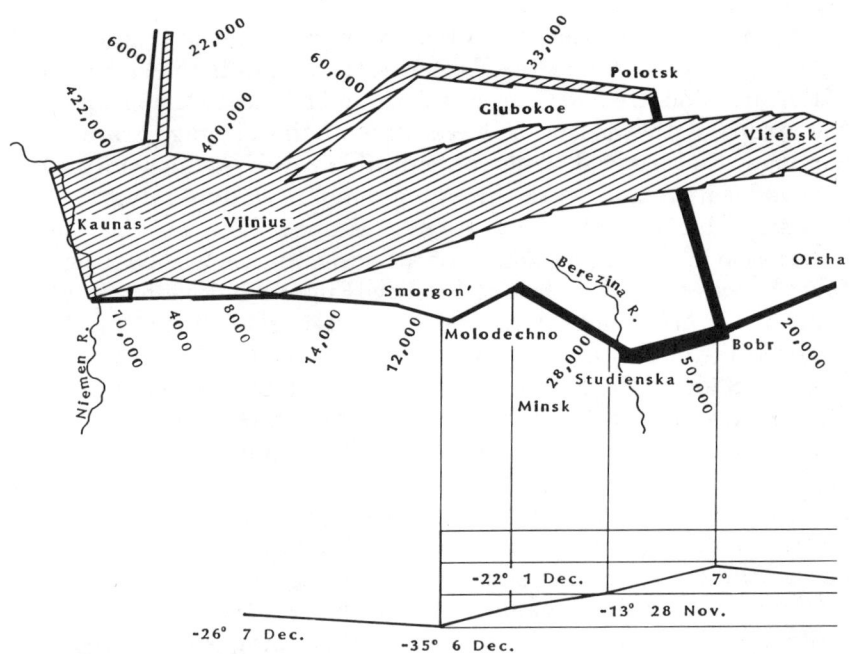

This flow map is famous for the amount of information it conveys in such a limited space. It plots six variables:
  (1) the size of the French army depicted by the width of the bands;
  (2) and (3) its location on a two-dimensional surface;
  (4) the direction of the movement of the advance (upper band) and retreat (lower band);
  (5) and (6) the temperature on certain dates during the retreat.

Note that various sources give somewhat different numbers and temperatures.

A FREEZING WINTER

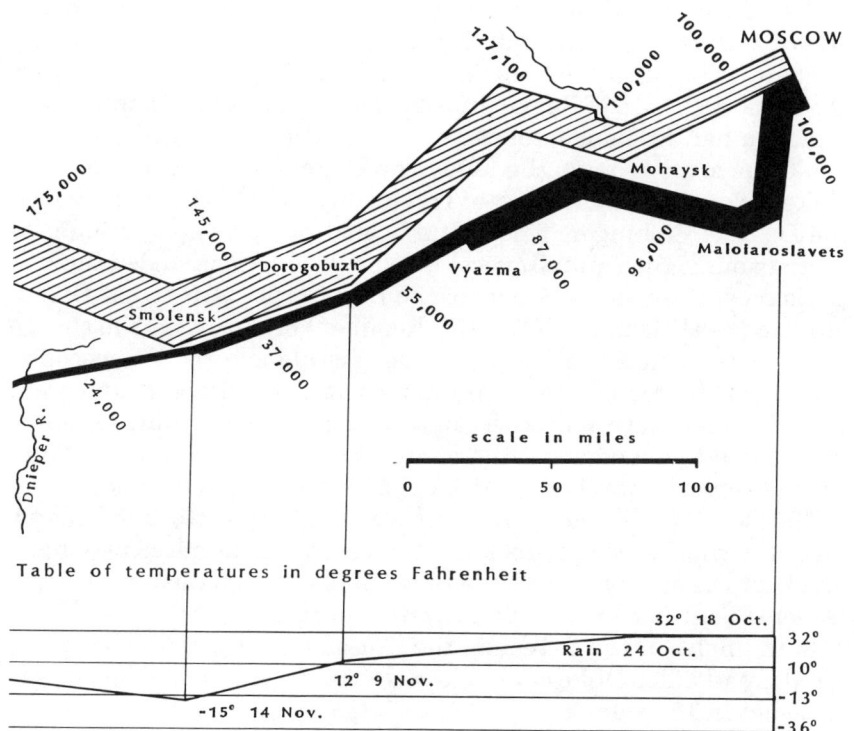

wounded. Throughout the 26th and 27th the army crossed the Berezina....

After the entire army had crossed by the morning of the 28th, the Duke of Belluno [Marshal Victor] guarded the bridgehead on the left [east] bank; the Duke of Reggio was on the right [west] bank with the entire army behind him.

With Borisov evacuated [by the French], the [Russian] armies of the Dvina and Volhynia communicated with each other and planned a joint attack [against the French on both sides of the river]. At dawn on the 28th, the Duke of Reggio informed the EMPEROR he was under attack; a half an hour later, so was the Duke of Belluno on the left bank; the army took up the fight. The Duke of Elchingen aided the Duke of Reggio; and the Duke of Treviso [Marshal Mortier] reinforced the Duke of Elchingen. The battle heated up; the enemy sought to overrun our right flank; General Doumerc, who commanded the Vth Division of *Cuirassiers*, a part of the IInd Corps stationed at Dvina, ordered the IVth and Vth Cavalry Regiment of *Cuirassiers* to charge at the same time as the Legion of the Vistula entered the woods to pierce the center of the enemy forces, which collapsed and were routed. These brave *cuirassiers* in turn smashed six infantry squares and routed the enemy cavalry coming to aid the infantry; six thousand prisoners, two flags, and six cannon fell into our hands.

The Duke of Belluno, for his part, had his troops attack the enemy vigorously, defeated him, took five hundred to six hundred prisoners, and kept the enemy beyond the range of the cannon near the bridge. General Fournier made a fine cavalry charge.

In the fight on the Berezina, the [Russian] army of Volhynia suffered greatly. The Duke of Reggio was wounded, but not seriously. He was shot in the side.

The next day, on the 29th, we remained on the battlefield. We had to choose one of two routes, that of Minsk or that of Vilna. The Minsk route passes through a forest and swampy wasteland, and it would have been impossible for the army to live off the land. On the other hand, the Vilna route passes through very good land. The army, without cavalry, lacking ammunition, dreadfully fatigued by a fifty-day march, dragging along the sick and the wounded of so many battles, needed to reach its stores. On the 30th, the headquarters was at Pleshchenitsy; on December 1, at Slaiki; and on December 3, at Molodechno, where the army met the first supply columns from Vilna.

The wounded officers and soldiers, and all that was difficult to transport, luggage, etc., were sent off toward Vilna.

That the army must reestablish discipline, refresh itself, replenish its cavalry, artillery, and supplies is the consequence of the events just described. Its fundamental need is rest. Supplies and horses are arriving. General Bourcier has already more than twenty thousand fresh horses in various depots. The artillery has already made up its losses. The generals, officers, and soldiers have suffered much from fatigue and a shortage of food. Many have lost their equipment as a result of losing their horses; some because of Cossack ambushes. The Cossacks have captured a number of isolated individuals, surveyors who were mapping positions, and wounded officers who marched recklessly, preferring to take risks rather than marching deliberately and with escorts.

The reports of the general officers commanding the corps will announce the officers and soldiers who most distinguished themselves and will furnish detailed accounts of all these memorable events.

In all these troop movements, the EMPEROR has always traveled in the middle of his Guard—the cavalry commanded by Marshal [Bessières] Duke of Istria and the infantry commanded by the Duke of Danzig [Marshal Lefebvre]. The high morale of his Guard has continued to please HIS MAJESTY. It has always been ready to go anywhere the circumstances would require; but the circumstances have always been such that its simple presence was enough and to attack was unnecessary. . . .

Our cavalry had lost so many horses that it was possible to join together the officers who still had mounts into four companies of 150 men each. The generals served as captains, and the colonels as noncommissioned officers. This Sacred squadron, led by General Grouchy and under the orders of the King of Naples [Murat], never lost sight of the EMPEROR wherever he went.

HIS MAJESTY'S health has never been better.[1]

[1][This last sentence was not simply an insensitive, arrogant statement. Napoleon was trying to reassure his subjects that, despite rumors to the contrary, he was healthy and that the recent coup d'état by General Malet had failed.—Eds.]

David G. Chandler (1934–   ), a clergyman's son, was born in England. He attended the University of Oxford and served as an officer in the British Army from 1957 to 1960. He teaches in the Department of War Studies and International Affairs at the Royal Military Academy at Sandhurst, England. He has published three massive books on Napoleonic warfare, The Campaigns of Napoleon *(1966)*, a Dictionary of the Napoleonic Wars *(1979)* and Napoleon's Marshals *(1986)*, as well as other books about Napoleon and military history in general.

NAPOLEON'S ERRORS OF JUDGMENT
David G. Chandler

The first result of the Russian Campaign was the irretrievable shattering of the legend of Napoleonic invincibility. Defeat in Russia, added to Britain's unquestioned command of the seas and the progressive deterioration of the Peninsular War [Spanish War] where the Emperor's subordinates were soon vainly attempting to contain the new advance of Wellington's army, did much to build a new confidence among the governments and peoples of the submerged powers of continental Europe. This was to lead to a new effort by Prussia and the other states of North Germany to throw off the conqueror's yoke. In the course of a few months, Austria too would abandon the French alliance and throw in her lot with Russia and Prussia. Thus the immediate consequences of 1812 were the preparation of the War of German Liberation and the rapid diminution of the French sphere of influence in Europe.

The disasters of 1812 also exercised a most detrimental influence on French military potential. Because of the magnitude of the losses sustained, Napoleon was to experience the greatest difficulty in reconstructing his armies to face the coming Russian and German challenge. The scale of his losses were formidable by any standards. No less than 655,000 troops crossed the Vistula during the summer months of 1812 (including second line forces and reinforcements), but this vast multitude was reduced to a mere 93,000 men by the new year of 1813. By far the greatest proportion of casualties was borne by the central army group, which in its heyday numbered 450,000 combatants; of this vast armament, only 25,000 bedraggled survivors re-

---

From David G. Chandler, *The Campaigns of Napoleon* (New York: Macmillan, 1966), pp. 852–861. Reprinted by the permission of Macmillan Publishing Company. Copyright © 1964 by David G. Chandler.

crossed the Niemen. The flanking forces were rather more fortunate; between them, Schwarzenberg and Macdonald, Augereau and Reynier brought 68,000 combatants out of Russia, but a considerable proportion of the XIth Corps had never stirred out of Prussia or Poland. In round figures, therefore, Napoleon lost 570,000 soldiers. Of these, perhaps 370,000 died on the battlefield, of illness or exposure. The remaining 200,000 including 48 generals and 3,000 other officers, fell into Russian hands, but at least half of these unfortunates subsequently perished. Besides manpower, the Emperor had also lost over 200,000 trained horses (cavalry, artillery and transport services included). In some ways this was even more significant than the loss of his men, for although Napoleon would prove capable of filling most of the gaps in his ranks by arming pensioners and schoolboys in 1813, he was never to be able to reconstitute his cavalry arm effectively. This deficiency was to be gravely felt during his remaining campaigns. Furthermore, of the 1,300 cannon taken into Russia, only 250 remained in French hands at the end of the campaign (most of them belonging to the flanking corps). The Russians captured 929 of the remainder according to their records; the rest must have been destroyed or lost in rivers and swamps. However, the resources of the Empire were to prove capable of replacing much of this loss of metal before the next campaign; it was to be experienced men, and above all horses that presented the main problems, and French military strength never recovered from the losses incurred in Russia.

Russian losses over the same period were also far from light; it is estimated that at least 150,000 perished from all causes, and at least twice as many more must have been crippled by wounds or frostbite. An incalculable number of Russian civilians must also have suffered during the seven months of bitter fighting. However, by the end of the year, the Tsar's forces enjoyed the great advantage of a strategical victory over Napoleon with which to boost their morale—the soil of Holy Russia was clear of the invader. The French forces and people had no such compensation. If it were possible, France's allies had even less reason for comfort or complacency.

The reasons for Napoleon's cataclysm have often been analyzed and enumerated, and it may be useful to list the most important of them together with general remarks concerning his conduct of operations under the main headings of national policy, strategy and grand tactics. In this way it will be possible to build up a picture of French and Russian strengths and weaknesses which between them account for this tremendous reversal in Napoleon's fortunes.

From the very outset, the Emperor made grave errors of policy and suffered the consequences of several unfavorable diplomatic developments before even a single soldier placed foot on the Russian bank of the River Niemen. It can be argued that his cause was doomed from the moment the executive order was issued to invade Russian soil. If the threat posed by over half a million men massed along his frontiers was insufficient to persuade the Tsar to seek an accommodation, it was unlikely that Alexander would be brought to terms by battle or occupation of ground once war had been joined; for military reverses only seemed to steel Russian determination, while the huge extent of the Tsar's possessions made effective conquest virtually impossible. However remote Napoleon's chances of ultimate success might have been on account of the very nature of the people and the land which he set out to overthrow, there were even more telling grand strategical reasons that doomed him to probable failure from the very outset. First, there was the mistake of trying to wage war on two widely separated fronts at one and the same time. Napoleon should have taken steps to bring the Peninsular War to some form of conclusion before undertaking his even greater Russian project; to try to mount and maintain two such massive campaigns at once proved the height of folly. Not only did the continuation of the Spanish war tie down 200,000 veteran French soldiers and place an impossible strain on French resources, it also forced the Emperor to bully unwilling allies into producing large contingents for the war with Russia. This, in itself, was a potent cause of weakness. The Prussian and Austrian courts bitterly resented Napoleon's inflexible decision to involve them in a French war designed to enforce the economic sanctions of the Continental System which were as inconvenient to Berlin and Vienna as to St. Petersburg. Their cooperation, therefore, was at best unwilling, and this atmosphere of resentment and distrust inevitably percolated to the generals and even the rank and file. On a purely practical level, the multiplicity of languages and types of military equipment included in the *Grande Armée* of 1812 made the maintenance of discipline, passing of orders and logistical support even more problematical.

Nor was allied cooperation assisted by the fact that Austrian and Prussian forces were called to serve alongside Poles and Lithuanians. The Polish question formed another source of severe friction between Berlin, Vienna and Paris. In consequence, Napoleon fell between two stools. For the sake of allied solidarity, he dared not reconstitute the ancient Kingdom of Poland despite the entreaties of Poniatowski and other accredited Polish leaders; as a result he never received complete Polish or Lithuanian support, while Austrian and Prussian suspicions of his ultimate intentions remained as sharp as ever. Thus Napoleon's alliances were riddled with inconsistencies and damaging, unsolved dilemmas; despite his army's magnificent outward appearance in June 1812, the giant had feet of clay.

If Napoleon's diplomatic preparations for the campaign were weak, those of his rival the Tsar were unexpectedly successful. The Emperor could expect the development of an Anglo-Russian *entente*, but he considered that this would have little practical influence on the campaign apart from possible naval intervention in the Baltic. However, he never anticipated that the Tsar would prove able to make peace with his inveterate Turkish enemy, or invoke the assistance (or at least friendly neutrality) of an ex-Prince and Marshal of the Empire, Bernadotte of Sweden. These two Russian diplomatic coups had a decided bearing on the course of military events in 1812. Not only were Napoleon's calculations that large Russian forces would be tied down in Moldavia and Finland proved utterly erroneous, but large numbers of troops were abruptly made available for active operations against the French; both Admiral Tshitshagov and General Steinheil made notable contributions to the French defeat by mounting telling attacks on Napoleon's overextended flanks. At the level of grand strategy, therefore, Napoleon was consistently outmaneuvered or hoodwinked by his opponents.

It is on the strategical level, however, that we find most reasons for the French catastrophe of 1812. Without a doubt the greatest single reason for Napoleon's defeat was the unsurmountable logistical problem. In the simplest terms, the task of feeding and equipping 600,000 troops in a hostile land proved too much for the administrative devices of the period. . . . The Emperor made unprecedented efforts to provide his forces with adequate logistical support for the Russian venture, but these proved hopelessly insufficient. In the first place, his staff made gross miscalculations regarding the traffic capacity of the atrocious Polish and Russian roads, and this meant that every convoy was weeks and even months late in reaching its specified destination. Similarly, the local grain and fodder resources of Russia were overestimated, and the speed at which the vast herds of cattle accompanying the army could move was incorrectly assessed. All these problems, present from the outset of operations, steadily grew in severity as the campaign progressed, and in the end the overstrained French transport services broke down completely. The depots were sited too far away to the rear, the Russian scorched-earth policy deprived the army of even rudimentary local supplies, and the mud roads could not take the necessary volume of traffic. The main weakness lay in the inadequate arrangements for supplying the forward units; it is of significance that the retreating relics of Napoleon's army found huge quantities of supplies of every description at Smolensk, Vilna and Kovno, and that the Russians captured further well-supplied depots at Minsk and Vitebsk. It was not so much shortage of supplies, therefore, as the inability to move and distribute them to the forward areas that doomed the *Grande Armée* to virtual elimination. Napoleon's well-known maxim that "an army marches on its stomach" was never better illustrated than during his own Russian campaign.

The logistical problem underlies the second grave strategical error on the part of Napoleon which compromised his chances of success. His decision to press on from Smolensk to Moscow proved the proverbial "straw that broke the camel's back" as far as his supply services were concerned; it also revealed the complete failure of his original plan of campaign. Before he set foot in Russia, Napoleon had no expectation of marching to Moscow. His avowed aim was to force the Tsar's armies to accept major battle at the earliest possible moment, ideally in scattered detachments, if necessary united together. The rather unusual means to this end was to be an all-out French offensive from the very start; no geographical target was specifically laid down, nor was the enemy to be encouraged to make the first move—as Napoleon usually preferred. This he proved incapable of achieving. In the first three months of the campaign . . . [there were] four successive attempts to trap the Russians into battle, but each failed in turn. [The Russian generals] Barclay de Tolly and Bagration successfully eluded the traps laid for them separately or collectively in the maneuvers of Vilna, Vitebsk, Drissa and Smolensk. These failures led Napoleon ever further into the depths of Russia, and when at length he reached Smolensk without finding his big battle he took his final gamble and decided to press on immediately for Moscow. All subsequent difficulties stemmed from this decision. The experts mostly agree that the French should have spent the winter of 1812–13 around Smolensk, building up their strength and supplies, preparatory to resuming the campaign the following spring. . . . During this further advance he certainly found his big battle [Borodino], useless though it proved (owing to inadequate numbers of troops being available to harass and destroy [Russian Field Marshal] Kutusov's retreating columns), and also occupied his adversary's religious capital, but these successes did nothing to win the campaign or end the war; they only made the probability of ultimate French defeat still stronger. Impatience and a refusal to accept the realities of the strategic position lured Napoleon and his army onward to their doom.

As the Emperor hounded his army eastward by ever longer forced marches, destroying the cohesion of his exhausted cavalry and dislocating his administrative arrangements, a third strategic factor came noticeably into play, that of strategic consumption. Every mile that Napoleon advanced implied a further decrease in his battle power, until the point was reached on September 7 when he no longer had enough men in hand to win his decisive victory. As the lines of communication inexorably grew and the length of his protective flanks extended, more and more first-line troops had to be diverted to perform secondary roles—the protection of depots, staging posts, the mounting of road patrols and internal security guards, the provision of city garrisons and escorts for couriers and convoys. Increasing suspicion of Prussian intentions also deprived the army of the greater part of Augereau's XIth Corps. This steady drain of manpower explains the relative failure experienced on the field of Borodino; the Russians received rude handling, but Napoleon did not possess the resources to convert victory into triumph. Once he had shot his bolt he found it impossible to retain the vast area of territory technically under his control. His resources were overextended, and thus hopelessly exposed to the danger of Russian counterattack.

The decision to spend a full month in operational inactivity around Moscow is a further indictment of Napoleon's strategy. Periods of frantic forward movement inevitably alternated with phases of deadening inactivity throughout the first half of the campaign. The lull at Vilna enabled Barclay and Bagration to make good their escape towards Smolensk; the pause at Moscow enabled the Tsar to rally his forces and await the approach of "General Winter." If Napoleon really hoped that the Tsar might be inclined to make peace in September, he would have been better advised to mount some form of further operations against Kutusov to back up his proposed terms. Instead, his inaction revealed the real extent of his weakness, and wasted four vital weeks of good weather into the bargain. In any case, he was misguided in believing that possession of Moscow would, of itself, lead to peace. French occupation of Vienna in 1805 and 1809 had not per se induced the Austrian Emperor to come to terms, nor had the fall of Berlin in 1806 brought the hapless Frederick William to his knees. Why then should Moscow in 1812, especially as the Tsar possessed a second capital of almost equal standing in St. Petersburg?

The ultimate strategical error committed by Napoleon occurred a week after quitting Moscow. His decision to march south from the Russian capital towards the fertile and unspoiled areas of Kaluga province was sound enough, but this wise and well-considered move was summarily abandoned when the army ran into resistance at Malojaroslavets, even though the outcome of that action was a French success. It is very doubtful whether Kutusov, mindful of Borodino, would have accepted another major action in defense of Kaluga; according to General Wilson, he had already determined on retreat if Napoleon pushed on. However, a fit of over-caution also infected Napoleon, and he threw away his best opportunity of survival, and certainly of ultimate victory, by falling back along the ravaged northern route to Smolensk. From that moment the issue of the campaign was never in doubt.

Another strategic factor that played a large part in this campaign was, of course, the Russian climate. This is the most often quoted reason for Napoleon's catastrophe, and yet it is generally misinterpreted. It is true that Napoleon was guilty of failing to order sufficient preparations for meeting the changes in Russian weather, but it is erroneous to attribute his failure to the Russian winter to any large degree. Napoleon was already decisively beaten before the serious frosts began; they served only to increase the scale of his disaster; the cold was not in itself even a major contributory factor to his strategic defeat. Napoleon tried to explain away his losses by blaming the weather, but this was largely propaganda. "My army has had some losses," he modestly admitted to the Senate on December 20, "but this was due to the premature rigors of the season."[1] From these words and the tone of the 29th Bulletin a celebrated historical myth has emerged.

In point of fact, Napoleon's army suffered as much damage from the heat of the Russian summer as from the rigors of the winter. Tens of thousands of cavalry and artillery horses died before Napoleon ever reached Moscow; tens of thousands of men dropped out of the ranks through sickness and heat exhaustion before the battle of Borodino was fought. The hot weather of July and August was as much to blame for Napoleon's defeat as the frosts of November and December. Indeed, the conditions pertaining at the outset of the retreat were far more favorable than might have been hoped for. The first severe frosts were encountered only on November 12, and these gave way to an unseasonable thaw that proved even more embarrassing to the French as they approached the crucial Berezina crossing, producing muddy roads, impassable countryside and swollen waterways instead of firm going and frozen rivers. This fact explains the importance of Borisov's bridges, and the reason for the apparently suicidal burning of the French pontoon train at Orsha (at a time when the hard frosts seemed established). "As it happened," recorded Marbot, "the frost, which at this time of the year should have transformed the water of the Berezina into an easy road, had left them almost entirely fluid when we wanted to cross. Hardly were we over before a severe frost froze them to a point when they were solid enough to carry cannon."[2] Indeed, the real effects of winter were experienced only after December 4, when the temperature plunged many degrees below zero. Well before that

---

[1]F. Markham, *Napoleon* (London: 1963), p. 187.
[2]Baron M. de Marbot, *Mémoires* (Paris: 1891), Vol. III, p. 208.

date, the *Grande Armée* had been reduced to a shadow of its former self. However, it is true that the cold served to increase the scale of the disaster during the final stage of the retreat when the strategic outcome had already been long decided.

It is also necessary to mention the record of the Russian forces to obtain a balanced view of the campaign. Although they deserve praise for dogged endurance and considerable skill in action, the Russian generals were really more fortunate than they deserved. Although there is no doubt that the Russian strategy of trading space for time was the most effective one possible for dealing with Napoleon and exhausting the impetus of his offensive, it is by no means certain whether this was the outcome of deliberate Russian policy or sheer military necessity. The fortification of the Dvina and the Dnieper river lines before the declaration of war would seem to indicate a more static strategic intention. Barclay and Bagration showed considerable skill in successfully uniting their armies at Smolensk without being forced to give battle, but their subsequent half-hearted attempt to launch a counter-offensive would seem to suggest that their retreat was the product of weakness rather than of design. Moreover, Kutusov's decision to stand and fight before Moscow would seem to indicate divided counsels at Moscow and St. Petersburg, for this was not militarily a sound idea, whatever its political and national motivation, and the Russians were fortunate to escape with so large a proportion of their fighting strength from the battlefield.

Thus it is difficult to detect a consistently applied strategy underlying Russian operations in the period up to the loss of Moscow. Thereafter a definite plan does emerge. It was clearly a matter of policy to keep Napoleon lingering near Moscow for as long as possible, and then implement a strategy to trap his army at a convenient river line when at last he began to retreat. The plan was sound, but its execution was faulty. Kutusov seems to have had no desire to try conclusions with Napoleon on the field of battle, and he appears to have deliberately set out to ruin the Tsar's plan by failing to push Napoleon's retiring columns to the uttermost. Similarly, his colleagues, Wittgenstein and Tshitshagov, do not come very well out of the events around the Berezina. It can be argued that Napoleon owed his defeat to a combination of his own miscalculations and the dogged strength of character displayed by Tsar Alexander in repeatedly refusing to entertain the idea of a settlement. The contribution of the Russian soldiery was only of secondary importance; the raids of Cossacks and partisan bands did more harm to the Emperor than all the endeavors of the regular field armies of Holy Russia.

Any study of the campaign's grand tactics will also reveal grave deficiencies on the French side. Napoleon is personally to blame for most of his subordinates' errors that compromised his repeated attempts to secure victory. His system of command was gravely at fault. It was beyond the powers of any one man to control the movements of half a million men, and yet Napoleon was insistent that he should be the sole source of authority. His marshals were not allowed to think or act for themselves, and consequently when the exigencies of distance separated them from Napoleon's all-controlling presence their showing was often far from impressive. As Caulaincourt related, "The staff foresaw nothing, but on the other hand, as the Emperor wanted to do everything himself and give every order, no one, not even the general staff, dared to assume the responsibility of giving the most trifling order."[3] Jerome [Bonaparte] accordingly failed to carry out his proposed role in the maneuver of Vilna; Macdonald, Oudinot, Victor and St. Cyr failed to coordinate effectively their efforts against Wittgenstein on the River Dvina, thereby missing several opportunities of annihilating the Russian right wing; Davout and Eugène hesitated when temporarily cut off on the retreat toward Vilna; and [Austrian, Field Marshal] Schwarzenberg [an ally of Napoleon during this campaign] acted with complete disregard for the moves of the main army through lack of proper supervision.

And yet, although the Emperor insisted on his own omnipotence, there are many signs that his physical and moral energy were no longer sufficient for the calls he placed upon them. He lingered for two weeks at Vilna instead of supervising the vital enveloping moves by his corps. En route for Smolensk, he wasted a crucial day holding a review to mark his birthday; he dallied for a month at Moscow instead of busying himself devising new methods of bringing pressure to bear on the Tsar. His record on the field of battle was often even less impressive. At Smolensk he retired to his quarters at 5:00 P.M. before the outcome was settled, and thus was not at hand to force Junot to take his opportunity. At Borodino, he scoffed at Davout's suggested encircling move, imposed his own idea of an unsubtle and wasteful frontal attack, and then spent the whole day in complete inactivity making little contribution to events apart from repeatedly refusing to send up the Imperial Guard. At Malojaroslavets, he was sufficiently disconcerted by a near-brush with a party of Cossacks to prevent his generals conducting a reconnaissance beyond the nearby ridge which would have revealed the road to Kaluga completely empty of Russians. These are evidences of a decline in his military powers, but conversely he must be awarded full credit for this conduct of the brilliant actions at Krasnoe and Berezina which were masterpieces of the military art.

---

[3]General de Caulaincourt, *Mémoires*, pocket edition (London: 1950), Vol. I, p. 155.

NAPOLEON'S ERRORS OF JUDGMENT

In the last analysis, Napoleon's defeat can be explained in terms of two circumstances. First, a general decline in the quality of his generalship, shown first of all in a lack of energy which led to poor supervision of subordinates and repeated failure to intervene personally at the decisive point (as had ever been his practice in the years of his prime); this is also reflected in growing indulgence in wishful thinking concerning the military capabilities of his troops (which he persistently overestimated) and the character of the Tsar (whom he consistently underestimated). The second circumstance was the sheer size of the enterprise he attempted to undertake; it is doubtful whether any other soldier in history would have achieved a larger measure of success, both in the preparatory and the executive phases under the military conditions of 1812. But, in the words of the philosopher Montaigne, quoted by the American historian, Dodge: "Great and distant enterprises perish from the very magnitude of the preparations made to ensure their success."[4] The problems of space, time and distance proved too great for even one of the greatest military minds that has ever existed, but it was the failure of a giant surrounded by pygmies.

[4] T. A. Dodge, *Napoleon* (New York: 1904), Vol. III, p. 696.

10
NAPOLEON AND THE ARTS AND SCIENCES

For centuries before 1800 the rulers of France regarded the advancement of learning as a duty and a source of glory. Napoleon too expressed this sentiment. But did his rhetoric exceed his performance, and how substantial were the gains from his actions?

Dora B. Weiner argues that Napoleon paid little attention to medicine. He distrusted physicians and neglected most medical institutions. The consequences were, paradoxically, not so bad as one might expect. Military battle casualties from untreated wounds and illnesses proved to be enormous, but Napoleonic France still achieved great progress in such fields as clinical medicine, public health, and surgery.

On the other hand, Maurice P. Crosland advances a more favorable view of Napoleon as a patron. Although Napoleon had little appreciation of art and literature, he did value science and technology. He may have failed to stress the teaching of science in the secondary schools, but he did give posts, honors, and subsidies to scientists, technologists, and industrialists, who in turn promoted agriculture, industry, and scientific knowledge.

During the period from 1799 to 1815, France was a leader in medicine and science. It also was the home of such distinguished artists as Jacques-Louis David and of such eminent men of letters as Chateaubriand. Did all this creativity flourish largely because of Napoleon or despite him?[1] Before trying to answer such a broad question, it might be useful to ask such preliminary questions as these: To what extent did the Napoleonic regime support medicine, science, art, literature, and other branches of learning? What motivated this support? What limitations existed on freedom of expression in the arts and sciences?

[1]For more detailed information on this question than the two short selections that follow, see Crosland's entire book and the articles "Architecture," "Art," "Economy, French," "Literature," "Medicine," "Science," "Sculpture," "Symbolism and Style," and "Theater" in the *Historical Dictionary of Napoleonic France, 1799–1815*, ed. Owen Connelly (Westport, Connecticut: Greenwood Press, 1985).

Dora B. Weiner (1924–), born in Germany, received her secondary school degree in France in 1941 and her Ph.D. from Columbia University in 1951. She has taught at several American colleges and universities. At present she holds a joint appointment in the schools of medicine and liberal arts at the University of California at Los Angeles. Her chief research interest is the history of French medicine and public health since 1750. She is the author of Raspail, Scientist and Reformer *(1968) and many learned articles, including several on the Napoleonic period.*

MEDICINE
Dora B. Weiner

The evidence suggests that the beginning of the Consulate marks a dividing line between eight years of republican rule when the welfare of citizens and soldiers—including their health—was of genuine concern to the government, and fifteen years of Napoleonic autocracy when the needs of strategy, administrative efficiency, and economy gradually gained ascendance over humanitarian and medical considerations. The first period is marked by official gratitude toward the maimed and wounded, by some deference toward the competence of medical men, by idealistic experiments in medical education and in prompt assistance to casualties on the battlefield. Even in this early period there is evidence that, despite the enlightened tenor of the law, the traditional prejudice against doctors was already reasserting itself and that the military resisted the intrusion of professionals with a higher allegiance than to the god of war.

In the Napoleonic era only "battle surgery" (the phrase is [the renowned Napoleonic surgeon P. F.] Percy's) met with any kind of success. Other medical assistance was gradually rendered impossible. Indeed, from Austerlitz to Leipzig, the battlefields lay far from home, problems of logistics became insuperable, supplies were scarce, many soldiers were foreigners (making communication with French doctors difficult and often eliciting less dedicated efforts than French patients), the army "health officer" was of increasingly doubtful competence since the army medical schools had been abolished, until

---

From Dora B. Weiner, "French Doctors Face War, 1792–1815," *From the Ancien Régime to the Popular Front,* ed. Charles K. Warner (New York: Columbia University Press, 1969), pp. 56, 67–73. Reprinted by permission of the author and the publisher. Copyright © 1969.

finally, in the merciless Russian winter of 1812, mere survival remained the only aim of the hale, and the wounded died in the snow, of cold and starvation. . . .

Napoleon disliked doctors and distrusted medication. His experiences in Italy and Egypt had convinced him that most drugs were worthless. This confirmed his view that clean water, fresh air, moderation, and will power were the best therapeutic agents. He had also found that doctors tended to have minds of their own and this, as his power grew, he increasingly resented. Once First Consul, he muzzled the "Ideologues," those "idea-mongers," many of them physicians, who believed in observation, experiment, and the power of the individual mind.[1] While one might attempt to portray Napoleon as a patron of science, one could not possibly depict him as encouraging medicine.[2] Once emperor, he surrounded himself with medical courtiers such as Corvisart who had independent judgment but was a therapeutic skeptic like His Majesty.

As for his own health, Napoleon was unconcerned. He *knew*, from boyhood on, that because his father and grandfather had died of cancer of the stomach this would be his fatal illness as well. He would therefore die of nothing else. He participated fearlessly in sixty major battles; he had nineteen horses shot from under him. He thought himself invulnerable. He died of cancer of the stomach.[3]

Napoleon's attitude toward medicine was thus solidly rooted in prejudice. His *Correspondence* and his remarks to the Council of State suggest that he gave medicine little attention. His directives for the soldiers' well-being emphasized preventive and hygienic measures: healthful encampments, adequate rest, solid shoes and warm clothing, sound food, fresh air, and good spirits—these were his preferred medications. One can hardly quarrel with these precepts. High casualties depressed him. As for the wounded, his main concern—like any general's—was their return to active duty. He had little sympathy with men who, like Percy, urged the creation of an Army

---

[1] See G.Rosen, "The Philosophy of Ideology and the Emergence of Modern Medicine in France," *Bulletin of the History of Medicine*, XX (1946), 328–39; and O. Temkin, "The Philosophical Background of Magendie's Physiology," *Ibid.*, 10–35.

[2] In an excellent recent study of the Société d'Arcueil, the author attempts to show that Napoleon furthered science. A more convincing case could be made for Napoleon as a champion of technology. See M. Crosland, *The Society of Arcueil: A View of French Science at the Time of Napoleon I* (London, 1967).

[3] See, for example, A. Braun, "Napoleon I und die Medizin," *Zeitschrift für ärtzliche Fortbildung*, XXX (1933), 628–29; B. Sokoloff, *Napoleon: A Doctor's Biography* (New York, 1937); and J. Kemble, *Napoleon Immortal: The Medical History and Private Life of Napoleon Bonaparte* (London, 1959). [In a controversial book, Ben Weider and David Hapgood, *The Murder of Napoleon* (New York: St. Martin's, 1982), claim that Napoleon died of poisoning.—Eds.]

Medical Corps with career officers, special schools, a distinctive uniform, and appropriate salaries.

Lest one be tempted to condemn too categorically Napoleon's shabby treatment of his army doctors, it should be remembered that the Imperial Guard had a medical service which was judged excellent by contemporaries. Each battalion of infantry or squadron of cavalry had its surgeon; the Guard had its own hospital, its light maneuverable ambulances, its special personnel, uniformed down to the male nurses. Morale was high, to the end, at Waterloo. True, this medical service was the work of [the surgeon D. J.] Larrey, but it was not only Larrey's work: the chief physician, surgeon, and pharmacist of the Guard's medical service were paid 9,690 francs a year, more than three and a half times the salary of the highest paid army doctors with thirty years' service.

Much could have been done with money, a little time, and a will. It is true that excellent improvements in battle surgery were planned and, had the plans been carried out, French soldiers would have received prompt and efficient succor on the battlefield. Given the opportunity offered Napoleon Bonaparte in the Year VIII [1799–1800], subsequent legislation concerning army medicine comes as a shock.

By a succession of decrees from 1800 to 1804[4] hundreds of medical officers were discharged with a small sum of money as their only reward, the army medical schools were abolished, and the staffs of the army hospitals sharply reduced. The health council was replaced by six inspectors and the authority of doctors strictly limited to medical matters. The administrative officials of the war department would make the decisions regarding army medicine. As a result of these measures, "the entire medical corps of the army gradually disintegrated."[5] The number of army physicians declined from 210 doctors and 1,665 surgeons in 1800 to 62 doctors and 842 surgeons in 1802. "As far as any other health personnel was concerned the situation was very much worse, indeed, such personnel practically no longer existed,"[6] and the army medical services were seething with "discouragement, rage, and revolt."[7]

[4]The main relevant decrees were dated: 4 Germinal and 24 Thermidor, Year VIII; 16 Frimaire and 15 Nivôse, Year IX; 18 Vendémiaire, Year X; 20 Vendémiaire, Year XI; 9 Frimaire, Year XII; and 14 Fructidor, Year XIII. The decree of 15 Nivôse, Year IX, ended by stating: "The army medical service is based on temporary commissions only and . . . strictly speaking, *there is no medical corps*" (italics mine).
[5]A. G. Chevalier, "Hygienic Problems in the Napoleonic Armies," *Ciba Symposia*, III, No. 6 (Sept., 1941), p. 974.
[6]*Ibid.*, p. 975.
[7]Dr. Brice and Captain Bottet, *Le Corps de santé militaire en France, son évolution, ses campagnes, 1708–1882* (Paris, 1907), p. xviii.

Why did Napoleon Bonaparte choose to face fifteen years of warfare without an adequate medical service? Chevalier argues that he anticipated "a long peace."[8] This theory is hardly tenable. Some aver that his medical service was adequate. The evidence is meager indeed.[9] He may have thought that, in case of war, he might work another miracle of 1793 and assemble another Army Medical Corps by an appeal to patriotism. How wrong he was, if he considered the campaign of Austerlitz a mere sequel to the victory of Valmy! The stark truth is that army medicine under a military dictator is really a paradox, since warfare and healing serve diametrically opposed purposes: generals court death; doctors preserve life. Napoleon would have composed his differences with Russia and England had the true welfare of his men been his paramount concern.

Perusal of the numerous medical accounts of the Spanish campaign of 1808 and the Russian campaign of 1812 soon makes it clear that medical care gradually became an irrelevant luxury. The heat and drought of Spain, the cold and snow of Russia, the poor logistic preparation resulting in lack of food and supplies were more effective killers than battle wounds or sickness. The diaries of Blaze[10] and Percy[11] in Spain, of Larrey,[12] de Kerckhoffs, and Roos[13] in Russia are heartrending documents. The hunger, thirst, cold, and pain were indescribable. Out of an army of over half a million men which invaded Russia in 1812, 350,000 died or "disappeared." A doctor of the Imperial Guard complained that "there was a drastic lack of transportation, food, medical supplies, and drugs. Several days after a battle

---

[8]Chevalier, "Hygienic Problems in the Napoleonic Armies," p. 113.
[9]S. Haendcke, "Beiträge zur Hygiene in der Armee Napoleons I," *Sudhoffs Archiv für Geschichte der Medizin*, XXVI (1933), 47–64; F. Helme, "Napoléon et la médecine: La prophylaxie et le service de santé," *La Presse médicale*, XXIX Annexe (June 15, 18, 1921), pp. 853–55, 177–80; R. Lacronique, "Mesures d'hygiène et de prophylaxie prescrites à l'armée d'Allemagne, 1810–1812," *La France médicale*, 51st year (October 25, 1904), pp. 377–84.
[10]S. Blaze, *Mémoires d'un apothicaire sur la guerre d'Espagne pendant les années 1808 à 1814* (2 vols.; Paris, 1828). In one of his lighter moods, Blaze classified military personnel as follows: First class, glory and wealth (imperial marshals and generals); second class, glory without wealth (most officers); third class, wealth without glory (war commissioners, employees of the treasury, the supply corps, the hospitals . . .); fourth class, neither wealth nor glory (health officers, doctors, surgeons, pharmacists). Vol. II, pp. 220–28.
[11]P. F. Percy, *Journal des campagnes du baron Percy, chirurgien-en-chef de la grande armée (1754–1825)* (Paris, 1904).
[12]D. J. Larrey, *Clinique chirurgicale exercée particulièrement dans les camps et les hôpitaux militaires depuis 1792 jusqu'à 1829* (Paris, 1829–36), 5 vols.
[13]J. R. L. de Kerckhoffs, *Histoire des maladies observées dans la grande armée française entre 1812 et 1813* (Anvers, 1836); H. Roos, *Souvenirs d'un médecin de la grande armée* (Paris, 1913).

one could still find wounded men who had not been helped. They would die of hunger rather than of their wounds . . . ."[14] In the frenzied retreat from Moscow casualties were a handicap: "Everyone had the same idea: get rid of the wounded. Whenever the soldiers stopped to camp or to rest and these unfortunates needed to get out of the carriage or to have their dressings changed, they were abandoned."[15] One history of the French Army Medical Service comments:

> The Empire scorned humanity. . . . The abandonment and disdain of the wounded was the rule in its armies. The decadence of the medical service is one of its major faults. Though this service included the most famous doctors and surgeons, they were hampered by changing and incoherent laws; they lacked encouragement and support and could act only as individuals. How remarkable would their work have been if the all-powerful Emperor had supported them, if their prescriptions of drugs and hygienic measures had been acted on by well-trained assistants! They could thus have curtailed the horrendous expenditure in French lives extracted by the Great Epic![16]

Many French army doctors, it would seem, would gladly have followed Napoleon into battle, had the Army Medical Service been better organized.

Civilian French medicine reaped considerable benefits from Napoleon's disdain and neglect—albeit benefits of a negative nature. Phy-

---

[14]M. Bouvry, "Services de santé et ravitaillement de la grande armée pendant la campagne de 1812," *La Presse médicale*, LXIV (1956), 1804. (This is a review of a Paris thesis [1955] by Pierre Blouin, which I have not yet been able to examine.)
[15]*Ibid.*
[16]Brice and Bottet, *Le corps de santé militaire en France* . . . , p. xix.

The following statistics need no comment: "Of the 4½ million soldiers engaged in the Revolutionary and Napoleonic Armies during 1792–1815 about 2½ million died in hospitals and 150,000 were killed in action . . . . In the Egyptian campaign Bonaparte lost 4,758 out of 30,000 in action and 4,157 from disease, of whom 1,689, including 40 medical officers, died from bubonic plague. In the Russian campaign his total forces, increased to 533,000 by reinforcements, had shrunken to 95,000 when he reached Moscow, although there had been only two battles. . . .

"The losses in the principal battles from Austerlitz to Waterloo were:

Austerlitz: 12,000 French killed and wounded out of 94,000;
Jena-Auerstadt: 6,000 out of 96,000;
Eylau: 15,000 out of 79,000;
Friedland: 12,000 out of 86,000;
Aspern: 8,000 killed, 24,000 wounded out of 70,000;
Wagram: 23,000 killed and wounded, 7,000 missing out of 181,700;
Smolensk: 20,000 out of 180,000;
Borodino: 32,000 out of 130,000;
Leipzig: 30,000 out of 145,000;
Waterloo: 30,000 killed and wounded, 6,000 prisoners, out of 72,000."
From F. H. Garrison, *Notes on the History of Military Medicine* (Washington, D.C., 1922), pp. 169–70.

sicians were not drafted into the army in huge numbers. The medical schools and the hospitals suffered relatively little interference. And it is in these medical schools, especially in Paris and in the Parisian hospitals, that clinical medicine now blossomed. Born of the ideas held by the reformers of the late eighteenth century (Condillac, Helvétius, and their circle), freed from the shackles of tradition by the bold destructive blows of the Revolution, channeled into creative teaching by the imaginative reforms of Pinel, Hallé, Thouret, and other professors at the new Paris "Health School," enlivened by clinical conferences in the various hospitals, and enriched by laboratory work, the new French medicine made Paris the medical center of the world. The new methods of percussion and auscultation were taught [to determine the condition of the heart and other internal organs]; mass autopsies were performed. Laënnec's stethoscope was used. Medicine had emerged into the modern world.

While official disdain and neglect thus gave medicine much needed freedom, the wars entailed more positive stimuli. The benefits to surgery are obvious. Newly developed methods included the ligation of blood vessels, the tourniquet, the extraction of foreign bodies in gunshot wounds through a counter-opening, the dipping of bandages in water (Percy) or in camphorated hot wine (Larrey).[17] According to an experienced army surgeon, the most valuable lesson was speed, and simplicity of instruments and medication.[18] The large number of available cases stimulated the use of statistics in medicine. The government had applied them to problems of health and population since the seventeenth century.[19] Now they were increasingly used by doctors—who were led to view diseases as entities and to subject them to statistical analysis.[20]

Statistics were also applied to public health and hygiene.

> The Napoleonic wars . . ., [writes Ackerknecht] seem to have increased rather than stifled knowledge and understanding of hygienic problems, private and public, and their application. Former and active army medical officers supplied a considerable contingent of . . . hygienists. . . .
> When the "veterans" of 1815 started their study of hygiene, they found in Paris

[17]A. G. Chevalier, "The Physicians and Medical Service of the Revolutionary Armies," *Ciba Symposia*, VII, No. 11 (1946), p. 254.

[18]P.-F. Briot, *Histoire de l'état et des progrès de la chirurgie militaire en France pendant les guerres de la Révolution* (Besançon, 1817), pp. 4–5.
   Cf. also Biron, "Discours sur les progrès de la médecine militaire en France depuis un demi-siècle," *Journal de médecine militaire*, I (Paris, 1815).

[19]G. Rosen, "Problems in the Application of Statistical Analysis of Questions of Health, 1770–1880," *Bulletin of the History of Medicine*, XIX (1955), 31.

[20]See, for example, the use of statistics by Philippe Pinel (1745–1826) in his *Résultat d'observations et construction des tables pour servir à déterminer le degré de probabilité de la guérison des aliénés* (Paris, 1807).

the unparalleled institution of a regular chair of hygiene, one of the many creations of the revolution in the medical field.[21]

These "veterans," with their solid and varied experience and their new interests were a major influence, of course, on French medicine after 1815. It may be sufficient to mention that both Larrey and Desgenettes became inspectors general in the army medical service, that the great hygienists Fodéré[22] and Réveillé-Parise[23] as well as the despotic Broussais[24] had years of military duty to their credit.

Most subtle, but perhaps most lasting, was the effect of the Napoleonic wars on the feelings of the French public concerning its medical men. Although, among the military, discrimination against army medical personnel continued for two generations longer, the attitude of the public at large toward physicians changed. Gone from French literature are Molière's pompous robed doctors who speak Latin, quote Galen, and would not deign to touch a patient. The physicians of Balzac and Flaubert, of Beyle and Sainte-Beuve are knowledgeable, respected, kindly men like Dr. Benassis, Balzac's "Country Doctor." Many Frenchmen owed their lives to the selfless dedication of physicians such as he. The wars of the Revolution and Empire had won for French doctors the respect and admiration of their countrymen.

[21] E. H. Ackerknecht, "Hygiene in France: 1815–1848," *Bulletin of the History of Medicine*, XXII (1948), 119.
[22] F. E. Fodéré (1764–1835).
[23] J. H. Réveillé-Parise (1782–1852).
[24] F. J. V. Broussais (1772–1838).

Maurice P. Crosland (1931–) received his Ph.D. from the University of London and teaches the history of science at the University of Kent at Canterbury. His publications include The Society of Arcueil: A View of French Science at the Time of Napoleon I *(1967),* Historical Studies in the Language of Chemistry *(rev. ed., 1978), and* Gay-Lussac: Scientist and Bourgeois *(1978).*

SCIENCE AND THE ARTS
Maurice P. Crosland

One could, like Chateaubriand, smile at Bonaparte's pleasure in being made a member of the Institute.[1] But in so far as it is indicative of the scale of values of the future Emperor, it is highly relevant in any discussion of his attitude to science. When Napoleon divorced Josephine to marry Marie Louise, he was proud to be the husband of an arch-duchess and this pride was reflected in his pleasure in recruiting his staff from among the old nobility. In a similar way Bonaparte, member of the First Class of the Institute, was permanently prejudiced in favour of men of science in a way in which no subsequent ruler of comparable power has been. An example of this can be seen in the recruitment of his government and administration. For ministers he chose [the mathematician and astronomer] Laplace and [the chemist] Chaptal. In reorganizing education the chemist Fourcroy was invaluable and he was helped by the zoologist Cuvier. The naturalist Lacépède proved a capable administrator of the Legion of Honour, of which he was put at the head. On the other hand the republican general and mathematician Lazare Carnot was excluded from any part in the government except for two short periods in 1800 and 1815. Whether by appointing the mathematician Fourier[2] as prefect of Isère, Bonaparte was contributing to the progress of science is a debatable point. Yet by their positions in the Senate others such as Berthollet and Monge

---

From Maurice P. Crosland, *The Society of Arcueil: A View of French Science at the Time of Napoleon I* (London: Heinemann; and Cambridge: Harvard University Press, 1967), pp. 49–54. Reprinted by permission of the author and Harvard University Press.

[1] [A learned society sponsored by the government, including some of the leading men of letters, scholars, and scientists of the time.—Eds.]
[2] Bonaparte arranged for Berthollet to discuss this appointment tactfully with Fourier before it was made official on 2 January 1802 (J. J. Champollion-Figeac, *Napoléon et Fourier*, 1844, p. 22).

were able to make some contribution to government and still have leisure for the pursuit of scientific research.

Bonaparte went out of his way to encourage foreign men of science to reside in France. When Rumford arrived in Paris at the end of October 1801 he had spoken of his very flattering reception by the scientists of the capital. In November he wrote:

> I have had the opportunity of making the acquaintance of several of the most distinguished characters now in power in this country. I am very intimate with Chaptal, the Minister of the Interior, and frequently see Talleyrand, the Minister for Foreign Affairs; I have dined with both of them and visit them often. Laplace and Berthollet are very civil and attentive to me and have each of them given me a dinner, where I have met most of the men of science of distinction in Paris.[3]

In short, Rumford was genuinely impressed by the new men who had come to the fore under the Consulate. On the reorganization of the Institute in January 1803 Rumford was nominated one of the seven foreign associates of the First Class. When he visited France again later that year, he sent one of his memoirs on heat to Bonaparte. Bonaparte took the trouble to read this memoir and compose a letter in which he attempted to discuss it intelligently.[4] The First Consul clearly wished to create the impression that France's new government was particularly favourable to science.

Some of Bonaparte's statements and actions suggest that he believed that science transcends national frontiers. If the record is examined more critically, however, it shows that he was really concerned with enhancing the reputation of his government. In a few cases, notably those of Blagden and Humboldt, Bonaparte's customary welcome of foreign scientists was tempered by suspicions of spying. He was not prepared to allow his self-appointed role as an international patron of science to be used as a means of threatening state security. Yet there can be no doubt that he did care about the international prestige of French science.

During the Consulate and Empire there was no one year comparable to the republican year II (1793–4), in which a national emergency brought about a great mobilization of talent and the successful application of science to a fairly wide range of industry. Yet, although the concentration of effort was less remarkable, its steady application for more than a decade built up the strength of French industry. Bonaparte had a genuine concern for the state of agriculture and industry which he was prepared to support by subventions and other awards. Furthermore France under Bonaparte enjoyed a period of political stability which to many was a welcome alternative to the anarchy

[3]British Museum, Add. MS. 8099, f. 108v.
[4]Napoléon, *Correspondance*, vol. ix, no. 7141.

which had followed the Revolution. The Continental system was a further stimulus to industrial development and the exploitation of France's natural resources. Freedom from competition allowed the cotton industry to rise from nothing to be almost the equal of that of England and in the chemical industry the Leblanc process could only come into operation sheltered by the prohibition of foreign soda.

Napoleon encouraged industry not only by subsidies and loans but also by the much cheaper reward of honour. Placing a high value on honour as a motivating power in society, he had inaugurated the Legion of Honour in the face of opposition from many of his advisers. If the majority of the awards went to men who had distinguished themselves by their bravery on the field of battle or by their competence in the civil service, Napoleon did not neglect men who had made important contributions to industry or technology, such as Oberkampf and Delessert. Yet when money was required, Napoleon was usually prepared to advance it. He was particularly generous to the textile manufacturer Richard (of the famous company Richard-Lenoir), to whom he lent a total of one and a half million francs. Although there are a few outstanding cases where the offer of a prize led to a new discovery or significant development, much more important was the provision of sums of money over a sufficiently long period to give the freedom to concentrate on particular problems. Financial backing was important in technology and in the field of pure science the value of a steady income is illustrated by Berthollet's ability to finance the work of the Society of Arcueil [a center for the study of science].

Napoleon's attitude to science may be contrasted with his attitude to literature. Evidence comes from various sources including Bourrienne,[5] Bonaparte's secretary up to the autumn of 1802. Himself a man of literary interest and accomplishment, Bourrienne complained of the slight esteem in which Bonaparte held men of letters. His attitude was roughly that such men could make up fine phrases or could arrange words to give a striking effect to the ear and yet be empty of meaning. Bonaparte had once thrown away a book he had started to read and complained to his secretary of the emptiness of much literary production:

> ... These men are good for nothing under any government. Yet I will grant them pensions as is my duty as head of state; they provide an occupation for the idle and amuse them; but I will make [the mathematician and astronomer] Lagrange a senator—there's a brilliant man.

---

[5]Bourrienne, *Mémoires*, vol. v, pp. 126–7.

This antithesis of Bonaparte's toleration of literature and admiration of science is brought out in a document sent by the Emperor in 1807 in reply to the request of Champagny, then Minister of the Interior, who had asked for the authorization of a special school of literature and history at the *Collège de France*.[6] Napoleon contrasted the progress of science with the apparent lack of advance in literary studies. For this reason higher education was desirable in the former but of little use in the latter:

> Mathematics, physical and natural science, medicine, and jurisprudence are sciences because they are built on facts, observations, comparisons; because discoveries that they make successively accumulate from century to century and come to increase daily the domain of science . . . [yet] we have not surpassed the Greeks either in tragedy, comedy or in epic poetry.

Under the Consulate and Empire literary works and theatrical presentations were subjected to such an intolerant system of censorship that Napoleon should not have been surprised that no outstanding work was done in these fields when France was under his control. The two most distinguished French writers of the Napoleonic era, Chateaubriand and Madame de Staël, were strongly opposed to Napoleon and lived in virtual exile.

This situation may be contrasted with the state of affairs in science. It is not only that distinguished French scientists were not driven out of France; on the contrary they were loaded with honours and given pensions. Bonaparte went out of his way to attract scientists from other countries. Rumford was encouraged to stay in France, Volta was given a medal, Chladni was given money. When in 1802 the *Bureau des Longitudes* awarded a prize of 6,000 francs to the Austrian astronomer Bury for his lunar tables, Bonaparte doubled the prize and Chaptal wrote Bury a letter telling him of the favourable treatment he would receive if he came to France.[7] The most famous example of the special place of science in the Napoleonic regime is the visit of the English scientist Sir Humphry Davy to France in 1813, a time when the French armies were particularly hard-pressed.

If Napoleon's attitude to science contrasts with his appreciation of literature, his appreciation of the graphic arts was even more limited.[8] He would judge a painting or a statue as a replica of nature and he saw little merit in the process of copying nature. Artists, nevertheless, were useful to Napoleon to the extent that they were able to portray his military victories and produce monuments to his glory. To a limited extent he may have valued the arts as a facet of national

---

[6]Napoléon, *Correspondance*, vol. xv, no. 12416.
[7]Aulard, *Paris sous le Consulat*, vol. iii, p. 136.
[8]Chaptal, *Mes souvenirs sur Napoléon*, 1893, pp. 269–70.

achievement but this was not something which he personally could understand. He had often said that the two things that had impressed him most were the pyramids of Egypt and the size of a circus giant. In other words, a feat of engineering and a question of magnitude were closer to Napoleon's sympathies and understanding than the greatest achievements of the arts.

There is substantial evidence that Napoleon favoured the pursuit of science. Sometimes his contact and influence was direct, often it was more remote. Yet French science, which came to the fore towards the end of the eighteenth century, continued to flourish under the Consulate and Empire and Napoleon claimed some of the credit for this. In retrospect one of the major weaknesses of the thesis that Napoleon supported the cause of science was the failure of the French educational system to provide adequate secondary education in science.[9] In the *lycées*, founded by Bonaparte in 1802, the emphasis was on humanities, although mathematics also figured quite prominently. By 1808 forty-four *lycées* were in existence but only eight of these offered instruction in physics, chemistry or natural history and these courses were not well-attended. Even in Paris where the standard of science teaching was probably better than in any other part of France, a study of prizes awarded to senior pupils in the years 1809–12 shows that science played only a minor role. Pearce Williams has argued that "when viewed against the provisions for the teaching of science in the Napoleonic schools" Napoleon's attempts to play the part of a patron of science can hardly be regarded as sincere. While there may be some justice in attributing to the head of state the imperfections of one aspect of one of his ministries, one can also see that the question of education only becomes of crucial importance from the long-term point of view.

[9]See especially the indictment by L. Pearce Williams: "Science, Education and Napoleon I," *Isis*, xlvii (1956), 369–82, particularly pp. 371–2, 379–380. The record of the Consulate and Empire on *technical* education is rather better.

11
NAPOLEON'S LEGACY

Was Napoleon one of the shapers of modern Europe? Since his death, as Jean Tulard points out, he has captured the popular imagination not only in Europe but elsewhere. He has represented, for good or ill, different things to different people: the destroyer of feudalism, the defender of the French Revolution from its opponents, the father of nationalism and liberalism, the personification of the pursuit of glory, the consolidator of order, the soldier of fortune, the enlightened despot, the imperialist, and the military dictator.

When measuring and judging Napoleon's legacy, historians have been more judicious than has the general public. Yet many do believe he had a great impact. Jacques Godechot surveys Napoleon's relationship to the Revolution and discusses how he spread to various parts of Europe most of the institutional changes the Revolution had brought to France. These included new law codes, financial, administrative, and judicial reforms, the abolition of feudalism, but did not include the introduction of the revolutionary ideals of freedom of speech and press. After 1792, these freedoms were limited in France. Abram Leon Sachar confines himself to one aspect of the Napoleonic heritage—its effect on the Jews. The revolutionaries had emancipated the French Jews by granting them full citizenship on September 27, 1791. Napoleon, although not sympathetic to Jewish culture, extended the emancipation to most places he conquered, and Jews no longer had to live in ghettos.

Other historians consider Napoleon's impact on Europe as less decisive. Gunther E. Rothenberg tries to demonstrate this regarding military affairs. Marcel Garaud and Romuald Szramkiewicz discuss the family and the status of women. The legal provisions of Napoleon's codes as to the rights of women are shown to be nowhere near so liberal as those of the Revolution. Finally, Louis Bergeron argues that the age of Napoleon was not a major crossroad in French history. Concentrating on the French economy, social structure, and size of population, Bergeron finds that France in 1815 was not very different from France in 1800 and that the Revolution had brought much greater change.

How do we go about answering a question so vague as the nature of Napoleon's legacy? Would it be useful to analyze this problem by dealing with it country by country, social class by social class, and institution by institution? In addition, before even beginning, do we need to establish various standards for measuring the impact of an extraordinary person on history?

For biographical information on Jean Tulard, see Chapter 6, "The Common People in France."

A LEGEND
Jean Tulard

Now that he [Napoleon] had gone from the world's stage which he had occupied for nearly twenty years, was the fallen Emperor destined to oblivion? He was too clever a propagandist not to be aware of the effect of absence on men's memories, and so was to launch his last battle from the rock of St. Helena and to shape the image he hoped to leave to posterity.

Undoubtedly, the legend was not born on St. Helena. It was forged during the first Italian campaign in the newspapers which were destined to raise the morale of the troops, but which taught France about Lodi and Rivoli. The Napoleonic legend blossomed with the official cult of the Emperor which the imperial catechism established—the festival of St. Napoleon and endless thanksgivings. But it was after 1815 that its real nature developed.

New social conditions were a determining factor. Popular loyalty to Napoleon was undeniable under the Empire. The workers from the Parisian districts, at least some of them, were still ready to fight the invader in 1815. All the police reports underline their attachment to the Emperor. Among the peasants, Napoleon's prestige was equally great, although it was somewhat clouded over in the last years by the *droits réunis* [excise taxes] and conscription.

This prestige was to grow steadily after the fall of the Eagle. The industrial revolution, which had been slowed down by war during the Revolution and the Empire, upset the former structures as old artisans were laid off in favour of machines, cheap labour in the shape of women and children was employed, and a slump in wages occurred on a labour market which was already overcrowded with demobilized men. The Empire, a time of full employment, high wages, plentiful and cheap bread, became for all these outcasts a veritable golden age. Napoleon became, without difficulty, "the father of the people." The same reaction took place in the countryside where, at least until the law on the émigré millions was passed, the peasants trembled for the

---

From Jean Tulard, *Napoleon: The Myth of the Saviour*, trans. Teresa Waugh (London: George Weidenfield and Nicolson Ltd., 1984), pp. 344–349. Reprinted with some changes in translation by permission of the publisher.

national property they had acquired under the Revolution.[1] Furthermore Napoleon's glory was also the glory of that army of peasants who had conquered Europe. These old soldiers, condemned by their wounds to idleness, justified their social uselessness through the tales of war which they told their neighbours of an evening—Balzac has shown this clearly. They were the best protectors of the cult, the true authors of the legend as they relayed their tales, for the book peddlers were now forbidden and the new mayors were destroying the municipal collections of the Grande Armée bulletins.

Concern spread to the bourgeoisie. With its new privileges forever threatened by a return to the past, the bourgeoisie discovered, on a political level, that legitimacy had miscarried and that a return to stability was precarious. Undoubtedly Charles X succeeded Louis XVIII without difficulty in 1824, but the sneers which accompanied the coronation showed that the monarchy had lost its old charisma. Béranger wrote:

> Charles s'étend sur la poussière
> Roi! crie un soldat, levez-vous!
> Non, dit l'évêque; et par saint Pierre,
> Je te couronne; enrichis-nous.
> Ce qui vient de Dieu vient des prêtres,
> Vive la légitimité![2]

Seventeen eighty-nine marked a definite turning point. A Republican and liberal opposition endlessly made points to the detriment of the throne. Napoleon's stroke of genius lay in using this opposition to his advantage, in his taking hold of the rising forces which were shaking old Europe.

Curiosity about the outlaw was unending. In 1817, the *Manuscrit venu de Sainte-Hélène d'une manière inconnue* had a tremendous success until it was forbidden. These apocryphal memoirs of Napoleon were probably by a Genevan friend of Madame de Staël, Lullin de Châteauvieux. But they were eclipsed by Las Cases's publication in 1823 of the *Mémorial de Sainte-Hélène*. The *Mémorial* was probably the greatest bestseller of the nineteenth century. Between the first edition in 1823 and Charlet's illustrated edition in 1842 four more editions appeared with additions and corrections. Between 1815 and 1816, Las Cases had collected Napoleon's confidences—and what confidences they were!

[1][This Law of 1825 indemnified émigrés who had lost their property during the Revolution. The total amount was about one billion francs, payable in government bonds earning 30 million francs (3 per cent) each year.—Eds.]

[2]"Charles lies down in the dust. 'King!' shouts a soldier, 'get up!' 'No,' says the bishop; 'and by St. Peter, I crown you; make us rich. What comes from God comes from the priests. Long live legitimacy!' "

A LEGEND

Royalist pamphlets had depicted Napoleon as the inheritor of the Terror, and as Robespierre's disciple. Far from rejecting such an heritage, Napoleon accepted it: "The Emperor," Las Cases noted, "said that despite all its horrors, the Revolution had nevertheless been the real cause of our moral regeneration." The same man who had broken with the ideologues[3] affirmed "the irresistible ascendance of liberal ideas". "Nothing could destroy or wipe out the great principles of our Revolution," he added. "These great and beautiful truths must last for ever, we have so interwoven them with lustre, with monuments and with wonder. . . ." Liberator of peoples, Napoleon would also be their unifier: "The impulse has been given and I do not think that after my fall and the disappearance of my system, any great balance will be possible in Europe other than that provided by the conglomeration and the confederation of great peoples." The defence of revolutionary conquests and the unification of the peoples of Europe are the two essential causes of the long wars for which Napoleon has been blamed, but which were in fact desired by the absolute monarchs.

In 1816 these remarks, if indeed they were made, were addressed to the Whigs, the English liberals whom the prisoner hoped would improve his lot. The choice of spokesman was judicious. Napoleon knew that his confidant was taking notes and that this former émigré who had lived in London would be able to find the right words to sway British opinion. But such affirmations, which were probably altered by Las Cases and adapted to the political circumstances of 1823, were also aimed at international opinion. By these declarations, Napoleon laid claim to the two rising forces of the nineteenth century—the nationalism and the liberalism against which he had fought. As a prisoner of the Holy Alliance, the fallen sovereign could bury the anti-liberal Caesar in favour of a democratic Napoleon, the soldier of a Revolution which belonged no longer to the bourgeoisie alone, but which encompassed the Fourth Estate [poorer city workers and peasants].

The operation would have been difficult without the emotion which arose from the Emperor's martyrdom on St. Helena. This miserable and lonely end on a rock lashed by the sea struck the imagination of the Romantics. A whole generation, the "children of the century," brought up on the bulletins of the Grande Armée, found in the *Mémorial* the noise of battle of which it was deprived by the restored monarchy. Victor Hugo's father had served in Italy and Spain, Alexandre Dumas's in Egypt. Initially Royalist, Romanticism swung

---

[3][The ideologues were a group of intellectuals who supported the liberal ideals of the early years of the French Revolution.—Eds.]

towards a poetic Bonapartism which provided the Napoleonic legend with the literary support without which its success could not have been so brilliant. Hugo and Balzac, Musset and Vigny with more subtlety, Dumas and Eugène Sue with less genius, all became poets of the Empire. At the same time, the world of employees [office clerks] was mourning the golden age of bureaucracy over which Napoleon had reigned. And the people remained convinced that it was their cause which Napoleon had espoused at Brumaire. Louis Geoffroy wrote a *Napoléon apocryphe* in which the Emperor, having conquered Russia and the East, became Master of the world. Returning to the Cape from Sydney he passed by St. Helena but ordered Admiral Duperré not to put in there! Nerval was fired with enthusiasm but Flaubert remained indifferent.

The legend reached its height in 1840 at the time of the return of the ashes [Napoleon's remains]; it ensured Napoleon III's success. "It is quite something," grumbled Guizot, "to be all at once a national glory, a revolutionary guarantee and a principle of authority." Napoleon III's defeat at Sedan [1870] occasioned an eclispe of the legend and put an end to dreams of a Napoleonic dynasty. But the idea of the plebiscite and of appealing to the people survived as the only way in which to reconcile democracy and the strong power of a saviour. France was awaiting this saviour in order to have her revenge on Prussia and to reconquer Alsace-Lorraine; her hope was inspired by Jena; she thought she had found another Bonaparte in Boulanger, and in 1900 Edmond Rostand wrote *L'Aiglon*, a prelude to the warlike assaults of 1914 whose authors had been nurtured on Daudet's *La dernière classe* and Marbot's *Mémoires*. Napoleon was popular again. From Job to Detaille, from Sardou to Esparbès, he inspired soldiers, painters and writers. It was a new conquest. A literary and artistic Brumaire. Gone were the reservations of old republicans, readers of Quinet and Lanfrey; voiceless were the supporters of the old legitimacy who believed in Taine and his [book] *Régime moderne* in which Napoleon was painted as a soldier of fortune. Never were more books, or more engravings derivative of Charlet and Raffet, devoted to the saviour, than between 1885 and 1914.

Napoleon had, in fact, like Tristan or Don Juan, taken on a new dimension. The legend had become a myth. Napoleon's universality meant that he could inspire Dostoevsky ("Yes, I wanted to become Napoleon. That is why I have killed," declares Raskolnikov) and Tolstoy (*War and Peace* is dominated by Napoleon), Nietzsche in *Die fröhliche Wissenschaft* and Thomas Hardy in *The Dynasts*. Kipling composed *A Saint Helena Lullaby* and Emerson has Napoleon appear in *Representative Men*. Conan Doyle abandoned Sherlock Holmes for *The Great Shadow*. Nor did the world of music remain indifferent.

A LEGEND

Beethoven removed his dedication to Napoleon from his Third Symphony, but Berlioz composed a cantata in 1835 on *Le Cinq Mai*; in 1943 Schoenberg was to write an *Ode to Napoleon* in which Napoleon was to be likened to Hitler, but to Robert Schumann we owe *The Two Grenadiers* with words from the poem by Heine; Tchaikovsky branded 1812 with his *1812 Overture*, but Prokofiev is more balanced in his opera *War and Peace*. More films have been made about Napoleon than about Joan of Arc, Abraham Lincoln and Lenin combined. He has been the subject or the target of each and every nationalism: Austrian (*The Young Médard* by Curtiz), German (Grune's *Waterloo* and Wenzler's *The Hundred Days* around 1930), English (*The Iron Duke* or *Lady Hamilton*), Nazi (*Kolberg* made in 1944 by Harlan on instructions from Goebbels), Stalinist (*Kutuzov* in 1943), Polish (Vajda's *Ashes* in 1968) and of course, French with Gance and Guitry. Neither has he been overlooked by Hollywood directors (Ford, Walsh, Vidor, Sidney and Mann). He has been used in the period of the "détente" (*Waterloo*, shot in Russia in 1970 by a Russian, Bondartchouk, for an Italian director with Orson Welles as Louis XVIII) and in pornography (*L'Auberge des plaisirs*, on the Emperor's alleged impotence).

Chaplin thought of interpreting Napoleon as a character who had become a myth of the cinema, like Arsène Lupin, Garbo (who played Marie Walewska), Mickey Mouse or Laurel and Hardy. Caran d'Ache used him in his comic strip at the *Pieds Nickelés*, and he even features in science fiction (*Le voyageur imprudent*). No art form, has remained indifferent to the man of whom Balzac wrote "he could do everything because he wanted everything."

The myth is inexhaustible, then, and open to every interpretation; (for Marx, the destroyer of feudalism; for Freud, the frustrated younger brother) it is one which other myths enhance: myths of women (the frivolous Josephine, the faithless Marie-Louise and the touching Marie Walewska); of Talleyrand, the prince of diplomats and Fouché the inventor of the modern police; of soldiers on half pay, of the Bugeauds, Bros, Fabviers, Pougets and others like Parquin, dedicated to boredom or to plotting; the King of Rome coughing up blood like Marguerite Gautier (*La Dame aux Camélias*); and finally the Revolution. Through the *Mémorial*, the fall of the Bastille and the victory at Austerlitz became part of the same historical movement.

Jacques Godechot (1907–   ), the son of a businessman from Lorraine, studied history at the University of Nancy and the University of Paris, and then taught at the University of Toulouse for most of his academic career. He is a prolific writer on many historical topics. Two of his books about Napoleon have been translated into English: The Napoleonic Era in Europe *(1971), written in collaboration with Beatrice F. Hyslop and David L. Dowd; and* The Counter-Revolution: Doctrine and Action, 1789–1804 *(rev. ed., 1981). He has also published* Napoléon *(1969) and the classic* Institutions de la France sous la Révolution et l'Empire *(3rd ed., 1985).*

INSTITUTIONS

Jacques Godechot

It may be appropriate at the beginning of this discussion to define an institution and the place institutions have in general history. As I see it, institutions are the framework within which men compete; they are therefore the product of struggles among classes or social groups. Institutions are the translation into laws, decrees, orders, regulations, or just into habits or customs, of the equilibrium achieved among the opposing forces at a particular point in time. A man, whoever he may be, cannot impose on society institutions that it has rejected. Perhaps what is most characteristic of the *hero* is to sense and understand better than his contemporaries what the masses want and to translate these desires into institutional forms. It is therefore necessary, when studying institutions, to go beyond simply examining legislative or regulatory texts, but to investigate their application carefully. The only way to do this is to examine documents preserved in archives, in France not only documents in the national, departmental, and communal archives, but also those in private and specialized collections; this should be done because personal correspondence, memoirs, and the records of men who made the institutions operate or observed them are especially valuable. If we lack access to archival documents, we must use the works of those who have studied these documents directly, notably doctoral theses.

From Jacques Godechot, "Sens et importance de la transformation des institutions révolutionnaires à l'époque napoléonienne," *Revue d'histoire moderne et contemporaine* 17 (1970): pp. 795–813. The entire article is printed by permission of the author and the general secretary of the *Revue d'histoire moderne et contemporaine*. Editors' translation.

In studying Napoleonic institutions, we cannot forget that at the beginning of the Consulate Bonaparte was faced with certain earlier decisions *that could not be reversed*. The "principles of 1789," that is, equality before the law, abolition of the feudal system (in the sense that the National Assembly understood it), and constitutional and representative government, could no longer be rejected. In addition, General Bonaparte received such widespread support because it was understood that he would uphold these principles. Of course, one can point out that if three million Frenchmen voted "Yes" to the Plebiscite of the year VIII [results announced February 7, 1800] while only fifteen hundred voted "No," there were about four million abstentions.[1] But were all these abstentions hostile to Bonaparte? Surely not. Many people were biding their time. They wondered whether the young general would really respect the "principles of 1789" or whether he would try to destroy them and reestablish the Old Regime, a regime which a minority of the French, perhaps even an important minority, hoped would return. Consequently, the study of the meaning and importance of the transformation of revolutionary institutions during the Napoleonic period brings us back to the classic question: did Napoleon destroy or continue the Revolution? Many historians have dealt with this problem, and their answers often depended more on their political opinions and on the situation at the time they were writing than on truly scientific research. Among those who depicted Napoleon as the destroyer of the revolutionary achievement, we can mention Michelet in his *History of the XIXth Century*, published in 1875 after his death, Edgar Quinet in his *Revolution* (1865) and especially in his *Campaign of 1815* (1865), Pierre Lanfrey in his *History of Napoleon I* (1867–1875), Colonel Jung in *Bonaparte and His Times* (1880), and Henri Guillemin in a brilliant but superficial pamphlet published this very year [*Napoleon as He Was* (Paris, 1969)].

On the other hand, Thiers in the *History of the Consulate and the Empire* (1846–1862), Taine in the *Origins of Contemporary France* (3rd part, 1887), Aulard in the *Political History of the French Revolution* (1901), and Albert Soboul in *The Directory and the Consulate* (1967) and *The First Republic* (1968) judge that, in general, Napoleon did continue the Revolution, although their reasons for reaching this conclusion often differ.

An examination of Napoleonic institutions will permit us to form an opinion. We shall study in succession in what ways Napoleon destroyed revolutionary institutions, which ones he preserved (some-

---

[1][For an analysis of these so-called three million "Yes" votes, see the selection in this book by Claude Langlois, pp. 57–65.—Eds.]

times after modifications), and finally the new institutions that he created himself. In concluding we shall not omit the role Napoleon played in spreading throughout Europe certain principles and ideas that he had inherited.

It cannot be denied that Napoleon sharply reduced, if he did not destroy, liberty, the most important principle of 1789. "Men are born and remain free" proclaims the first article of the Declaration of the Rights of Man and the Citizen of 1789. The Consulate and the Empire were dictatorial regimes. But had not liberty disappeared well before 18 Brumaire? Actually it had lasted barely more than three years, from 1789 to August 10, 1792. This is obvious for the periodical press: the first three years of the Revolution witnessed the publication of a large number of newspapers of all political complexions. After August 10, 1792 counterrevolutionary papers were not permitted.[2] In all areas liberty vanished. Its eclipse was, certainly, inevitable in order that France, attacked on all fronts, could defeat the immense coalition that attacked it. After Robespierre's fall on 9 Thermidor, year II (July 27, 1794), the regime liberalized, but not so much that full liberty was granted to individuals, religions, or the press. The coup d'état of 18 Fructidor, year V (September 4, 1797) again restricted liberty. Following this affair, the Directory ordered the arrest of the "authors and printers" of 32 Parisian and 44 provincial newspapers. In practice, after the coup d'état of Brumaire, neither freedom of the press nor freedom of conscience was reestablished, and individual freedom remained uncertain. Bonaparte only perpetuated a regrettable situation. During his reign arbitrary arrests continued, but we can still repeat the classic observation that if some half a million people were arrested as suspects during the Terror, there were, in state prisons in 1814, only twenty-five hundred persons held arbitrarily. Liberty was therefore suppressed, but it had been since 1792.

The Constitution of the year III [1795] was, of course, abolished. This was the first effect of the coup d'état of Brumaire. All the revolutionary constitutions had been ephemeral. That of 1791 was in force for a year; that of 1793 never was applied; and the Law of 14 Frimaire, year II (December 4, 1793), which may be considered the actual constitution of the "revolutionary government," was fully respected for eight months and lasted another fourteen months after many changes. The Constitution of the year III lasted four years. The constitutions of the Consulate and the Empire were also ephemeral. That of the year XII (1804) lasted the longest, ten years, but only after undergoing many amendments.

[2][For a different view, see Jeremy D. Popkin, *The Right-Wing Press in France, 1792–1800* (Chapel Hill, North Carolina, 1980).—Eds.]

INSTITUTIONS

Napoleon introduced some limitations on equality. The creation of the Legion of Honor was a first step in this direction, for this distinction brought certain honorific privileges to its members. The founding of the Empire marked the appearance of the princes, who were members of the imperial family, a new step toward the reestablishment of the nobility. And it did reappear in 1808. We must point out, however, that the Imperial nobility conferred no tax advantages, that it was open to a wide spectrum of citizens, and that it did not restore the "society of orders" abolished in 1789. Despite all this, the new nobility was a major attack on the principle of equality to which the French people, as we shall see, were so attached.

But it was in the area of foreign policy that Napoleon broke most definitely with revolutionary principles. Of course the Revolution, after declaring "peace to the world" on May 22, 1790, initiated a war on April 20, 1792, a war which was to last twenty-three years. But the Convention and the Directory had maintained some principles rather strongly: the right of people to self-government, announced for the first time in the National Assembly in regard to Corsica on November 30, 1789 and then proclaimed with more vigor by Merlin de Douai on October 28, 1790; the right of France to expand to its "natural frontiers" if the inhabitants of the newly annexed regions gave their approval; and, finally, the creation around France of a defensive belt of "sister republics." Napoleon repudiated all of these principles. He never applied the "right of people to self-government." As early as the Treaty of Campo Formio (October 18, 1797) he had forced the Directory to annex the Ionian Islands, which were located beyond France's frontiers. One could, of course, consider them a colony, and the Revolution certainly did not renounce colonies. But on September 11, 1802, by annexing Piedmont to France without consulting its inhabitants, he showed that he completely abandoned one of the fundamental principles of the foreign policy that France had followed since 1792. As for the sister republics, he changed these into vassal states for the benefit of his family members. Consequently, it was in the principles of foreign policy—principles that should be considered as resembling an institution—that Napoleon departed the most from the Revolution.

Napoleon preserved the legacy of the Revolution in a large number of areas. The first to be examined is that of social organization. In 1789 the National Assembly had established the equality of all French people before the law, that is, abolished privileges and began the destruction of the feudal system, which was completed by the Law of July 17, 1793. Most of the French were fervently attached to these two fundamental transformations. Some, of course, regretted that the Revolution had stopped at equality of "rights," but efforts made in the year II [1793–1794] to go further and establish economic equality ran afoul of strong opposition and failed. Equality of rights, on the contrary, seemed a decisive and conclusive "conquest." The same was true for the abolition of the feudal system, that is, the system of landholding involving feudal and manorial dues to which ecclesiastical tithes were added. By 1799 it was already apparent that no French government could reverse these gains. This is what Bonaparte meant, when right after 18 Brumaire he declared, "Citizens, the Revolution has made permanent the principles that began it and it is now over." Louis XVIII in 1814 could not eliminate these "conquests of 1789"; and when the people of Paris suspected Charles X of wishing to do this, they overthrew him in the Revolution of 1830. So Napoleon maintained the new social system established in 1789, and he even buttressed it, as we shall see, with the Civil Code. As for equal rights, he breached this only slightly by creating the Imperial nobility, but even this breach contributed to alienating the mass of the French from him.

Another great change that came in 1789 concerned the source of power. Under the Old Regime authority was based on divine right. The king ruled by God's will, which implied heredity confirmed by a coronation. The king represented God in the temporal world, which meant, consequently, governmental absolutism. The monarchy itself had struck the first blow against this system by calling for an Estates General elected by a very extensive suffrage. Then it had yielded to this Estates General when, at the end of June 1789, the deputies declared themselves the "national constituent assembly." That title implied that they possessed greater power than the "constitutional" power of the king. The source of power henceforth resided in the Nation [the people], which expressed itself by electing deputies and by the referendum, then called a plebiscite. Thereafter the Revolution for ten years experimented both with limited suffrage, by which the wealthier citizens voted (from 1789 to 1792 and from 1795 to 1799), and with universal manhood suffrage.

Bonaparte could not reverse this major innovation; it formed the very essence of the Revolution in the political domain. But he resolved to allow the people only the appearance of power while keeping the reality for himself. Here he was very well advised by Sieyès, who as early as 1789 made subtle distinctions between "active" and "passive" citizens and had thus introduced limited suffrage to France. Sieyès had proclaimed, at the time of writing the Constitution of the year VIII [promulgated December 1799], "Confidence comes from below, power comes from above." So the citizens would be asked only for their support, and the government would use its power without any constraints. Bonaparte had already experimented with such an arrangement in the Cisalpine Republic, where in 1797 he had named the deputies himself. He had selected them from his supporters, of course, and as such they comprised only assemblies of yes-men.

Given conditions such as these, there was no harm in reestablishing universal suffrage. All citizens were therefore supposed to vote, but they elected only "notables" who were expected to put their "trust" in the government. They later chose from lists of people known as notables or men of confidence the members of the communal, departmental, and national assemblies. Consequently, there was practically no way for opposition to exist in these assemblies. That complicated system was used only once, and in 1802 Bonaparte replaced it with a different one. This time all the voters elected only the members of the cantonal assemblies, and these men elected the electoral colleges of the arrondissement and the department. The members of these colleges, elected for life, had to be chosen from among the "most heavily taxed," that is, the richest. A notable, therefore, could be only a rich person, and this idea characterized French political life until 1881. The electoral colleges did not elect the members of departmental or national assemblies directly, but only nominated candidates from whom the Senate or the government appointed those they wanted. As in the system of the year VIII, that of the year X [enacted August 2, 1802] allowed the citizens only the appearance of sovereignty.

National assemblies comprising deputies that were appointed and not elected could hardly be dangerous for the government. However, Sieyès was careful not to suggest a unicameral legislature. There were serious reservations about certain hasty decisions taken by the National Assembly, the Legislative Assembly, and the Convention in the heat of enthusiasm but without adequate reflection. As under the Directory, Sieyès had provided for two councils, but of small size and possessing different powers. A Tribunate of one hundred members (rather than the 250 of the Council of Elders) would debate the bills. A Legislative Body of three hundred deputies (rather than the "Five Hundred" of the Directory) would vote on them without discussion. Sieyès also had introduced into the Constitution of the year VIII the constitutional court that he had vainly proposed in 1795 under the name "constitutional jury." But this court, which took the title "Senate," appeared as a third assembly; it was more powerful than the other two, because its members—limited in numbers (60 to 80) and holding their seats for life—were chosen by co-optation and enjoyed a high salary. The Senate was supposed to judge the constitutionality of laws—which it did rarely—and handle revisions of the constitution by *"senatus consulta"*—which were, on the contrary, frequent. The Senate, a new type of assembly whose members enjoyed independence because of their irremovability and their wealth, could have opposed the executive power. It did not do so until the last days of the Empire and demonstrated, on the contrary, an extreme servility.

The executive power that Bonaparte, not Sieyès, established was very strong. In appearance it was still a committee, as it had been under the Directory, but smaller, with three members rather than five. In fact all power was concentrated in the First Consul. Article 42 of the Constitution provided that "the decision of the First Consul is sufficient." The other two consuls were only advisers at a salary (150,000 francs per year) much below that of the First Consul (500,000). The Constitution of the year X, in granting life tenure to the First Consul, and that of the year XII [enacted May 18, 1804], in conferring on him the title of Emperor, increased only very slightly his already immense prerogatives. In sum, the constitutions of the Consulate and the Empire preserved the "conquests" of the Revolution, but only in appearance. Nevertheless they bequeathed to future generations two principles which, like equality and the abolition of feudalism, could not be withdrawn: a representative system and constitutional government. They even preserved, although in attenuated form, universal suffrage; the parties of the Left would demand its full restoration after 1830, and it would reappear in 1848.

In the area of administration, Napoleon brought only mild adjustments to the revolutionary institutions. As consolidated by Consular and Imperial decrees, they would be assured a very long life.

The framework of governmental administration had been set in place by the National Assembly as early as 1790: this was the system of departments, divided into districts, cantons, and communes. Napoleon barely touched this. Within the frontiers of 1792 only one new department was created. This was the Tarn-et-Garonne, created in 1807 to allow Montauban, the former capital of the province of Haute-Guyenne, to become a departmental capital. The districts, eliminated in 1795, were reestablished—but decreased in number and increased in size—and called arrondissements. The cantons were retained with a few changes. Innovation came with the installation of prefects and sub-prefects at the head of the departments and arrondissements. But this innovation was not so great as is commonly believed. The Directory [in 1795] had replaced the prosecuting attorney, elected since 1790, with an appointed central commissioner, and this commissioner was given the title of prefect in the Roman and Helvetic Republics organized in 1798. The only difference between the central commissioner and the prefect lay in the fact that the commissioner had to be chosen from the citizens of the department, but the prefect could be selected from outside the department. In addition, as centralization of the government grew, the powers of the prefect continued to increase. So, in the area of local administration, Napoleon simply followed the efforts at centralization undertaken by the Convention and maintained by the Directory. This was to be accentuated even more after 1815. As for the administrative boundaries of France, other than the changes due to wars (creation of the departments of Savoie, Haute-Savoie, and Alpes-Maritimes in 1860 after the Italian war, of the department of Meurthe-et-Moselle and the territory of Belfort in 1871 after the loss of Alsace and Lorraine, and then the formation of the departments of Moselle, Haut-Rhin, and Bas-Rhin after the return of Alsace and Lorraine in 1918), we must wait until 1964 with the redivision of the Paris region to see new departments appear.

Napoleon altered the organization of justice more significantly. The National Assembly had rebuilt justice on three principles: bring justice and the people involved closer together and therefore make the judicial boundaries coterminous with administrative boundaries; assign the responsibility of justice to elected judges and to juries chosen by lot, not to professional magistrates; and reduce as much as possible the hierarchy of tribunals to avoid the reappearance of courts as powerful as the old parlements. Bonaparte maintained almost all of the first part of the judicial work of the National Assembly. It had established justices of the peace in the cantonal capitals, civil and police tribunals in the district capitals, a criminal tribunal in the departmental capital, and a Tribunal of Cassation [the highest court] in Paris. In the year VIII [1800] Bonaparte kept this organization while, of course, changing the districts to arrondissements. But he was hostile to elected judges and even to juries. This sytem seemed too democratic to him, and he suspected that elected judges might arrive at decisions aimed at pleasing the voters. Such studies as have been made concerning justice during the Revolution—and there have really been only a few of them—show that the elected judges were competent (they had to be chosen from men with legal training, possess five years of professional experience, and be at least thirty years of age) and only rarely did they allow themselves to be inappropriately influenced. Some exceptional cases, however, came to the attention of the First Consul and confirmed his revulsion against electing judges or other public officials. Since Bonaparte excluded any return to the sale of judicial offices as practiced under the Old Regime, a procedure vigorously denounced in 1789, there was no other system possible than appointed judges. To guarantee their independence, they were given tenure for life. Bonaparte also wanted to abolish juries, but the opposition that this proposal aroused led him to abandon it. In 1811 he introduced it again, but only to eliminate grand juries, which he replaced by an investigating judge; he retained the petty jury.

As we indicated, the National Assembly had wanted to avoid reestablishing courts of justice as powerful as the parlements. So it limited the right of appeal in civil cases, which led to complaints. In 1800 Bonaparte considered establishing a tribunal of appeal in each department, but this would have been too expensive. He created one for each three or four departments. Most of these tribunals of appeal had jurisdictions smaller than the old parlements and could not hope to enjoy the power and prestige of their predecessors. In 1804 there were sound reasons for giving them and the Tribunal of Cassation the name of courts. Criminal tribunals would be called courts of assizes from 1811 on. The salient change brought by Napoleon to the judicial reforms of the Revolution, therefore, was in substituting appointed magistrates for elected judges; justices of the peace, however, continued to be elected.

In the year VIII these tribunals rendered justice according to the laws approved by the revolutionary assemblies. But gradually these laws were replaced by new law codes, especially the Civil Code that soon took the name Napoleonic Code. One might believe that Napoleon was responsible for the great work of legal codification completed during his reign and which supplied the framework for the new society. Such was not the case. As early as September 2, 1791 the National Assembly had decreed: "A code of civil laws applicable to the entire kingdom will be prepared." The Legislative Assembly, the Convention, and the assemblies of the Directory all worked on this code. They decided above all to produce something very different from what was called a "code" in the Old Regime and instead to prepare a vast synthesis of all legislation—customary, written, or revolutionary—and the jurisprudence regulating society. A task of this extent could not be accomplished quickly. It was quite well advanced, but not finished, when Bonaparte became First Consul. He speeded up the completion of the job; this was his primary achievement. The men he chose to expedite the preparation of the code, Tronchet, president of the Tribunal of Cassation, Bigot de Préameneu, government commissioner at this Tribunal, Portalis, commissioner at the Prize Court,[3] and Maleville, judge on the Tribunal of Cassation, were fine jurists to be sure, but they never would have been able to finish their work in four years without the tremendous efforts of Cambacérès (who had already prepared three drafts of a civil code), Jacqueminot, Merlin de

---

[3][The Prize Court was the judicial body that determined the ownership of the ships—the prizes—captured in maritime warfare.—Eds.]

Douai, Berlier, and Treilhard. Of course, Bonaparte did enter into the Council of State's discussion of the code, but his comments, although not trivial, were more famous than really important. However, in the discussions about some controversial articles he won his point: he made sure of the father's authority over children and of husband over wife, of the interest of legitimate children over those who were illegitimate, and of the domination of employers over workers. But he also insisted that divorce be retained, although Portalis favored ending it. Actually, Bonaparte himself was thinking about divorcing Josephine.

So Napoleon pushed the Civil Code in the direction of authority and hierarchy and harmonized it with the regime that he was establishing. We repeat that, by means of the Civil Code, Napoleon consecrated the great social conquests of the Revolution of 1789: abolition of the "feudal regime" and the privileged "orders"; equality before the law; and full and complete property holding in the Roman sense of the word property.[4] He added to this the control of vital statistics by the civil authorities [rather than the clergy] which had been decreed on September 20, 1792.

The Code of Civil Procedure was promulgated in 1806 and the Code of Criminal Instruction on November 27, 1808. They marked a reaction against the procedures used since 1789 and a partial return to the royal ordinances of 1667 and 1670. The major innovation in the Code of Criminal Instruction was, as we have mentioned, the substitution of an investigating judge for the grand jury and the resumption of secret procedure.[5] The Penal Code was completed two years later, in 1810, and replaced the code of September 25, 1791. It differed from the earlier version by providing for harsher penalties—reestablishing general confiscation and civil death[6]—but it instituted "extenuating circumstances," which allowed a better adaptation of punishments to particular offenses and crimes. It also was much clearer in language than its predecessor. But the great principles adopted in 1789, which were those proclaimed by the famous Italian *philosophe* Beccaria, were maintained. The 1807 Code of Commerce offered little new. The revolutionary assemblies had done nothing in this area, and the 1807

---

[4][The Roman sense of private property gave the owner greater control over it than does American or English law.—Eds.]

[5][Secret procedure meant that the investigating official could interrogate witnesses privately in the absence of the suspect, who could also be interrogated before knowing the charge and the evidence against him.—Eds.]

[6][General confiscation permitted the state to seize all the property of a criminal. Such confiscation was used frequently during the Old Regime and was reestablished from 1810 to 1814 and again occasionally after 1918. Civil death meant the loss of citizenship rights.—Eds.]

code generally followed Colbert's edict of 1673 and his ordinance of 1681. It did not therefore take into account the considerable development of commercial techniques over more than a century. Napoleon also wanted a rural code and an industrial code. The first of these was prepared during his reign and published only after his fall in 1814. The second never appeared. On the whole, Napoleon's action on the codes represents the completion of an effort rather than an original creation. But these codes, more than the constitutions, ratified the existence of the new society born in 1789.

In the financial and monetary realm, Napoleon limited himself to finishing the work of the Revolution. The immediate cause of the Revolution had been the disorderly state of French government finances under the Old Regime. The National Assembly had entirely destroyed the old fiscal system and had based the revenues of the French government on the collection of three direct taxes: on land, on personal property, and on business licenses. The Assembly had determined that indirect taxes were unjust because they weighed more heavily, relatively, on the poor than on the rich, and it authorized, in addition to customs duties, only a small number of minor indirect taxes such as registration fees and stamp duties. The Directory decided that these resources would not bring in enough money; so it created a fourth direct tax, the one on doors and windows. Napoleon preserved this tax system, and with only minor adjustments it lasted until 1914. These were the "four old" direct taxes. But as the income from them remained insufficient, Napoleon, in a move that quickly became unpopular, sharply raised indirect taxes by creating duties on alcoholic beverages, salt, and tobacco. They were administered by the office called the *droits réunis*. Detested at the end of the Empire, the indirect taxes would be greatly reduced or abolished by the Restoration.

Napoleon performed a useful and durable service especially in the matter of collecting direct taxes. The National Assembly had arranged for the municipalities to collect these taxes. They often proved to be incompetent and were never zealous enough. The Directory had put above them a "direct taxes office" partly staffed by government officials. Bonaparte assigned the collection of all direct taxes to specialized public officials: communal tax collectors, arrondissement treasurers, and departmental treasurers. This organization performed well and has remained essentially the same to the present.

Napoleon is often praised for stabilizing the franc and giving it the definition [5 grams in weight of .9 pure silver] that it retained until 1926, the "franc of Germinal." This is not correct. The National Assembly, to fill the huge budget deficit, had nationalized the clergy's property and issued paper money, assignats, based on it. The war, beginning in 1792, required enormous expenditures; the state issued assignats whose face value far exceeded the value of the nationalized church land. This brought inflation. In 1796 the Directory abandoned the assignat and returned to "metallic money." The franc was declared equal to five grams of silver. Napoleon's Law of 7 Germinal, year XI (March 28, 1803) only made this more precise. The Directory also relieved itself of the debt by a veritable bankruptcy on September 30, 1797: only one-third of the face value of each government bond remained inscribed on the Convention's "great book of the public debt" [remained an obligation of the government]. This was known as the "consolidated third." The other two-thirds were paid off in bonds theoretically valid for the purchase of national land, but which in fact quickly lost most of their value. In any event Bonaparte in 1799 inherited a healthy situation and was always careful not to increase the debt. He fought all his wars without borrowing and financed them by huge war taxes imposed on conquered countries.[7] He never believed in the immense possibilities that credit might have supplied him and always considered England on the brink of defeat because it lived on loans.

This way of thinking explains why Napoleon did not give a strong impetus to the Bank of France. Indeed, soon after his accession to power, he created it on January 6, 1800, but it was really more a conversion of the Caisse des comptes courants, which dated from June 29, 1796. The first banknotes of the Bank of France (whose smallest denomination was five hundred francs, an enormous sum for the period, equal to at least two thousand francs in 1970 [almost $350 in 1970]) were also exactly identical to those of the Caisse des comptes courants, which had been accepted at par with coined money from their first issue. The innovation consisted in granting to the Bank of France in 1803 a monopoly to issue banknotes in Paris and thus withdrawing this privilege from other Paris banks (Caisse d'escompte, Comptoir commercial). In addition, the Bank of France was more closely linked to the state than the Caisse d'escompte. Still, under the Empire, the Bank of France was neither the bank of the state nor the official [central] bank of France. It remained, as the Caisse des comptes courants had been, the leading bank of Paris, or more exactly the bank of its large merchants and bankers.

The Revolution had been forced to provide new institutions for the army, the navy, and the war economy. Napoleon hardly touched them. This may seem paradoxical but should not surprise us. Because of the army forged by the Revolution, Bonaparte won the victories of 1796 and 1797 that made him famous and allowed him to seize power. Why

[7][For a different view, see Owen Connelly, *Napoleon's Satellite Kingdoms* (New York, 1965), p. 341.—Eds.]

should he change so perfect an instrument? As for the war economy that had been constructed by the Convention, he had only to extend it to all of Europe.

The superiority of the revolutionary army over its enemies came from the principle of compulsory and universal military service, which had been established in principle by the Convention on August 23, 1793. The famous decree regarding the *levée en masse* was published on that day and had given France the "mass" army that allowed it to win its first great victories in 1794. The Jourdan-Delbrel Law of September 5, 1798, instituted conscription—the application of the principle of compulsory and universal military service with the possibility of hiring a replacement. Napoleon barely touched the conscription system that enabled him to meet the enormous manpower needs of his armies. The Jourdan-Delbrel Law actually remained in force, with some modifications, until 1872. The training of soldiers continued to follow the system established during the Revolution, the *amalgame*: recruits were sent directly to fighting units; they learned from the old hands. The Convention had provided for promotion by means of election to various ranks; the Directory had practically abandoned this and replaced it by appointment. Napoleon retained promotion by appointment along with a certain proportion of promotions based on seniority. He also established military schools from which sons of the bourgeoisie and nobility graduated with the rank of second lieutenant. Napoleon did not change the army's weapons: the 1777 model musket and Gribeauval's artillery were used in all the campaigns of the Empire. Excellent at the beginning, these weapons came to be outclassed by the English musket and the Russian cannon. On the other hand, Bonaparte did not maintain the military observation balloons created by the Convention. The army's organization was hardly modified. Already in 1792 regiments were grouped in divisions. The army corps appeared sporadically under the Directory. Napoleon made extensive use of it and created the cavalry corps; but especially he made the Guard, derived from the Guard of the Directory, into an elite corps that numbered up to sixty thousand men. The only innovations of some importance concerned the support services. The civilian wagon trains and the military hospitals, which worked poorly, were replaced by the artillery train, the equipment train, and a real "military medical service."

The navy, after being badly mauled at Aboukir Bay on August 1, 1798, was almost destroyed at Trafalgar on October 21, 1805. Napoleon endeavored to rebuild it, but on the old model. He would have been able to rejuvenate it, however, if he had accepted the steamboat and the submarine that Robert Fulton had personally proposed for his consideration in 1802. Neither strategy nor tactics changed. Although mustering in 1814 over 70 ships of the line and 40 frigates, the fleet built by Napoleon remained unused. After Trafalgar, Napoleon actually gave up fighting England at sea. He wanted to subdue the country by the Continental Blockade, that is, by stopping it from selling its products on the European continent. The colossal measures taken by Napoleon (the Berlin decree of November 21, 1806, the Milan decree of December 17, 1807, and the Trianon decree of August 1, 1810) were really only a systematic extension to the European continent of measures taken by the Convention. As early as October 9, 1793 it had forbidden entry of British manufactured goods to French territory; and on September 21, 1793, a "navigation act" had restricted all French foreign trade to French ships, which signified a close control over neutral shipping. These regulations had been enforced (with varying degrees of rigor) throughout the war, that is, until 1802; and as soon as the war resumed in 1803, Napoleon reestablished them. Although the deputies to the Convention had generally favored free enterprise for domestic commerce, when scarcities began to appear in 1793 they had voted to fix prices of food; at the time they called this the "maximum." The "maximum" was abolished at the end of a year. Napoleon, who favored economic freedom as much as the members of the Convention, also turned to price fixing in 1812 after the bad harvest of 1811 had brought price increases. Price fixing was abandoned several months later, after the abundant harvest of 1812. Although Napoleon encouraged the cultivation of French products (sugar beets, chicory, and woad [a plant used to make a blue dye]) to replace colonial goods, he did not require this. The domestic economy remained, as under the Revolution, unregulated.

In which institutional areas was Napoleon a real pioneer? We can, it appears, mention only two: relations with the churches and also education, both secondary and higher.

The issue of the relations between the State and the Catholic Church was one that had shaped the history of the Revolution. The National Assembly had wanted to complete the work begun long before by the Gallicans: integrate the Catholic Church into the State and create a Gallican Church nearly independent of Rome. To this end it had prepared the "Civil Constitution of the Clergy." But the Pope had rejected this. The result was a serious schism. Those clergymen opposed to the Civil Constitution, the "refractories," soon joined the camp of the counterrevolutionaries. In addition, an anti-religious movement derived from the "philosophy" of the Enlightenment began to develop. Robespierre established a deist cult inspired by the ideas of Rousseau, while the atheists tried to spread a "cult of reason." On February 21, 1795 the Convention took a position diametrically opposed to that of the National Assembly and established the separation of Church and State. The Republic no longer paid the salaries of any religious cult, but guaranteed the free exercise of all of them. Still religious struggles went on. The refractories continued to be viewed as the most unrelenting opponents of the Revolution. To consolidate the Revolution, it was necessary to eliminate the refractories or to end the schism by negotiating with the Pope. Bonaparte already had attempted this as early as his first victories in Italy in 1796, but he had failed. He resumed discussions with the new Pope, Pius VII, immediately after [the French victory of] Marengo. They resulted in the Concordat of July 16, 1801, which reestablished the unity of the Catholic religion in France and seemed to return to the National Assembly's ideas of integrating the Catholic Church into the State. In fact, because the Pope asked for and obtained the resignation of all French bishops, "refractory" as well as "constitutional," his power over the Church in France increased considerably. Gallicanism would disappear, and the Church of France would become more and more "ultramontane." This would lead to new religious quarrels, developing only after 1880 and leading, on December 9, 1905, to the reestablishment of the separation of Church and State. The Concordat, an entirely original action by Bonaparte, lasted no less than a hundred years. It was followed by similar agreements with the Protestant churches and with Judaism, agreements which lasted as long as the Concordat. For the moment, and for the period of the Consulate and Empire, these accords ended all religious opposition and contributed greatly to the consolidation of the Napoleonic regime.

Coming to terms with the churches eliminated opposition forces that could have been extremely dangerous, as was true from 1791 to 1801. Yet, was it not also necessary that citizens receive, beginning in their childhood, an education based on open criticism of men and institutions? This was exactly what the revolutionaries had tried to do by reorganizing public education. Of course, concerning primary schools, they never moved beyond the stage of principles and desires. On June 24, 1793, the Convention had added the right to an education onto the Declaration of the Rights of Man and on the following December 19, had decreed that primary education would be free of charge and compulsory. But the lack of money—and also of teachers—meant that these principles remained only expectations and were applied neither under the Convention nor the Directory. The Napoleonic regime displayed no interest in primary education, which in 1814 was less extensive than in 1789.

In the realm of secondary education, the Convention had, on the contrary, carried out important and original achievements. To replace the former *collèges*, inspired by Jesuit methods and based on the teaching of Latin, it established Central Schools, where the curriculum emphasized first the sciences of observation (drawing, natural sciences), then mathematics and physics, and finally history, philosophy, and literature. This completely reversed the educational system of the Old Regime, and the parents of students as well as the teachers adapted poorly to the changes. Some schools flourished (in Paris, Nancy, Besançon, and Grenoble), others vegetated. Undoubtedly this system, which allowed students (12 to 18 years of age) freedom to choose their courses and did not have boarding students, could have been improved. But it was viable and original. It produced independent and energetic spirits. Stendhal for example. Napoleon, however, wanted secondary education to supply him with submissive civil servants. He therefore abolished the Central Schools and replaced them with State-operated *lycées* and private *collèges*; they were newly created, but resembled in part those of the Old Regime. Although the curriculum did include mathematics and physics, literature and especially Latin regained dominance. The major differences from the Old Regime were the secularizing of education—the majority of the teachers were not clerics; its uniformity—all the *lycées* and *collèges* in France thereafter followed the same programs; its increased centralization—when in 1806 the Imperial University was established; and the military character of the discipline imposed on the instructors and on the students—they marched to class to the beat of drums. For a century and a half thereafter, secondary education for boys would provide the state with personnel and officers cast from the same mold.

The Convention had also overturned higher education. It had abolished the old universities, which were moribund anyway by the eve of the Revolution. Believing that general education was provided by the Central Schools, it had offered only specialized higher education in *grandes écoles* called "special schools": law, medicine, pharmacy, public works (Ecole polytechnique), and teacher education (Ecole normale). The Collège de France was retained.[8] Napoleon allowed these schools to continue and even added a "special military school." He did not reestablish the universities, but instead reestablished groups of faculties, together with *lycées*, in an "Imperial University" covering the entire country. In fact, only the special schools, and the faculties of medicine, pharmacy, and law, former special schools, thrived. The faculties of letters and sciences vegetated and did nothing more than serve as examining boards for the baccalaureat [secondary school] degree. But here too uniformity and centralization were the rule. And so was born the Napoleonic University, hierarchical and centralized,

---

[8][The Collège de France is still an institution composed of eminent scholars who engage in research and give public lectures. It does not award degrees.—Eds.]

which survived in its basic principles, despite important modifications between 1880 and 1896, until May 1968. In any event, in its early years the Imperial University trained only submissive subjects and involved only a tiny proportion of the population.

We see then, how Napoleon, by consolidating the major part of the revolutionary reforms and by creating new institutions, left his mark on France, in many cases for two centuries. He not only marked France, but the greater part of Europe. The revolutionary armies had already exported the new institutions to Belgium, the Netherlands, Rhineland Germany, Switzerland, and Italy. Napoleon's soldiers brought them to the rest of Germany, Poland, Spain, and even the Balkan peninsula.

The abolition of the "feudal system," that is, the end of serfdom, of seignorial and feudal dues, of labor service, and of the tithe, was extended in theory everywhere in the Grand Empire. In theory only, for Napoleon tried more and more to gain support from the nobility of the vassal states and tended to make more or less serious exceptions to this principle, particularly in southwest Germany, where many seignorial dues remained in force, and in the Duchy of Warsaw, where seignorial dues, labor service, and tithes continued. Nevertheless, in peoples' memories the Napoleonic regime remained linked to the abolition of the feudal system, and in regions where feudalism did not disappear entirely, its complete abolition remained a major objective during the first half of the nineteenth century.

If Napoleon placed a great importance on the abolition of the feudal system, hoping to gain from this gratitude and support among the masses, he pursued no less vigorously the spread of the Civil Code. He did this partly through pride, of course, because the Civil Code was the "Napoleonic Code," but also because the Code really established civil equality and allowed all capable persons an opportunity to win administrative, judicial, and military positions. The Napoleonic Code was introduced, sometimes with significant modifications, in most of the vassal states. By 1812 almost all of the "Grand Empire" was under its sway.

All the states of the Grand Empire also adopted constitutions, more or less inspired by French constitutions. Certainly these constitutions in no way established democracy, but they gave to the countries where they were introduced the experience of representative government. When they were eliminated in 1814—as in Germany and Italy—the call for a constitution became the leading demand of revolutionaries and liberals.

Administrative, judicial, financial, and military institutions generally were organized on the French model; and in most of the vassal states, they brought a rational and efficient organization to replace decrepit and sclerotic administrations. Only education escaped reform on the French model. Primary schooling in Germany, Holland, and Switzerland was certainly more highly developed than in France. Milan had a public secondary school for girls where none existed in France. French-style *lycées* were introduced in many countries. On the other hand, the old universities were retained because they had modernized themselves during the eighteenth century and managed, more than French universities, to contribute to the advancement of research.

It can be argued either that Napoleon destroyed or continued the Revolution in France, but there is no doubt that beyond the French frontiers he was, as a result of the institutional organization of the new governments, the propagator of the principles and institutions of the Revolution.

By consolidating the essential features of the revolutionary legacy, Napoleon gave to the new society of classes a solid framework within which this society would develop and create a novel economic system, capitalism. In France, he was forced to maintain the "conquests of 1789" and keep the institutions that embodied them so as to retain the confidence of the people; abroad, through his foreign policy, he spread these conquests to the greater part of Europe. He was, therefore, one of the founders of modern Europe.

Abram Leon Sachar (1899–), a native of New York City, received his B.A. and M.A. from Washington University, St. Louis, and his Ph.D. from Cambridge University in England. After teaching history at the University of Illinois, he became a leader in Jewish cultural affairs. From 1933 to 1948, he was the National Director of the B'nai B'rith Hillel Foundations in American universities. He then served as the President of Brandeis University from 1948 to 1968 and has since been its Chancellor. His best-known publication, A History of the Jews, *which first appeared in 1929, is in its fifth edition and remains a standard survey of the subject.*

NAPOLEON AND THE JEWS

Abram Leon Sachar

It is difficult to estimate his [Napoleon's] personal attitude to Jews. Often he was quite friendly and there are many legends of his benefactions in France and Germany. More often he was distinctly hostile, and a number of his edicts smacked of the spirit of the meanest Jew-baiters. Yet, at least indirectly, his actions had undeniably useful consequences for Jewish life. Wherever his victorious legions came, the walls of the ghetto fell and the Jews walked forth free and unafraid. To this day German Jews look upon him as the father of their emancipation.

He won his first glorious victories in Italy, against the flower of the Austrian forces. He struck with bewildering speed, with deadly accuracy, and within a few months the fairest cities of the peninsula lay at his feet. The Italians greeted him as a saviour, for he had, at least temporarily, destroyed the hold of the hated Austrian. The Jews rained blessings upon him, for he destroyed the barbarities that made their lives miserable. The ghettos fell in Venice, in Livorno, even in Rome, where, in 1775, the benighted Pope Pius VI had again reduced the Jewish community to virtual serfdom.

After his Italian success Napoleon dreamed of a French empire in the East, with Egypt and the Holy Land as a nucleus. Perhaps he would be able to cut the artery that connected England and India and reconquer the lost provinces for France. The jealous Directorate was only too happy to be rid of a popular hero and gave him all the rope he

---

From Abram Leon Sachar, *A History of the Jews* (5th ed., rev.; New York: Alfred A. Knopf, 1964), pp. 281–284. Copyright 1930, 1940, 1948, 1953 © 1964 and renewed 1958 and 1968 by Alfred A. Knopf, Inc. Reprinted by permission of the publisher.

needed with which to hang himself. He transported an army to the East and won several impressive victories, but the project was too vast, even for a Napoleon. Nelson destroyed his fleet and the British navy dogged his heels wherever he attempted to force the issue. For months the little general struggled valiantly against inevitable disaster. He seized upon every straw to bolster up his wobbling structure. There is a persistent newspaper tradition—not authenticated, however—that after capturing Gaza and Jaffa, in 1799, he appealed to the Jews of Asia and Africa to rally to the French standard, promising them a homeland in Palestine when he had completely conquered it. If the appeal had been made, it would have been a spectacular moment in Jewish history. A new world-conqueror was offering the ancient homeland to the Jews as a French protectorate. The Jews were not dazzled, however. They continued to support their sovereign with loyalty, and those who lived in Jerusalem worked feverishly to throw up earthworks to repel Napoleon's invasion.

Late in 1799 Napoleon deserted his army and slipped back to France, where his personal magnetism enabled him to cover his defeats and to make himself master of the country. He soon atoned for the disasters in the East. A rejuvenated French army scattered to the four winds every foe that dared to contest his supremacy. He conquered half of Europe in half a dozen battles. Then he sheathed his sword for a moment to consolidate the fruits of the Revolution in France.

The Jews were now equal before the law [since September 27, 1791], but the outcry against them continued. The Alsatians remained their bitterest critics, for a period of depression had set in and the peasants were at the mercy of their creditors, many of whom were Jews. They besieged Napoleon with tales of Jewish usury, of brutal, inhuman exploitation. Others who bore the Jews no goodwill hinted that the Jews were avoiding conscription. The gifted writers Chateaubriand and Bonald added their dignified philosophic objections to Jewish equality.

At the outset Napoleon was very angry. In his council, early in 1806, he spoke like a Capistrano [St. John of Capistrano was a notorious anti-Semite], repeating the rubbish ten thousand times chewed over by every enemy of the Jews. Jews were not like decent Catholics or Protestants; they were unassimilable; they formed a state within a state; they had no loyalty. Alsace and Strassburg, the keys of France, must not be left in their hands; they were a nation of spies. They ought to be punished or scattered.

Fortunately he was mollified by friendlier members in the council and contented himself by suspending for one year all debts due to Jews in the eastern departments. Then he determined to call together an assembly of Jewish notables from all the provinces under French control for the purpose of getting a promise of civil patriotism, and of putting an end to the "unfair" practices of the Jews. He would revive, he said, "the civic morality of the Jews, lost during the long centuries of a degraded existence."

It was a frightened and thoroughly subservient gathering that met in Paris, in 1806, at his request—a hundred and twelve of the leading Jews of France, Italy, and Germany. Twelve questions were presented to them publicly, dealing with patriotism, social morality, intermarriage, and other national and religious problems. The assembly completely reassured Napoleon, answering all charges with as much ability as dignity. The leaders pledged their loyalty to France and to Napoleon and asserted their determination to enter fully into the life of the country, although they would never sacrifice their loyalty to Jewish traditions.

Now the brilliant imagination of Napoleon seized upon the idea of making the body permanent, modelling it on the ancient [supreme Jewish judicial body, the] Sanhedrin of Temple days. Perhaps such a dramatic move would rally the Jews of the enemy countries to his support. At any rate it would be useful to have a representative Jewish body always at hand through which the Jews of France could be reached for every imperial purpose. The project was enthusiastically received by the French Jews, who were carried away by the romantic thought that the ancient glory of Jewish life was being resurrected.

The first Sanhedrin met in Paris in 1807 and re-emphasized the pledges of loyalty which had been given by the previous assembly. It was not destined to become a permanent body, however. It had no real work to perform and even the emperor, now completely absorbed in a new Prussian war, forgot his early grandiloquent designs. The Sanhedrin therefore died of inanition.

That Napoleon was not motivated by any special love of Jews in these organizing projects was clear from the special legislation which followed the dissolution of the Sanhedrin. Consistories [religious councils] were created in every department which had more than two thousand Jews. These imperial bodies were material aids in regulating religious life, but their primary purpose was to facilitate conscription. Further, by the "infamous decrees," restrictions were placed for ten years on Jewish loans to peasants and new trading-enterprises were forbidden without express permission. In the majority of the departments the Jews obtained exemption from the operation of these measures, but not until thousands of families had been ruined by them. The consistorial organization of Jewish life remained in force until State and Church were separated, in 1905.

So far Napoleon had brought nearly as much evil to the Jews as he had alleviated. During the remainder of his carer he proved to be a magnificent Jewish benefactor.

After the collapse of the Third Coalition [in 1805], he carved out of the western German provinces the kingdom of Westphalia and placed his tolerant and well-meaning brother Jerome on the throne. By the royal edict of the new king, issued in 1808, the Westphalian Jews were made full citizens of the new State. Their special taxes were abolished and they were admitted to all means of livelihood. They were then organized into a consistory, on the French model, which was to regulate their congregational activity and to serve as intermediary between them and the government.

From the ruins of the Holy Roman Empire Napoleon created another important unit of government, the Confederation of the Rhine, of which Frankfurt was the centre. Here lived five hundred Jewish families, in mediæval degradation. The Frankfurt ghetto had already been bombarded and partially destroyed during the earlier Napoleonic campaigns in Germany. Now, in 1811, when the duchy of Frankfurt was created, serfdom came to a sudden end and the Jews were made full citizens. The archduke and the populace were violently opposed to the edict, but Napoleon's guns thundered too effectively not to be promptly obeyed. The archduke submitted and was compensated for the loss of his special taxes by a payment of four hundred and forty thousand gulden from the Jewish community.

In most of the other German communities edicts of equality, with some reservations, were also decreed. In Baden all Jews except money-lenders and petty traders were granted citizenship; in Hamburg, Lübeck, Bremen, and other Hanse cities, the restrictions of centuries were abolished as soon as the French troops entered. In the Prussian communities, where Napoleon's influence was much more superficial, the battle for emancipation took longer. The king and his advisers could not overcome their personal animosities. After the humiliation of Jena, however, in 1806, the State was reconstituted by liberal administrators, and many mediæval abuses were swept out in the general cleaning. In 1812, on the eve of the War of Liberation, equality was granted to the Jews, with the qualification that they were not eligible for State offices.

A few German states, however, resisted to the bitter end all efforts to destroy the existing system. Catholic Bavaria, where thirty thousand Jews lived, remained adamant, and when citizenship was extended to the Jews, it was full of restrictions. Saxony, because of its mediæval attitude, became known as the Protestant Spain of the Jews, and even the degrading poll-tax was not abolished until the allied armies compelled its repeal, in 1813.

Meantime the Napoleonic forces spread their conquests to every corner of Europe, and the ancient ghettos continued to fall. Even Spain was affected when Napoleon annexed the Peninsula [in 1808] and placed his brother Joseph upon the throne. The Inquisition was at once destroyed, and, though there were no Jews to be freed, the *marranos* [Jews converted to Christianity] probably breathed easier. In 1820, when complete freedom was decreed, a number of *marrano* families in the Portuguese cities of Lisbon and Oporto openly proclaimed their long-hidden Jewish faith.

The French Revolution and its heir, Napoleon, inaugurated a new era in Jewish history. Despite later reactions, which temporarily rescinded the earlier liberal legislation, the Jews became a definite part of the European world. Henceforth it became the leading motive in Jewish history to readjust Jewish life to the new situation.

For biographical information on Gunther E. Rothenberg, see Chapter 9, "The Main Causes for the Defeat in Russia."

MILITARY AFFAIRS
Gunther E. Rothenberg

The Revolutionary and Napoleonic wars left a mixed military legacy. By the end of the period most armies had adopted some forms of Napoleonic strategy and tactics, and these were retained. On the other hand, as soon as the conflict ended all governments, even the Prussian, realizing that radical innovations in the military sphere were closely linked to changes in the political, social and economic framework, returned as much as they could to military establishments resembling those of the pre-revolutionary period.

When the *ancien régime* had vanished and the state had become a nation, there had been a departure from the older traditions of dynastic wars with limited participation. Resting on conscription and patriotic fervour, and with war nourishing war, the new French armies were larger and more mobile than those of the eighteenth century. At the same time new methods of organization, divisions and later corps, and new tactics, skirmishing and charging in columns, not only could be taught more easily than linear evolutions, but they also proved highly effective. To fight the French the other European powers had to adopt similar methods and organizations; as Frederick William III of Prussia said, it was necessary to "make our army more like the French."[1]

Yet, in the end, the reforms adopted were limited and partial. Generally speaking, French military organization, strategy, and tactics were adopted. Armies manoeuvred in corps, divisions and brigades, and fought in columns and skirmish lines supported by massed batteries of mobile field artillery. But on the question of whether armies should become "national," that is whether they should be constituted by citizens with rights and obligations, or whether the traditional forms of officers procured from the upper classes in society and a rank and file enlisted from the opposite end of the social

---

From Gunther E. Rothenberg, *The Art of Warfare in the Age of Napoleon* (Bloomington: Indiana University Press, 1978), pp. 241–245. Reprinted by permission of Indiana University Press and Batsford Limited.

[1] W. O. Shanahan, *Prussian Military Reforms, 1786–1813*, Columbia University Press, New York, 1945, 84.

spectrum should be continued, the powers, except for Prussia proved extremely conservative. England had always continued the system of raising troops by voluntary enlistment; there also had been no change in the Russian army. Austria, to be sure, had experimented with the *Landwehr* [national guard] concept in 1809, but had discarded it by 1813. Only Prussia, keenly aware of her manpower weakness compared to the other powers, had in 1814–15 introduced universal conscription legislation preserving the *Landwehr* as a permanent part of her military establishment.

The tendency to retain, or revert to, the traditional pattern was reinforced by the international situation. The fall of Napoleon ushered in a period of relative stability in Europe, based primarily on the balance of power established by the treaties of 1815 and the rigorous suppression of all domestic disorder. Except for a continuing suspicion of French designs, the armies of the great continental powers were designed primarily for use against nationalist and liberal uprisings and not for use against each other. Governments after 1815 feared that the ghost of revolution had only been inadequately banished and they believed that Jacobinism, nationalism, and the nation in arms were interlocking revolutionary concepts. Therefore even where changes in the military establishment had been made, the governments returned as soon as possible to the spirit and forms of the eighteenth century.

Even where extensive changes had occurred, there was a determined effort to insulate soldiers once again from the political, social, and economic problems around them. In France the restored Bourbons returned as soon as they could to a professional long-service army, though retaining conscription on paper. And in Prussia, too, the reformers [, who included Gneisenau and Scharnhorst], regarded as military Jacobins by the reactionaries, first scaled down their hopes and then almost became reactionaries themselves. In any case, most of these professional officers had been uneasy about the idea of a "people's army" and the citizen-soldiers. As one of Gneisenau's assistants wrote even before the army had been withdrawn from France, "it was quite proper to use them as *piqueurs* who, with the moral hunting-whip, drove the lazy dogs as long as the hunt lasted. But when they sat down to dine with the hunting society . . . it became time to show them the door."[2] By 1819, most of the radical officers associated with the innovations of the Scharnhorst period either had recanted or had been driven from office.

In tactics, however, there was considerable continuity between those of the Napoleonic era and the second quarter of the nineteenth

---

[2]Cited in A. Vagts, *A History of Militarism*, W. W. Norton, New York, 1937, 175–6.

century and beyond. To be sure, the British clung to their refined linear system, in many ways the ultimate perfection of eighteenth century warfare. But in the other armies combat methods evolved by the end of the Napoleonic wars remained in use, even though new technological developments rapidly diminished their effectiveness. This in part was due to the prevailing conservatism in ruling circles, but also due to the fact that all military establishments were dominated by men who had gained their experience, and sometimes fame, in the Napoleonic wars. In France there were Soult, Marmont, and St. Cyr; in England Wellington; and in Austria Radetzky. And while Scharnhorst had died in 1813 and Blücher in 1819, Prussian tactical methods continued to be dominated by Gneisenau and Clausewitz, and after them by men like Wrangel and others. And in Russia, finally, Paskievich, promoted to Lieutenant-General at Leipzig, dominated the military scene into the Crimean War. None of these men were disposed to abandon the tried and true methods and they did not encourage their subordinates to question them. As a result, tactics became ossified and the manoeuvres of the wars in the mid-nineteenth century in Europe, and for that matter those of the Civil War in America, would have been perfectly familiar to any Napoleonic general. Indeed, the European commanders during these wars had seen their last active service in 1813–15.

There was, in fact, some regression. Emphasis on squadrons of glittering cavalry and long lines of infantry wheeling with precision on the parade ground became common in all armies. The economic exhaustion following the long war played a role here. Mechanical drill, the manual of arms, and parade-ground exhibitions were less expensive than realistic training and also more in line with the return of the concept of the officer as gentleman or aristocrat and not a professional.

Except for Prussia, and even here there was a marked decline, the general staff was neglected. Everywhere there was a resurgence of the old antagonisms between the "quill-pushers" and the men of the sword, many of whom retained an essentially pre-industrial conception of the army, distrusting all scientific and technological developments likely to upset the status quo. Emperor Francis Joseph of Austria put this feeling into words. "The quality of my army," he remarked, "does not depend on learned officers, but on brave and chivalrous men." Loyalty, unquestioning obedience, literal observance of regulations, and above all personal courage were considered the most essential soldierly qualities.

As a result there was little progress in military theory, though there now arose a considerable literature attempting to interpret the lessons of the Napoleonic past. Baron Jomini, who had served on Ney's staff before deserting to the Russians, became the most influential interpreter until the 1860's. His many writings, prescribed readings in most military academies, provided little more than a clear and schematic exposition of Napoleonic strategy, culminating in the elaboration of 10 major maxims and three general combinations emphasizing mass, mobility, and pressure against the decisive strategic point. Jomini was completely silent on the issue of motives and political objectives, and he frequently confused the categories of strategy and tactics. In fact, he said little about tactics, though when he did, he emphasized the attack. By contrast, Clausewitz's writings, especially his uncompleted work *On War*, were far more sophisticated and complex. He did not believe in the validity of rigid systems and dogmas, but stressed instead the interaction of war, politics and society. He described war as "an act of force to compel our enemy to do our will," and since war was the continuation of state policy by other means, it was subject to certain limitations. Nonetheless, Clausewitz scorned the thought that there was "some ingenious way to disarm or defeat an enemy without too much bloodshed," and while he warned against escalating the level of force beyond that required to attain the political aim, he also felt that battle, an act of will and moral force as much as that of skilled generalship and manoeuvre, was the decisive act.[3]

Although Clausewitz's work soon became accepted as authoritative in Prussia, translated into French by 1849 and into English by 1873, it was not always clearly understood. Most military men read his sentiments not as a subordination of warfare to state policy, but as an ideological superstructure for their profession. And as far as tactics went, Clausewitz too was but little removed from the Napoleonic era. When he did his writing, all armies had achieved an approximately equal technological level and therefore he concluded that "superiority in numbers becomes every day more decisive, and that the principle of assembling the greatest possible numbers may therefore be regarded as more important than ever."[4]

On the operational level, therefore, despite his profound sociopolitical insights which became more important than ever in the twentieth century, Clausewitz had only limited impact. All military commentators were agreed on the importance of morale, though Clausewitz, to be sure, extended this morale factor from the private in the rear ranks to the commanding general and from the lowest civilian to the head of state. But the immediate military revolution on the operational level came through the perfection first of efficient and

---

[3]P. Paret, *Clausewitz and the State*, Oxford University Press 1976, 204–5, 382–95. Cf. Vagts, *op. cit.*, 192–6.
[4]*Ibid.*, 195.

relatively cheap percussion rifle-muskets, later breech-loaders, and rifled artillery, together with the development of dense railroad and telegraph networks. Although these innovations were accepted by the military everywhere in the 1850s, there was no realization that they created a dichotomy between firepower and the existing tactics. Despite the fact that massed charges yielded constantly diminishing returns against the new weapons, faith in the mass attack remained constant until the 1870s and beyond. At the same time, there was some hesitation to adopt the new strategic mobility conferred on armies by railroads and telegraph, and much preoccupation with secure operational bases, good positions, and safe lines of communications. This, of course, represented a regression to the eighteenth century, but generals commanding old-fashioned armies were unprepared for the new, and revolutionary, implications in strategy and tactics created by the new weaponry and communications.[5]

The Prussian general staff, directed since 1857 by Helmuth v. Moltke, was perhaps the first to realize that the forces unleashed by the Industrial Revolution provided the means to mobilize, equip, and direct huge armies, and that this required both a complex and highly professional staff and the support of the entire sociopolitical potential of the nation. But, with conscription becoming once again universal in Prussia in the 1850s, and with an all pervasive and effective state controlled educational system, for the first time Clausewitz's conception of the national will could be transmitted to the entire population. Meanwhile, realizing the potentialities of rail transportation, Moltke developed new strategies which demonstrated, and on an even larger scale, the Napoleonic principle of forcing a quick and decisive battle within a few weeks after the outbreak of war.

Prussia's surprising victories in 1866 and 1870–1 induced all continental armies to adopt the Prussian, and now German, system of mass mobilization through conscription, professional staffs, strategic railroads, and extensive telegraphic communications. Yet, although he had promoted the adoption of a breech-loader—the famous needle gun—into the Prussian army, achieving a decisive fire-superiority over the Austrians in 1866, Moltke, too, did not fully comprehend the necessity to adopt tactics suited to the radically changed circumstances. In fact, there was little realization of the growing gap between weapons and tactics, and between tactics and strategy in all European countries. All of the 1914 war plans of the continental general staffs were offensive and based on the expectation of achieving a quick and decisive decision on the Napoleonic-Moltkean pat-

[5] W. McElwee, *The Art of War from Waterloo to Mons*, Weidenfeld and Nicolson, 1974, 1–69 *passim*.

tern. All of these schemes failed, creating a bloody stalemate, a war of attrition and not a war of quick annihilation of the opposing forces.

The development of new tactics, and especially the rise of air and armour, seemed to revive the possibilities for quick decisions. During the Second World War, and in the smaller conventional wars of the post-war period, there was a revival of Napoleonic strategy—feints, penetrations, flank attacks, and envelopments, conducted by armoured and motorized armies under the cover of air umbrellas. But at the same time, the emergence of nuclear arsenals and missile-delivery system seems to have undercut the viability of conventional wars and Napoleonic strategy. Instead some writers suggest that the guerrilla warfare which plagued the French in the Vendée, the Tyrol, and above all in Spain, may well dominate the spectrum of future conflict. To be sure, there are others who disagree. They argue that while military planners in the past often made the mistake of underestimating the guerrilla, the danger now is that this type of warfare will be overrated and be considered a military panacea. Guerrilla wars, they maintain, remain only one form of conflict and they believe that there will be future wars in which Napoleonic doctrines, suitably adapted to modern conditions, still retain validity. The issue remains unresolved.

Whatever the outcome, it seems likely that as long as soldiers survive and men follow the profession of arms, Napoleon will continue to exert a powerful attraction and his achievements will continue to be studied. Few understood as well as he did the possibilities and limitations of time and space, and few commanders had his ability to inspire devotion and courage amidst peril and confusion. In recognizing and honouring these qualities, one also recognizes the qualities of his adversaries.

Marcel Garaud (1885–1972) was Professor of Law at the University of Poitiers and the author of many books and articles on medieval and modern French law. Romuald Szramkiewicz (1936–   ) is a professor at the University of Paris-Sorbonne. He has written about the Napoleonic period in Les Régents et censeurs de la Banque de France nommés sous le Consulat et l'Empire *(1974); one of his main research interests is French commercial law in the eighteenth and nineteenth centuries.*

WOMEN AND THE FAMILY
Marcel Garaud
Romuald Szramkiewicz

THE CIVIL CODE AND THE FAMILY

In the case of the family, the Civil Code of 1804 was a compromise between the old legal tradition and revolutionary legislation. Those who drafted it, "veterans of the Revolution," as Esmein called them,[1] could not repudiate the Revolution's work. The principles of liberty and equality that were the essence of the Revolution were supported by the majority of the French people and had brought reforms that deserved to be kept. There was no question of abolishing them. Nevertheless, the pursuit of the revolutionary ideal had produced changes that were inappropriate for the customs of the time. "The story of the Revolution is over," Bonaparte said to the Council of State. "We must decide what can be applied, practically speaking, from these principles and not concern ourselves with speculating and hypothesizing. To follow a different path today would be philosophizing, not governing." The drafters of the Civil Code had the same attitude. They worked judiciously to correct what was excessive and improper in the revolutionary legislation by going back to traditional jurisprudence, so long as it remained consistent with contemporary attitudes. Afterward, revolutionary legislation could be compared with that of the Old Regime, and from this juxtaposition a single and harmonious set of laws could be drafted. This is what they did.

The provisions of the Civil Code concerning the family differ

---

From Marcel Garaud and Romuald Szramkiewicz, *La Révolution française et la famille* (Paris: Presses universitaires de France, 1978), pp. 167–176. Printed by permission of the publishers. Editors' translation. Some of the footnotes have been omitted.

[1]A. Esmein, *Livre du centenaire du Code civil* (Paris, 1904).

greatly from the arrangements established by the intermediary [revolutionary] legislation. But the revolutionary inheritance was preserved in part.

MARRIAGE

In its essentials, the secularization of marriage was not challenged. This major reform had been prepared and begun during the Old Regime. The Edict of Toleration of 1787 had authorized the king's non-Catholic subjects to marry whomever they chose before a justice of the peace or before parish priests or vicars who would act not as clergymen but as public officials. The Revolution simply fulfilled the Edict of 1787, which had already been accepted in common practice and which was based on the principle of freedom of conscience that a large majority of the French wanted. Freedom of conscience had, as a corollary, the separation of the legal system from religion. This was the position of those who drafted the Civil Code.[2] They do not seem to have thought of recommending freedom for its own sake or the separation of the State from the Church, a doctrine supported by royalist jurists in the Old Regime.

In the Civil Code, as in the 1792 law, marriage is treated as a civil contract. The 1792 law, however, permitted any citizen to have his marriage sanctified by a clergyman either before or after the civil ceremony. The Civil Code did not confirm this provision. At the time of the Concordat [of 1801], the French state overlooked, as had the legislatures of the Revolution, the fact that the secularization of marriage entailed the independence of the Church on religious matters. Article 54 of the Organic Laws completing the Concordat's regulation of religion, which had been drafted by Portalis, provided that the civil marriage ceremony should precede the religious rites.[3] After the reestablishment of the Catholic religion in France and the reopening of the churches, there was concern that the faithful would consider only the religious ceremony as significant and jeopardize their legal status by omitting the civil ceremony.[4] There was an effort also to protect future couples from their own ignorance. For example, a seducer might trick a young woman into settling for a religious

---

[2]P.-A. Fenet, *Recueil complet des travaux préparatoires du Code civil* (15 vols.; Paris, 1827), IX, 141.

[3]"Priests will perform the wedding rites only for those who can prove that they had been married earlier by a civil official." Law of 18 Germinal, year X [April 8, 1802], Article 54.

[4]G. Bertier de Sauvigny, "Le Discrédit du mariage civil sous le Ier Empire," *Revue d'histoire de l'Eglise de France*, 1942, pp. 231f.

ceremony alone with the intention of abandoning her later. According to Portalis, this happened frequently.[5]

Article 54 aimed to eliminate these improper actions. But as it included only a prohibition without a penalty, it was ineffective. A punishment had to be added. The First Consul and Bigot-Préameneu recognized this as early as 1804. Articles 199 and 200 of the Penal Code of 1810 declared, in the same phrases as the report read to the Legislative Body, "a just punishment against clergymen who, by a criminal usurpation, attempt to substitute their services for those of the only officials recognized by public authority and who substitute religious ceremonies for those actions the law regards as purely civil acts." The punishment consisted of a fine for the first infraction, then prison, and then even a longer term in prison (substituted for deportation by the law of April 28, 1832, which amended the Penal Code of 1810 on this point).

This double ceremony of marriage has been criticized because, in some cases, it did not respect the principles of freedom of conscience and of religion that the legislators prided themselves on protecting. It could happen, for example, that after the civil marriage ceremony performed by a public official, one of the partners might refuse to take part in the religious ceremony. The marriage would still be valid from the legal point of view. One should not underestimate the seriousness of this situation, for the beliefs of the other partner might prevent her or him from considering the union as final until the religious rite was performed. Still, a remedy existed. The offended partner had the alternative of requesting a legal separation or divorce to undo a bond, such as it was, which was repugnant to her or his religious beliefs. Even so, cases of this sort were extremely rare. Also couples planning to marry had available a preventive device that consisted in having the civil ceremony followed immediately by the religious ceremony. Consequently, it has not been necessary to repeal Articles 199 and 200 of the Penal Code, whose application might cause the problem just discussed.[6]

[5]"It often happens," he said, "that a clever seducer appears before a priest with the woman that he pretends to choose for his bride, lives with her as man and wife, but then later refuses to go through a civil marriage ceremony. When the seducer grows tired of a union that has become irksome to him, he forsakes his so-called wife and leaves her in despair, for this unhappy woman has no way to establish her rights and those of her children."

[6]For a commentary on this matter, see L. Desforges, *Etude historique sur la formation du mariage en droit romain et en droit français* (Paris, 1887), pp. 291f. Most European states have adopted civil marriage. The law is much the same for France, Germany, and the countries of the Soviet bloc, which recognize only civil marriages as valid.

DIVORCE

Along with the secularization of marriage, the acceptance of divorce was the major bargaining concession made, though not easily, by the drafters of the Civil Code to the legislators of the Revolution in the area of family law. The revival of Catholicism during the Consulate had increased the disrepute of divorce and worked in favor of abolishing it.[7] Although it had been legal for ten years, divorce had not yet become an accepted French custom. Still, it had many partisans. Despite their view that divorce was not beneficial, some of the French favored its retention as a remedy of some dubious merit for unfortunate couples on condition that it be kept within narrow limits. The drafters of the Civil Code reflected this judgment, permitting divorce only for certain specified reasons. It came up for discussion in the [legislative committee of the] Council of State on 14 Vendémiaire, year X (October 3, 1801).

Two groups of jurists, one favoring and the other opposing divorce, confronted each other. They disagreed less on the principle of divorce, which did not arouse opposition, than on the restrictions on it. Portalis, Malleville, Tronchet, and Bigot-Préameneu, going back to the traditional doctrine of the indissolubility of marriage, wanted a rigorous control over divorce, which in their view should be permitted only in desperate circumstances. Other committee members, such as Berlier, Regnault de Saint-Jean d'Angély, Thibaudeau, and Cambacérès, inspired by revolutionary principles, viewed divorce as a necessary complement to marriage. They believed divorce should be permitted with some safeguards, even on such grounds as mutual consent or incompatibility of temperament. Bonaparte's intervention in this discussion was decisive. Taking a somewhat negative view of divorce, he rejected the grounds of incompatibility. And yet his attitude, which was not free of some Jacobinism, made him oppose the indissolubility of marriage. He declared himself in favor of divorce by mutual consent. Perhaps he had a personal motive here. He wanted to make his rule hereditary, but recognizing with regret that his union with Josephine Beauharnais continued barren, he may have wanted to leave open a means of ending it. In any event, mutual consent was kept as one of the grounds for divorce in the committee's proposal.[8]

---

[7] One of the best-known contemporary works against divorce was Louis de Bonald, *Du Divorce* (Paris, 1801). . . . The unity and indissolubility of marriage found another eloquent defender in F.-R. de Chateaubriand, *Génie du Christianisme* (Paris, 1802), Book I, Chapter X.

[8] See D. Roughol-Valdeyron, "Le Divorce par consentement mutuel et le Code Napoléon," *Revue trimestrielle de droit civil*, no. 4, 1975, 482–487, which demonstrates the decisive influence of Bonaparte (against the appeals courts' views) on maintaining this procedure aimed at permitting families to avoid recourse to the

On the other hand, the drafters of the Civil Code tried to make divorce as rare as possible by surrounding it with restrictive conditions. Instead of the seven grounds for divorce authorized by the law of 1792, a case could be brought on only three grounds—adultery, physical violence or moral cruelty, and the sentencing of one partner to harsh and degrading punishment. For divorce by mutual consent, the husband had to be over twenty-five years of age, the wife over twenty-one and under forty-five; they must have been married more than two years and less than twenty years; if they had been minors when they married, they had to obtain the authenticated approval of the same persons who authorized the marriage; and finally, they had to agree in writing on custody of the children, on the place where the wife would live, and on the alimony that her husband would pay her during these legal proceedings. District courts were called upon to resolve matters relating to divorce rather than relying on family courts, which the drafters of the Code described as "a gang of toadies or cronies always ready to plot with husbands against the law."

The Civil Code included in its provisions physical separation, that is separation from the marriage bed, requested by Catholics and also demanded by several courts of appeal. Respect for freedom of conscience in effect required this reform. It was adopted despite opposition from Jacobins with anticlerical views. They believed that physical separation must form an obstacle to divorce because Catholics would use it as a substitute for divorce. Separation meant that neither of the partners could marry again, which presented difficulties. For this reason the Civil Code authorized the conversion of separation into a divorce under certain limited circumstances. The separation must have lasted for at least three years; in addition, the marriage partner who had obtained the separation must have been opposed to ending it.

Under the restrictive conditions of the Civil Code, divorce became rare, and the scandals which had occurred under the 1792 law ended.[9]

---

humiliating procedure of adultery. "The court," he said, "will grant a divorce not *because* there is mutual consent, but *when* there is mutual consent." Ultimately, this route came to be used only rarely.

[9][During the Empire, divorces averaged sixty per year in Paris, six per year in Marseille, and just two per year in Toulouse compared with twenty per year in that city under the Directory and Consulate. See J. Godechot, *Les Institutions de la France sous la Révolution et l'Empire* (3rd ed.; Paris: Presses universitaires de France, 1985). After the fall of the Empire, the Restoration government in 1816 abolished divorce but retained the right of separation. In 1884, divorce was legalized again in a measure similar to the provisions of the Napoleonic Code. Thereafter several changes made divorce somewhat less restrictive, and finally in 1975 the divorce law was thoroughly revised. The new system provided three general grounds for divorce: mutual consent, separation, and serious faults committed by one partner. The number of divorces in

Favorable to secularizing marriage and to dissolving it by divorce in exceptional cases, the drafters of the Civil Code reacted strongly against the revolutionary legislators' views concerning the legal status of women and against their views on the power of the father and the status of illegitimate children.

THE POSITION OF WOMEN

The Revolution had wanted to make women equal to men. This progress had already been nearly achieved for unmarried women by the end of the Old Regime. Single women enjoyed civil rights equal to men except in some provinces which followed written law and in Normandy, where the *sénatus-consulte* Velléien still prevailed. There a woman could not legally enter into a contract. But the inequalities of inheritance seemed contrary to natural rights, and the revolutionaries ended the special privileges of males. Women now could act as witnesses in cases of civil law and make valid contracts without running into the provisions of the *sénatus-consulte* Velléien. They were permitted to share in the division of property previously held in common.

Revolutionary legislators also understood the need to change the legal status of married women, a status which flouted the principles of liberty and equality. The first proposed Civil Code presented to the Convention by Cambacérès [in 1793] did not speak to the matter of male legal dominance in marriage, but seemed to eliminate it purely and simply. It also gave equal rights over property held in common to each partner. These reforms soon appeared incompatible with contemporary social attitudes, and the Convention rejected them. Later in the Revolution Cambacérès repudiated them in the third proposed Civil Code that he submitted to the Council of Five Hundred: "The management of property under joint control would always be hindered, and arguments over small details soon would lead to a dissolution of the marriage." He specified that if equality was "to serve as the standard in all acts of organized society, we should depart from it only to maintain the natural order of things and thereby avoid arguments that destroy the charm of domestic life." By this Cambacérès meant that the natural order gave to the husband the dominant role in the family.

France at various times are as follows: 1900, about 7,300; 1913, about 15,000; between the world wars, about 21,000 per year; early 1960s, about 33,000 per year; and early 1980s, about 95,000 per year. The French rate of about 1.7 divorces per thousand inhabitants in the early 1980s was considerably less than the U.S. rate of 5.1 per 1,000. Parental consent for marriages is now required in France only if one of the partners is under eighteen years of age.—Eds.]

Those who prepared the [Napoleonic] Civil Code held the same views. "There have been many discussions on equality and superiority of the sexes. Nothing is more useless than such disputes," Portalis remarked somewhat disdainfully. "Their physical differences imply differences in their respective rights and duties.... Not laws, but nature determines their fate. Women need protection because they are weaker; men are free because they are stronger."[10]

Based on these considerations, the drafters of the Civil Code went back to the legal traditions of the Old Regime, where the legal incapacity of married women rested on two principles: firstly, the husband's authority in the marriage, which was distinct from the matrimonial agreement; and secondly, the woman's need for protection due to her sex.[11]

As stated in the Civil Code of 1804, the wife owed obedience to her husband. She also had to live with him and follow him wherever he chose to establish his home. Certain inequalities also marked the legal status of the marriage partners. They owed fidelity to each other. But this duty was enforced differently for husbands and wives: "A wife's infidelity," observed Portalis, "implies more corruption and has more dangerous effects than that of her husband; so the man always has been judged less severely than the woman." According to Portalis, this was an "honorable and useful distinction," for it attempted to stop the wife from introducing outsiders into the legitimate family.

Either spouse could petition for divorce because of adultery. But a wife's petition would be permitted only if the husband maintained his mistress under the family roof. Moreover, on the demand of the public prosecutor, a wife convicted of adultery could be confined in a house of correction for a term of three months to two years. The husband convicted of keeping his mistress in the family home incurred only a fine of from 100 to 2,000 francs. Finally, if the husband caught his wife and her lover engaged in adultery in the family home and committed murder, the crime was excused, although the law did not excuse a woman's murder of her husband in similar circumstances. In addition, the husband alone managed property held in common. He was, as under the law of the Old Regime, the lord and master. The wife could not sue in court, sell or mortgage her own property, or contract a debt without her husband's consent.

Consequently, the Civil Code made the wife, whom the Revolution

---

[10] Portalis, quoted in Fenet, IX, 177–178. On Bonaparte's attitude, see R. Savatier, *L'Art de faire des lois: Bonaparte et le Code civil* (Paris, 1927), pp. 27f., 31f.

[11] In his *Droit commun de la France* (Paris, 1747), F. Bourjon speaks of the "healthy" lack of legal power of women, "a wise arrangement that keeps the peace and preserves the family property by protecting it from the independence, fickleness, and frivolity of women."

had wanted to make equal to the husband in civil law, completely dependent upon her husband.[12]

PATERNAL POWER

During the Revolution the first draft of a Civil Code presented by Cambacérès to the Convention announced the end of paternal power. As Berlier put it in his report on the draft: "The imperious voice of Reason has been heard; paternal power is no more; to establish its rights by force is to deceive nature. To keep watch and protect, those are the rights of parents; to nourish and raise their children, those are their duties." The second draft remained faithful to this position, "Among us the power of fathers over their children will only be the duty of protecting them." And likewise in the third draft, "For too long we have considered the duty of protection that nature has inscribed on our hearts as a source of paternal power. We must reduce the connections between fathers and sons to kindness and generosity on the one side, to respect and gratitude on the other."

Under the Consulate, there was a reaction influenced by Roman law and the Christian tradition in favor of a return to paternal power, a power considered enfeebled by revolutionary legislation. The fourth draft of the Civil Code, prepared by Jacqueminot, took this path. It sought to restore to paternal authority "the legitimate power that should never have been lost and which would permit the rewarding of filial loyalty and the punishing of ingratitude." It would be enough if paternal power were organized so as to respect the interests of the state. With this understood, paternal power, "which is a right based on nature and confirmed by law," but not established by it, should be effective. The state would only rarely have to intervene in the exercise of this power. There was no need to fear that fathers would abuse their authority, and it was appropriate that authority reign in the family as in the state. These principles were those of the drafters of the Civil Code. One can find them spelled out in an essay on the question, "What should be the extent and limits of a father's powers in a well-established republic," proposed as the basis of a competition by the Institute. Rejecting the wary attitudes of the revolutionary legislators toward fathers, the drafters believed that the power of fathers was tempered by their love. "Nature," remarked Portalis, "has given to

[12][The legal status of women improved gradually from the 1880s on. For example, a 1907 law permitted married women unlimited control of their own salaries and earnings. A wide-ranging law of 1965 granted women legal status equal to that of their husbands. Married women could now manage their own property without their husband's consent. Jointly owned property would be managed by the husband, but he needed the wife's consent for major transactions.—Eds.]

fathers and mothers a desire to see their children succeed, a desire that the children hardly felt themselves. The law can, without any second thoughts, follow nature's lead."[13]

Influenced by these considerations, the Civil Code of 1804 concentrated all power in the father's hands. He alone possessed the right to punish. Treilhard and Berlier preferred to revive the family courts that had been abolished by the law of 9 Ventose, year IV (February 28, 1796). But Cambacérès and Bigot-Préameneu opposed this. The former two argued that "too often hatred and self-interest divide those united by blood," and the latter two observed that any legal dispute between father and son should be avoided, especially in front of the family. It was finally decided that a civil court would have jurisdiction in circumstances provided by law. The father could have his children under the age of sixteen imprisoned for up to a month if they had neither an occupation nor personal property. The presiding judge of the court had to comply with this request. But, for children sixteen to twenty-one years of age, the judge made the final decision on a request that they be imprisoned and on the question of how long, up to a maximum of six months.

Sons up to twenty-five years of age and daughters up to twenty-one years had to obtain their father's consent to marry, or should he not be present, the mother's consent was necessary. Sons from twenty-five to thirty and daughters from twenty-one to twenty-five had to ask for consent. If they did not gain permission, they could ignore their parents only following the submission of three monthly documents respectfully notifying them. Sons over thirty and daughters over twenty-five still had to send notice by a respectful document. If fathers and mothers were not available, grandparents had to be asked for their mutual consent. To justify the parents' role, Gillet argued in the Tribunate that, after major political upheavals, social stability could be strengthened only "by increasing precautions to maintain family order."

So, there can be no doubt that, as far as the consent of parents and other elder relatives in the marriages of sons and daughters of the family, the Civil Code conferred on paternal power a strength that approached the old *patria potestas* [the absolute power of the father in Ancient Rome]. Still, on a few essential points, the Code incorporated some of the reforms of the Revolution. Paternal power had its limits. The right to punish required the intervention of the civil court in circumstances specified by law. Secondly, the Civil Code rejected

---

[13]Fenet, IX, 144. The First Consul, taking a more realistic position, wanted to provide a counterweight to paternal power by increasing that of the grandparents, even that of the mother, "the natural teacher of her children," and that of the courts. But, absent from Paris, he could not watch over the changes in the text. See Savatier, pp. 16, 29.

disinheritance as a means of punishment. The highest court made this a corollary of paternal power. It wished to keep the right of disinheritance in certain situations, particularly in the case of a marriage contracted between the ages of twenty and twenty-five without parental consent. But this punishment, which created the drawback of harming the guilty son through his innocent posterity, appeared to be unjust; and therefore the son could always be sure of obtaining the remainder of his inheritance that the legislators had assigned to him unless he was declared disqualified from the inheritance.

Louis Bergeron (1929–   ) is a graduate of the Ecole normale supérieure and has been a teacher at the Ecole des hautes études en sciences sociales since 1971. A specialist in economic and social history, he completed a thesis on Parisian bankers, merchants, and manufacturers from 1799 to 1815. He has also written or collaborated on many other books. These include Grands notables du Premier Empire *(1978–   ),* Les "Masses de granit": cent mille notables du Premier Empire *(1979), and* L'Episode napoléonien: aspects intérieurs, 1799–1815 *(1972). This last work, which has been translated as* France Under Napoleon, *is striking for its concentration on Napoleon's times, rather than on Napoleon as an individual.*

NO TURNING POINT

Louis Bergeron

The importance of the period [1800–1815] and of the man [Napoleon] are unavoidably reduced when seen in the light of long gradual movements, deep tendencies, or elements of resistance. The period in this way may seem only an episode. The régime never had time to consolidate its base; perhaps it never had more than the appearance of stability. The demographic behavior of the French people escaped it; population growth slackened although Napoleon would have wished a high fecundity to strengthen his empire. It was only with reservations that the social body adapted itself to the Napoleonic structure; the fusion of elites was only imperfectly realized. One of the pillars of the State, the Catholic clergy, defected, undermined by the progress of ultramontanism. In the deeper life of the nation it was economic activity that showed the most independence, or the least capacity for adaptation to a régime whose ideal was for everything to be perfectly controlled. The agricultural and rural world evolved at its own rhythms, which had little to do with the political universe. Deeply marked by the Revolution, it was hardly affected by the Empire. Industrial production and commercial exchanges reacted immediately to the shifts in international politics, but the renovation of industrial structures depended on a combination of conditions that was modified only slowly. Let us not deceive ourselves—France changed very little from 1800 to 1815. Paradox-

From Louis Bergeron, *France Under Napoleon*, trans. by R. R. Palmer (Princeton: Princeton University Press, 1981), pp. xiii–xiv, 125–134, 204. Reprinted by permission of Princeton University Press.

ically, Napoleon was both behind and ahead of his time, the last of the enlightened despots, and a prophet of the modern State. . . .

THE FATE OF THE OLD NOBILITY

Fluctuat nec mergitur . . . .[1]

The Revolution did indeed found a society of landed proprietors subject to the same rules of the Civil Code, which fixed the conditions for the exercise of property rights with much precision. And one of the essential and conclusive results of the Revolution, achieved in the legislation of the Consulate, was to render all transfers of property originating in the Revolutionary confiscations henceforth untouchable. While the returning émigrés escaped persecution in their persons, and the amnesty restored them to public life, their confiscated estates remained in the hands of the new owners, whose rights were guaranteed in the same way as for any form of private or inherited property; and the extinction of seigneurial revenues without indemnity was confirmed. At the same time, returned émigrés could regain possession of confiscated property that had not yet been sold. In regions where the sale of émigré lands had been feeble—in the west, center, and south—"the nobility easily recovered its former importance on the land" (Tulard). Restitutions through assumed names, and amicably arranged retrocessions, in some departments reached a height of millions of francs. Such operations, of course, and the necessary rehabilitation of property whose maintenance had often been neglected, especially when real estate speculators were content with simply collecting the rent, represented so much heavy expense to be paid out of reduced fortunes. It might even happen, with generally opposite effects, that old nobles were obliged to sell some of the estates that they had preserved or recovered.[2] As late as 1809, the "personal and moral statistics" of Paris showed many a great old family in the Faubourg Saint-Germain "uniquely concerned with reestablishing a large fortune," or "restoring a fortune that had once been considerable" or "essentially occupied in improving its property."

It is an important fact, from an overall and quantitative point of view, that the bourgeoisie had a preponderant part in the purchase of nationalized property, and in landed property itself. But it is important also, and necessary, to admit that the old nobility remained very prominent in the uppermost bracket of landed fortunes, and preserved in many cases not only considerable wealth but a large social

---

[1]"Tempest-tossed but never sinks." The motto of the city of Paris, applied here to the pre-Revolutionary nobility. (Trans.)

[2]Robert Forster, "The Survival of the French Nobility," in *Past and Present*, 1967, pp. 71–86.

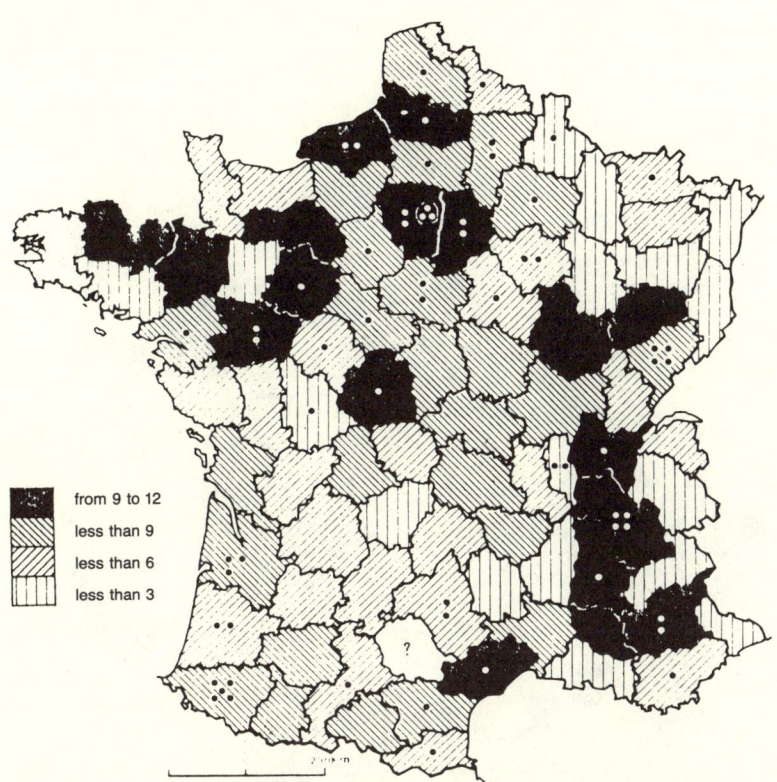

SURVIVAL OF ARISTOCRATIC LANDOWNERSHIP IN 1803

Of the twelve persons in each department paying the highest real estate tax, the map shows the number of such persons who were of the pre-Revolutionary nobility. The dots show the number, among the twelve, who had also been members of the pre-Revolutionary Parlements or sovereign courts. Note the predominance in this respect of the former privileged classes in the Paris region, Normandy, the west, and parts of the southeast.

and political influence. This conclusion emerges, at least on first study, from a document in the National Archives, a list by departments of the twelve persons in each department [in 1803] paying the largest real property tax.[3] In most cases old nobles are in the majority in the sample, and in some cases the only ones. Of even more interest, they occasionally appear as the largest owners of property confiscated during the Revolution.

The accompanying map is worth the trouble of analysis as a sketch of the social geography of France. Some departments show an abso-

[3]Archives Nationales, AF IV 1076.

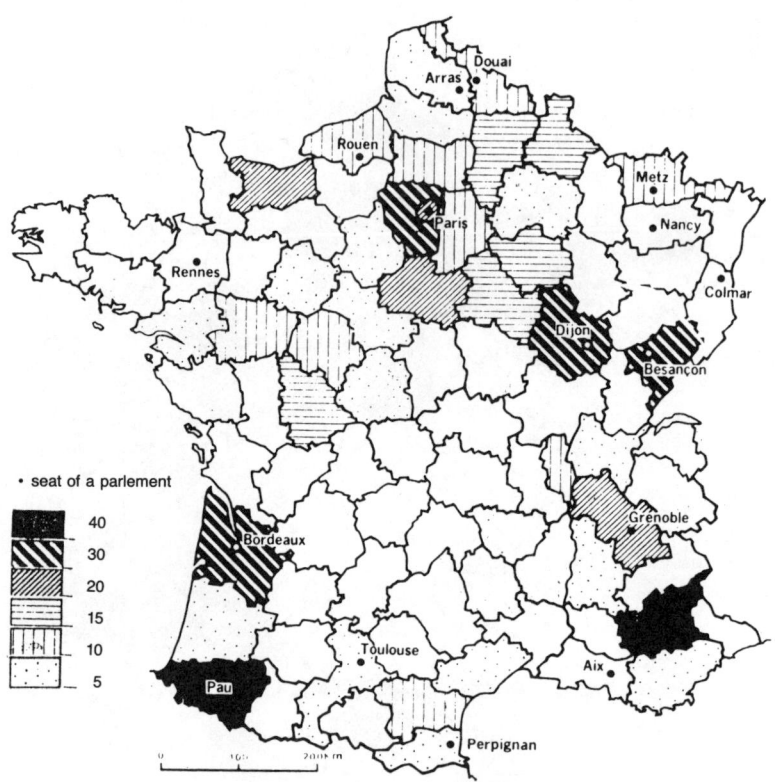

LANDOWNERSHIP IN 1803
BY MEMBERS OF THE PRE-REVOLUTIONARY PARLEMENTS

The map shows, within each department, the land owned by members of the old Parlements expressed as a percentage of the land owned by the twelve highest taxpayers. Though their ranks had been trimmed by the guillotine and by emigration, these former *parlementaires* were very much present during the Napoleonic years, some occupying posts in the high magistracy, others living in retirement on their estates, and in either case often being among the richest landowners among the old aristocracy. The towns whose names appear are those where a Parlement had been located.

lute noble predominance. In the Isère, the sale of confiscated noble land must have been small, since at the time of the famous "billion for the émigrés" (in 1825), there were only 128 cases of indemnification, while the average for all departments was 240. Among our twelve noble proprietors in the Isère we find four who had been members of the old [pre-revolutionary] Parlement of Dauphiny (de Barral-Montferrat, a former presiding judge; Moidieu, former attorney; de Meffrey and de Chaléon, former councillors), two ex-lieutenants-general of the army, and three other military men.

In the Sarthe the duke of Choiseul-Praslin heads the list by paying over 27,000 francs in taxes, followed by duke d'Albert de Luynes at almost 16,000. The former, incidentally, also paid over 30,000 in the Seine-et-Marne (where he also headed the list), and the latter paid over 15,000 in the Seine-et-Oise (where he was third). Then come du Bouchet de Tourzel, formerly first equerry of France, and Dreux-Brézé, who had been Louis XVI's grand master of ceremonies. Thus we have a total of eleven nobles out of twelve, and the twelfth, a navy contractor, was the former business agent and steward of M. de Luynes.

While differently composed, the sample for the Indre is no less significant. Along with cavalry officers and brigadier generals (a Moreton de Chabrillant, a de Poix), we find a pre-Revolutionary intendant of finances and an intendant of the generality of Dijon (Amelot de Chaillou), and at the head of the list (with a tax of 21,600 francs) Legendre de Luçay, a survivor of the old General Farm, and now a prefect, as we have seen. One of the commoners on the list operated an iron works. In the Hérault ten places out of twelve were occupied by noble rentiers, by former "barons of the Estates of Languedoc," by a president of the former Chamber of Accounts, and by a Faventine doubtless mistakenly classified as a "bourgeois." In the Basses-Pyrénées almost all the places were filled by ex-military men and especially by ex-members of the Parlement of Navarre. The department of the Seine was a special case, because its highest taxpayers, belonging to complex elites, were listed only for their houses and buildings located in the department, whereas many "Parisians" owned land in the "provinces," that is, other departments. The Seine-et-Marne, Seine-et-Oise, Eure-et-Loir, Oise and Aisne in fact contained many estates of great families that resided alternately in their country homes and in the capital. Much of the Seine-et-Oise remained in the hands of families famous before the Revolution in the robe and in ministerial functions—Molé at Champlâtreux, Machault at Arnouville, Lefèvre at Ormesson, Morel de Vindé at Magnanville. The old duke de Noailles was the largest taxpayer in the Eure-et-Loir, at 14,600 francs, and also in Aisne, at 7,000. The list for the Oise included a Crillon and a La Rochefoucauld-Liancourt alongside a Delahante.

The place held by members of the former privileged classes is no less surprising in departments where one would expect to find signs of a commercial capitalism able to exert its power by the ownership of land. In the Gironde the first place was indeed held by the elder Bonaffé, listed however as a "rentier" and not as a Bordeaux merchant, but Cabarrus was only in eighth place, and Mareilhac only in the tenth, while two former presidents and a former councillor of the Parlement of Bordeaux occupied the second, third and fourth places, and the other names were of officers of the Old Régime. In the Seine-Inférieure the situation was even more clear: the duke of Luxembourg, the duke of Tancarville and a former secretary to the king led the list by a wide margin; two members of the former Parlement of Normandy were in fifth and seventh places; and in tenth place, the only one of his kind, and paying only half as much in taxes as the dukes, came Begouën-Demeaux, the great merchant and shipowner of Le Havre. In the Loire-Inférieure the commerce of Nantes was represented only by the names of Geslin, Lamaignière and Tatin, but it is true that two others, Leroux and Bertrand, probably belonged to merchant families that had penetrated the old nobility, as Jean Meyer has shown. In second place, thanks to purchases of property nationalized in the Revolution, we find the house of Schweighaüser-Dobrée, one of the few which instead of declining had begun its rise during the Franco-English wars [1793–1815]. In the adjoining Maine-et-Loire the largest landowner was Petitpierre, the great cotton manufacturer of Nantes. Only at Marseilles is the list dominated by large-scale commerce, some of whose representatives had been ennobled at the end of the Old Régime. Here the largest taxpayer was also the largest soap manufacturer in the city.

The greatest landed fortunes were, finally, in the hands of the bourgeoisie in only a fairly limited number of cases. Rural commerce might provide a firm enough base; thus in the Calvados we see two beef merchants slipping into our sample among former officers of justice and notable military men. In the Nord there were a few, like Olry, de Vézelise and the Delannoy brothers, who had in reality become contractors for the army or navy. Closely bound to rural society, and in fact to the former seigneurs whose managers or lessees they might have been, were various ironmasters who were also considerable landowners. Some of them, such as Raux and Gendarme, were among the few electors in the Ardennes whose income in 1810 exceeded 10,000 francs, and they were surpassed by the cloth manufacturers of Sedan, where Jean-Antoine Poupart de Neuflize, the second highest taxpayer in 1802, had an income of 100,000 francs in 1810. In the Haute-Marne four ironmasters occupied the second, sixth, eighth and ninth places. By way of exception, large-scale merchants and manufacturers might take first place in departments generally dominated by the property of Parisian aristocrats, as in the Somme, where Dottin, of Amiens, the largest purchaser of nationalized properties, outdistanced even the duke d'Albert de Luynes and the count de Choiseul-Gouffier. In the Aube, Duchâtel-Berthelin, of

Troyes, was well ahead of an assortment of ex-members of the Parlement of Paris and old court nobility, and we find here also the banker and manufacturer Worms, of Romilly. In the Bas-Rhin bankers and commission merchants of Strasbourg (Mesnet, Turckheim, Reichshoffer, Saum) were clearly in the lead, along with the miller Ulrich and the ironmaster Dietrich.

THE OLD NOBILITY AND THE NEW SOCIETY

There is another point on which anecdote or a few famous examples might too easily give a false picture of social reality, namely the question of how the old nobility made a place for itself in a society without legal ranks and orders. Here, too, beyond the collapse of caste barriers in the Revolution, we should probably stress the continuity of social structures in France, rather than see two sharply contrasting societies, one feudal and the other bourgeois, divided by an insuperable gulf of rancor and enmity that opened up between the Fourth of August [1789] and the condemnations to the guillotine [1793–1794].

It must be pointed out, with all possible emphasis, that retirement to their estates or to the privacy of their townhouses, as stubbornly and deliberately practiced by a certain number of returned émigrés or of nobles who had never left the country, was no more than a marginal phenomenon, largely confined to one generation. There is no valid way to extrapolate from the attitude of a part of the aristocratic population of the Faubourg Saint-German to the actual behavior of a social group throughout the whole of France; nor should we confuse the determination of a handful of irreconcilables, or the secret nostalgias of a probably greater number, with the pragmatism and—why not say so?—the national feeling that finally prevailed in most cases.

Of course there existed on the Left Bank in Paris a few dozen families which, while hoping to enjoy the peace they had found again, vegetated in the prejudices of old times and in a malevolent silence. The duchess of Châtillon, described in the "personal statistics" as "pious and very proud of her ancient lineage," and whose daughters were the duchesses of La Trémoille and Uzès, lived in her magnificent hôtel in the rue du Bac (so Mlle de Boigne tells us), amid a collection of clocks, birdcages, and portraits of her numerous lovers, souvenirs of an amorous youth. Others shut themselves up in an austere retirement, which in some cases reflected a resurgence of religious ferver in a class as marked by its misfortunes as by its reduced circumstances, and would not leave the house except for the exercise of religious devotions or practice of charity; such were the Juignés, the Forbin-Jansons and the Laval-Montmorencys, one of whose sons apparently did not hesitate to employ the formula, "We saints." Between the government and the society that it promoted, on the one hand, and the old families of the faubourg, on the other, it was no doubt difficult to have any warm understanding when it was a question of the Polignacs, one of whose members was a state prisoner at Vincennes, or of the duchess of Luynes, whose daughter-in-law, Mme de Chevreuse, had been exiled by Napoleon when she refused to serve the Empress as a lady-in-waiting. The two kinds of "good society" engaged for a while in a petty war of coteries who ignored or sniped at each other in the salons. Those who accepted a place at court were scorned by others as "deserters."

But time was on the side of Napoleon. After the Austrian marriage [to the Archduchess Marie-Louise], as Mlle de Boigne goes on to say, "you could easily count the women who would not go to court. The number was so small that, if the Emperor's good fortune had lasted a few months longer, there would have been none." Rejection of imperial society, in short, was to be found mainly among elderly persons, whose whole existence attached them to the Old Régime or for whom no new career could reopen, or be of any interest. Outside Paris, among such people, there were large numbers of leisured gentlemen, old army officers, former members of the parlements and officers of finance, all abstaining from active life, and even from political life to the point of not attending the departmental electoral colleges even when they possessed the largest local fortunes.

On the other side were not only all those aristocrats who accepted Napoleon, and whose names fill the senatorial lists, the general councils of the departments, and the imperial and princely courts, but also all those sons of the old nobility who flocked into civil and military careers—officers, subprefects and civil servants of all kinds. The case of colonel and count Huchet de La Bédoyère, born in 1786, was no outstanding exception. The problem, moreover, should not be studied within the chronological limits of the Napoleonic period alone. It exists for the whole Revolution, from its very beginnings. The history of the nobility of the Old Régime cannot be written simply in terms of emigration, resistance and counterrevolution. Within so composite and multifarious a group we can discern an important current of faithful service to the State, to the Revolutionary State as well as to that of Napoleon. It was a highly significant current, for it made possible both impressive continuities in certain categories of government personnel and the first steps in that integration of elites of diverse social origins into a new leadership class, which was precisely at the center of Napoleon's thinking. In addition, it assured the reconsolidation of old aristocratic positions in a modernized state—in preparation for alliances with a modern capitalism that was to come.

THE WAYS OF BOURGEOIS ADVANCEMENT

"The Revolution of 1789," Georges Lefebvre once wrote, "brought the bourgeoisie to power, which the democracy then tried to take from them; under the Emperor's protection the notables recovered; their wealth and influence grew, and they prepared to govern and to restore liberalism."

In this summary by the last of the "great ancestors" in the historiography of the French Revolution, compacted to a surprising density in simple words, we can unhesitatingly recognize the whole effort, to tell the truth not very Revolutionary, of what had formerly been called the Third Estate. All told, from a point of view ten years after 1789, what was the "bourgeois Revolution"? It was a determined and successful attempt, in conditions of a social strategy that need not be recalled here, to break down the barrier of legal orders that blocked upward social mobility into the highest echelons, and to destroy "ministerial despotism," the final version of monarchical absolutism. It was a demand for infusing into the directing elites, substantially enlarged and enriched, a new social content in which the only passport would be a combination of fortune and ability. After the initial rupture, inevitable for coercing the most stubborn upholders of the old hierarchy, the action of the bourgeoisie absolutely lost its revolutionary character. Once the bars set up by the aristocracy had been broken, the bourgeoisie erected at the bottom of the social ladder, not barriers in a juridical or legal sense, but a screening mechanism—through access to property and education—behind which it was able to develop the cult of traditional values.

For what is striking in this victorious bourgeoisie is the preservation, before and after 1789, of economic, occupational and mental structures. The imperial society crowned the efforts of the bourgeois society of the Old Régime to ascend, identifying it with a new aristocracy without the monopolistic features of the old. We have just insisted on the limited character of the upheavals in the former privileged classes, for whom the abolition of the seigneurial and feudal regime was the beginning of a slow decline rather than a brutal collapse. We must insist equally on continuity in the efforts of the bourgeoisie to extend its control over all forms of power and property in the soil. In a France where there were still only sketchy and local signs of an industrial capitalism, and where, inversely, certain brilliant forms of the capitalism of the great colonial epoch were fading, there was a place, at the time of the Empire, for a short-lived apogee of a social model closer to the little lawyer-officials of the seventeenth century than to the Third Republic. . . .

DID NAPOLEONIC FRANCE MISS A TURNING-POINT?

... The First Consul and Emperor hesitated between two social models. By his intellectual formation, and by his taste for the power and efficiency of the State, Bonaparte was no stranger to the idea of a society that should enter upon industrialization, emphasizing technical skills in the popular culture and scientific skills in the culture of the bourgeoisie. But he was always absorbed by immediate preoccupations, chiefly political. For this reason, and considering his absolute opposition to a feudal and clerical restoration, the important thing for Bonaparte was a consolidation of the civil order. He sought it not merely by military victories but by choosing to support himself on property-owning and Catholic France. This France, after ten years of damaging blows [during the Revolution], and in the relative isolation from danger and competition that its armed power won for it, aspired to enjoy the benefits arising from its ordeal. More intent upon liberty for acquisition than upon liberty for production, seduced by the return of traditional values that would give "security," this France seemed eager, in sum, to take a long pause—one that would allow all possessors of real property to enjoy the fundamental conquest of the Revolution, the "democratization" of an aristocratic style of life which in previous ages had been both an object of envy and a source of oppression. And so the dominant classes of our country showed themselves ready for a lasting unfaithfulness to the very philosophy of progress that had opened the way to their success.

ANNOTATED BIBLIOGRAPHY

This bibliography includes a selection of some of the more important works on the Napoleonic period, with preference given to recent publications.

1. *Aids for Research*
Recently published textbooks provide excellent bibliographies for the revolutionary and Napoleonic epochs. See, for example, Owen Connelly, *French Revolution/Napoleonic Era* (New York: Holt, Rinehart and Winston, 1979); and D. M. G. Sutherland, *France 1789–1815: Revolution and Counterrevolution* (New York: Oxford University Press, 1986). Much more extensive is Jacques Godechot, *L'Europe et l'Amérique à l'époque napoléonienne* (Paris: Presses universitaires de France, 1967). Essential for sorting through the memoir literature is Jean Tulard, *Bibliographie critique des mémoires sur le Consulat et l'Empire* (Geneva: Droz, 1971). Also useful is *An Annotated Bibliography of the Napoleonic Era: Recent Publications, 1945–1985* (Westport, Conn.: Greenwood Press, 1987), comp. Jack A. Meyer.

The most important collection of Napoleon's words is the *Correspondance de Napoléon I* (32 vols.; Paris: Plon & Dumaine, 1858–70), but this is not nearly complete. Useful supplements are Arthur M. Chuquet, *Inédits napoléoniens* (2 vols.; Paris: Fontemoing, 1913–19); and Jean Tulard's edition of *Oeuvres littéraires et écrits militaires de Napoléon* (3 vols.; Paris: Société encyclopédique française, 1967–68). One can also sample his writings and opinions in James M. Thompson, ed., *Napoleon's Letters* (New York: Dutton, Everyman Edition, 1954); John E. Howard, ed., *Napoleon I, Letters and Documents: 1784–1802* (New York: Oxford University Press, 1961); and J. C. Herold, ed., *The Mind of Napoleon* (New York: Columbia University Press, 1955), a collection of his views taken primarily from his conversations and correspondence.

2. *Memoirs*
Among the most valuable memoirs of the period, one may consult Claude-François de Meneval, *Memoirs* (3 vols.; New York: D. Appleton, 1894), by a secretary to Napoleon and an administrator; André-François, comte Miot de Melito, *Memoirs* (New York: Scribner's, 1881), fundamental, and hostile to the Emperor; Étienne-Denis Pasquier,

Memoirs (3 vols.; New York: Scribner's, 1893–94), with a condensation (London: Elek, 1967), indispensable; the Austrian statesman Clemens von Metternich, *Memoirs* (5 vols.; New York: Scribner's, 1880–82), of which the first two volumes carry the tale to 1815. Other valuable recollections include Louise-M.-V., comtesse de Chastenay, *Mémoires* (2 vols.; Paris: Plon, 1896), for social life and the scientists of the period; A.-C. Thibaudeau, *Mémoires* (Paris: Plon, 1913), with an abbreviated version in English, *Bonaparte and the Consulate* (London: Methuen, 1908), by an informed bureaucrat; P.-L. Roederer, *Journal* (Paris: Daragon, 1909), and *Mémoires* (Paris: Plon, 1942), by a leading administrator of the regime; Mathieu, comte Molé, *Le Comte Molé, sa vie, ses mémoires* (6 vols.; Paris: Champion, 1922), and *Souvenirs* (Geneva: Milieu du monde, 1943); J.-M. de Montbreton de Norvins, *Souvenirs* (3 vols.; Paris: Plon, 1896–97), good for administrative life in Paris, the expedition to San Domingo, and the Friedland campaign. The last years of the Empire are recounted in Armand, marquis de Caulaincourt, *With Napoleon in Russia*, and *No Peace with Napoleon* (New York: Morrow, 1935–36); and A.-F. Villemain, *Souvenirs contemporains* (2 vols.; Paris: Didier, 1853–55). For royalists, see Eugène, baron de Vitrolles, *Mémoires* (2 vols.; Paris: Gallimard, 1950); and Louis V.-L. Rochchouart, *Souvenirs* (Paris: Plon, 1933). The best account of how Napoleon behaved and what he said while in exile on St. Helena is H.-G. Bertrand, *Cahiers de Sainte-Hélène* (3 vols.; Paris, A. Michel, 1949–51). Three of Napoleon's other companions in exile—Montholon, Las Cases, and Gourgaud—join Bertrand in the collection edited by Jean Tulard, *Napoléon à Sainte-Hélène: par les quatre évangélistes* (Paris: Laffont, 1981). Other memoirs will be found cited in the appropriate sections below.

3. *Biographies of Napoleon and Narratives of the Era*
The standard survey remains Georges Lefebvre *Napoléon* (6th ed.; Paris: Presses universitaires de France, 1969, orig. 1935). There is a translation in two volumes (New York: Columbia University Press, 1969). Jean Tulard is a leading French specialist on the Napoleonic period. His recent synthesis is *Napoléon ou le mythe du sauveur* (2nd ed.; Paris: Fayard, 1977), available in a flawed translation as *Napoleon: The Myth of the Saviour* (London: Weidenfeld and Nicolson, 1984). With colorful prose and illustrations is J. C. Herold, *Horizon Book of Napoleon* (New York: American Heritage, 1963). Even more sumptuous and with sections prepared by French specialists is *Napoléon et l'Empire*, ed. Jean Mistler (2 vols.; Paris: Hachette, 1968). Louis Madelin, *Histoire du Consulat et de l'Empire* (16 vols.; Paris: Hachette, 1937–54), is the most detailed recent account, usually favorable to the Corsican; there is a shorter, earlier version,

History of the Consulate and Empire (2 vols.; New York: Putnam, 1934–36). A recent one volume French survey is André Latreille, *L'Ere napoléonienne* (Paris: A. Colin, 1974). A fine, short study in English is Felix Markham, *Napoleon* (New York: New American Library, 1964); Maurice Hutt, ed., *Napoleon* (Englewood Cliffs: Prentice Hall, 1972), includes excerpts from the writings of Napoleon, his contemporaries, and historians. A classic and still valuable study is J. H. Rose, *Life of Napoleon I* (2 vols.; New York: Macmillian, 1901–02). More popular accounts are André Castelot, *Napoleon* (New York: Harper & Row, 1971); Vincent Cronin, *Napoleon* (New York: Morrow, 1972); and Louis Chardigny, *L'Homme Napoléon* (Paris: Perrin, 1987). For a fascinating analysis of how French historians up to 1939 interpreted Napoleon, see Pieter Geyl, *Napoleon, For and Against* (New Haven: Yale University Press, 1949). Two German views are Willy Andreas, *Napoleon: Entwicklung, Umwelt, Wirkung* (Constance: Thorbecke, 1962); and Walter Markov, *Die Napoleon-Zeit: Geschichte und Kultur des Grand Empire* (Stuttgart: Kohlhammer, 1985).

For particular periods or episodes, see the following: M. J. Sydenham, *The First French Republic, 1792–1804* (Berkeley: University of California Press, 1973), on the Consulate; J. C. Herold, *Bonaparte in Egypt* (New York: Harper & Row, 1962), offers a riveting and critical account; Albert Vandal, *L'Avènement de Bonaparte* (2 vols.; Paris: Plon, Nourrit, 1902–07), is favorable to Napoleon; Alistair Horne, in a splendid narrative, displays *Napoleon, Master of Europe, 1805–1807* (London: Weidenfeld and Nicolson, 1979); Jean Tulard surveys *Le Grand Empire, 1804–1815* (Paris: A. Michel, 1982); older, detailed, and exciting are H. Houssaye, *1814* (Paris: Perrin, 1888), and *1815* (3 vols.; Paris: Perrin, 1889–1905). For Bonaparte's legacy, see J. Lucas-Dubreton, *Le Culte de Napoléon, 1815–1848* (Paris: A. Michel, 1960).

4. *France under Napoleon*

Two handy reference works on the era are *Dictionnaire napoléon* (Paris: Fayard, 1987), ed. Jean Tulard; and the *Historical Dictionary of Napoleonic France, 1799–1815* (Westport, Conn.: Greenwood, 1985), ed. Owen Connelly and others. An essential encyclopedic work is Jacques Godechot, *Les Institutions de la France sous la Révolution et l'Empire* (3rd. ed.; Paris: Presses universitaires de France, 1985). A shorter treatment, Louis Bergeron, *France under Napoleon*, trans. R. R. Palmer (Princeton: Princeton University Press, 1981, orig. 1972), emphasizes institutional and social history, as does "La France à l'époque napoléonienne," a long special issue of the *Revue d'histoire moderne et contemporaine*, 17 (1970), 331–920. Robert Holtman, *The Napoleonic Revolution* (Baton Rouge: Louisiana State University Press, 1979, orig. 1967), is a clear and reliable survey of institutional reform; while Philippe Sussel, *La France de Napoléon Ier (1799–1815)* (Paris: Denoël, 1970), is strong on economic topics. Political studies include Werner Giesselmann, *Die brumairianische Elite* (Stuttgart: Klett-Cotta, 1977); Jean Bourdon, *La Constitution de l'an VIII* (Rodez: Carrère, 1941), and *La Législation du Consulat et de l'Empire: la Réforme judiciaire de l'an VIII* (Rodez: Carrère, 1942); Clive Church, *Revolution and Red Tape: The French Ministerial Bureaucracy, 1770–1850* (New York: Oxford University Press, 1981); Irene Collins, *Napoleon and His Parliaments, 1800–1815* (New York: St. Martin's, 1979); and Jean Durand, *Le Fonctionnement du Conseil d'Etat napoléonien* (Gap: Louis-Jean, 1954).

The police are treated in Eric Arnold, *Fouché, Napoleon, and the General Police* (Washington, D. C.: University Press of America, 1979); E. d'Hauterive, *Napoléon et sa police* (Paris: Flammarion, 1943); Henri Gaubert, *Conspirateurs au temps de Napoléon I* (Paris: Flammarion, 1962); and Jean Savant, *Les Espions de Napoléon* (Paris: Hachette, 1957).

For other important officials, see Edward Whitcomb, "Napoleon's Prefects," *American Historical Review*, 70 (1974), 1089–1118; J. Savant, *Les Préfets de Napoléon* (Paris: Hachette, 1958), and his *Ministres de Napoléon* (Paris: Hachette, 1959).

Useful recollections by contemporary officials include P.-M. Desmarets, *Témoignages historiques ou quinze ans de haute police sous le Consulat et l'Empire* (Paris: Garnier, 1900, orig. 1833), which are more reliable than those of another policeman, A.-J.-M.-R. Savary, duc de Rovigo, *Mémoires* (5 vols.; Paris: Garnier, 1900); and the account by a leading minister, J.-A. Chaptal, *Mes Souvenirs* (Paris: Plon, 1893).

Essential for domestic affairs is F.-N. Ravaisson-Mollien, *Mémoires* (4 vols.; Paris: Fournier, 1837). The view of an insider is A.-J.-F. Fain, *Mémoires du baron Fain, premier secrétaire du cabinet de l'Empereur* (Paris: Plon, 1908). An excellent memoir by a prefect is Adrien Plancy, *Souvenirs (1798–1816)* (Paris: Ollendorff, 1904). The first volume of Charles de Remusat, *Mémoires* (5 vols.; Paris: Plon, 1958), concerns life in a lycée and the end of the Empire. Fundamental for a study of the opposition is Jean-G., baron Hyde de Neuville, *Mémoires et Souvenirs* (3 vols.; Paris: Plon, 1888).

5. *Social and Economic History*

Bertrand Gille, "La Société française," in J. Mistler, ed., *Napoléon et l'Empire* (Paris: Hachette, 1968), 1:201–229, is a brief survey. Demographic aspects are treated in Marcel Reinhard, *Etude de la population pendant la Révolution et l'Empire* (Gap: Louis-Jean, 1961). Local studies with much social content are Jean Tulard, *Nouvelle histoire de Paris: le Consulat et l'Empire* (Paris: Hachette, 1970); Raymonde

Monnier, *Le Faubourg Saint-Antoine (1789–1815)* (Paris: Société des études robespierristes, 1981); and René Durand, *Le Département des Côtes du Nord sous le Consulat et l'Empire* (2 vols.; Paris: F. Alcan, 1926).

The upper levels of society have been analyzed most thoroughly in Jean Tulard, *Napoléon et la noblesse d'Empire* (Paris: Tallandier, 1986); G. Chaussinand-Nogaret, Louis Bergeron, and Robert Forster, "Les Notables du 'Grand Empire' en 1810," *Annales, E.S.C.*, 26 (1971), 1052–75; Louis Bergeron and G. Chaussinand-Nogaret, *Grands Notables du Premier Empire* (15+ vols.; Paris: CNRS, 1978–   ); Geoffrey Ellis, "Rhine and Loire: Napoleonic Elites and Social Order," in *Beyond the Terror*, eds. C. Lucas and G. Lewis (New York: Cambridge University Press, 1983), 232–267; and Robert Forster, "The French Revolution and the 'New' Elite, 1800–50," in *The American and European Revolutions, 1776–1848* (Iowa City: University of Iowa Press, 1980), ed. J. Pelenski, pp. 182–207.

Colin Jones takes a long view of the disinherited in *Charity and Bienfaisance: The Treatment of the Poor in the Montpellier Region, 1740–1815* (New York: Cambridge University Press, 1982). Alan Forrest examines "Conscription and Crime in Rural France during the Directory and Consulate," in *Beyond the Terror*, cited above, pp. 92–120; while Alain Corbin studies *Les Filles de noce: misère sexuelle et prostitution, 19e et 20e siècles* (Paris: Aubier-Montaigne, 1978).

In Fernand Braudel and Ernest Labrousse, eds., *Histoire économique et sociale de la France*, vol. 3, book 1 (Paris: Presses universitaires de France, 1976), Albert Soboul prepared the chapter on the Napoleonic period, where he finds that the Corsican continued the "bourgeois" revolution. An older and more detailed account is Alexandre Chabert, *Essai sur les mouvements des revenus et de l'activité économique en France de 1798 à 1820* (Paris: Librairie de Médicis, 1949). François Crouzet, "Wars, Blockade, and Economic Change in Europe, 1792–1815," *Journal of Economic History*, 24 (1964), 567–588, is a brilliant survey of the Continent. G. Ellis's case study, *Napoleon's Continental Blockade: The Case of Alsace* (New York: Oxford University Press, 1981), finds that, on balance, this region's economy benefited. Changes in transportation are described in Bernard Lepetit, *Chemins de terre et voies d'eau: réseaux de transports et organisation de l'espace en France, 1740–1840* (Paris: Ecole des hautes études en sciences sociales, 1984). Denis Woronoff examines an important sector in *L'Industrie sidérurgique en France pendant la Révolution et l'Empire* (Paris: Ecole des hautes études en sciences sociales, 1984). The histories of two important industrial firms are Reed Geiger, *The Anzin Coal Company, 1800–1833* (Newark, Del.: University of Delaware Press, 1974); and Claude Pris, *Une Grande entreprise française sous l'ancien régime: la manufacture royale des glaces de Saint-Gobain (1665–1830)* (New York: Arno, 1981). L. Bergeron examines businessmen in *Banquiers, négociants et manufacturiers parisiens: du Directoire à l'Empire* (Paris: Champion, 1975). There are few special studies of agriculture. We mention two: G. Dallas, *The Imperfect Peasant Economy: The Loire Country, 1800–1914* (Cambridge: Cambridge University Press, 1982); and Michel Vovelle, "Peut-on parler de 'mentalités paysannes' à l'époque napoléonienne?" *Annuario dell'Instituto storico italiano per l'età moderna et contemporanea* (Rome), vol. 33–34 (1981—82), 125–163.

6. *Intellectual History*

Two first-rate studies of education that deal with the Napoleonic period are R. R. Palmer, *The Improvement of Humanity: Education and The French Revolution* (Princeton: Princeton University Press, 1985); and Françoise Mayeur, *De la Révolution à l'école républicaine, 1789–1930* (Paris: Nouvelle libraire de France, 1981), vol. 3 of *Histoire générale de l'enseignement et de l'éducation en France*. A close look at the provinces is provided by Robert Gildea, *Education in Provincial France, 1800–1914: A Study of Three Departments* (Oxford: Oxford University Press, 1983).

Three views of the intellectuals are Georges Gusdorf, *La Conscience révolutionnaire: les Idéologues* (Paris: Payot, 1978); Emmet Kennedy, *Destutt de Tracy and the Origins of "Ideology"* (Philadelphia: American Philosophical Society, 1978); and J. C. Herold, *Mistress to an Age: Mme de Staël* (New York: Crown, 1979, orig. 1955). General accounts of literature and the arts are Gustave Merlet, *Tableau de la littérature française, 1800–1815* (3 vols.; Paris: Didier, 1878–83); André Michel, *Histoire générale de l'art* (Paris: A. Colin, 1926), vol. 8; and Louis Hautecoeur, *L'Art sous la Révolution et l'Empire en France, 1789–1815* (Paris: Le Prat, 1953). A brief look at a major institution is Cecil Gould, *Trophy of Conquest: The Musée Napoléon and the Creation of the Louvre* (London: Faber and Faber, 1965). In science much was accomplished in this period. Consult Maurice Crosland, *The Society of Arcueil: A View of French Science at the Time of Napoleon I* (Cambridge: Harvard University Press, 1967); Pierre Huard, *Sciences, médecine, pharmacie, de la Révolution à l'Empire* (Paris: Dacosta, 1970); and Roger Hahn, *The Anatomy of a Scientific Institution: The Paris Academy of Sciences, 1666–1803* (Berkeley: University of California Press, 1986, orig. 1971). A brief interpretation of one scientist is L. J. Jordanova, *Lamarck* (New York: Oxford University Press, 1984).

7. Religious History

Valuable surveys include the first volume of Adrien Dansette, *Religious History of Modern France* (2 vols.; New York: Herder and Herder, 1961); the second volume of André Latreille, *L'Eglise catholique et la Révolution française* (2 vols.; Paris: Hachette, 1950); Jean-Marie Leflon, *La Crise révolutionnaire, 1789–1846* (Paris: Bloud & Gay, 1949); and Bernard Plongeron, *Théologie et politique au siècle des lumières, 1770–1820* (Geneva: Droz, 1973). Margaret M. O'Dwyer has a recent biography of Pius VII, *The Papacy in the Age of Napoleon and the Restoration: Pius VII, 1800–1823* (Lanham, Md.: University Press of America, 1985). *The Concordat of 1801* (New York: Columbia University Press, 1933) by Henry H. Walsh is the standard account in English. See also the even-handed Bernardine Melchior-Bonnet, *Napoléon et le pape* (Paris: Amiot-Dumont, 1958).

Three local studies are Jean Godel, *Histoire religieuse du département de l'Isère . . . (1802–1809)* (Le Rondeau-Montfleury: the Author, 1968); Jacques Valette, "Le Clergé du diocèse de Poitiers en 1802," *Annales historiques de la Révolution française*, 55 (1983), 137–153; and Auguste Billaud, *La Petite Eglise dans la Vendée et les Deux-Sèvres (1800–1830)* (Paris: Nouvelles éditions latines, 1961). G. de Bertier de Sauvigny, *Le Comte Ferdinand de Bertier (1782–1864) et l'énigme de la Congrégation* (Paris: Presses continentales, 1948), sheds much light on the religious opposition to Napoleon, as does Comte Louis de Gobineau, *Mémoires* (Brussels: Erasme, 1955). The view from Rome can be found in Bartolommeo Pacca, *Mémoires du cardinal Pacca sur le pontificat de Pie VII* (2 vols.; Paris: Bray, 1860). The situation of Freemasonry can be examined in François Collaveri, "La Franc-maçonnerie sous le Premier Empire," *Souvenir napoléonien*, 46, no. 330 (1983), 4–26; and idem, *La Franc-maçonnerie des Bonaparte* (Paris: Payot, 1982). The standard work on this subject is Pierre Chevallier, *Histoire de la franc-maçonnerie française* (3 vols.; Paris: Fayard, 1974–75), of which part of the second volume deals with the Napoleonic period.

8. Diplomatic History

A survey of the diplomatic history of the period is André Fugier, *La Révolution française et l'Empire napoléonien* (Paris: Hachette, 1954). Studies of French diplomats are Edward A. Whitcomb, *Napoleon's Diplomatic Service* (Durham: Duke University Press, 1979); and Jean Ballou, ed., *Histoire de l'administration française: les affaires étrangères et le corps diplomatique français*, vol. 1, *De l'Ancien régime au Second Empire* (2 vols.; Paris: CNRS, 1984).

Concerned with much of Europe are Owen Connelly, *Napoleon's Satellite Kingdoms* (New York: The Free Press, 1965); Carlo Zaghi, *Napoleone e l'Europa* (Naples: Cymba, 1969); and Heinz O. Sieburg, ed., *Napoleon und Europa* (Cologne: Kiepenheuer und Witsch, 1971).

9. *The History of Individual Countries*
There is an extensive literature on individual countries. For Britain, see especially John S. Watson, *The Reign of George III* (Oxford: Oxford University Press, 1960); and François Crouzet, *L'Economie britannique et le blocus continental (1806–1813)* (Paris: Economica, 1987, orig. 1958). Germany is treated in T. C. W. Blanning, *The French Revolution in Germany: Occupation and Resistance in the Rhineland, 1792– 1802* (New York: Oxford University Press, 1984); Enno Kraehe, *Metternich's German Policy*: vol. 1, *The Contest with Napoleon, 1799–1814* (Princeton: Princeton University Press, 1963); Friedrich Meinecke, *The Age of German Liberation, 1795–1815* (Berkeley: University of California Press, 1977, orig. 1906); Karl O. Aretin, *Vom Deutschen Reich zum Deutschen Bund* (Göttingen: Vandenhoeck & Ruprecht, 1980); Kurt von Raumer and M. Botzenhart, *Deutsche Geschichte im 19 Jahrhundert*, vol. 3, *Von 1789 bis 1815* (Wiesbaden: Athenaion, 1980); Heinz O. Sieburg, "Napoléon et les transformations des institutions en Allemagne," *Revue d'histoire moderne et contemporaine*, 17 (1970), 897–912; Walter E. Simon, *The Failure of the Prussian Reform Movement, 1807–1819* (New York: Fertig, 1971, orig. 1955); Walter Hubatsch, *Die Stein-Hardenbergschen Reformen* (Darmstadt: Wissenschaftliche Buchgesellschaft, 1977); and Heinz K. Junk, "Das Grossherzogtum Berg . . . in napoleonischer Zeit," *Westfaelische Forschung*, 33 (1983), 29–83. Three biographical studies are especially important: Gerhard Ritter, *Stein* (3rd ed.; Stuttgart: Deutsche Verlaganstalt, 1958, orig. 1931); Peter G. Thielen, *Karl August von Hardenberg* (Cologne: Grote, 1967); and Peter Paret, *Clausewitz and the State* (New York: Oxford University Press, 1976). For Italy, see Carlo Zaghi, *Napoleone e l'Italia* (Naples: Cymba, 1966); and Livio Antonelli, *I prefetti dell' Italia napoleonica: Republica e regno d'Italia* (Bologna: Il Mulino, 1983). A detailed study of Spain is Gabriel H. Lovett, *Napoleon and the Birth of Modern Spain* (2 vols.; New York: New York University Press, 1965); and the Netherlands are covered in Simon Schama, *Patriots and Liberators: Revolution in the Netherlands, 1780–1813* (New York: Knopf, 1977). Three views of Russia in these years are Marc Raeff, *Understanding Imperial Russia, 1682– 1825* (New York: Columbia University Press, 1984); Patricia K. Grimsted, *The Foreign Ministers of Alexander I* (Berkeley: University of California Press, 1969); and Alan Palmer, *Alexander I* (New York: Harper and Row, 1974). For the United States, see C. L. Egan, *Neither*

Peace nor War: Franco-American Relations, 1803–1812 (Baton Rouge: Louisiana State University Press, 1983); and Alfred W. Crosby, Jr., *America, Russia, Hemp, and Napoleon: America's Trade with Russia and the Baltic, 1783–1812* (Columbus: Ohio State University Press, 1965).

Two memoirs are good for Belgium, François Dumonceau, *Mémoires* (3 vols.; Brussels: Brepols, 1958–63); and Henri Merode-Westerloo, *Souvenirs* (2 vols.; Brussels: Gruse, 1845–46); and for the Grand Duchy of Berg, see J.-C. Beugnot, *Mémoires* (Paris: Hachette, 1959, orig. 1866).

10. *Military History*

The essential starting place is *Napoleonic Military History*, ed. Donald D. Horward (New York: Garland, 1986), with chapters written by specialists. The English historian David G. Chandler has prepared several outstanding works: *The Campaigns of Napoleon* (New York: Macmillan, 1966); *Dictionary of the Napoleonic Wars* (New York: Macmillan, 1979); and *Napoleon's Marshals* (New York: Macmillan, 1986). A valuable analysis is Gunther E. Rothenberg, *The Art of Warfare in the Age of Napoleon* (Bloomington: Indiana University Press, 1978). Another recent survey is Michael Glover, *The Napoleonic Wars: An Illustrated History, 1792–1815* (New York: Hippocrene, 1979). Unexcelled for its maps is Vincent J. Esposito and J. Elting, *A Military History and Atlas of the Napoleonic Wars* (New York: Praeger, 1964). Other studies of the entire period are Georges Six, *Les Généraux de la Révolution et de l'Empire* (Paris: Bordas, 1947); Marcel Baldet, *La Vie quotidienne dans les armées de Napoléon* (Paris: Hachette, 1964); David Johnson, *Napoleon's Cavalry and Its Leaders* (New York: Holmes & Meier, 1978); and Isser Woloch, *The French Veteran from the Revolution to the Restoration* (Chapel Hill: University of North Carolina Press, 1979). An important subject is examined in Isser Woloch, "Napoleonic Conscription: State Power and Civil Society," *Past and Present*, no. 111 (May 1986), 101–129. See also Jean-Paul Bertaud, "Napoleon's Officers," *Past and Present*, no. 112 (August 1986), 91–111.

On particular episodes, see William Jackson, *Attack in the West: Napoleon's First Campaign Re-Read Today* (London: Eyre & Spottiswoode, 1953); Gabriel J. Fabry, *Histoire de l'armée d'Italie, 1796–1797* (3 vols.; Paris: Champion, 1900–03); James Marshall-Cornwall, *Marshal Masséna* (New York: Oxford University Press, 1965), also good for Italian operations; A. B. Rodger, *The War of the Second Coalition, 1798–1801* (Oxford: Clarendon Press, 1964); George A. Furse, *1800: Marengo and Hohenlinden* (London: William Clowers, 1903); and Norman E. Saul, *Russia and the Mediterranean, 1797– 1807* (Chicago: University of Chicago Press, 1970). The most authoritative work on the Egyptian adventure is Marquis Clément-Etienne de La Jonquière, *L'Expédition d'Egypte, 1798–1801* (5 vols.; Paris: Charles-Lavauzelle, 1899–1907); but also see the book by Herold cited in section 3 above.

Battles fought against the Third and Fourth Coalitions are described by Jean Thiry in several works, *Ulm, Trafalgar, Austerlitz* (Paris: Berger-Levrault, 1962); *Iena* (Paris: Berger-Levrault, 1964); and *Eylau, Friedland, Tilsit* (Paris: Berger-Levrault, 1964). In English there are the reissues of the classics by Francis Loraine Petre, *Napoleon's Conquest of Prussia, 1806* (New York: Hippocrene, 1972, orig. 1907); and *Napoleon's Campaign in Poland, 1806–1807* (New York: Hippocrene, 1975, orig. 1901).

The Spanish imbroglio can be followed in C.-A. Geoffroy de Grandmaison, *L'Espagne et Napoléon* (3 vols.; Paris: Plon, 1908–31); Juan Priego Lopez, *Guerre de la Independencia, 1804–1814* (5 vols.; Madrid: Libreria Editorial San Martin, 1972–82); the English classic, Charles W. C. Oman, *A History of the Peninsular War* (7 vols.; Oxford: Clarendon Press, 1902–30); and Jac Weller, *Wellington in the Peninsula, 1808–1814* (London: Vane, 1962). A tactical study is Donald D. Horward, *Napoleon and Iberia: The Twin Sieges of Cuidad Rodrigo and Almeida, 1810* (Tallahassee: Florida State University Press, 1984).

The Russian catastrophe continues to attract students. Recent accounts are Alan Palmer, *Napoleon in Russia, the 1812 Campaign* (New York: Simon and Schuster, 1967); Otto von Pivka, *Armies of 1812* (Cambridge, Eng.: Stephens, 1977); Curtis Cate, *The War of the Two Emperors* (New York: Random House, 1985); and Nigel Nicolson, *Napoleon 1812* (New York: Harper and Row, 1985).

The climactic battle in 1813 is described by Jean Thiry, *Leipzig* (Paris: Berger-Levrault, 1972); and in 1815 by Scott Bowden, *Armies at Waterloo* (Arlington, Texas: Empire Games Press, 1983). Another battlefield study is Harold T. Parker, *Three Napoleonic Battles* (Durham: Duke University Press, 1983, orig. 1944), that deals with Friedland, Aspern, and Waterloo.

The armies that Napoleon fought are described in Otto von Pivka, *Armies of the Napoleonic Era* (New York: Taplinger, 1979); Richard Glover, *Peninsular Preparations: The Reform of the British Army, 1795–1809* (Cambridge: Cambridge University Press, 1963); Peter Paret, *Yorck and the Era of Prussian Reform, 1807–1815* (Princeton: Princeton University Press, 1966); and Gunther E. Rothenberg, *Napoleon's Great Adversaries: The Archduke Charles and the Austrian Army, 1792–1814* (London: Batsford, 1982). For further investigation, consult Dennis E. Showalter, *German Military History, 1648–1982: A Critical Bibliography* (New York: Garland, 1984).

Among the hundreds of memoirs prepared by French military men, these are recommended: Marc Desboeufs, *Le Capitaine Desboeufs* (Paris: Picard, 1901); Victor Depuy, *Souvenirs militaires* (Paris: Calmann-Lévy, 1892); François Roguet, *Mémoires militaires* (4 vols.; Paris: Dumaine, 1862–65); J.-E. Macdonald, *Souvenirs du Maréchal Macdonald* (Paris: Plon, 1892); Étienne Choderlos de Laclos, *Le Fils de Laclos* (Lausanne: Payot, 1912); Joseph Guitard, *Souvenirs militaires du Premier Empire* (Paris: Guitard, 1934), by an enlisted man, and one of the most famous, Jean-Roch Coignet, *The Note-books of Captain Coignet* (New York: McBride, 1929, orig. 1853).

Additional memoirs that describe particular campaigns include Pamphile de Lacroix, *Mémoires pour servir à l'histoire de la révolution de Saint-Domingue* (2 vols.; Paris: Pillet, 1819); Philippe-Paul Segur, *History of the Expedition to Russia* (Boston: Houghton-Mifflin, 1958, orig. 1824); the volumes by Caulaincourt cited in section 2 above; Raimond de Montesquiou-Fezensac, *The Russian Campaign, 1812* (Athens: University of Georgia Press, 1970, orig. 1863); G. de Faber du Faur, *La Campagne de Russie (1812)* (Paris: Flammarion, 1895); and an English soldier's recollections, William Lawrence, *The Autobiography of Sergeant William Lawrence* (London: Low, Marsten, Searle, & Rivington, 1886).

Naval operations can be approached in Ernest H. Jenkins, *A History of the French Navy* (London: MacDonald & Janes, 1973); and Philippe Masson, *Histoire de la marine*, vol. 1, *L'Ere de la voile* (Paris: Lavauzelle, 1981). Bibliographical assistance is available in Jean Polak, *Bibliographie maritime française* . . . (Grenoble: Ed. des quatre seigneurs, 1976), and his *Supplément* (Grenoble: Debbane, 1983). Monographs by French authors include René Guillemin, *Corsaires de la République et de l'Empire* (Paris: France-Empire, 1982); Georges Bordonove, *Les Marins de l'an II* (Paris: Laffont, 1974); Jacques Aman, *Les Officiers bleus dans la marine française au XVIIIe siècle* (Geneva: Droz, 1976); Edouard Desbrière, *The Naval Campaign of 1805: Trafalgar* (Oxford: Clarendon, 1933). An important memoir is Jean-Baptiste Grivel, *Mémoires du vice-amiral baron Grivel* (Paris: Plon, 1914). Still valuable is Alfred Mahan, *The Influence of Seapower upon the French Revolution and Empire (1793–1812)* (2 vols.; Boston: Little, Brown, 1892).

British naval history has been much more extensively studied. Two surveys are C. Northcote Parkinson, *Britannia Rules: The Classic Age of Naval History, 1793–1815* (London: Weidenfeld and Nicolson, 1977); and Geoffrey J. Marcus, *The Age of Nelson: The Royal Navy, 1793–1815* (New York: Viking, 1971). On naval operations, see Christopher Lloyd, *St. Vincent and Camperdown* (London: Batsford, 1963); Piers Mackesy, *The War in the Mediterranean, 1803–1810* (London: Longmans, 1957); and Dudley Pope, *Decision at Trafalgar* (Philadelphia: Lippincott, 1960). For descriptions of the vessels and the men, see Charles H. Longridge, *The Anatomy of Nelson's Ships* (Annapolis: Naval Institute Press, 1977); and Michael A. Lewis, *A Social History of the Navy, 1793–1815* (London: Allen & Unwin, 1961). David Walder, *Nelson* (London: H. Hamilton, 1978) is the best biography; his associates are described in Ludovic Kennedy, *Nelson's Band of Brothers* (London: Collins, 1975); and Christopher Lloyd depicts a "Hornblower-type" character in *Lord Cochrane* (London: Longmans Green, 1947).

Less formal naval warfare is described in Donald MacIntyre, *The Privateers* (London: Paul Elek, 1975); and Seton Dearden, *A Nest of Corsairs: The Fighting Karamanlis of Tripoli* (London: J. Murray, 1976).

11. *Biographies*
In addition to the biographies already cited, the following are recommended: Felix Markham, *The Bonapartes* (New York: Taplinger, 1975); Ernest Knapton, *Empress Josephine* (Cambridge: Harvard University Press, 1963); Owen Connelly's study of Joseph, *The Gentle Bonaparte* (New York: Macmillan, 1968); Juan Mercador Riba, *José Bonaparte, rey de España (1806–1813)* (Madrid: Instituto Jeronimo Zurita, 1983); A. Pietromarchi, *Lucien Bonaparte* (Paris: Perrin, 1985); an account of Eugène Beauharnais by Carola Oman, *Napoleon's Viceroy* (London: Hodder & Stoughton, 1966); Elena Tessadri, *Il vicerè: Eugenio di Beauharnais* (Milan: Editoriale Nuova, 1982); Constance Wright, *Daughter to Napoleon* [Hortense Beauharnais] (New York: Holt, Rinehart & Winston, 1961); René, duc de Castries, *La Reine Hortense* (Paris: Tallandier, 1984); *Memoirs of Queen Hortense* (2 vols.; New York: Cosmpolitan, 1927); Hubert Cole, *The Betrayers: Joachim and Caroline Murat* (London: Eyre Methuen, 1972); Jean Tulard, *Murat ou l'éveil des nations* (Paris: Hachette, 1983); Patrick Turnbull, *Napoleon's Second Empress* (New York: Walker, 1972); G. Girod de l'Ain, *Bernadotte* (Paris: Perrin 1968); Jean Orieux, *Talleyrand* (New York: Knopf, 1974); Louis Madelin, *Talleyrand* (New York: Roy, 1948); François Papillard, *Cambacérès* (Paris: Hachette, 1961); Hubert Cole, *Fouché* (New York: McCall, 1971); John G. Gallaher, *The Iron Marshal* [Davout] (Carbondale: Southern Illinois University Press, 1976); Hellmuth Roessler, *Graf Johann Philipp Stadion* (2 vols.; Vienna: Herold, 1966), on the unlucky Austrian leader; John Ehrman, *The Younger Pitt*, vol. 1 (New York: Dutton, 1969), vol. 2 (Stanford: Stanford University Press, 1983), and volume 3, which will cover the Napoleonic years; and Elizabeth Longford, *Wellington* (2 vols.; New York: Harper & Row, 1969–72).

ABOUT THE EDITORS

FRANK A. KAFKER is Professor of History at the University of Cincinnati. He received his B.A., M.A., and Ph.D. from Columbia University. In collaboration with Serena L. Kafker, he has written *The Encyclopedists as Individuals: A Biographical Dictionary of the Authors of the Encyclopédie*. Also, he has edited *Notable Encyclopedias of the Seventeenth and Eighteenth Centuries: Nine Predecessors of the Encyclopédie*. Among the many journals to which he has contributed articles are *French Historical Studies, Revue d'Histoire Moderne et Contemporaine, Studies in Eighteenth-Century Culture, Eighteenth-Century Studies, Diderot Studies, Modern Language Review*, and *Studi Francesi*.

JAMES M. LAUX is Professor of History at the University of Cincinnati. He holds a B.S. from the University of Wisconsin, an M.A. from the University of Connecticut, and a Ph.D. from Northwestern University. He is the translator of *The Right Wing in France*, by R. Rémond, the author of *In First Gear: The French Automobile Industry to 1914*, and co-author and translator of *The Automobile Revolution*. His articles have appeared in *French Historical Studies, Le Mouvement Social, Business History, The Journal of Transport History, Aerospace Historian, Third Republic, French Review*, and the *Political Science Quarterly*.

Professors Kafker and Laux are co-editors of the journal *French Historical Studies* and of *The French Revolution: Conflicting Interpretations*, a companion volume to this one on Napoleon.